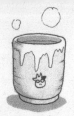

Great job on the anime.
Thank you very much.

I've been so busy since the *Fullmetal Alchemist: Brotherhood* anime started that I couldn't make it to a single voice recording session, but I was finally able to attend the one for the final episode.

At the after-party, we all laughed and cried and laughed again.

Thank you very much for all the delicious drinks.

—Hiromu Arakawa, 2010

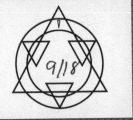

Born in Hokkaido (northern Japan), Hiromu Arakawa first attracted national attention in 1999 with her award-winning manga *Stray Dog*. Her series *Fullmetal Alchemist* debuted in 2001 in Square Enix's monthly manga anthology *Shonen Gangan*.

FULLMETAL ALCHEMIST VOL. 26

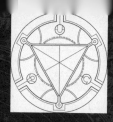

VIZ Media Edition

Story and Art by Hiromu Arakawa

Translation/Akira Watanabe
English Adaptation/Jake Forbes
Touch-up Art & Lettering/Wayne Truman
Cover Design/Julie Behn
Interior Design/Ronnie Casson
Editor/Alexis Kirsch

Hagane no RenkinJutsushi vol. 26 © 2010 Hiromu Arakawa/SQUARE ENIX. First published in Japan in 2010 by SQUARE ENIX CO., LTD. English translation rights arranged with SQUARE ENIX CO., LTD. and VIZ Media, LLC.

Printed in the U.S.A.

Published by VIZ Media, LLC
P.O. Box 77010
San Francisco, CA 94107

10 9 8 7
First printing, September 2011
Seventh printing, February 2018

www.viz.com

鋼の錬金術師

FULLMETAL ALCHEMIST

26

荒川弘

HIROMU ARAKAWA

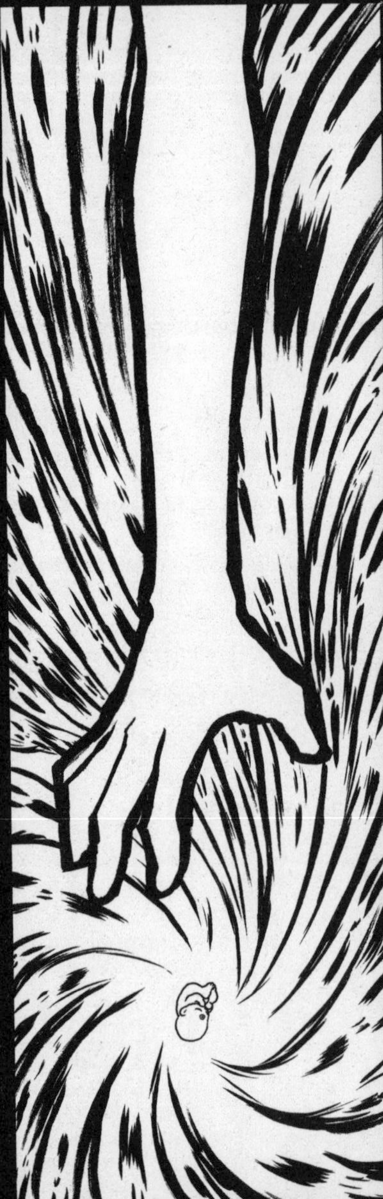

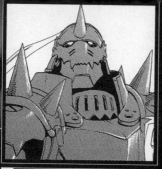

■ アルフォンス・エルリック

Alphonse Elric

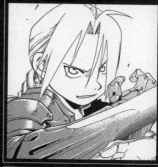

■ エドワード・エルリック

Edward Elric

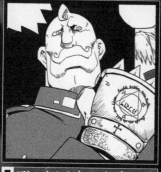

■ アレックス・ルイ・アームストロング

Alex Louis Armstrong

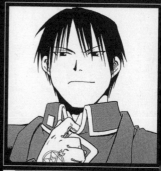

■ ロイ・マスタング

Roy Mustang

OUTLINE
FULLMETAL ALCHEMIST

Using a forbidden alchemical ritual, the Elric brothers attempted to bring their dead mother back to life. But the ritual went wrong, consuming Edward Elric's leg and Alphonse Elric's entire body. At the cost of his arm, Edward was able to graft his brother's soul into a suit of armor. Equipped with mechanical "auto-mail" to replace his missing limbs, Edward becomes a state alchemist in hopes of finding a way to restore their bodies. Their search embroils them in a deadly conspiracy that threatens to take the innocence, if not the lives, of everyone involved.

Edward, Al, Hohenheim and Izumi Curtis—the four Sacrifices who share the common curse of having performed human transmutation—have converged in the lair of the Dwarf in the Flask, the "father" of the Homunculi. They are joined by Roy Mustang, the final candidate, who was forced into participating in the same forbidden rite at the cost of his eyesight. The Day of

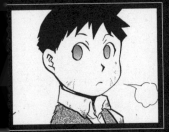

■ セリム・ブラッドレイ（プライド）

Selim Bradley (Pride)

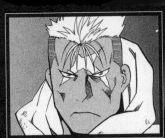

■ スカー

Scar

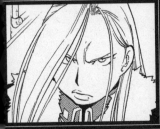

■ オリヴィエ・ミラ・アームストロング

Olivier Mira Armstrong

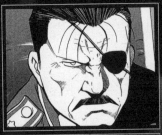

■ キング・ブラッドレイ

King Bradley

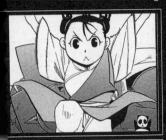

■ メイ・チャン

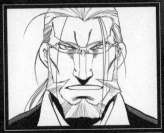

■ ヴァン・ホーエンハイム

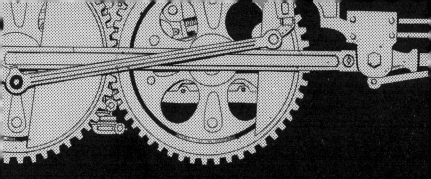

CONTENTS

Chapter 104: The Center of the World   7

Chapter 105: The Throne of God   61

Chapter 106: Pride's Abyss   131

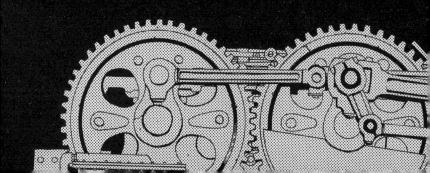

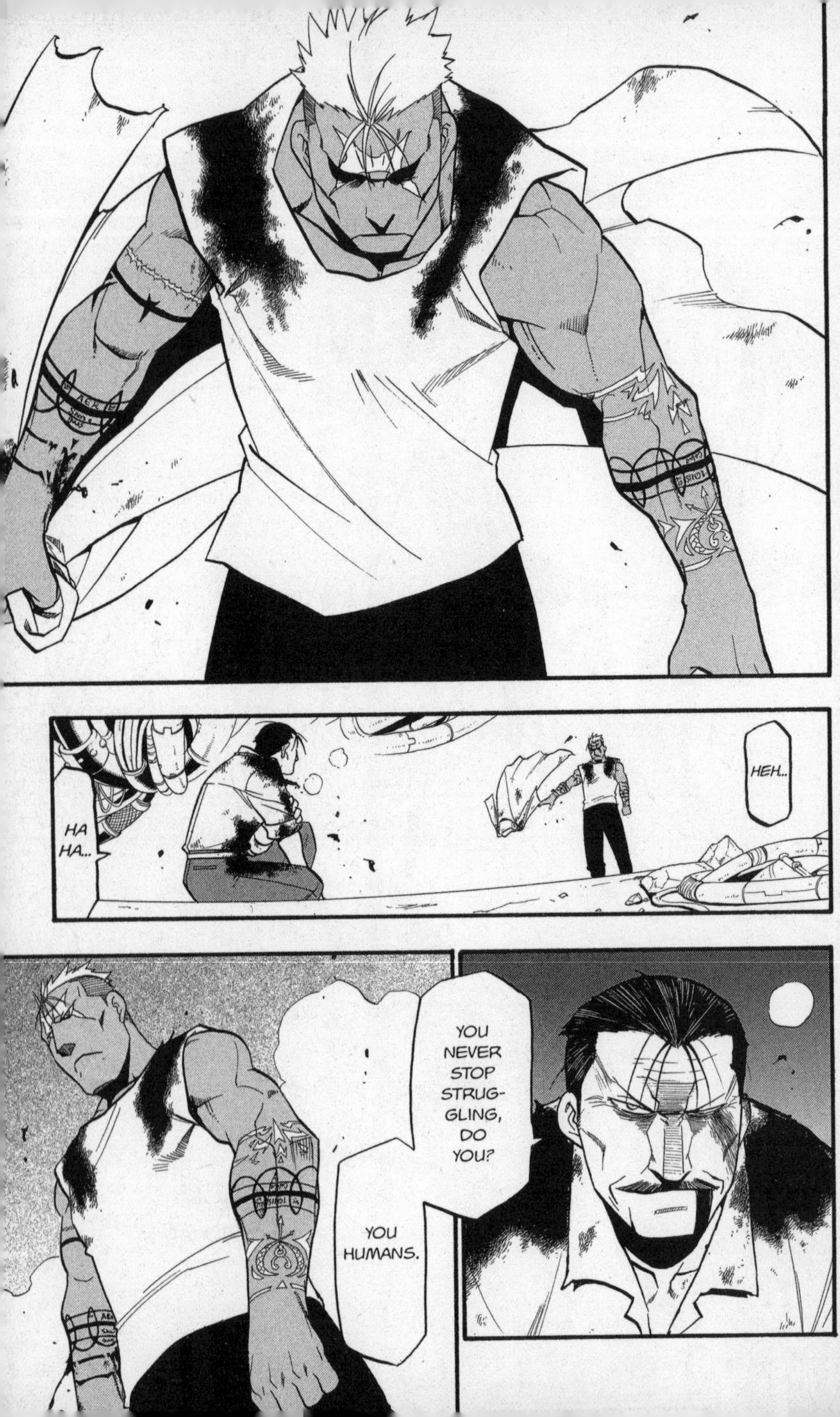
HEH...
HA HA...
YOU NEVER STOP STRUG-GLING, DO YOU?
YOU HUMANS.

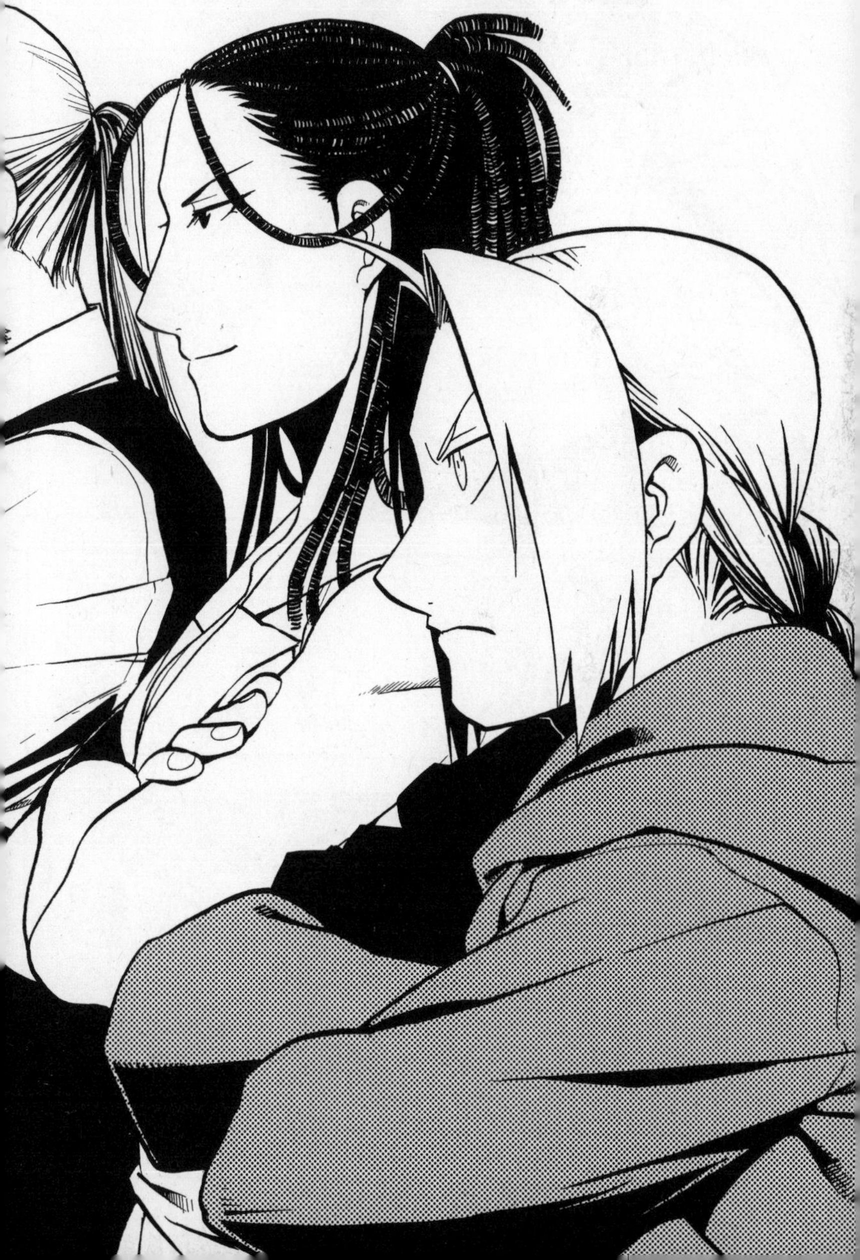

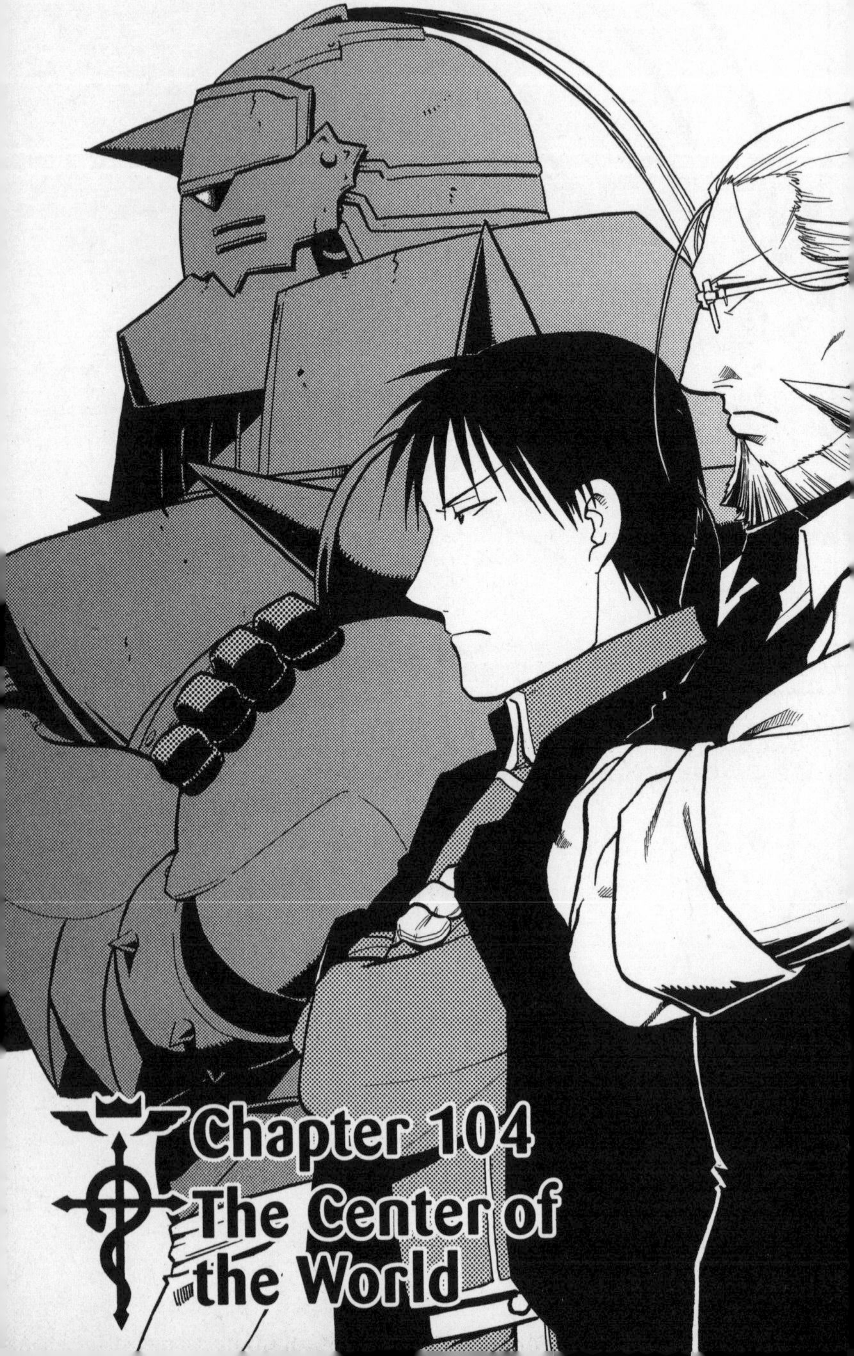
Chapter 104
The Center of the World

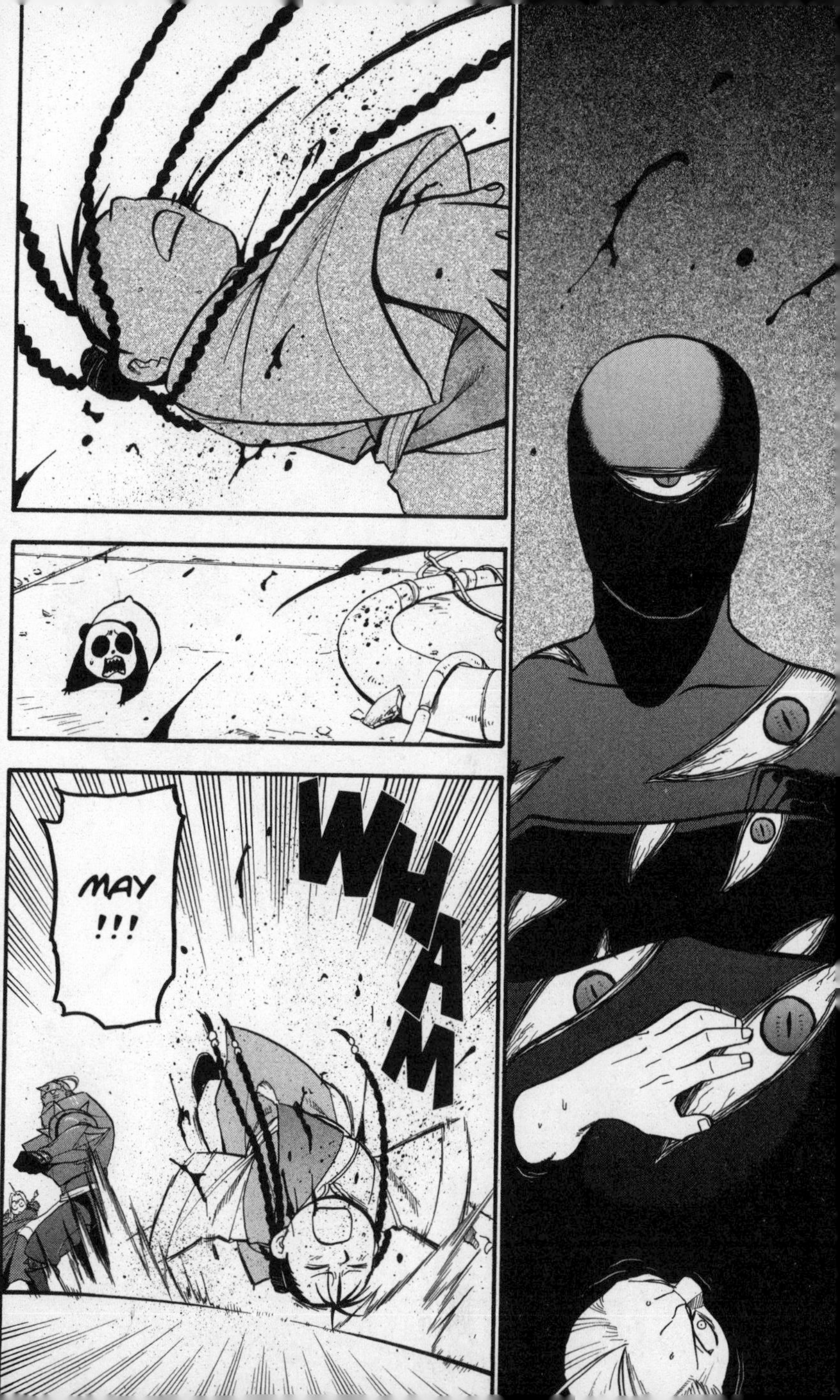
WHAM
MAY !!!

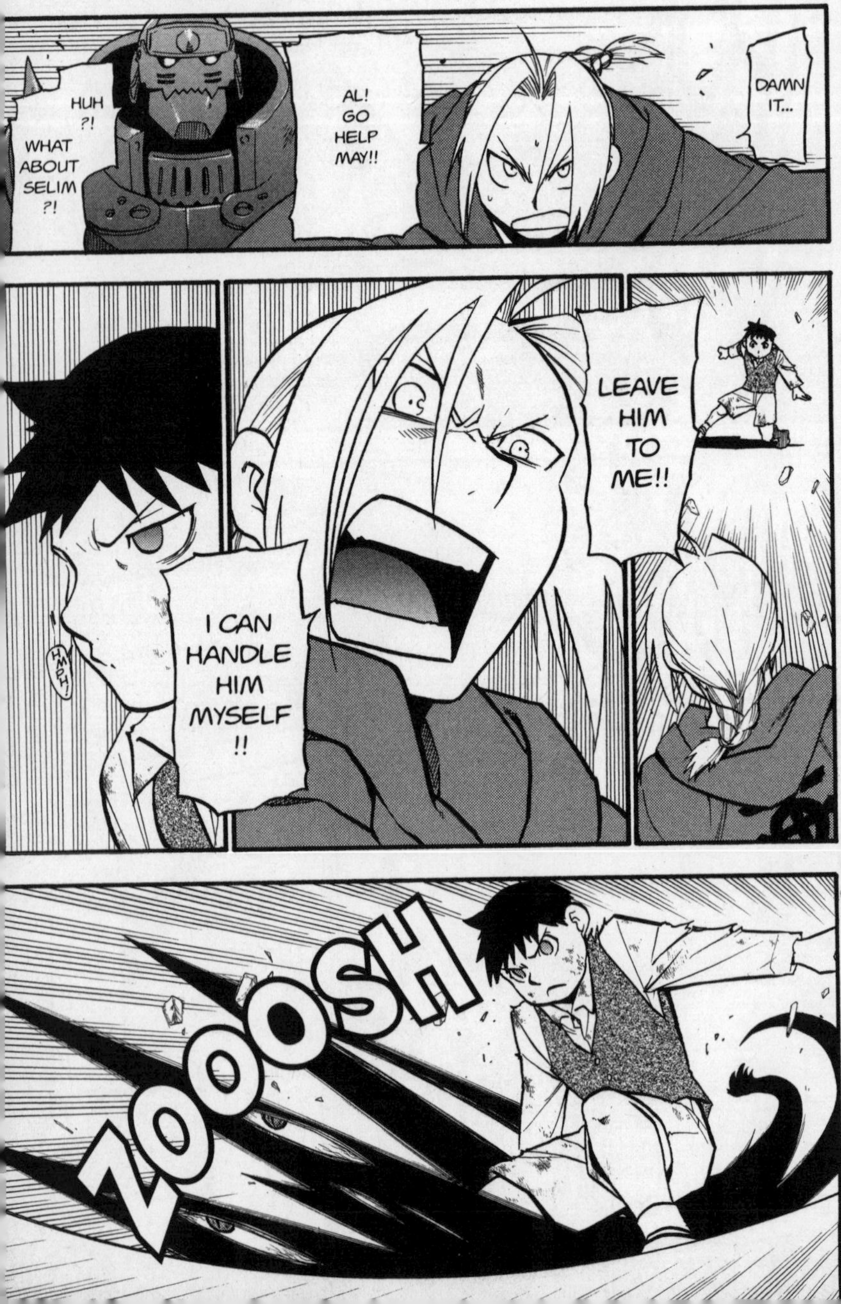
DAMN IT...
AL! GO HELP MAY!!
HUH ?! WHAT ABOUT SELIM ?!
LEAVE HIM TO ME!!
I CAN HANDLE HIM MYSELF !!
HMPH!
ZOOOSH

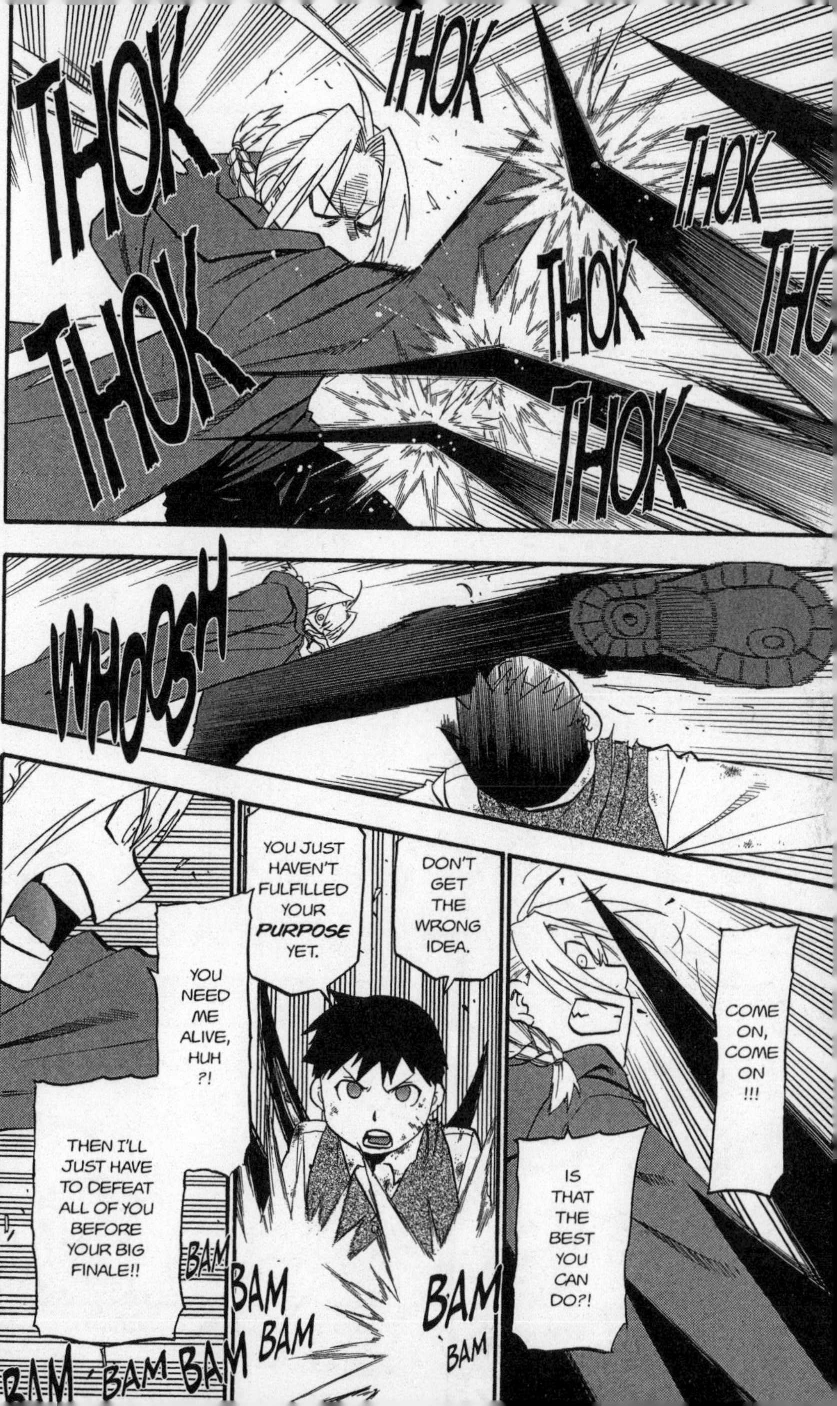
THOK
THOK
THOK
THOK
THOK
THOK
THOK
WHOOSH
COME ON, COME ON!!!
IS THAT THE BEST YOU CAN DO?!
BAM
BAM
DON'T GET THE WRONG IDEA.
YOU JUST HAVEN'T FULFILLED YOUR **PURPOSE** YET.
BAM
BAM
YOU NEED ME ALIVE, HUH?!
THEN I'LL JUST HAVE TO DEFEAT ALL OF YOU BEFORE YOUR BIG FINALE!!
BAM
BAM BAM
BAM

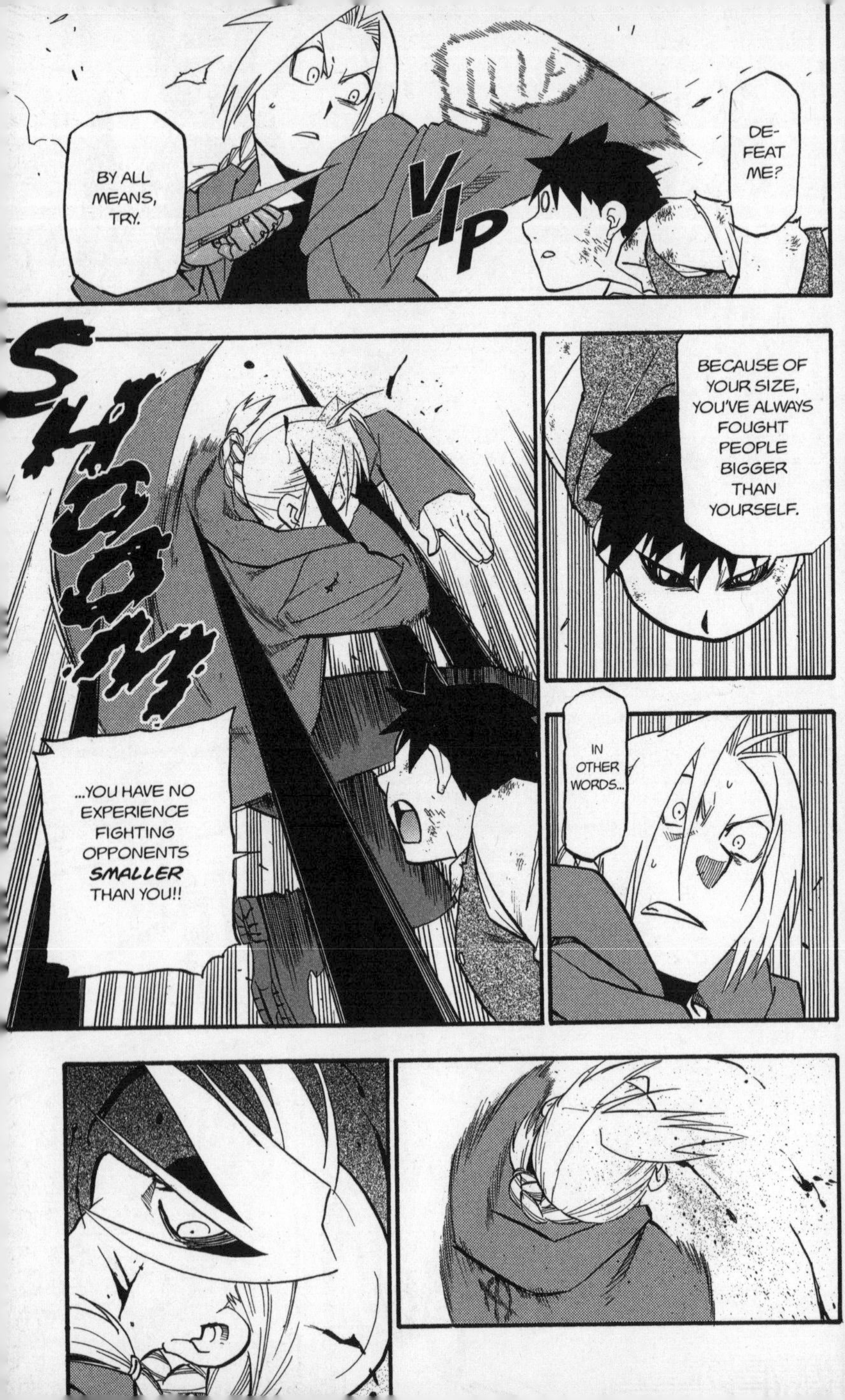
DE-FEAT ME?
VIP
BY ALL MEANS, TRY.
BECAUSE OF YOUR SIZE, YOU'VE ALWAYS FOUGHT PEOPLE BIGGER THAN YOURSELF.
SHOOM
IN OTHER WORDS...
...YOU HAVE NO EXPERIENCE FIGHTING OPPONENTS SMALLER THAN YOU!!

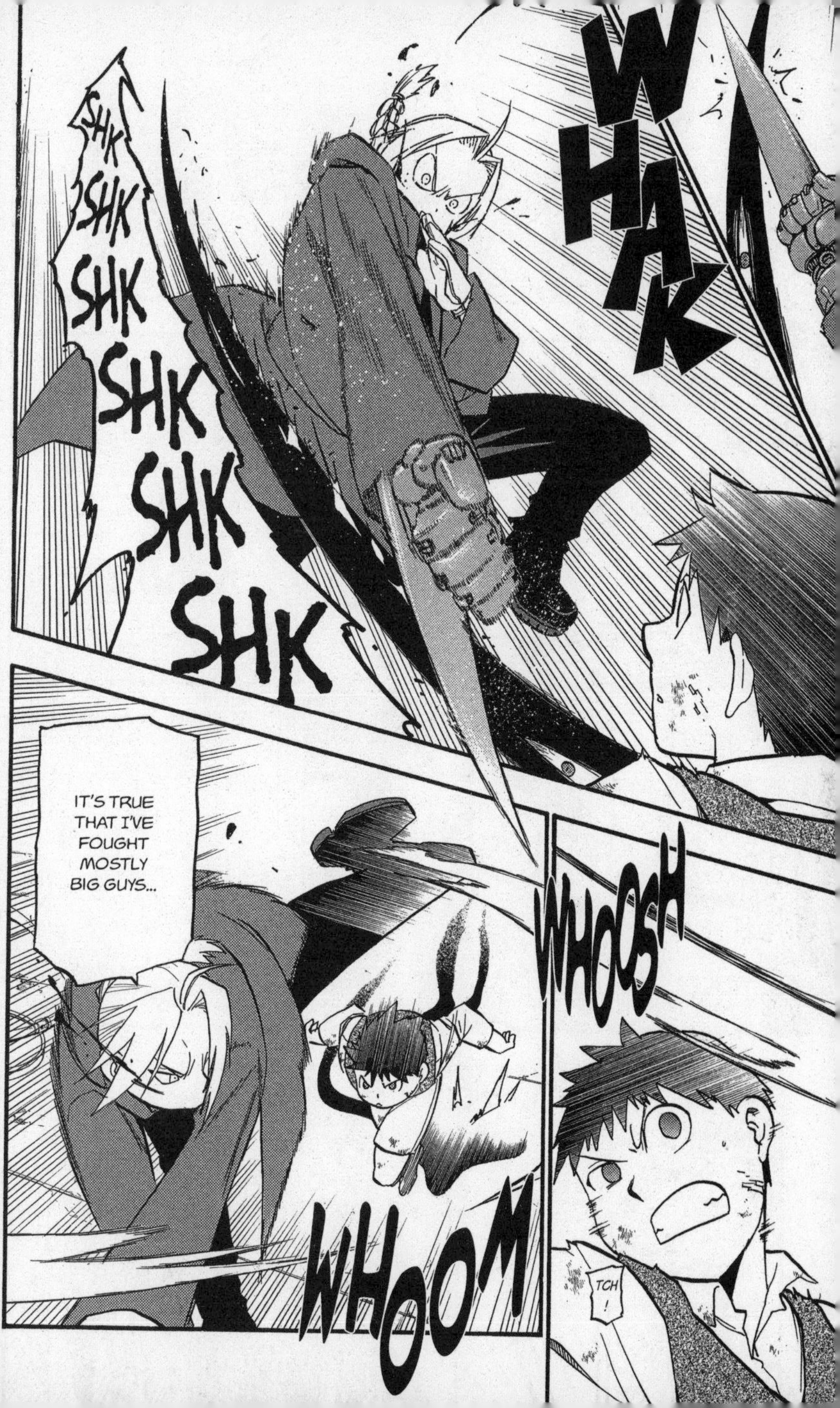
WHAK
SHK SHK SHK SHK SHK SHK
WHOOSH
TCH!
IT'S TRUE THAT I'VE FOUGHT MOSTLY BIG GUYS...
WHOOM

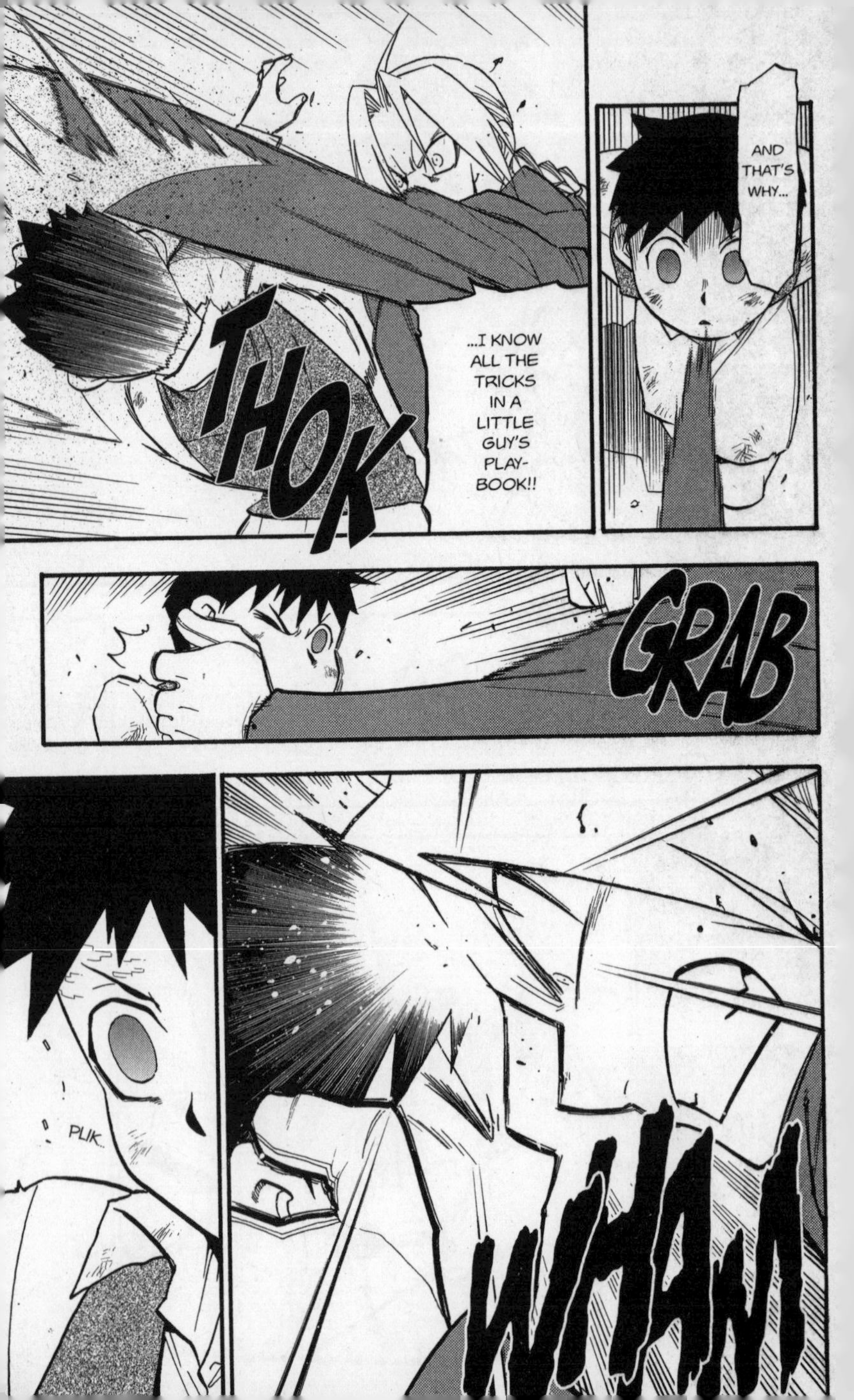
AND THAT'S WHY...
...I KNOW ALL THE TRICKS IN A LITTLE GUY'S PLAY-BOOK!!
THOK
GRAB
WHAM
PLIK..

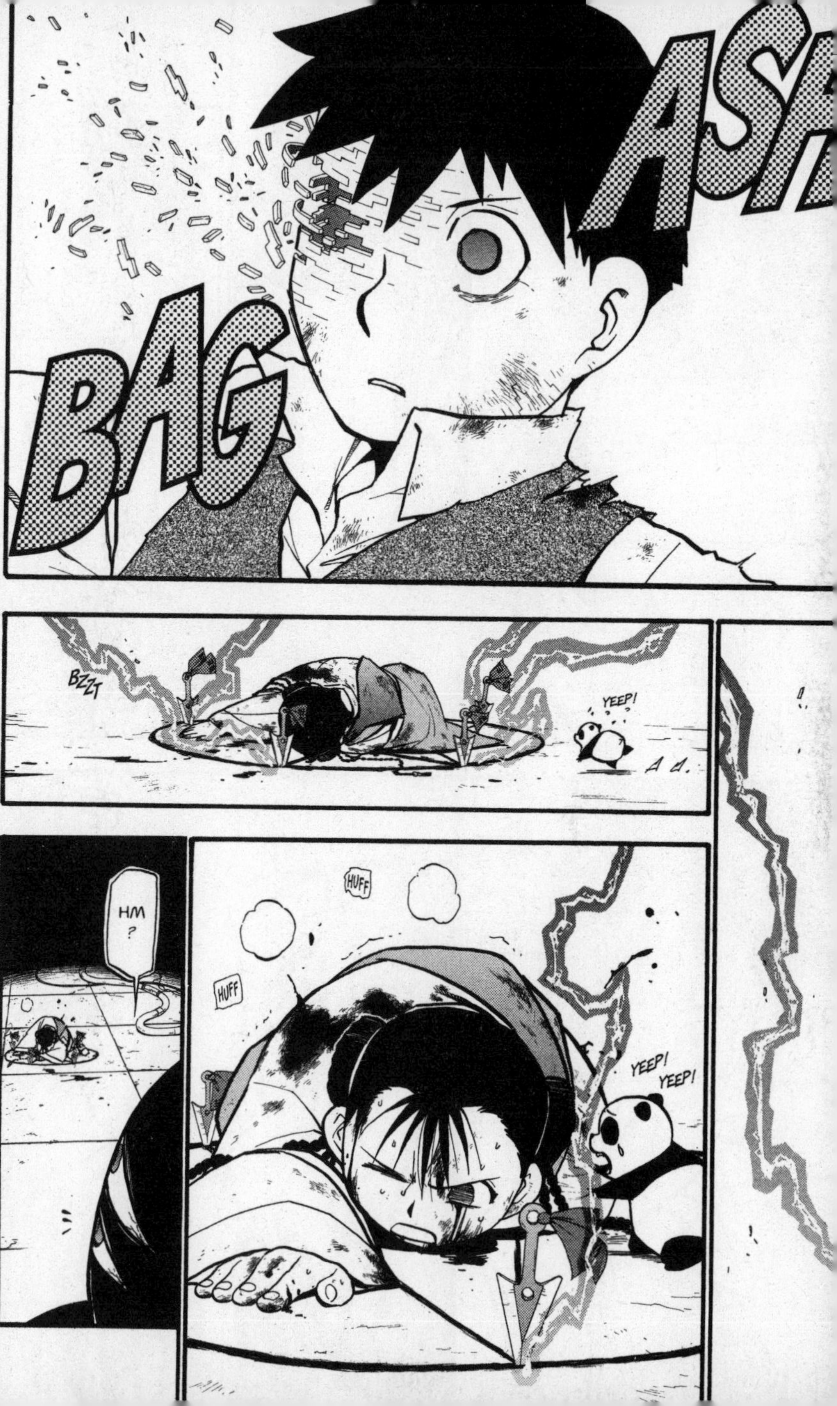
BAGASH
BZZZT
YEEP!
HUFF
HUFF
YEEP! YEEP!
HM ?

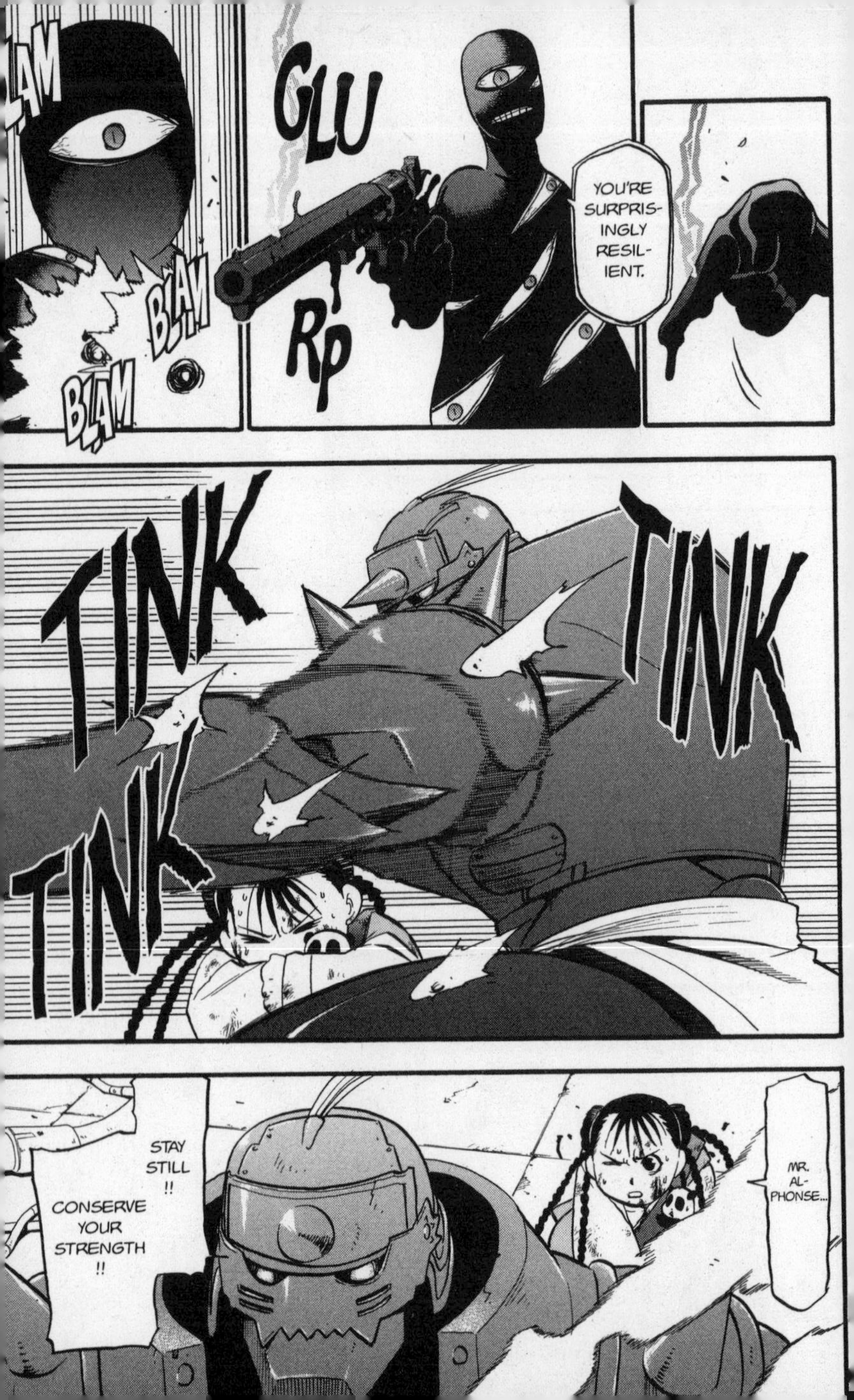

YOU'RE SURPRISINGLY RESILIENT.
GLU
RP
LAM
BLAM
BLAM
TINK
TINK
TINK
MR. ALPHONSE...
STAY STILL!!
CONSERVE YOUR STRENGTH!!

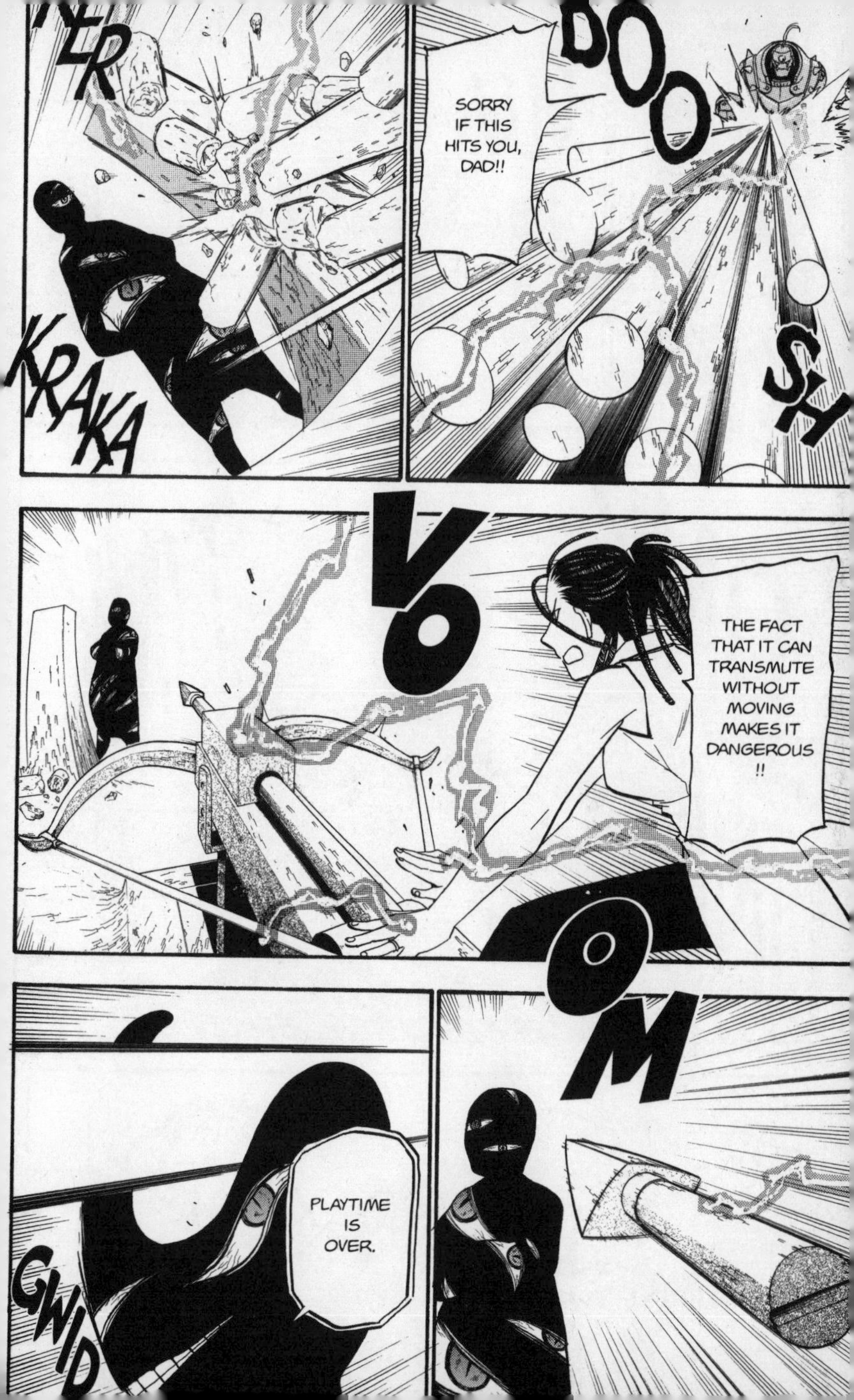
BOOOSH
SORRY IF THIS HITS YOU, DAD!!
KRAKA
VOOOM
THE FACT THAT IT CAN TRANSMUTE WITHOUT MOVING MAKES IT DANGEROUS!!
PLAYTIME IS OVER.
GWID

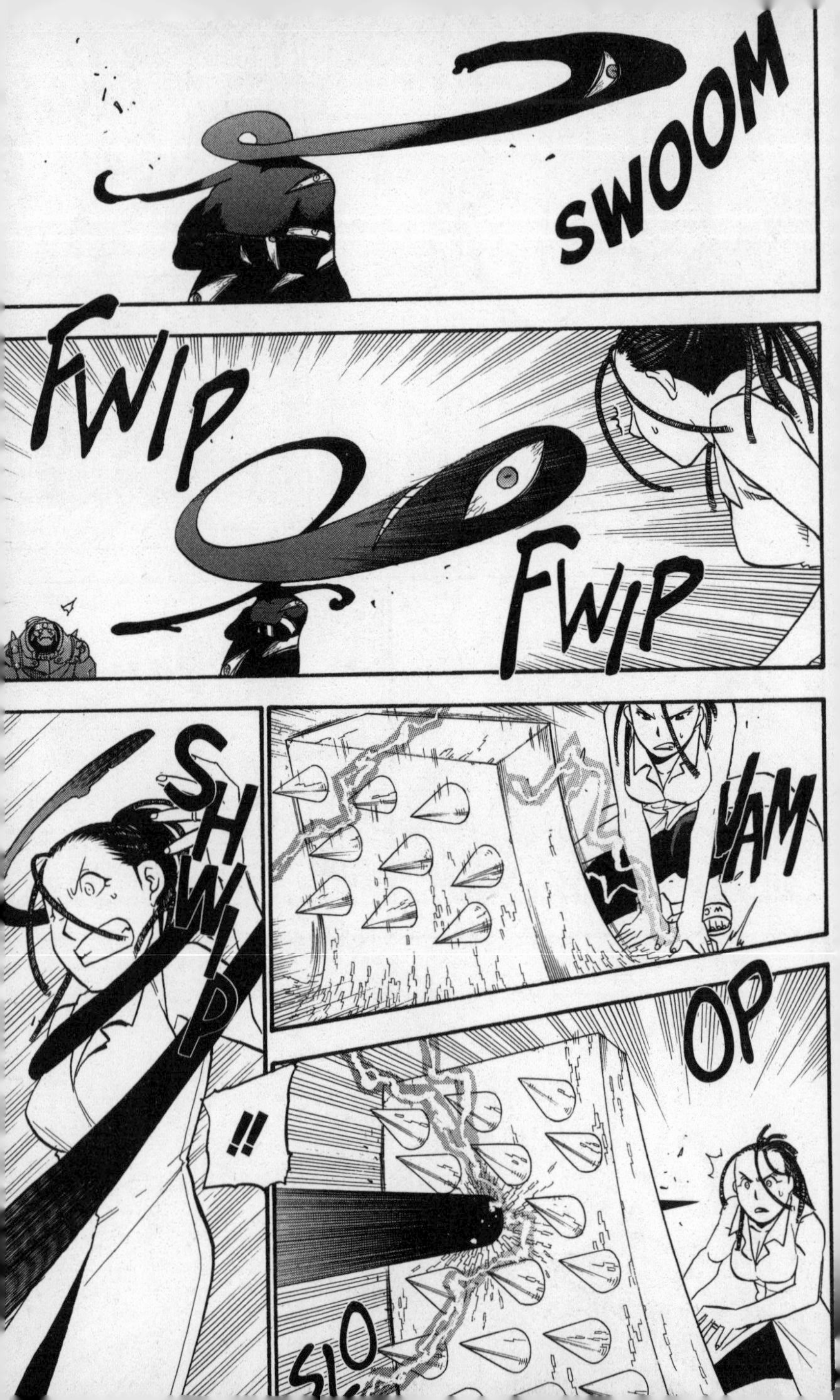

SWOOM
FWIP
FWIP
VAM
OP
!!
SHWIP

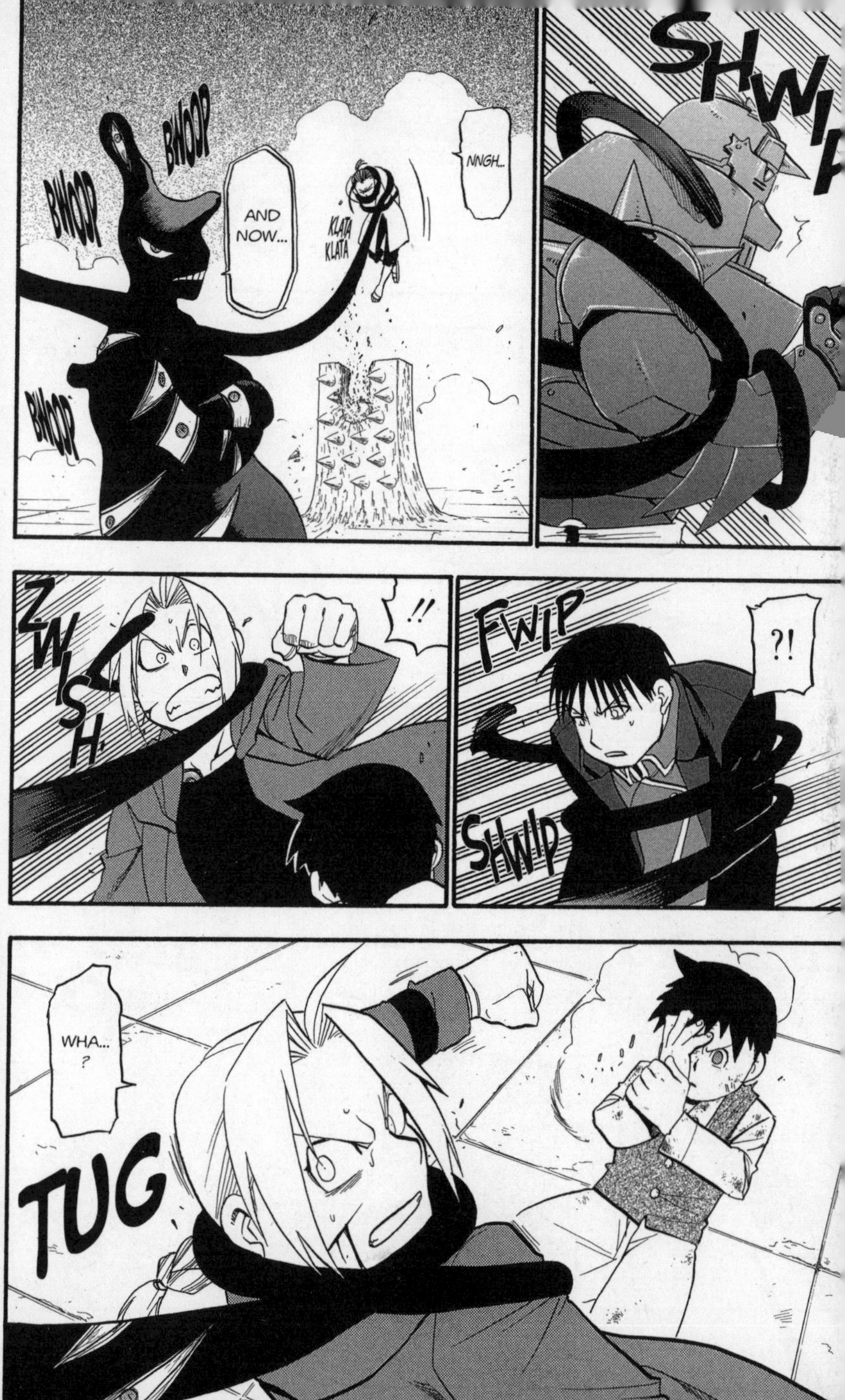
SHWIP
NNGH...
BWOOP
AND NOW...
KLATA KLATA
BWOOP
BWOOP
?!
FWIP
SHWIP
!!
ZWISH
WHA... ?
TUG

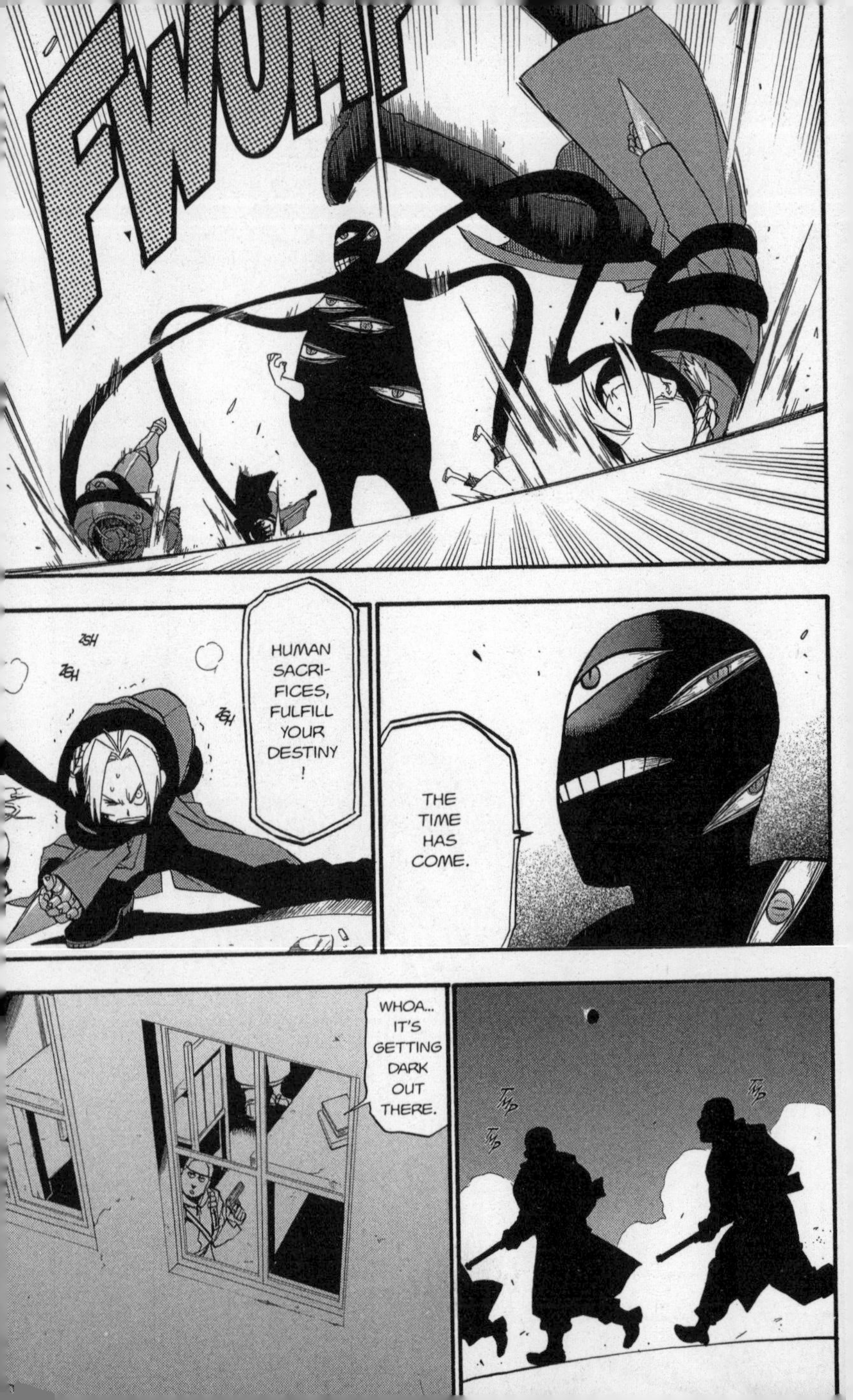
FWUMP
THE TIME HAS COME.
HUMAN SACRIFICES, FULFILL YOUR DESTINY!
ZSH
ZSH
ZSH
TMP
TMP
TMP
WHOA... IT'S GETTING DARK OUT THERE.

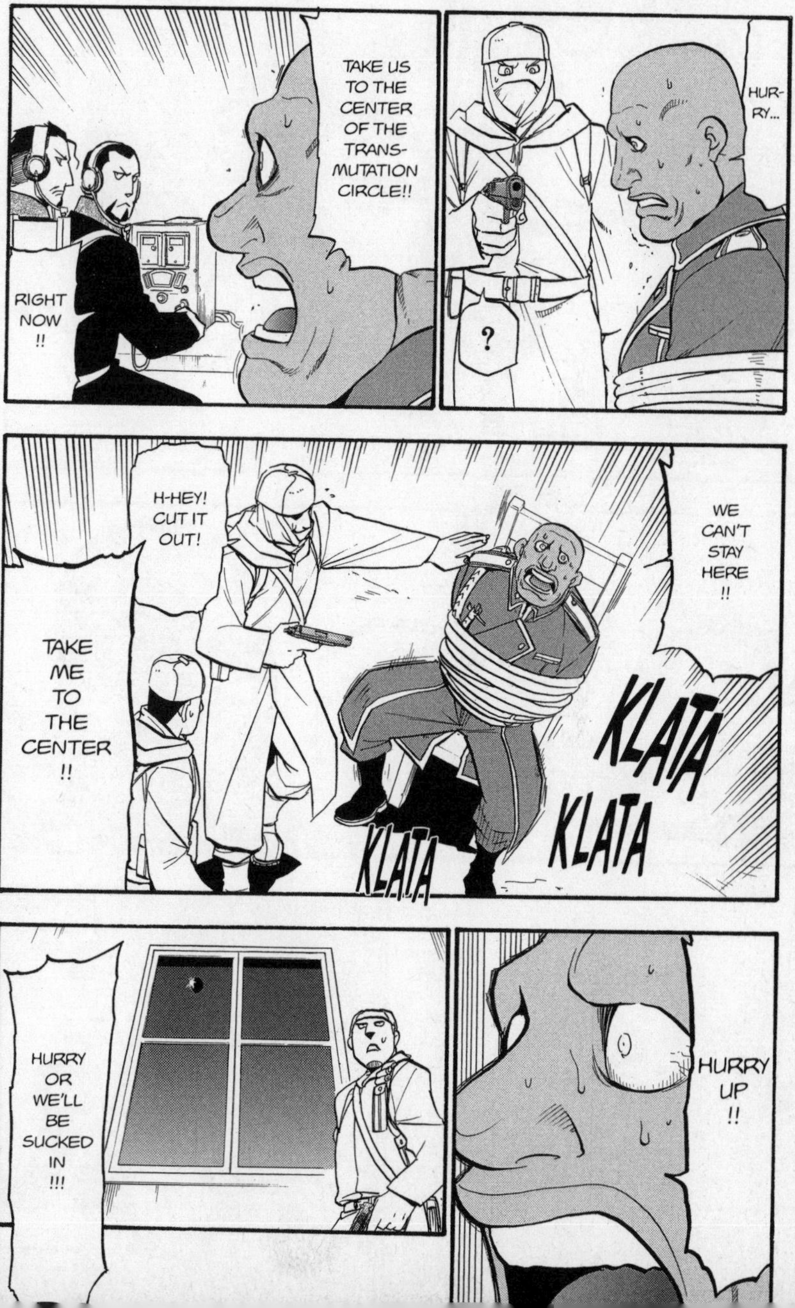
HURRY...
?
TAKE US TO THE CENTER OF THE TRANSMUTATION CIRCLE!!
RIGHT NOW!!
WE CAN'T STAY HERE!!
KLATA
KLATA
KLATA
H-HEY! CUT IT OUT!
TAKE ME TO THE CENTER!!
HURRY UP!!
HURRY OR WE'LL BE SUCKED IN!!!

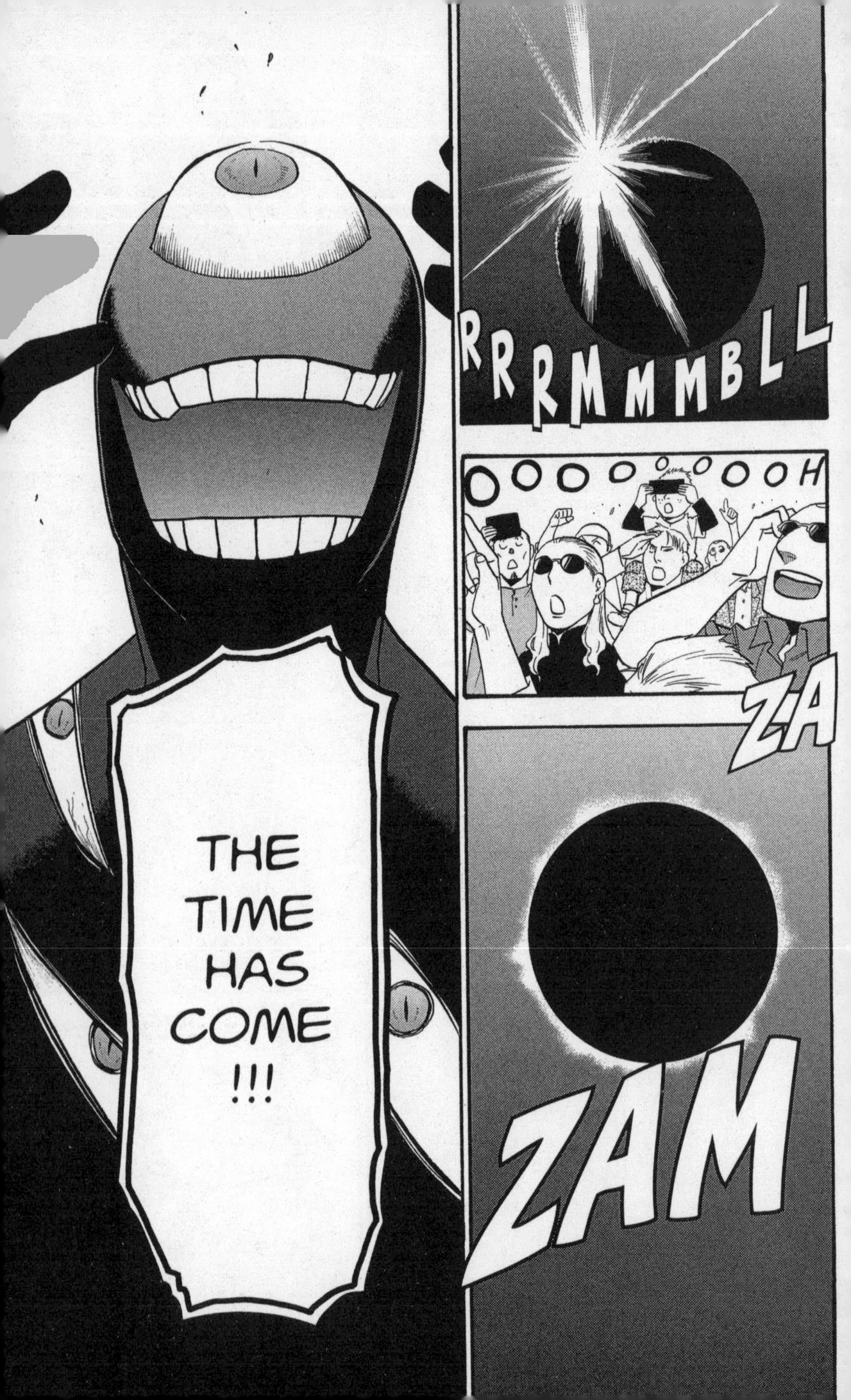
RRRMMMBLL
OOOOOOOOH
ZA
ZAM
THE TIME HAS COME !!!

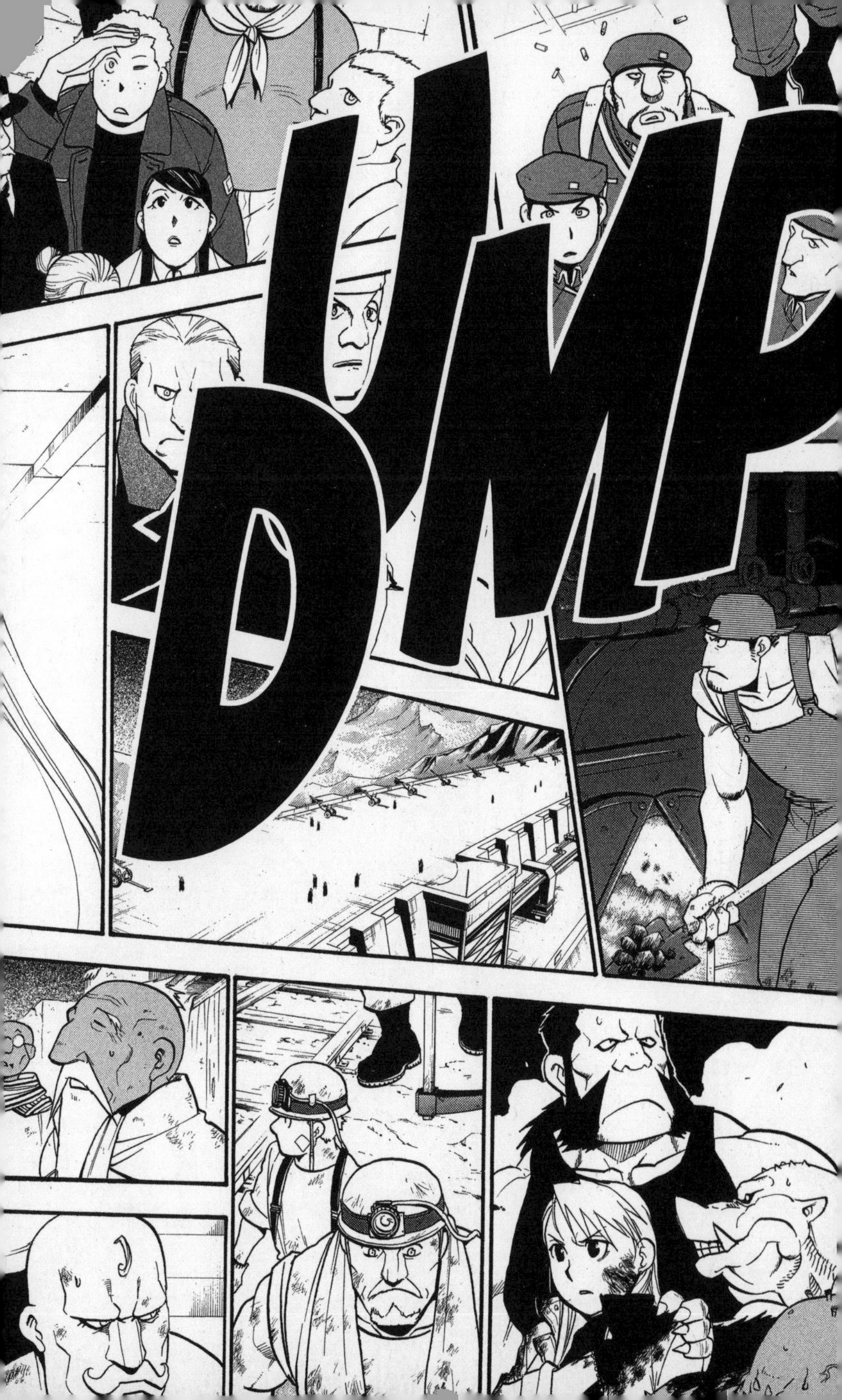
DUMP

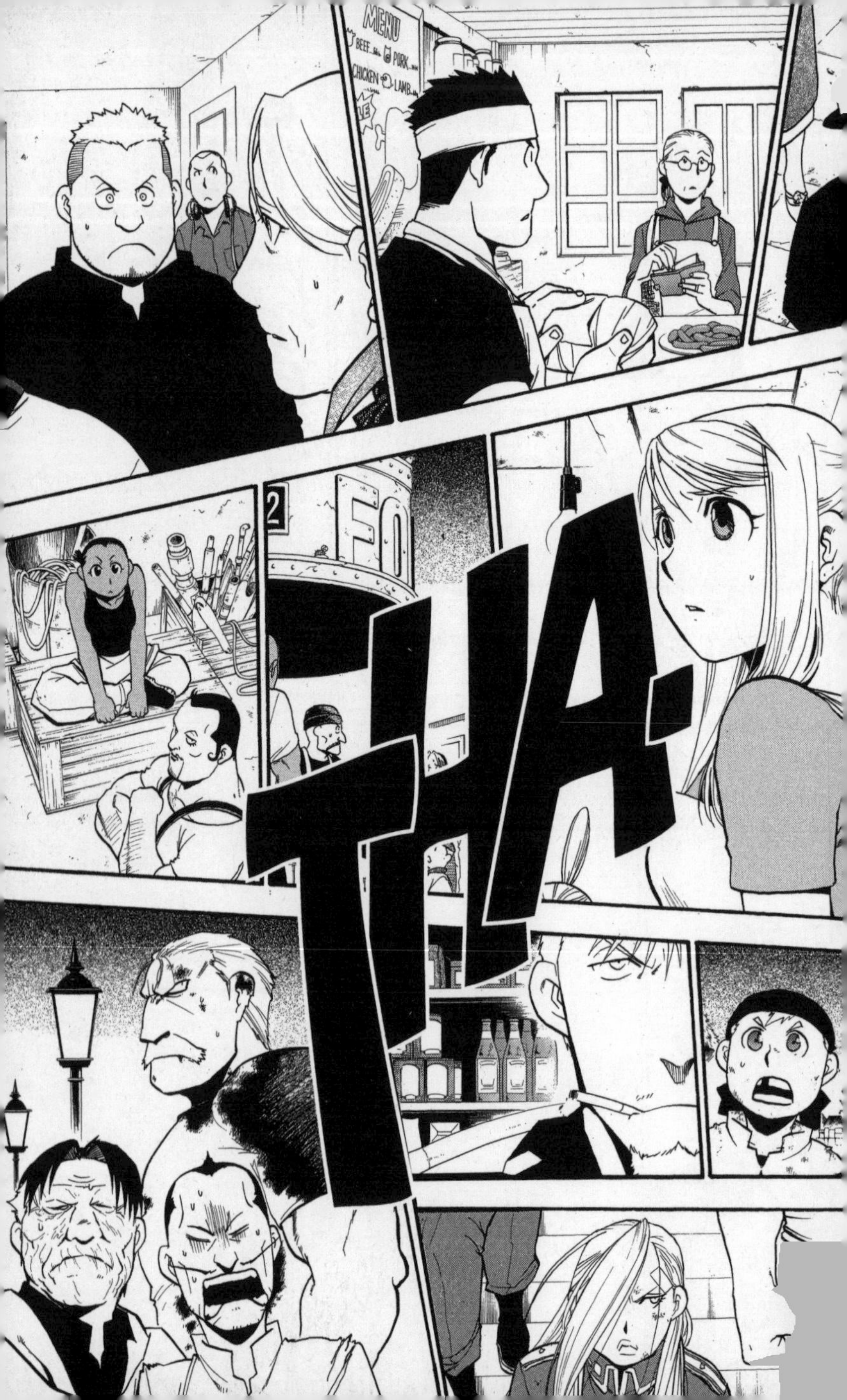
MENU
BEEF
PORK
CHICKEN
LAMB
2
FO
THA-

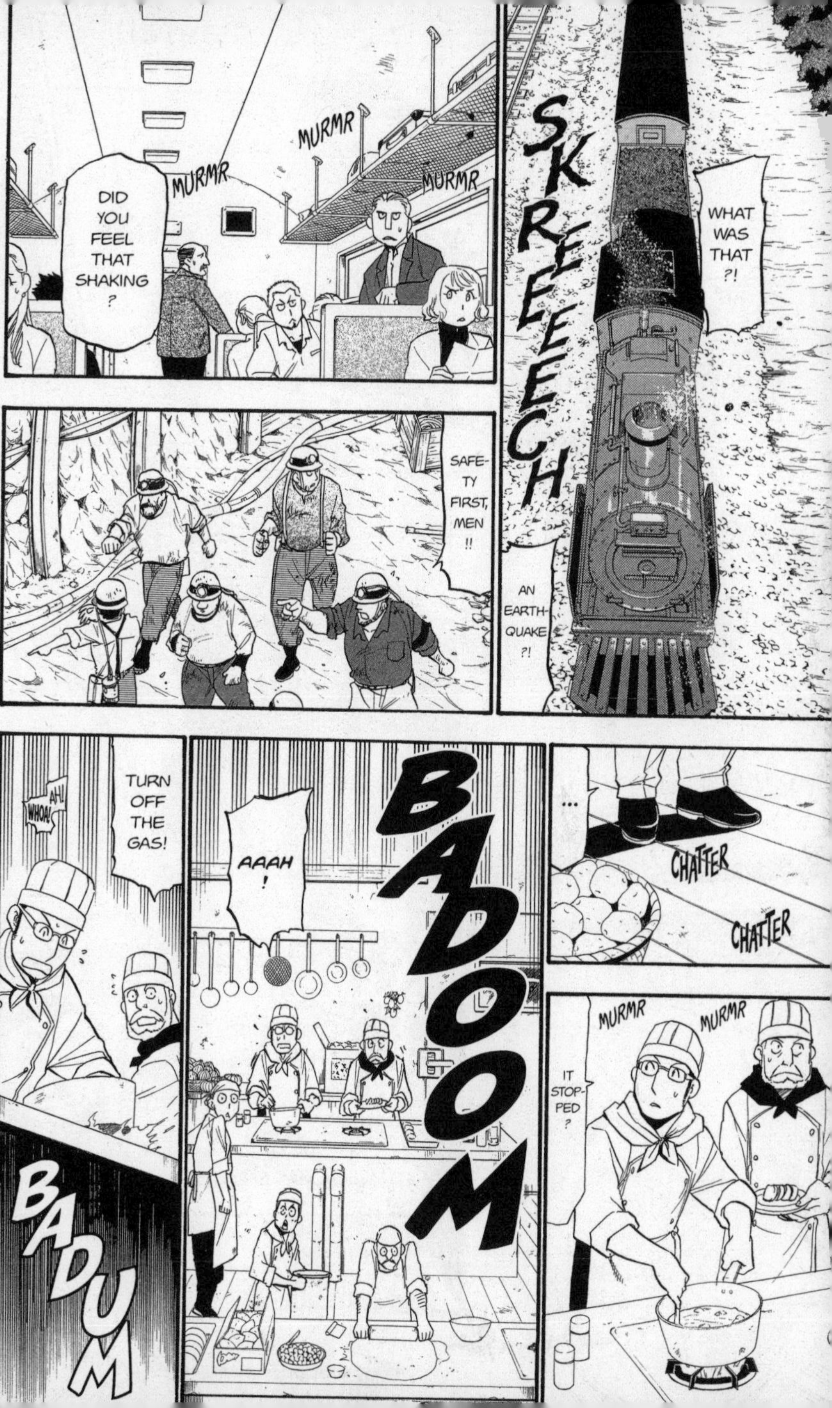
SKREEEECH
WHAT WAS THAT ?!
AN EARTHQUAKE ?!
MURMR
MURMR
DID YOU FEEL THAT SHAKING ?
MURMR
SAFETY FIRST, MEN !!
...
CHATTER
CHATTER
MURMR
MURMR
IT STOPPED ?
BADOOM
AAAH !
TURN OFF THE GAS!
AH! WHOA!
BADUM

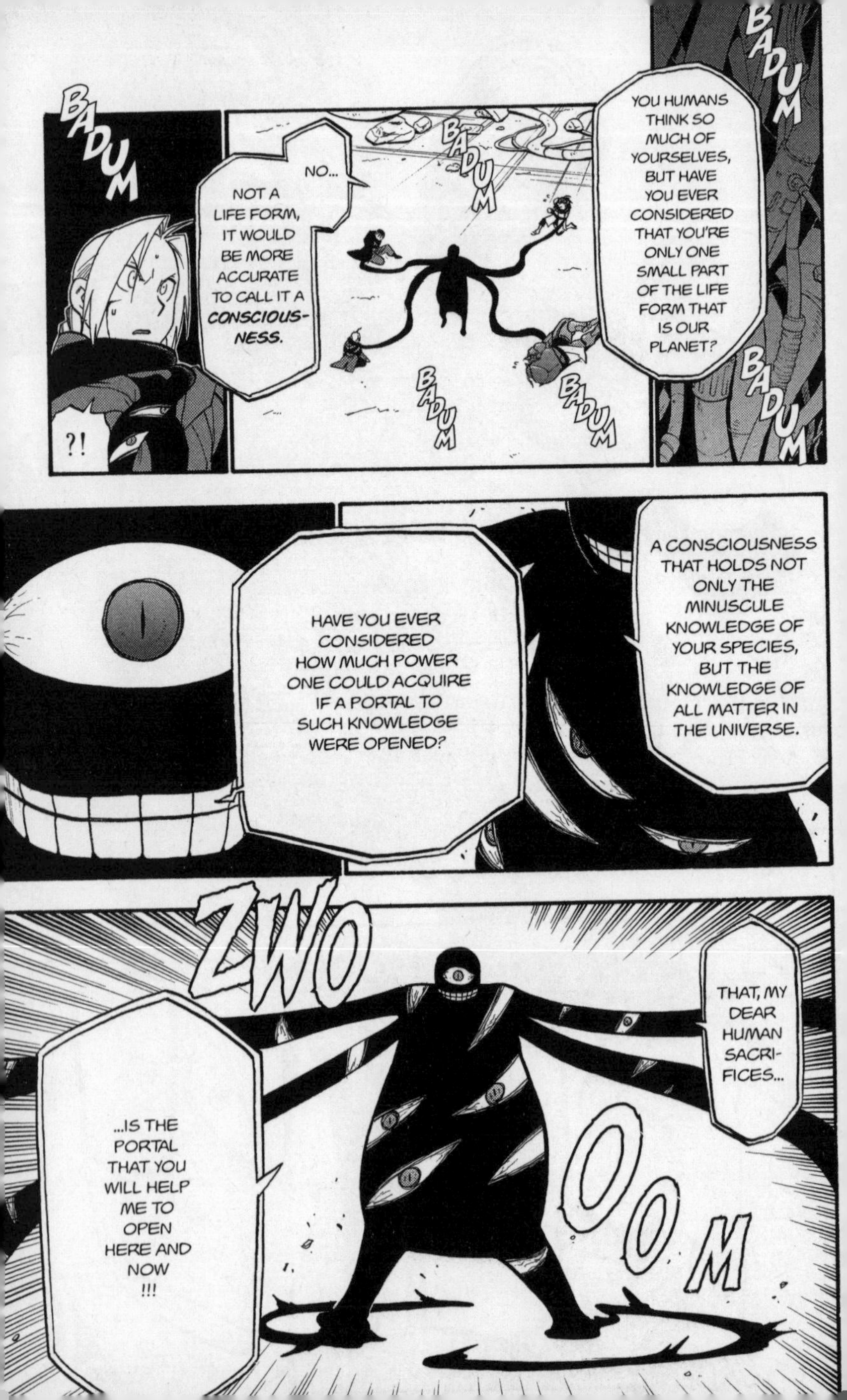
BADUM
BADUM
YOU HUMANS THINK SO MUCH OF YOURSELVES, BUT HAVE YOU EVER CONSIDERED THAT YOU'RE ONLY ONE SMALL PART OF THE LIFE FORM THAT IS OUR PLANET?
BADUM
NO... NOT A LIFE FORM, IT WOULD BE MORE ACCURATE TO CALL IT A CONSCIOUSNESS.
BADUM
BADUM
BADUM
?!
A CONSCIOUSNESS THAT HOLDS NOT ONLY THE MINUSCULE KNOWLEDGE OF YOUR SPECIES, BUT THE KNOWLEDGE OF ALL MATTER IN THE UNIVERSE.
HAVE YOU EVER CONSIDERED HOW MUCH POWER ONE COULD ACQUIRE IF A PORTAL TO SUCH KNOWLEDGE WERE OPENED?
ZWO
THAT, MY DEAR HUMAN SACRIFICES...
...IS THE PORTAL THAT YOU WILL HELP ME TO OPEN HERE AND NOW!!!
OOM

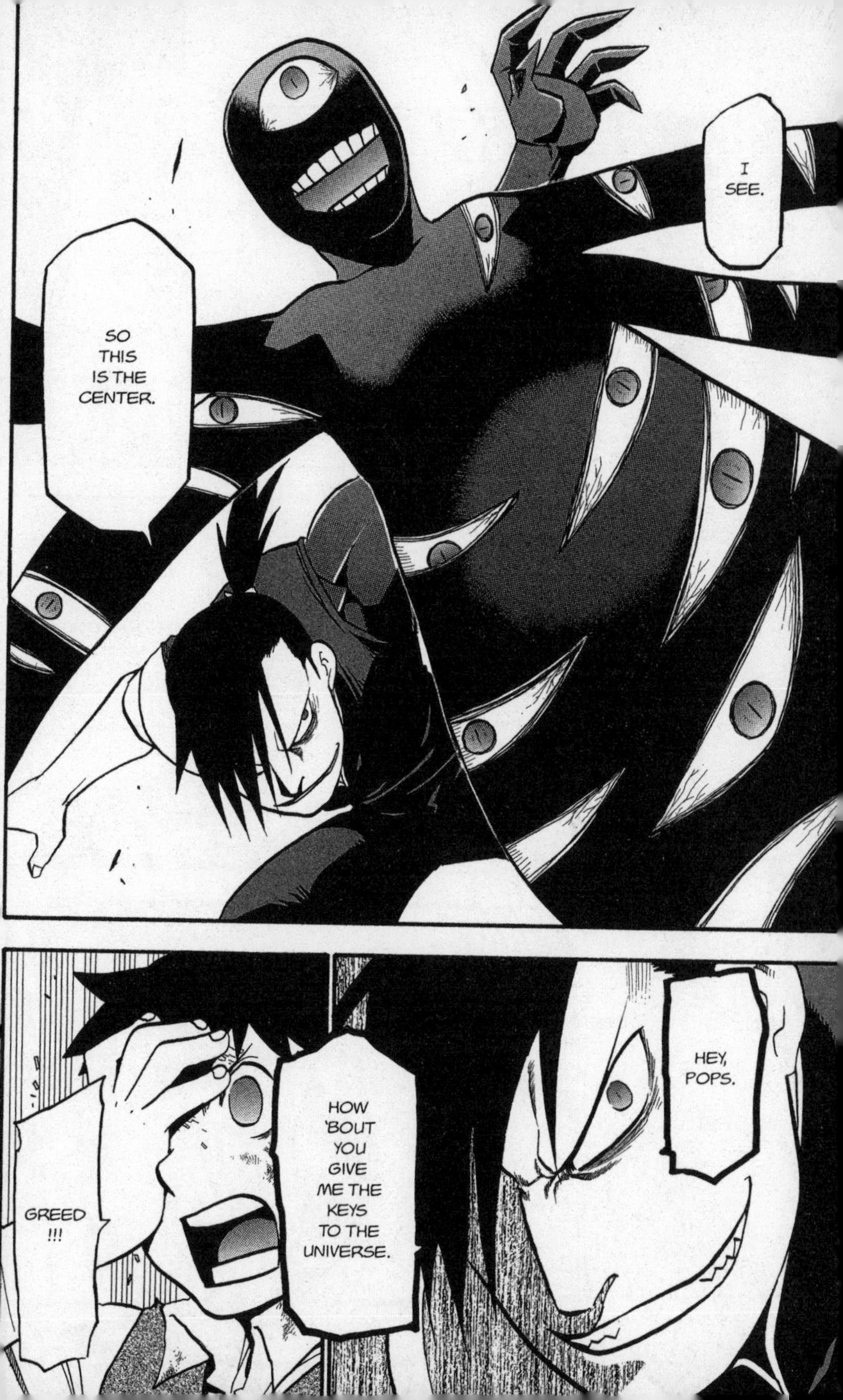
I SEE.
SO THIS IS THE CENTER.
HEY, POPS.
HOW 'BOUT YOU GIVE ME THE KEYS TO THE UNIVERSE.
GREED !!!

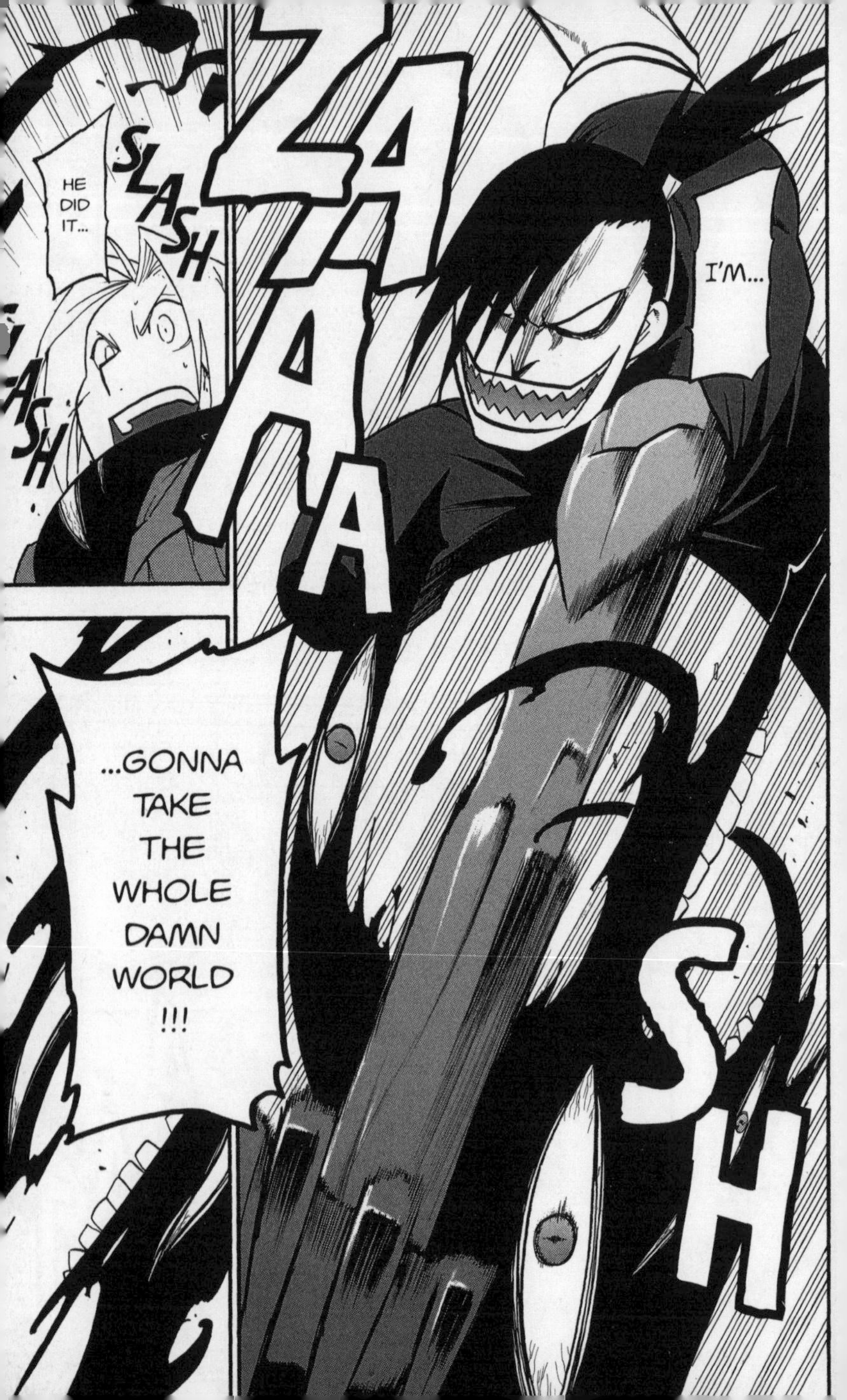
I'M...
ZAAAA
...GONNA TAKE THE WHOLE DAMN WORLD!!!
SH
HE DID IT...
SLASH
SLASH

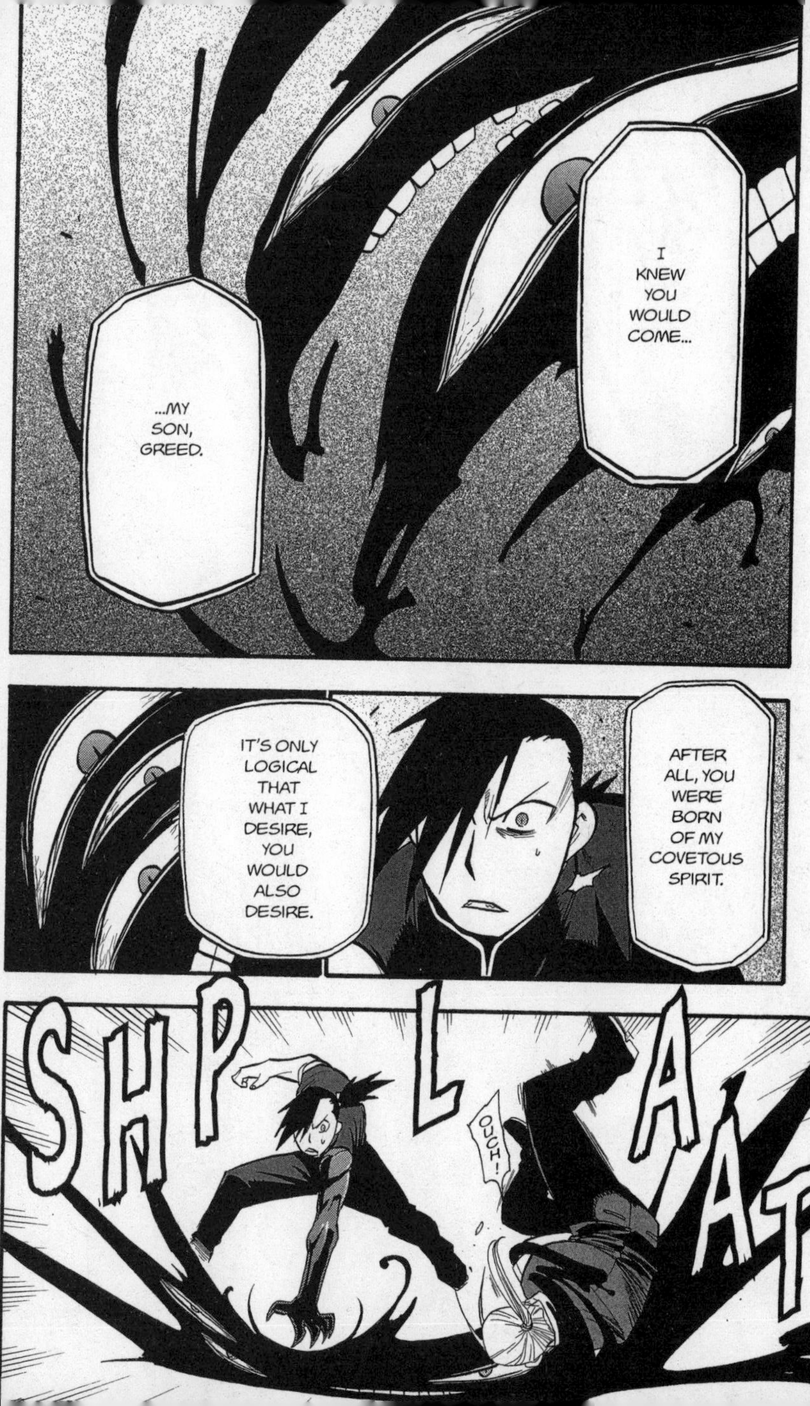
I KNEW YOU WOULD COME...
...MY SON, GREED.
AFTER ALL, YOU WERE BORN OF MY COVETOUS SPIRIT.
IT'S ONLY LOGICAL THAT WHAT I DESIRE, YOU WOULD ALSO DESIRE.
SHPLAAT
OUCH!

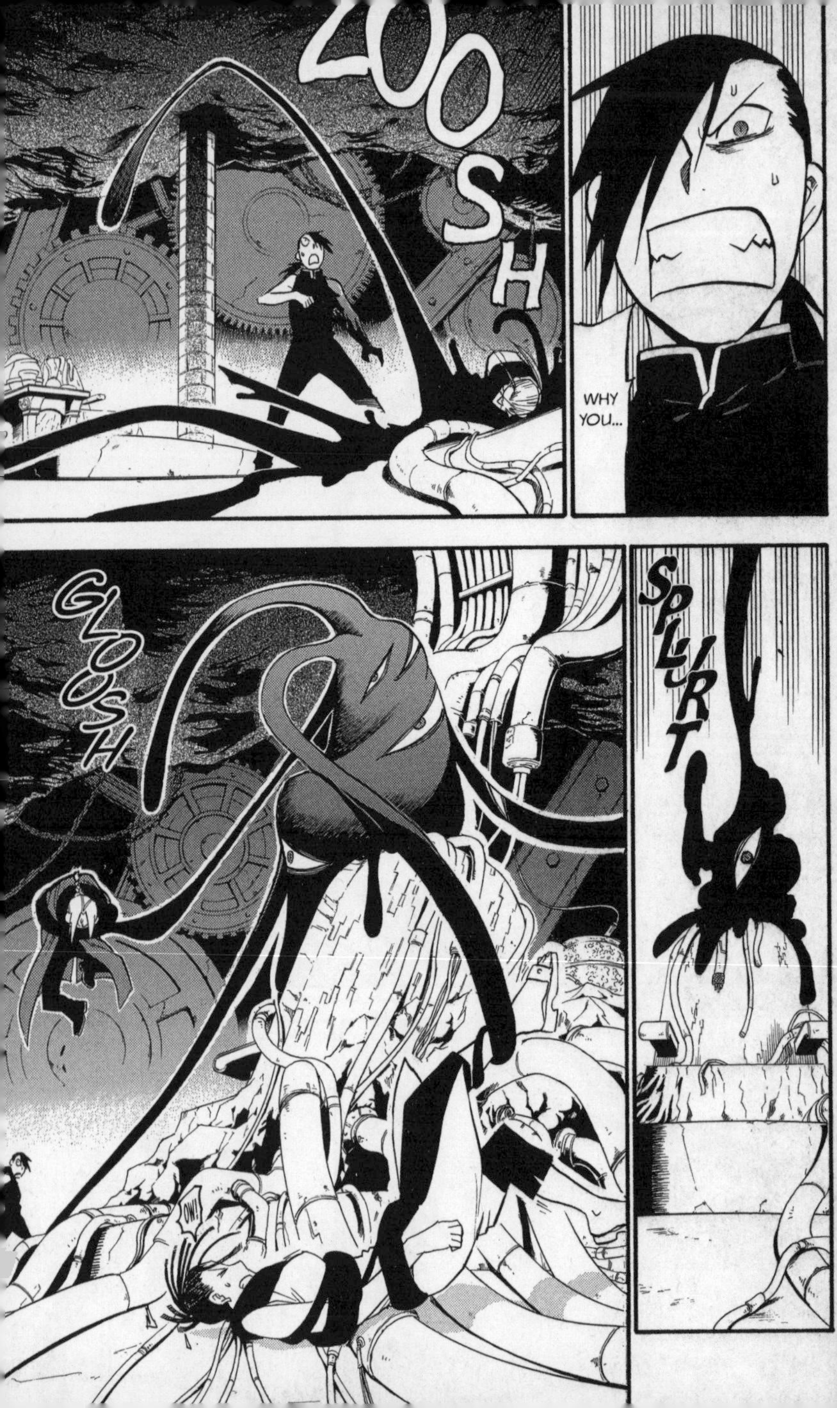
WHY YOU...
ZOOSH
SPLURT
GLOOSH
OW!

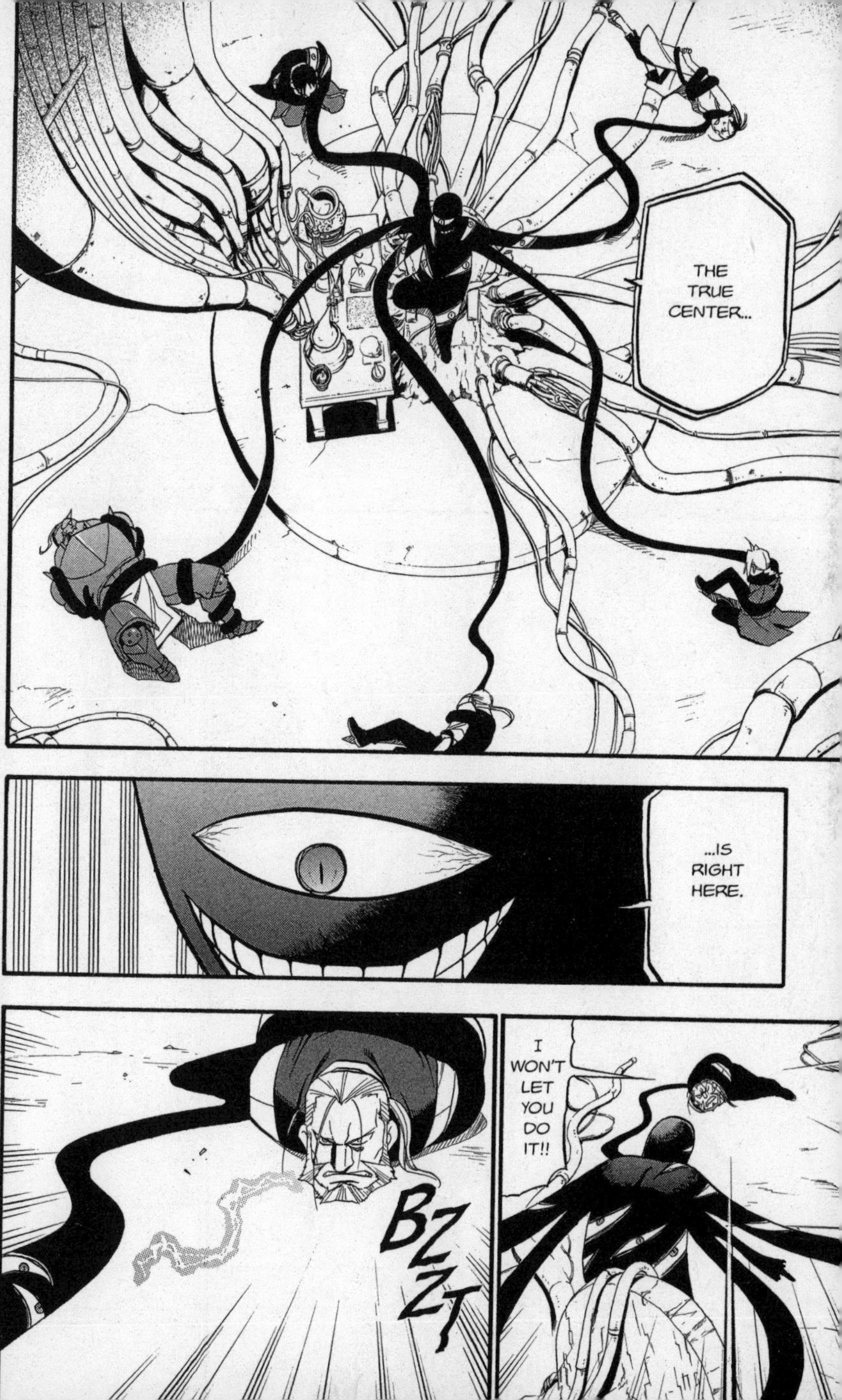
THE TRUE CENTER...
...IS RIGHT HERE.
I WON'T LET YOU DO IT!!
BZZT

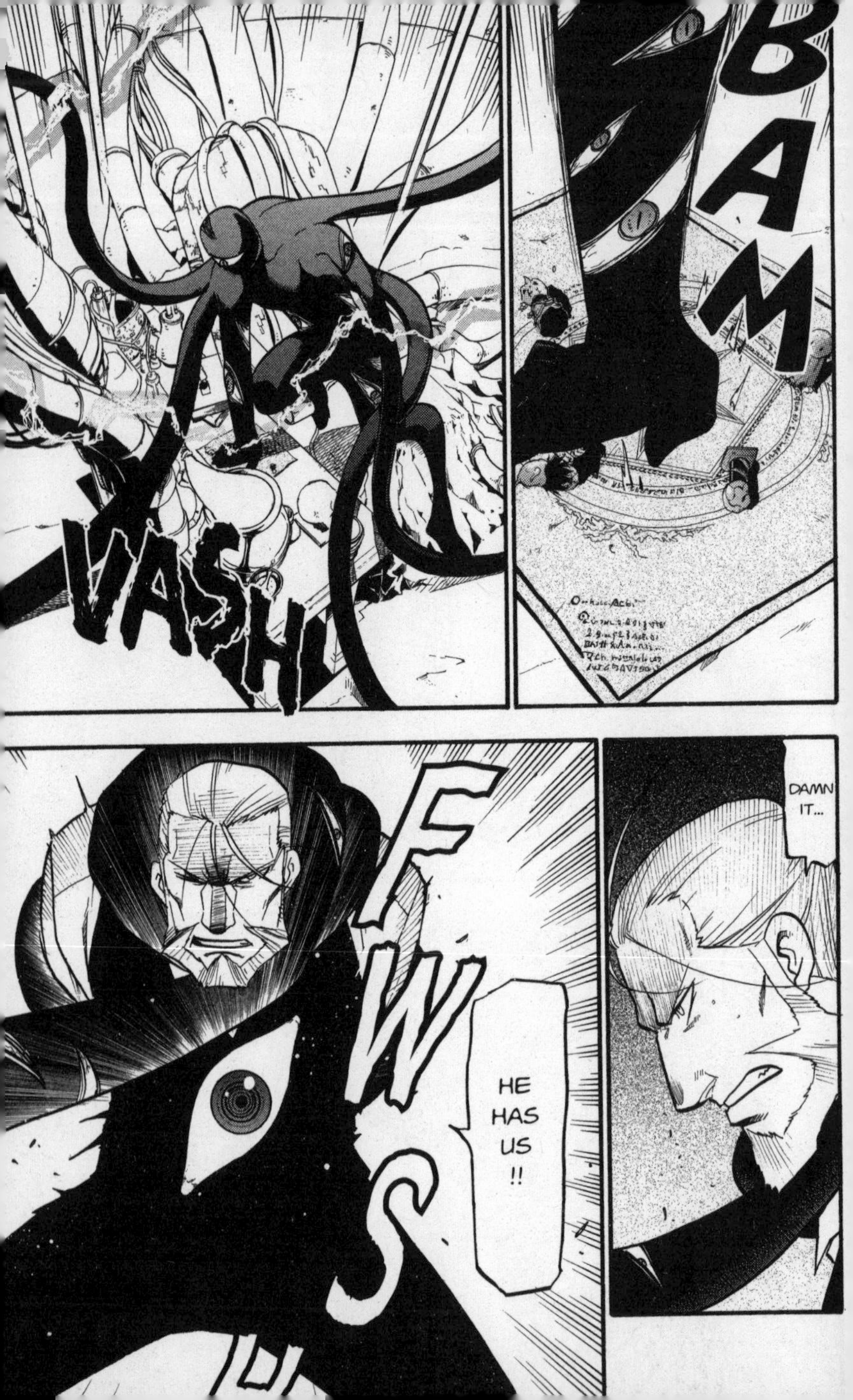
BAM
VASH
DAMN IT...
FWS
HE HAS US !!

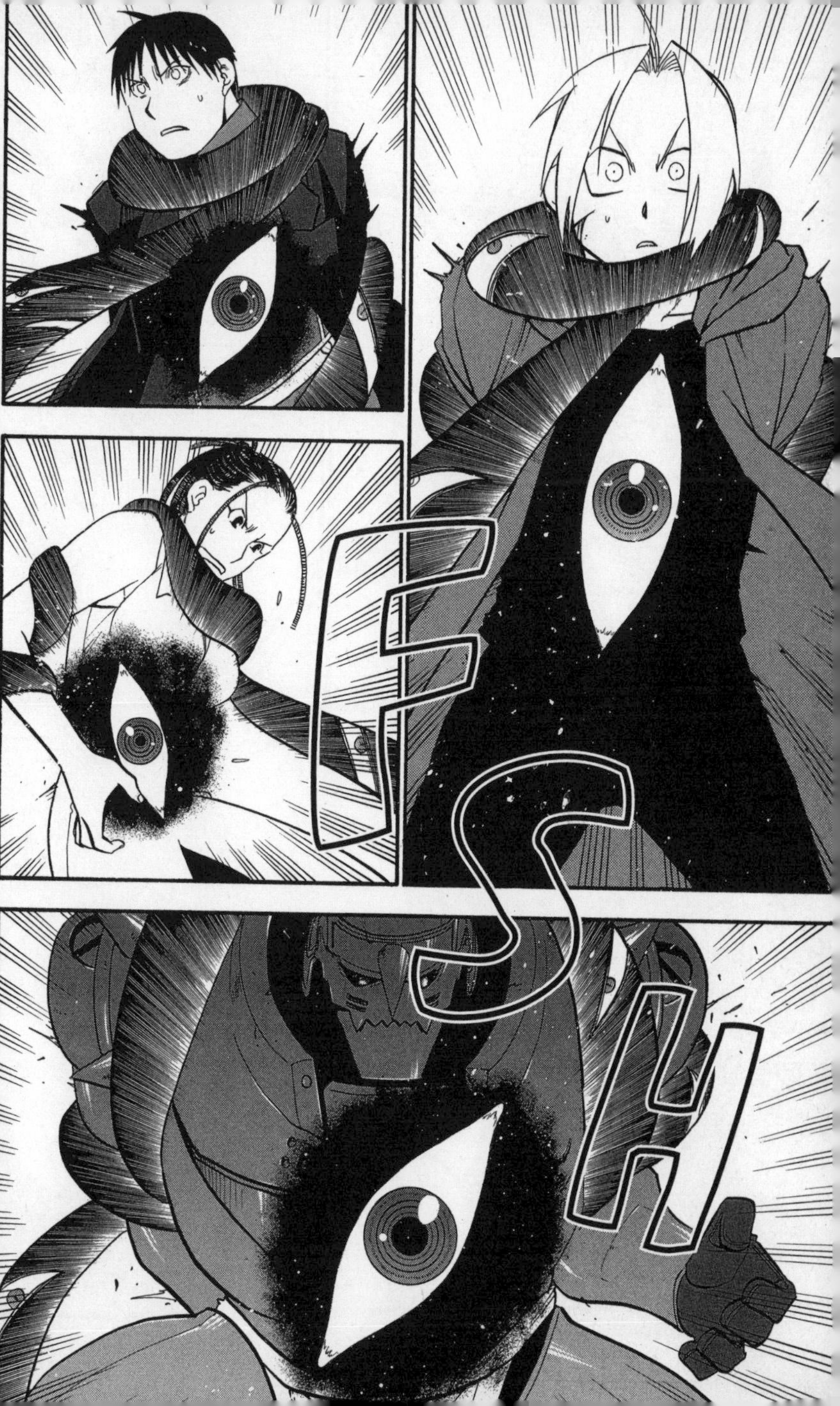
FSSH

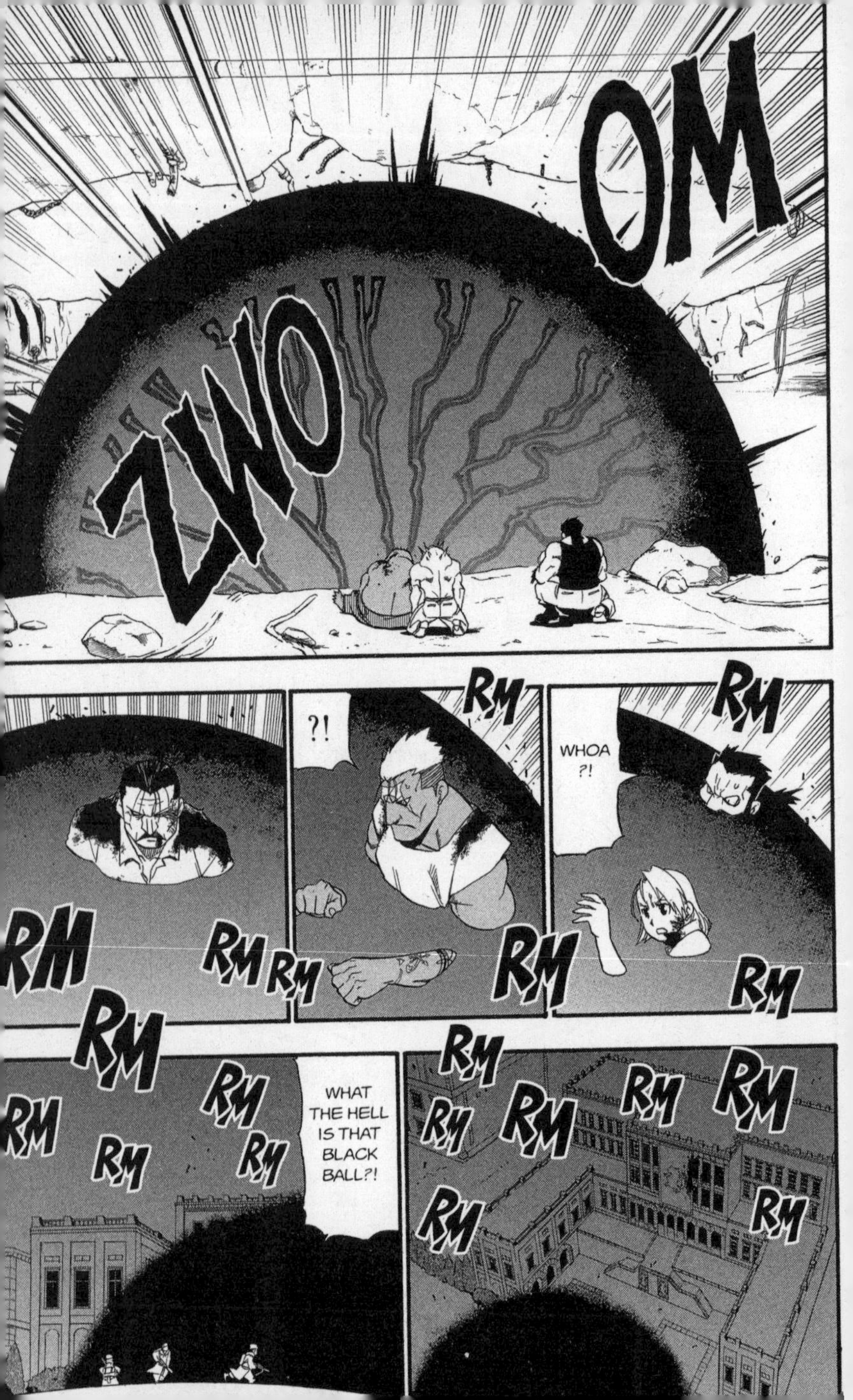
ZWO
OM
RM
WHOA ?!
RM
?!
RM
RM
RM RM
RM
RM
RM
RM
RM
RM
RM
RM
RM
WHAT THE HELL IS THAT BLACK BALL?!
RM
RM
RM
RM
RM

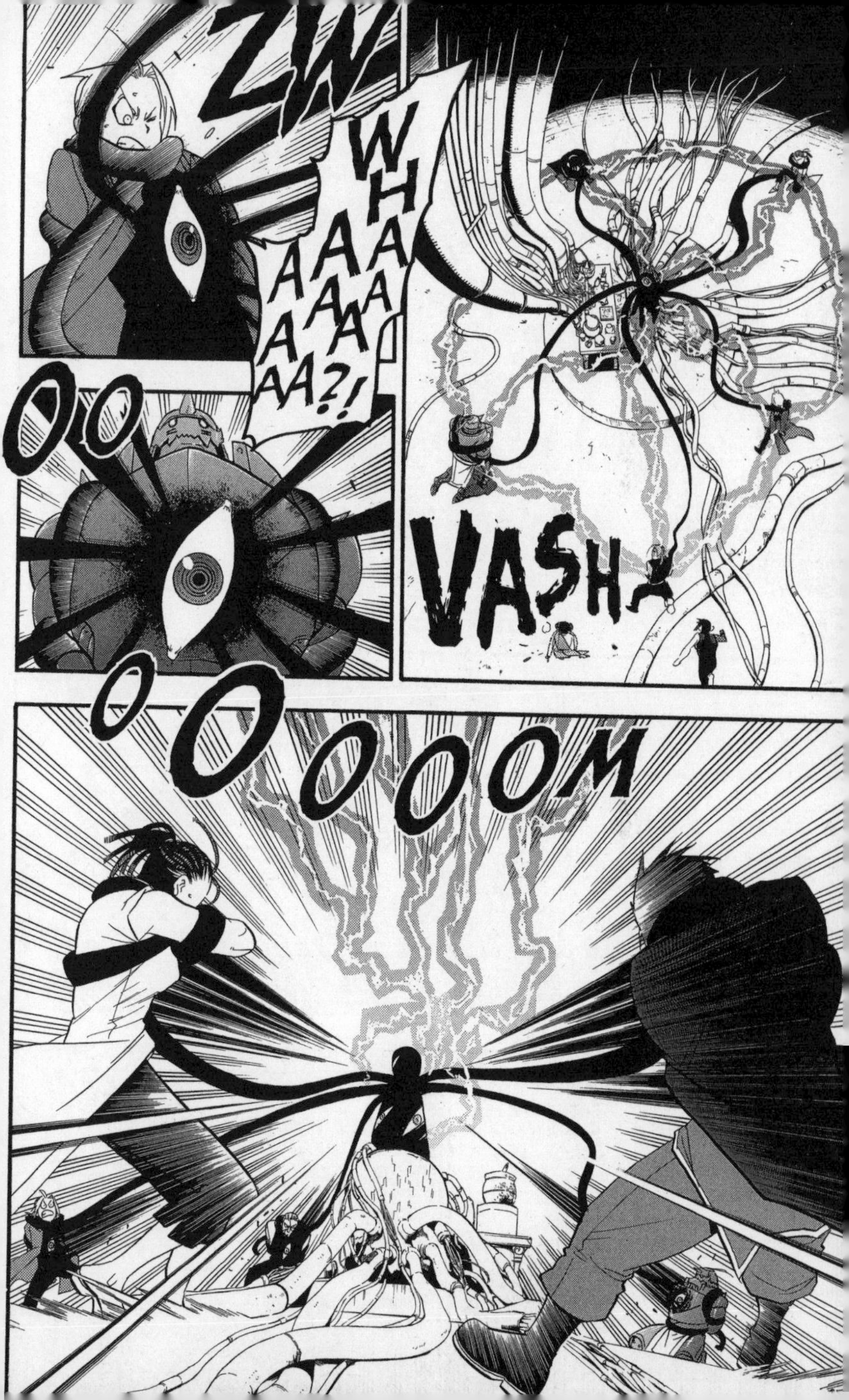
VASH
ZW
WHAAAAAAAAAA?!
OOOOOOOOOM

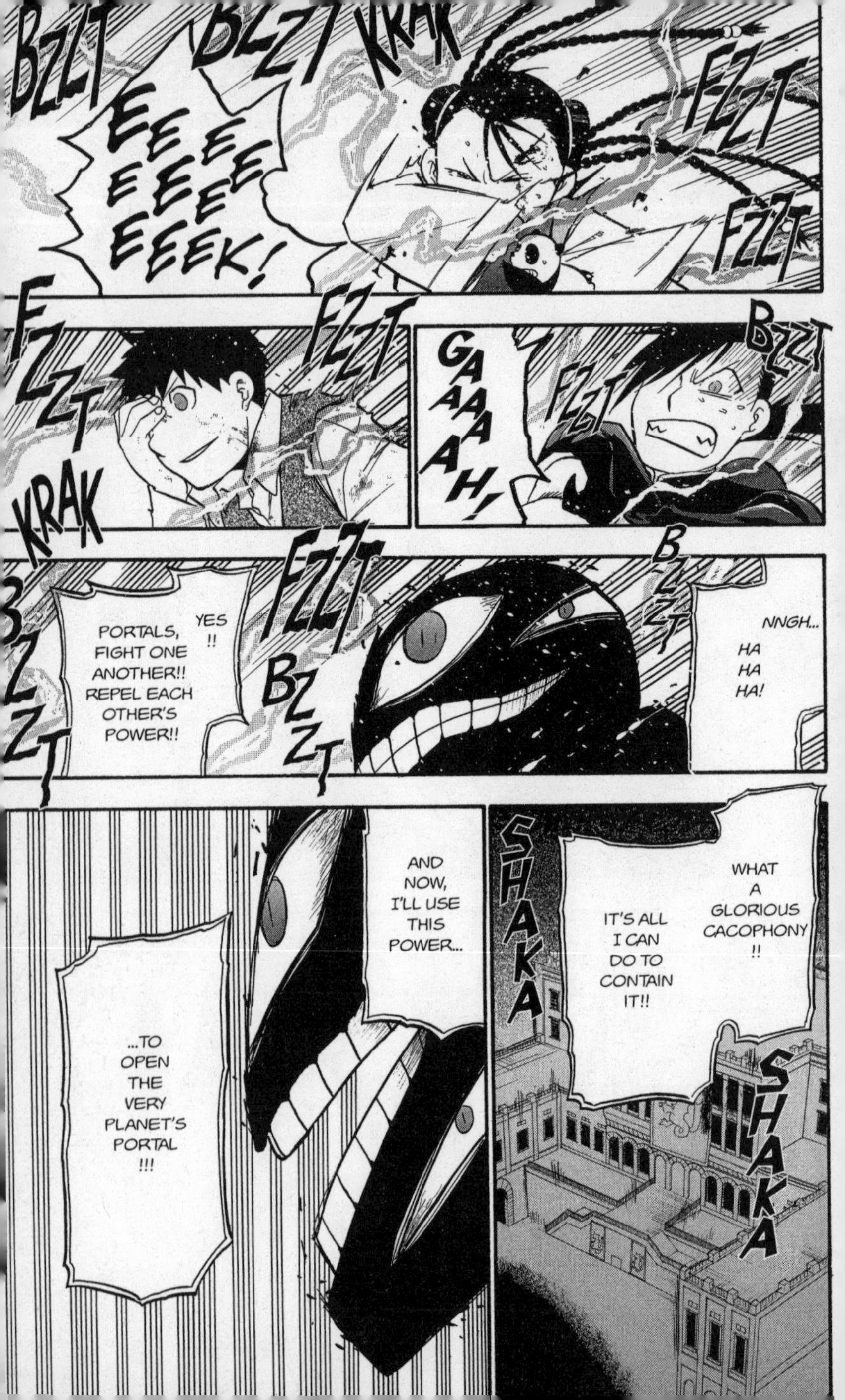
FZZT
FZZT
KRAK
BZZT
EEEEEEEEEEEEK!
BZZT
BZZT
GAAAAAH!
FZZT
FZZT
FZZT
KRAK
NNGH... HA HA HA!
BZZT
BZZT
FZZT
YES!!
PORTALS, FIGHT ONE ANOTHER!! REPEL EACH OTHER'S POWER!!
BZZT
WHAT A GLORIOUS CACOPHONY!!
IT'S ALL I CAN DO TO CONTAIN IT!!
SHAKA
SHAKA
AND NOW, I'LL USE THIS POWER...
...TO OPEN THE VERY PLANET'S PORTAL!!!

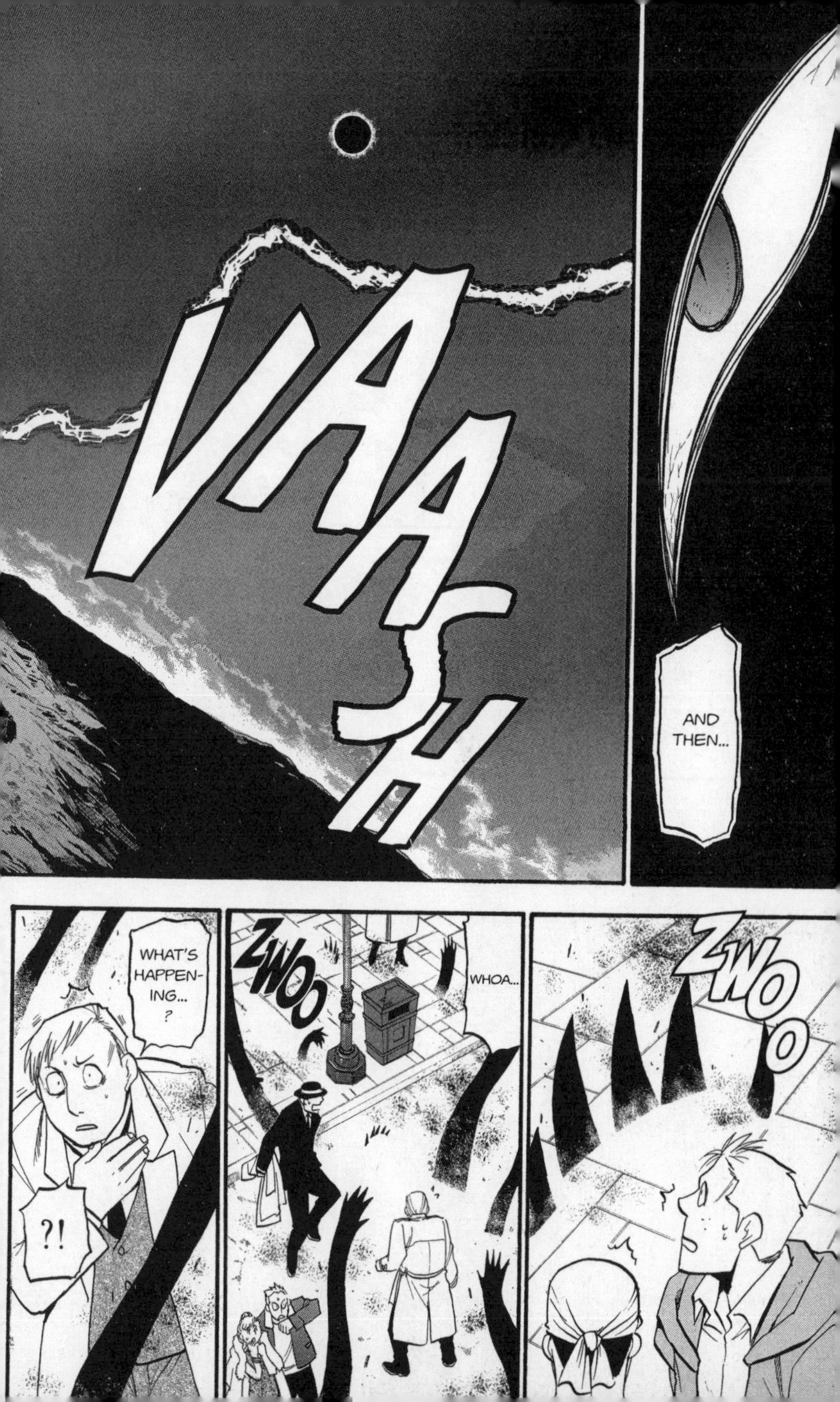
AND THEN...
VAASH
ZWOO
ZWOO
WHOA...
WHAT'S HAPPEN-ING... ?
?!

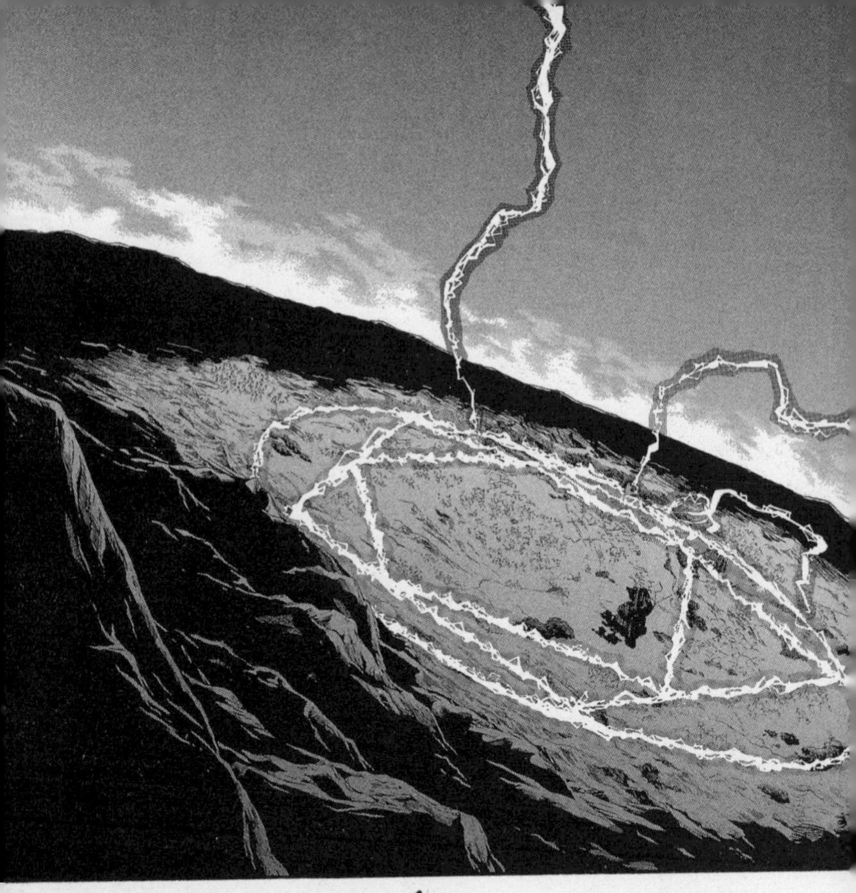

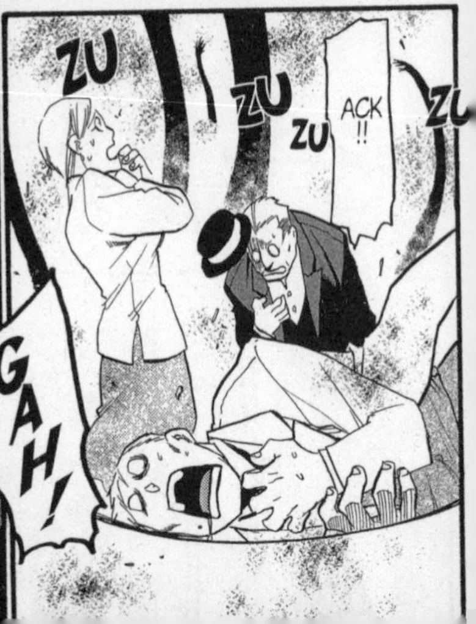
ZU
ACK!!
ZU
ZU
ZU
GAH!

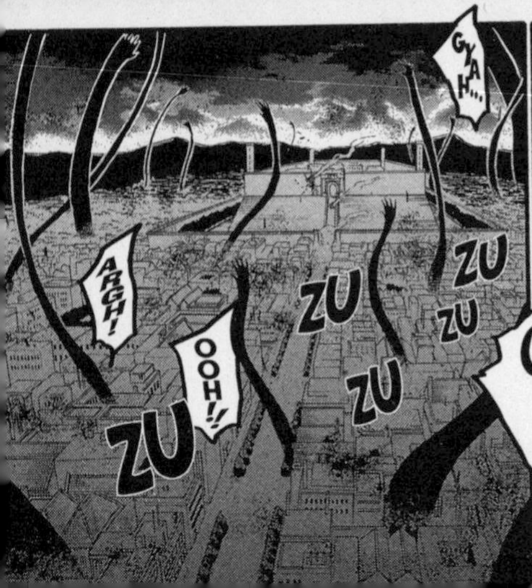
GYAH...
ZU
ZU
ZU
ARGH!
OOH!!
ZU
ZU

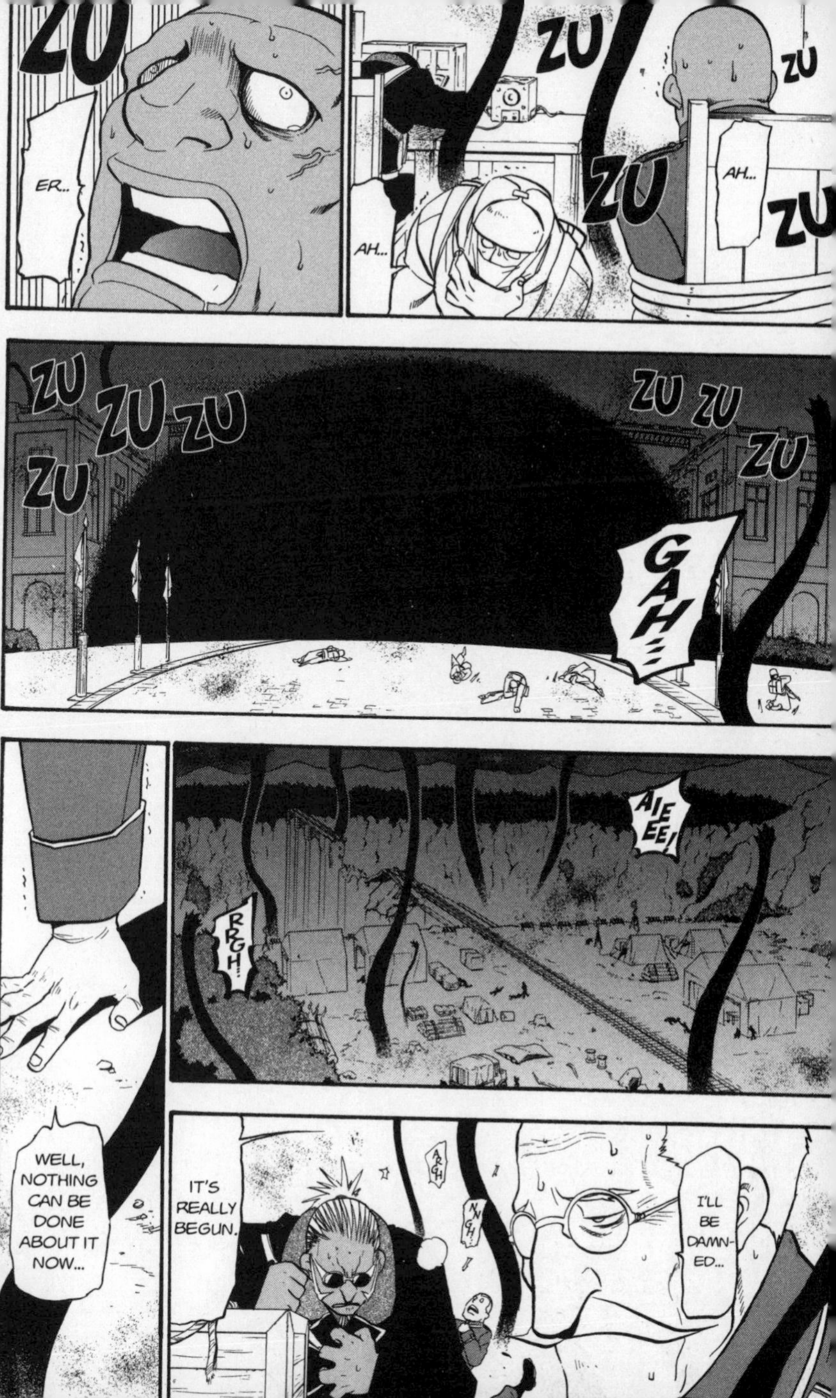
ZU
ZU
AH...
ZU
ZU
AH...
ZU
ER..
ZU ZU ZU
ZU ZU
ZU
GAH!!
ZU ZU ZU
ZU
AIEEE!
RRGH!!
I'LL BE DAMN- ED...
ARGH
NNGH!
IT'S REALLY BEGUN.
WELL, NOTHING CAN BE DONE ABOUT IT NOW...

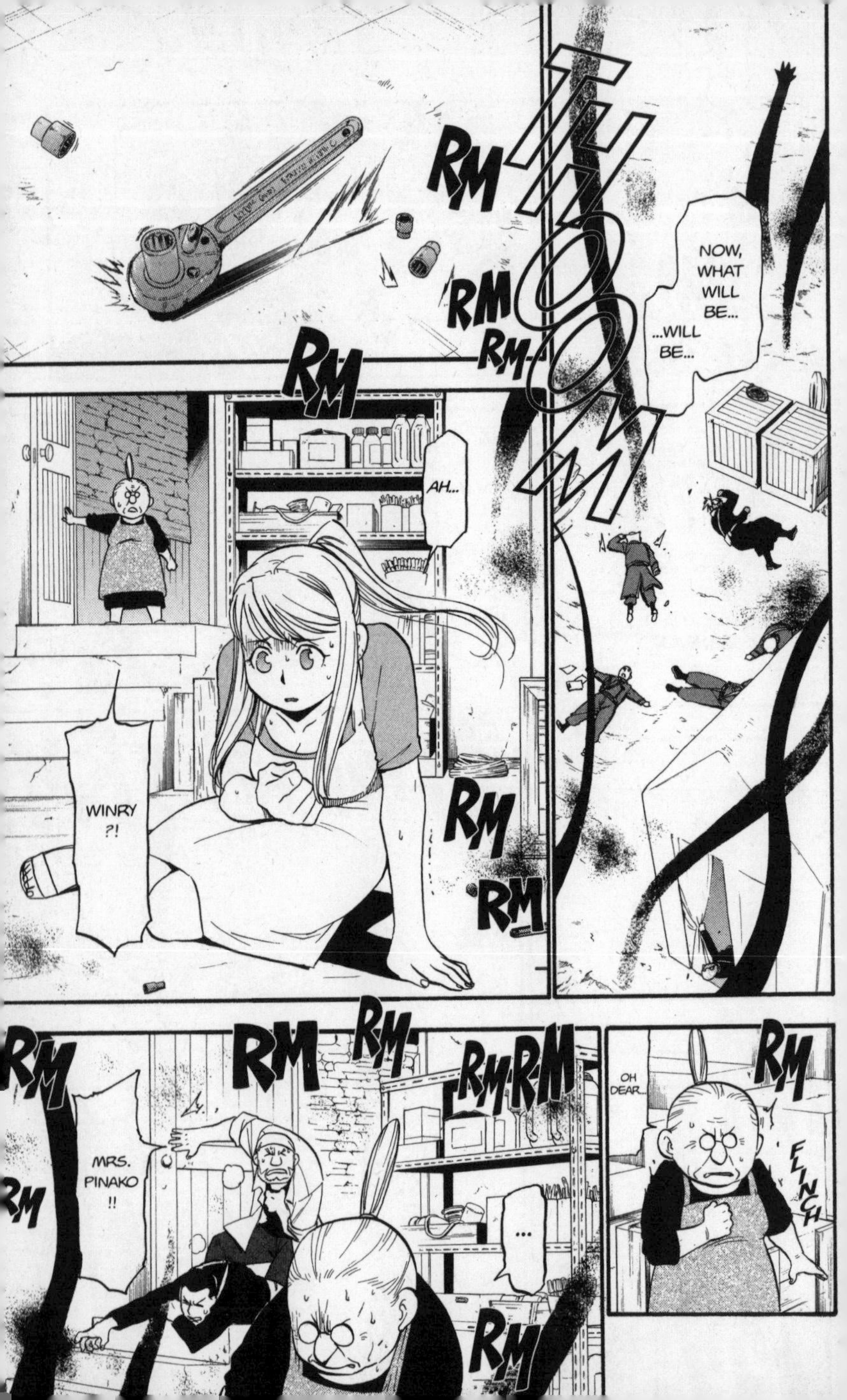
THOOOM
NOW, WHAT WILL BE...
...WILL BE...
RM
RM
RM-RM
RM
AH...
WINRY ?!
RM
RM
RM
FLINCH
OH DEAR...
RM
RM-RM-RM
RM
RM
MRS. PINAKO !!
...
RM
RM

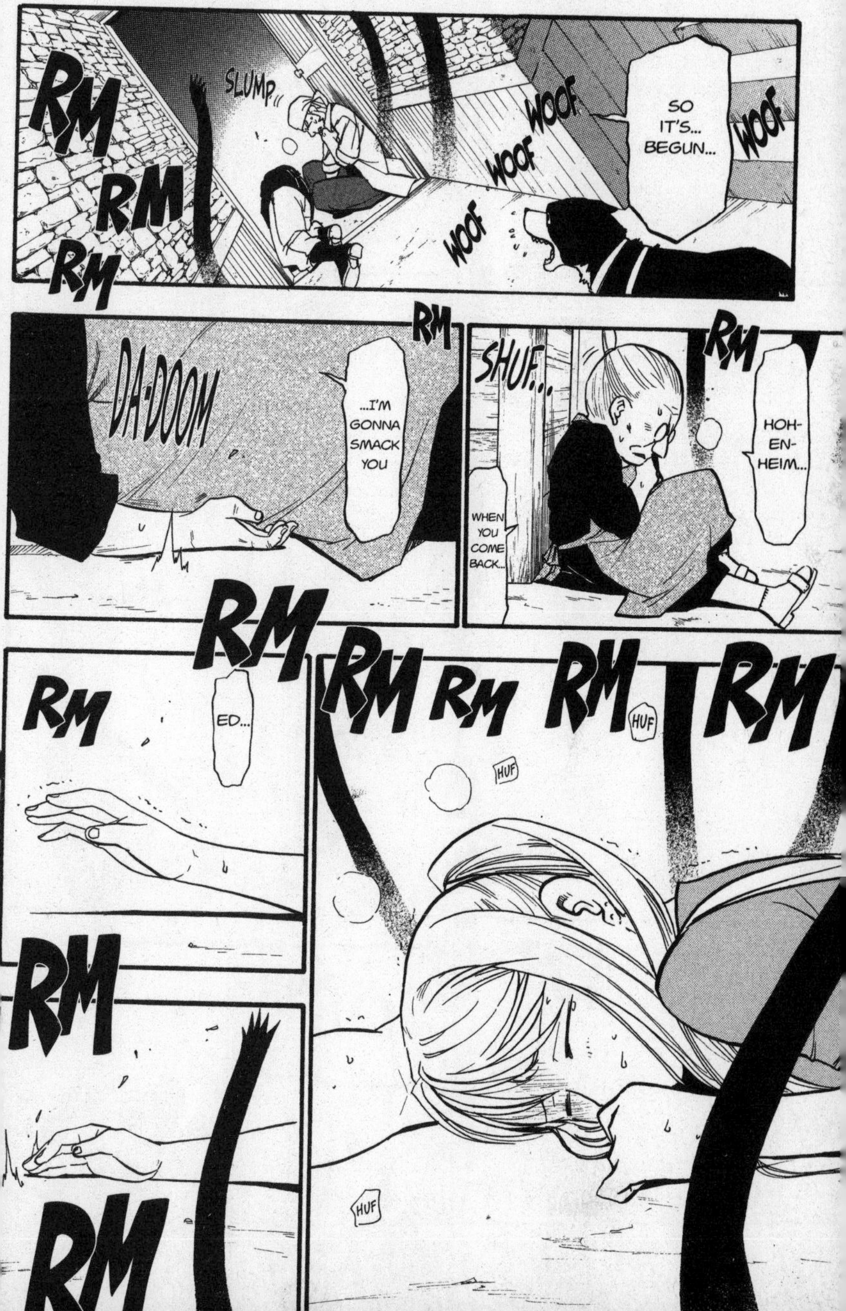
SO IT'S... BEGUN...
WOOF
WOOF
WOOF
WOOF
SLUMP
RM
RM
RM
RM
HOH-EN-HEIM...
SHUF...
WHEN YOU COME BACK...
RM
...I'M GONNA SMACK YOU
DA-DOOM
RM
RM
RM
RM
RM
HUF
HUF
HUF
RM
ED...
RM
RM

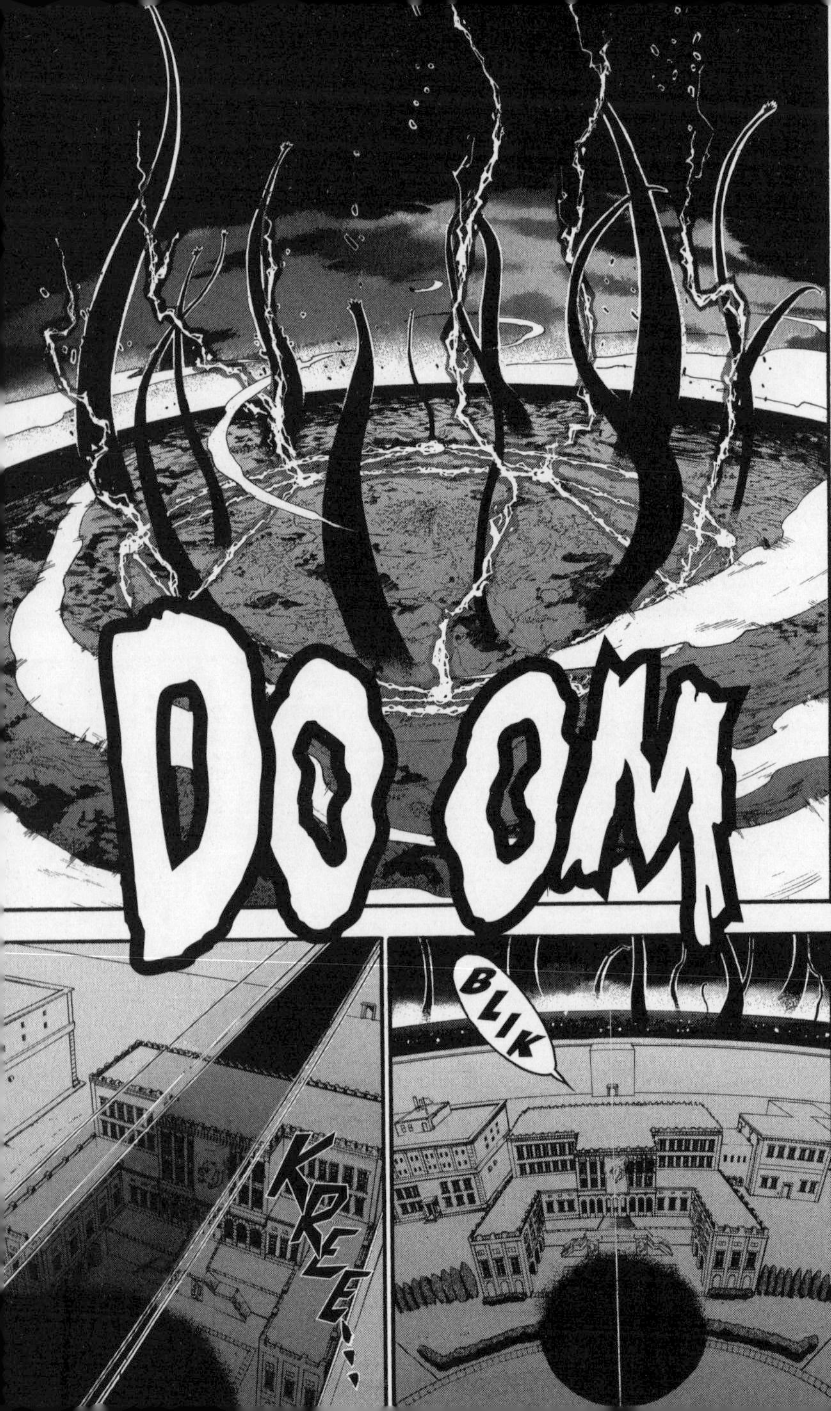
DOOM
BLIK
KREE..

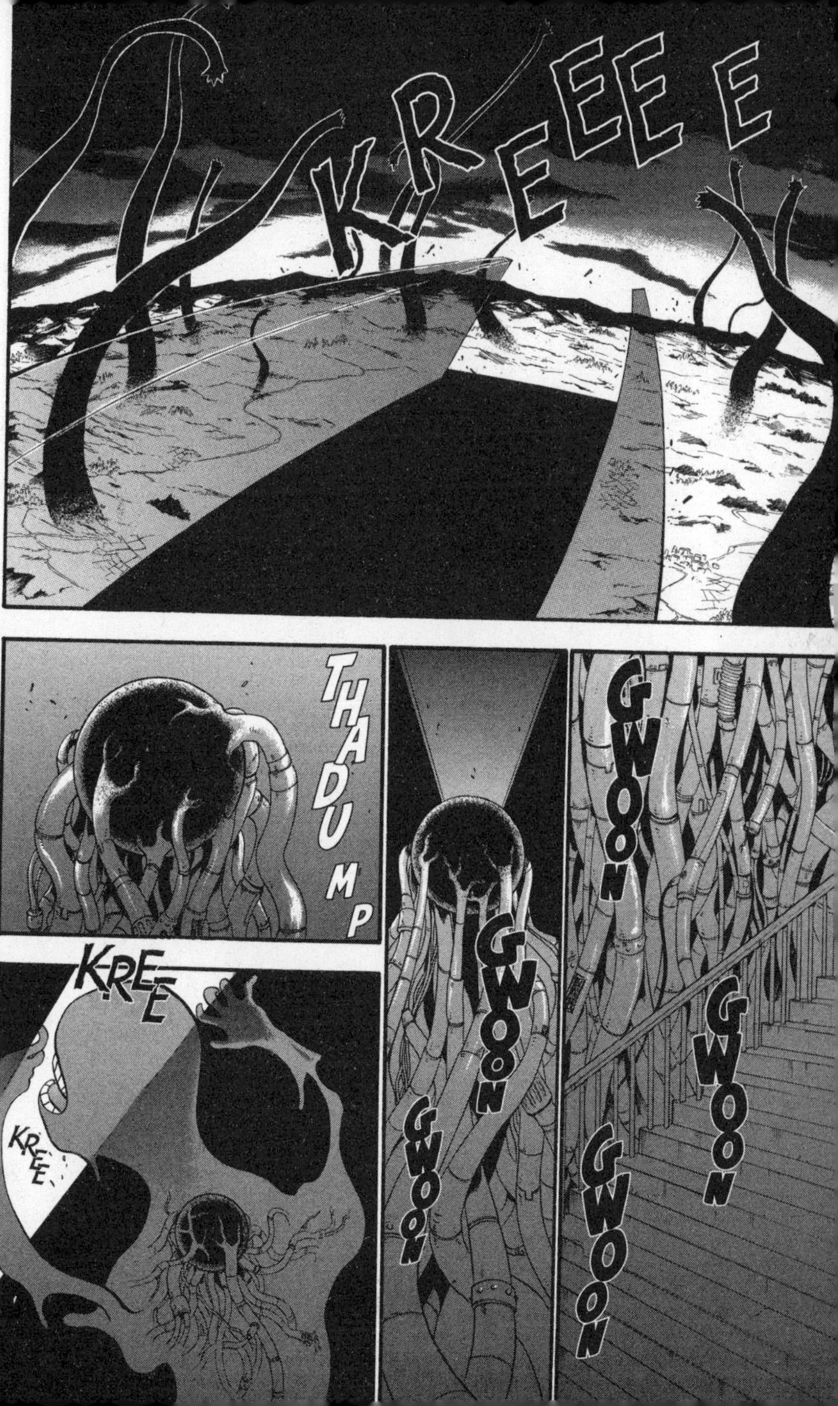
KREEEE
GWOON
GWOON
GWOON
GWOON
GWOON
THADUMP
KREE
KREE

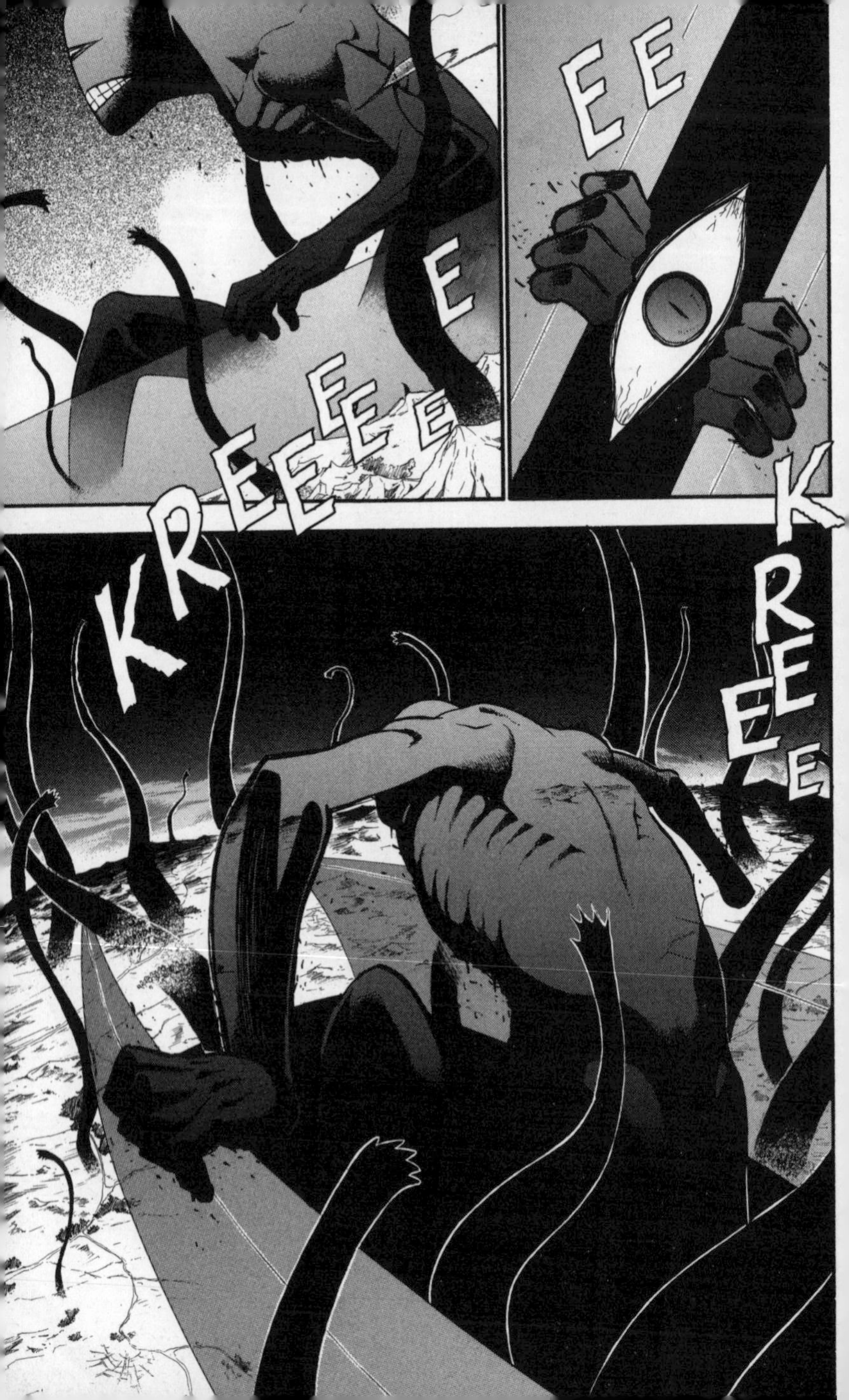
KREEEEEEEEEEE
KREEEE

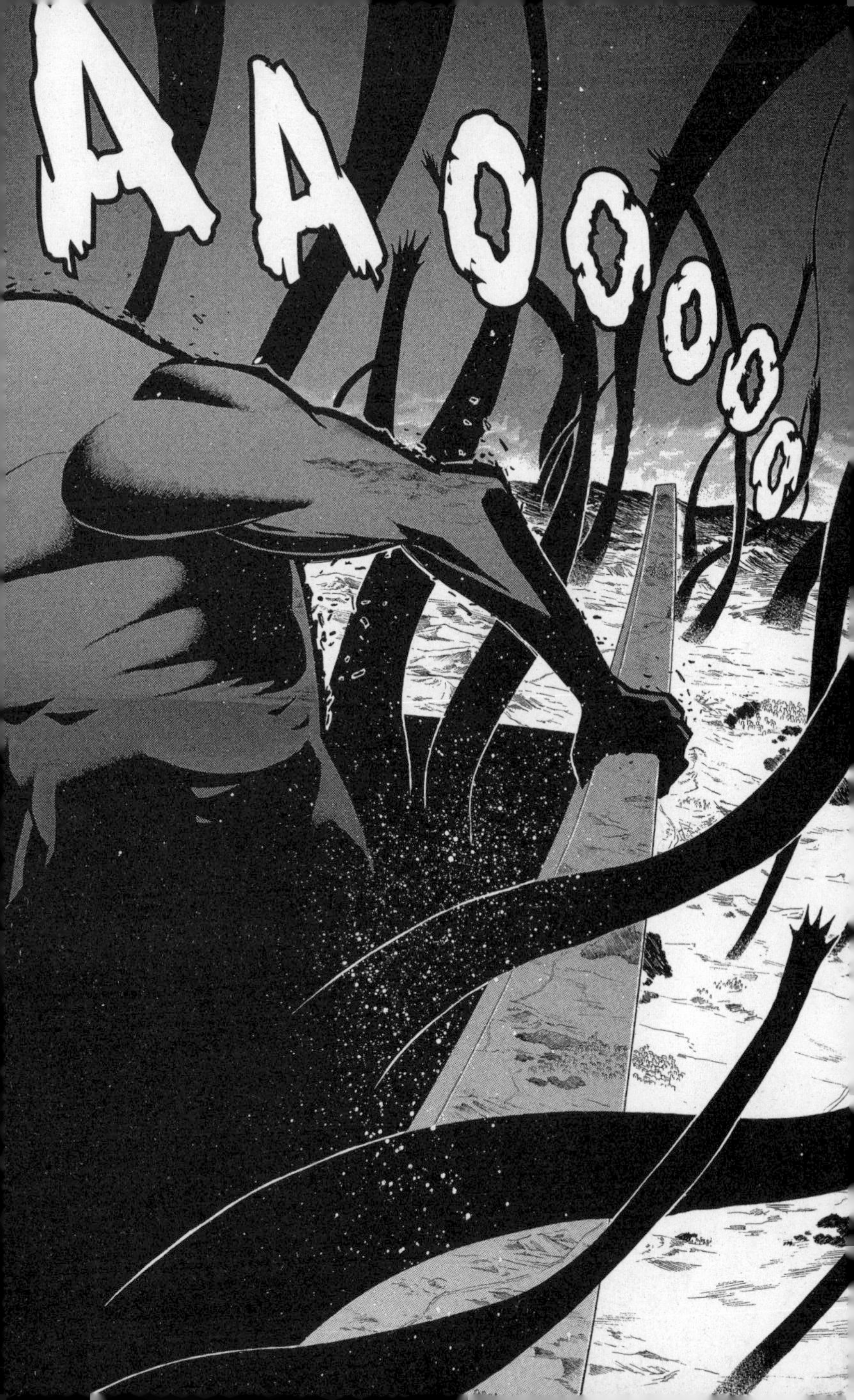
AAOOOOOO

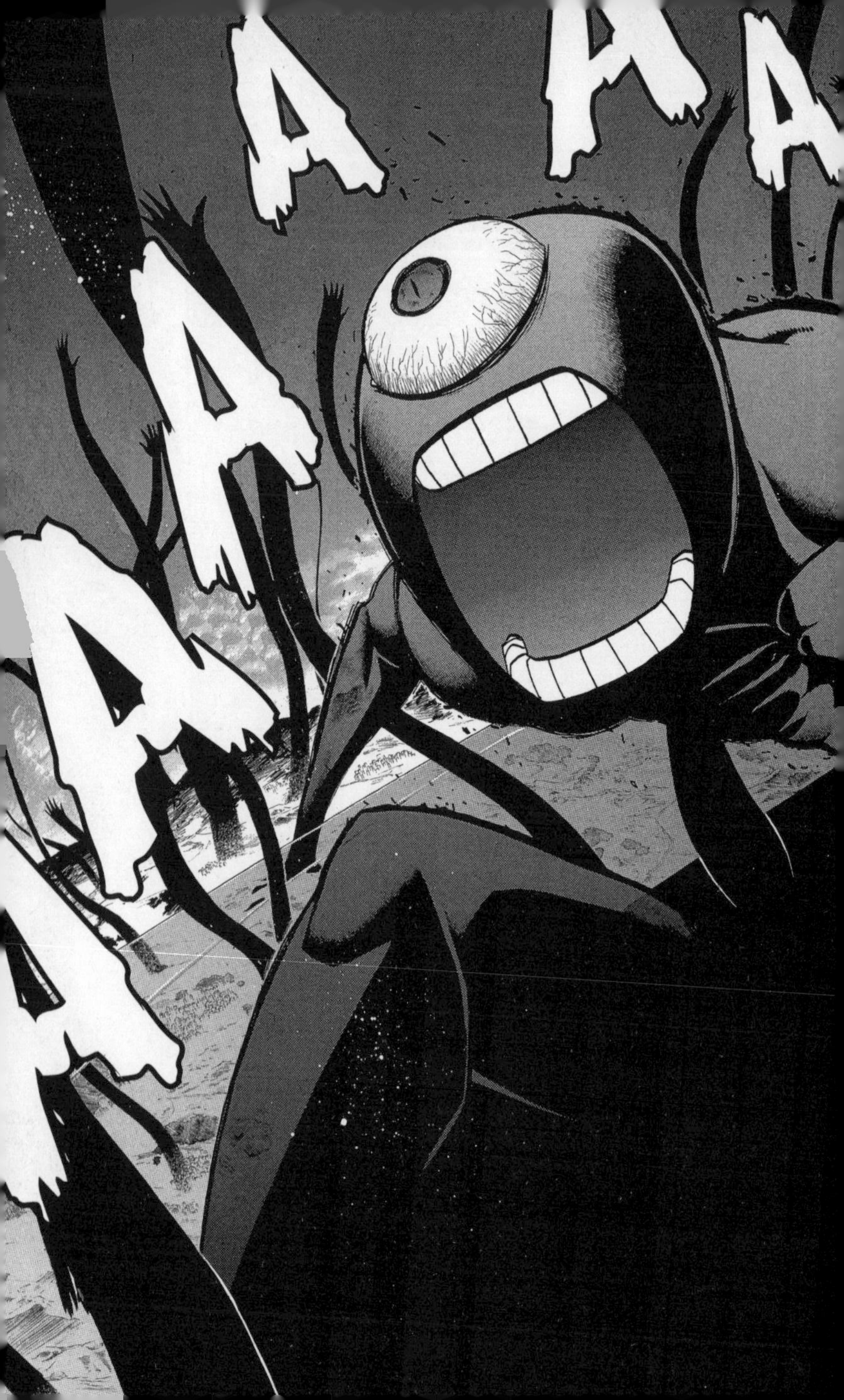
AAAAAA

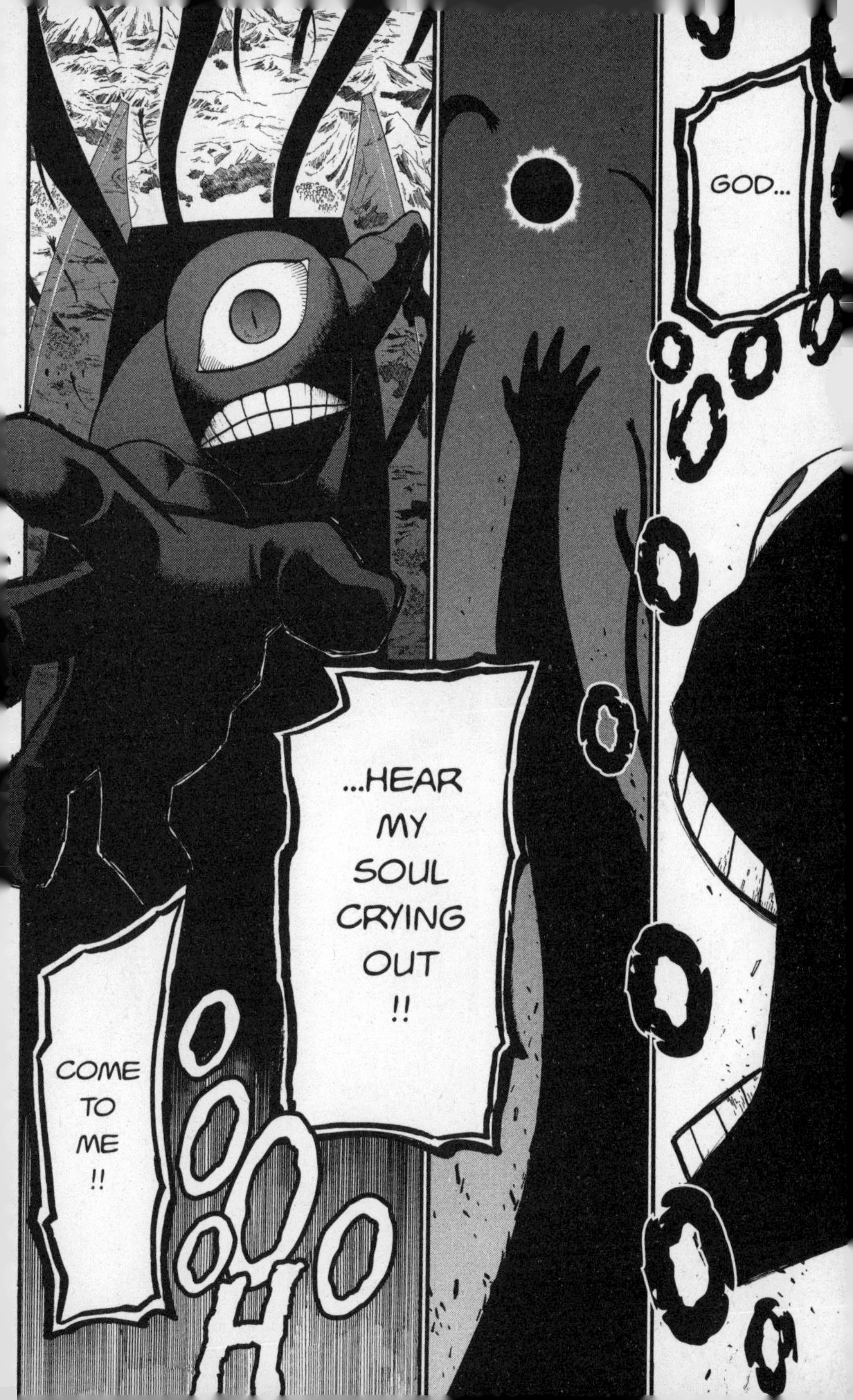
GOD...
...HEAR MY SOUL CRYING OUT !!
COME TO ME !!

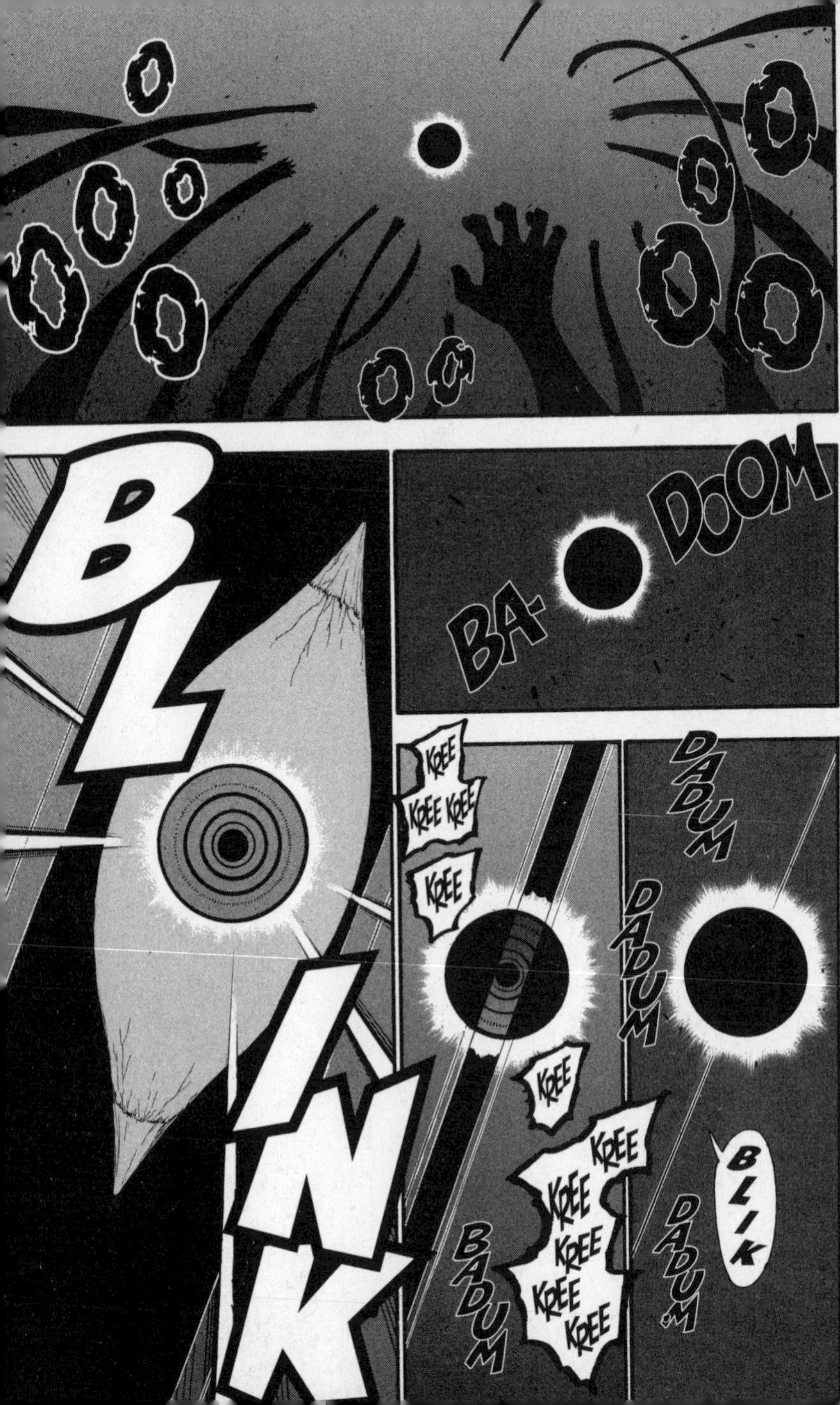
BA-DOOM
DADUM
DADUM
BLIK
DADUM
KREE
KREE KREE
KREE
KREE
KREE
KREE
KREE
KREE
KREE
BADUM
BLINK

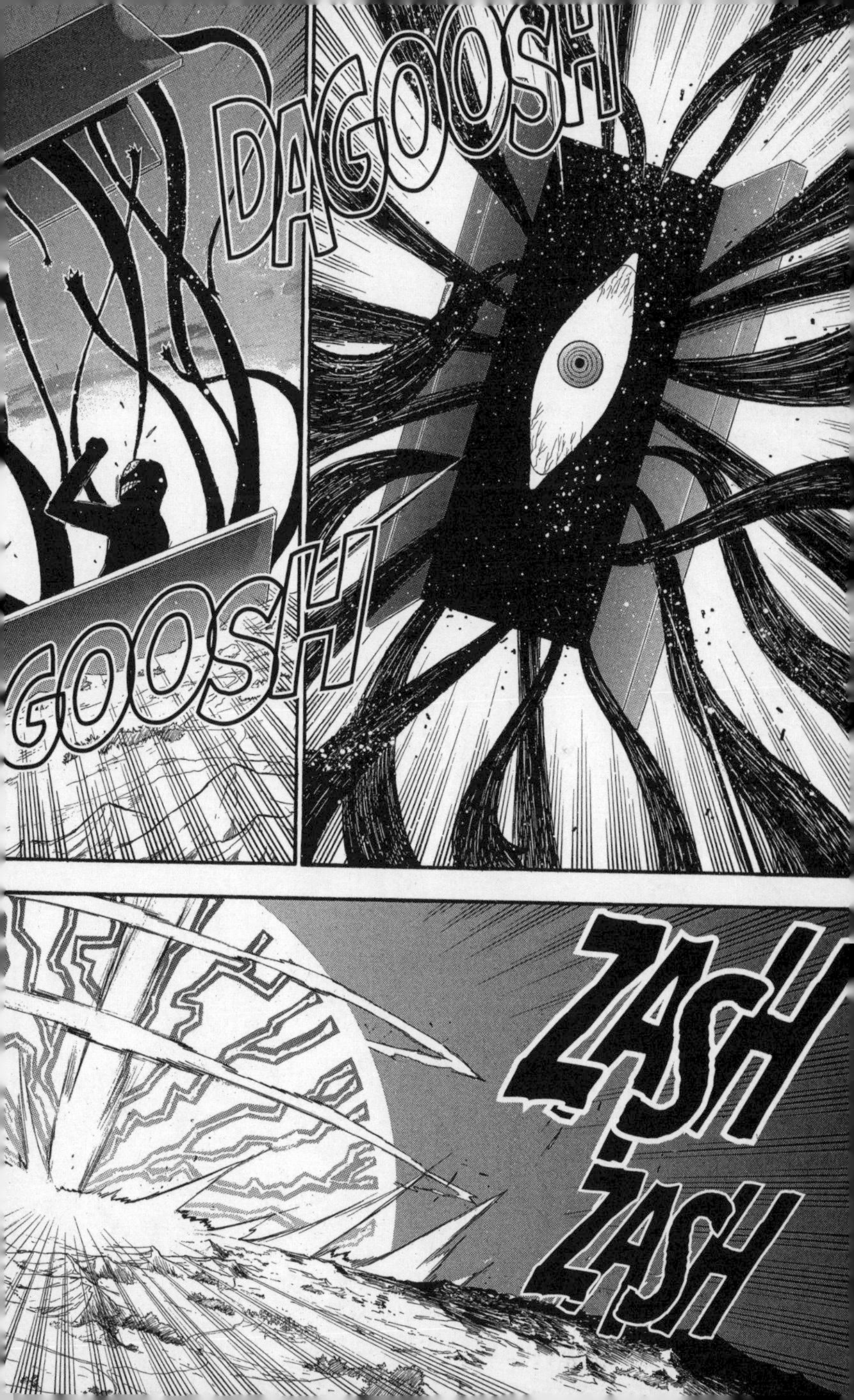
DAGOOSH
GOOSH
ZASH
ZASH

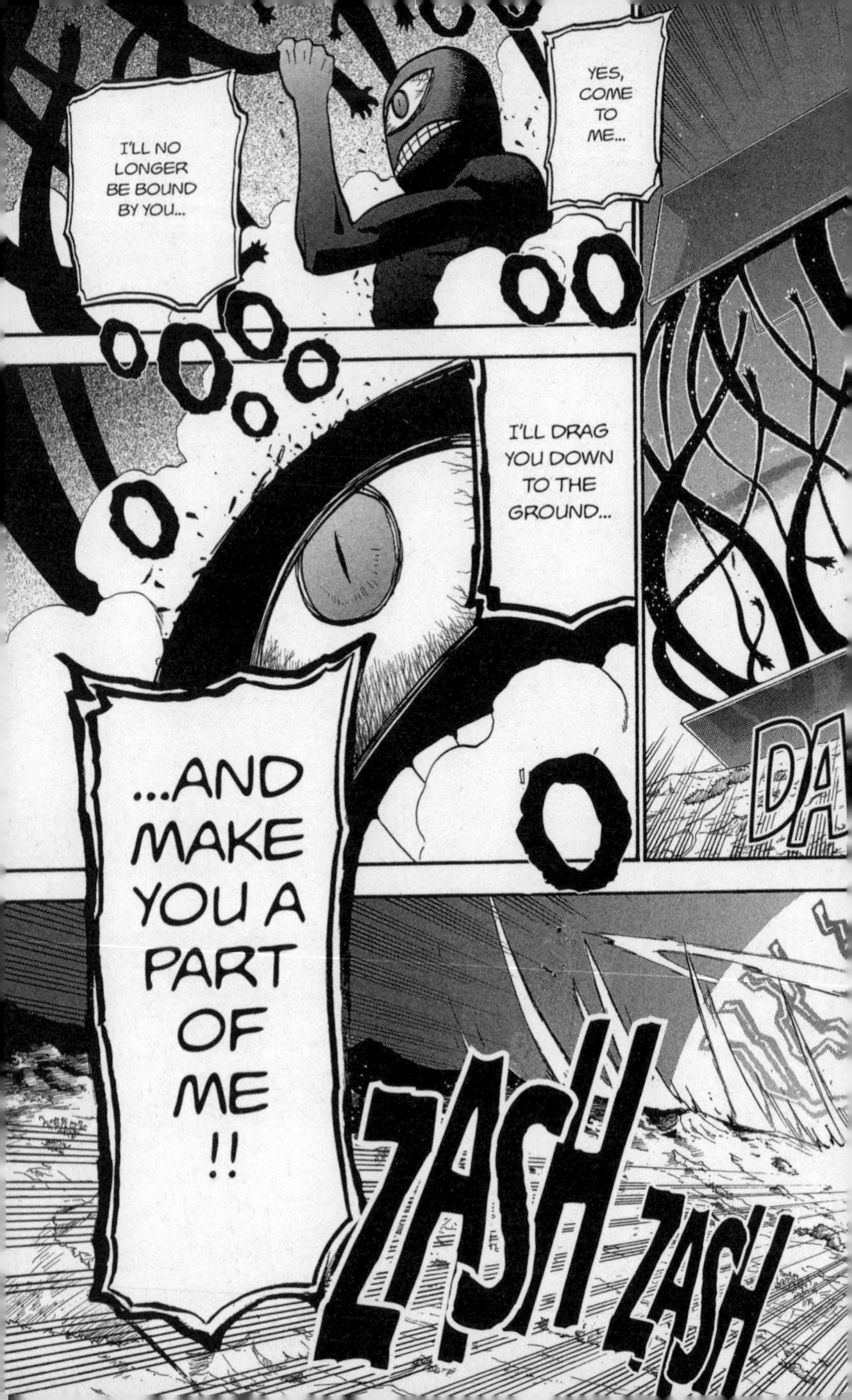
YES, COME TO ME...
I'LL NO LONGER BE BOUND BY YOU...
DA
I'LL DRAG YOU DOWN TO THE GROUND...
...AND MAKE YOU A PART OF ME!!
ZASH
ZASH

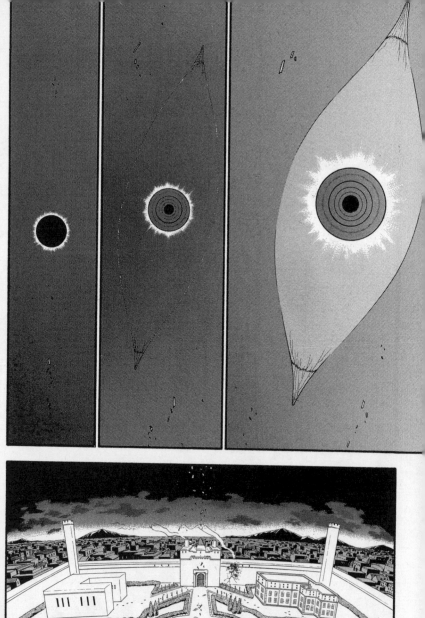
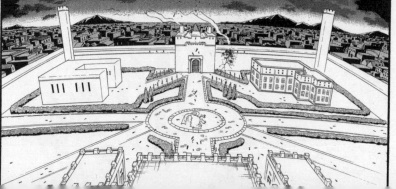

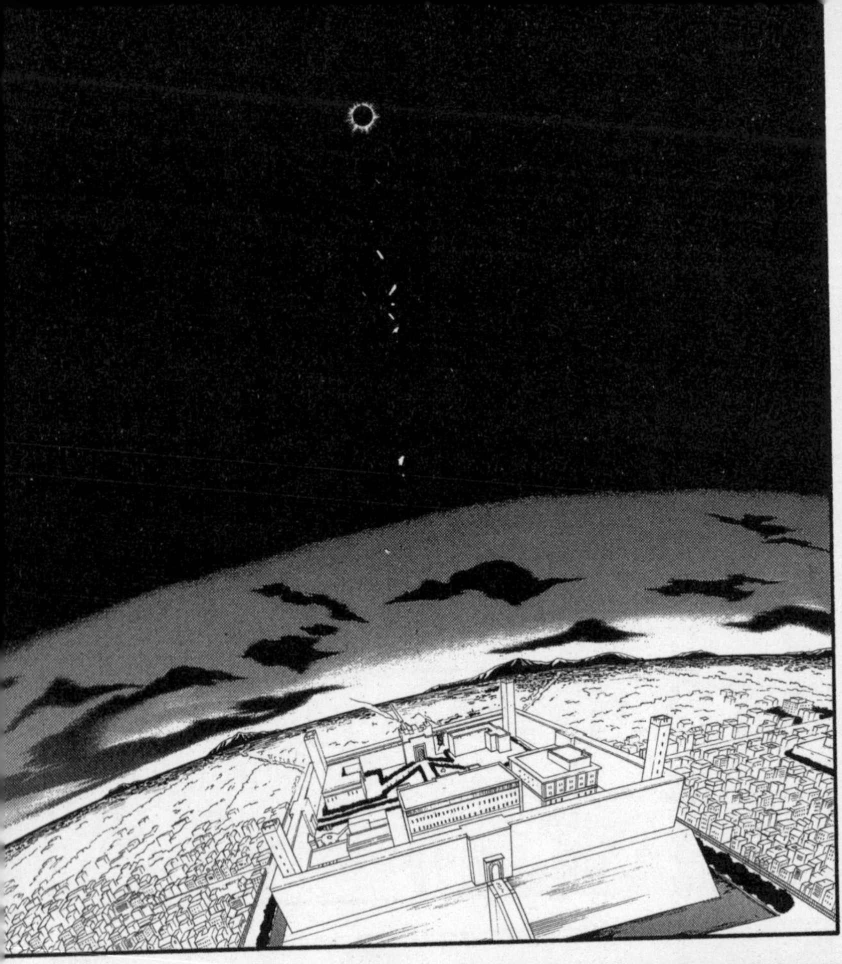
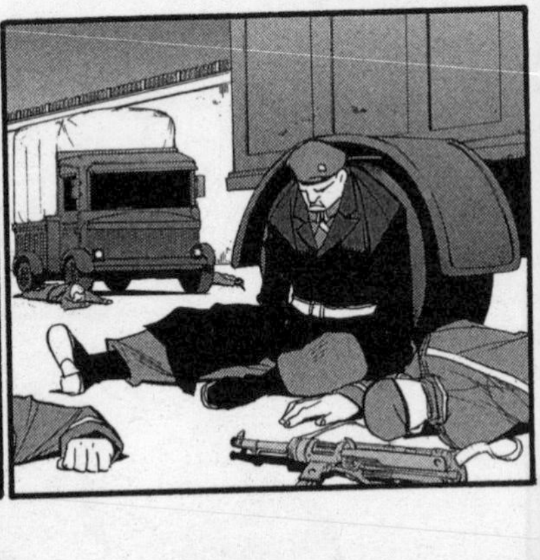
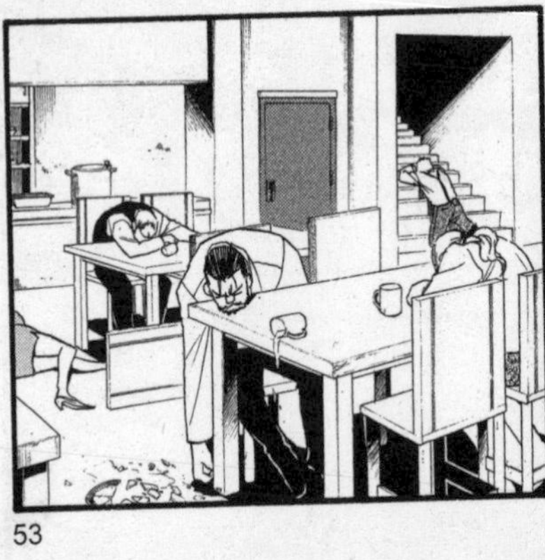

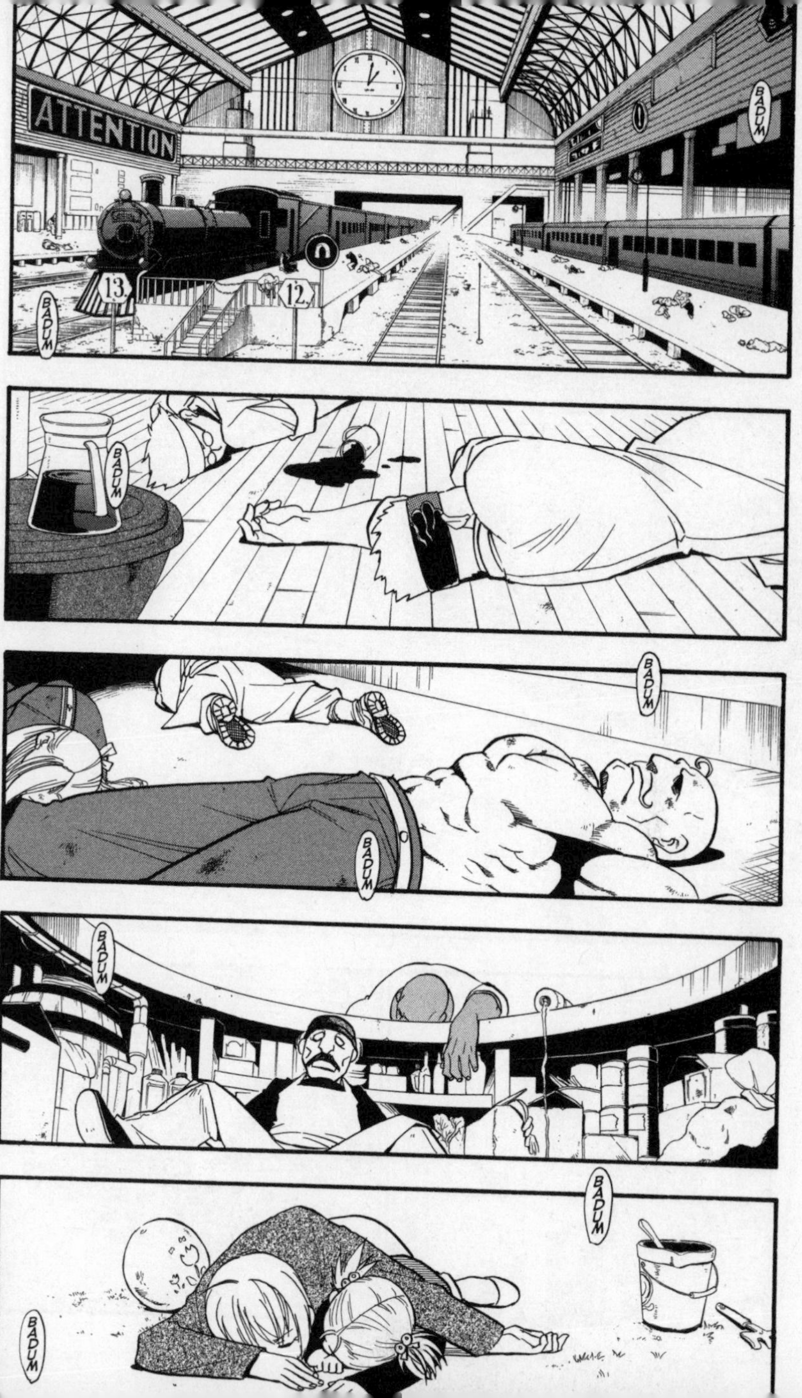
BADUM
ATTENTION
13.
12.
BADUM
BADUM
BADUM
BADUM
BADUM
BADUM
BADUM

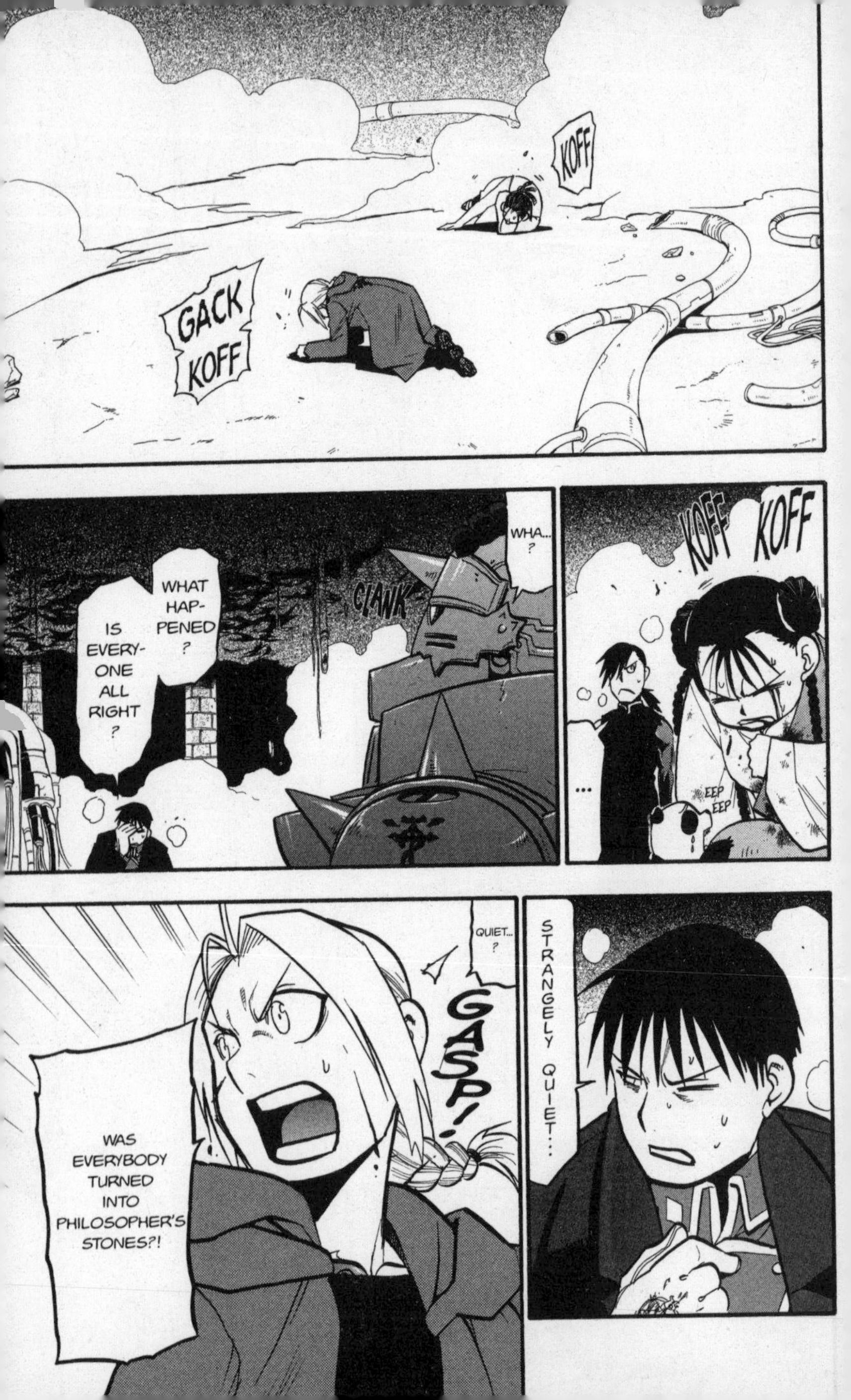
KOFF
GACK KOFF
KOFF KOFF
...
EEP EEP
WHA...?
CLANK
WHAT HAPPENED?
IS EVERYONE ALL RIGHT?
STRANGELY QUIET...
QUIET...?
GASP!!
WAS EVERYBODY TURNED INTO PHILOSOPHER'S STONES?!

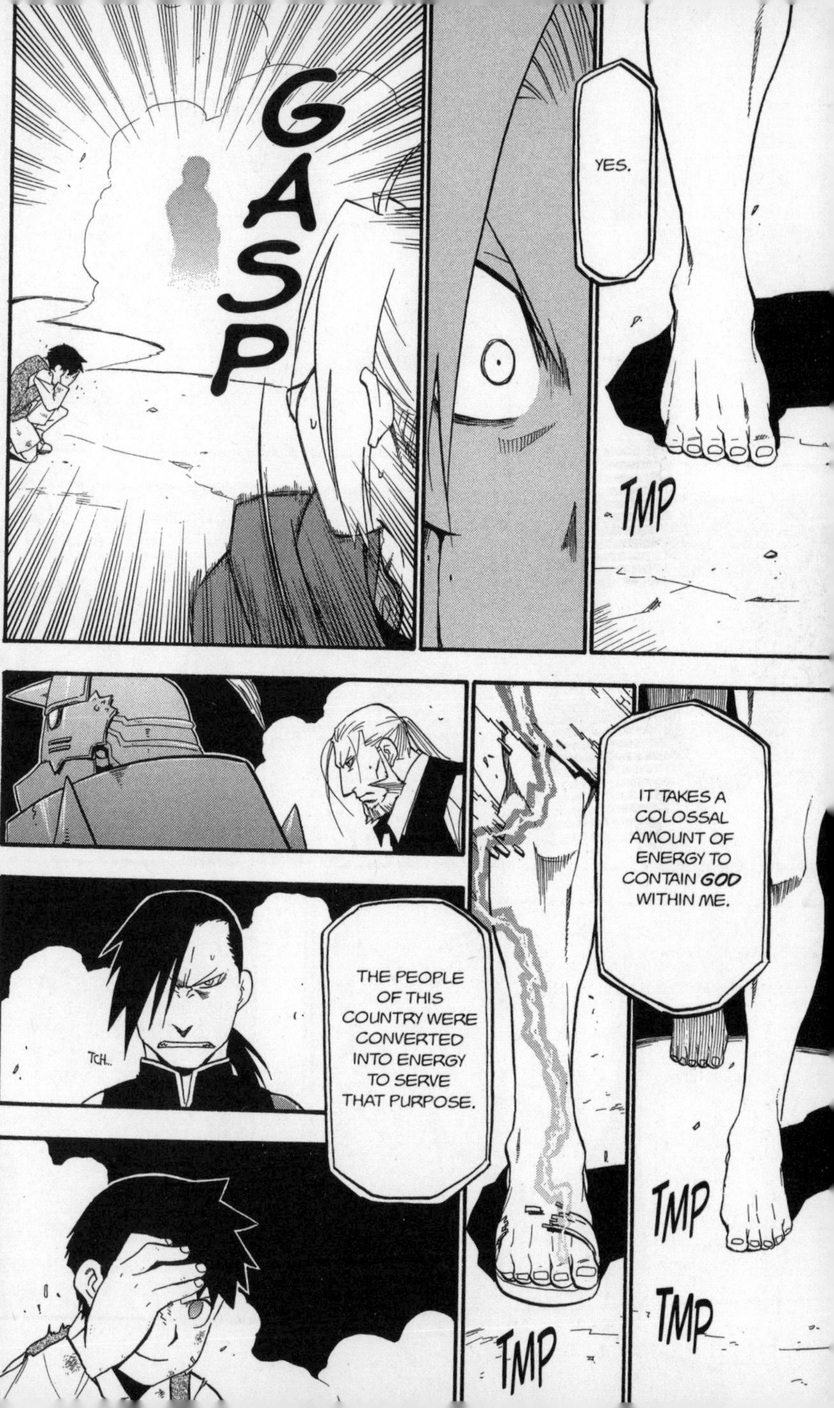
YES.
TMP
GASP
IT TAKES A COLOSSAL AMOUNT OF ENERGY TO CONTAIN GOD WITHIN ME.
THE PEOPLE OF THIS COUNTRY WERE CONVERTED INTO ENERGY TO SERVE THAT PURPOSE.
TMP
TMP
TMP
TCH...

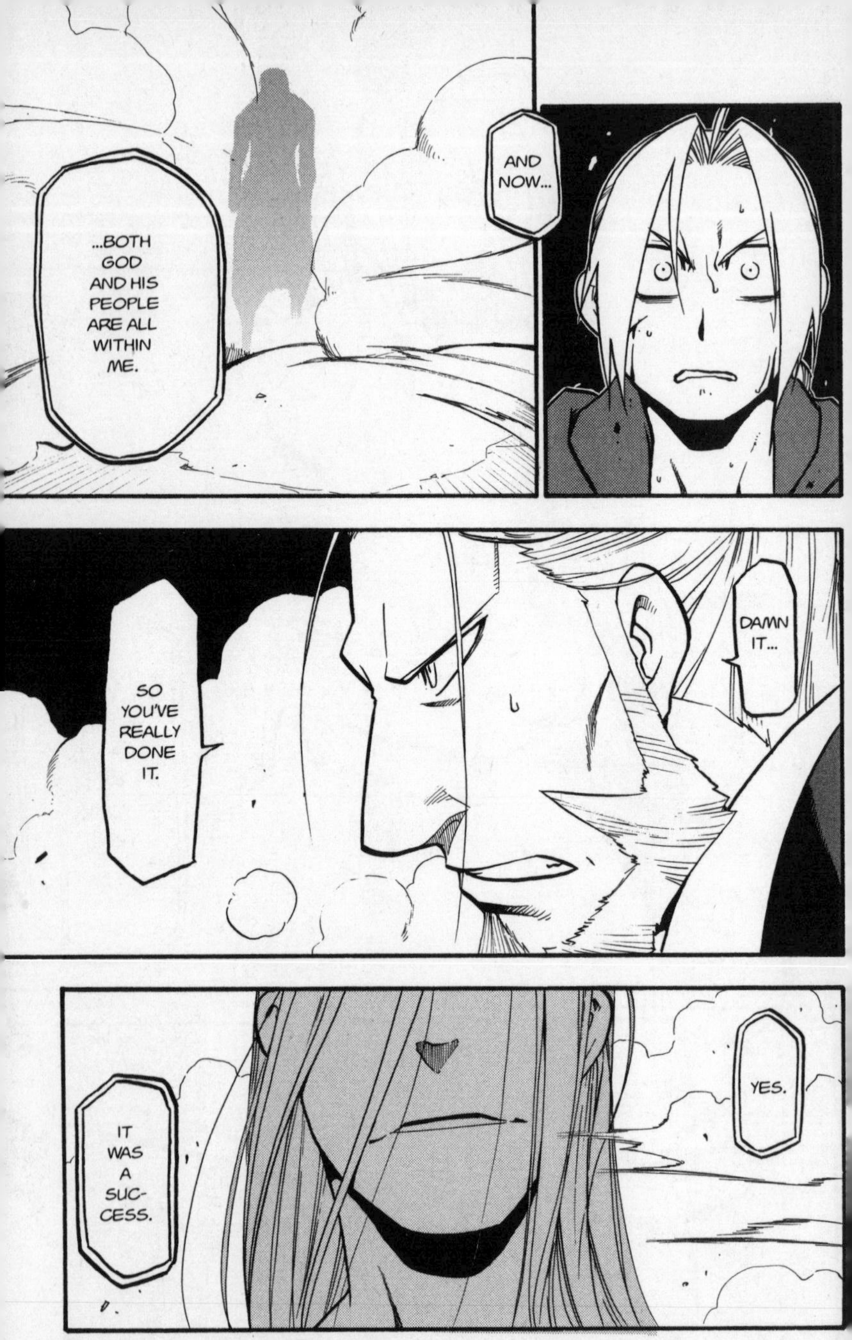
AND NOW...
...BOTH GOD AND HIS PEOPLE ARE ALL WITHIN ME.
DAMN IT...
SO YOU'VE REALLY DONE IT.
YES.
IT WAS A SUC-CESS.

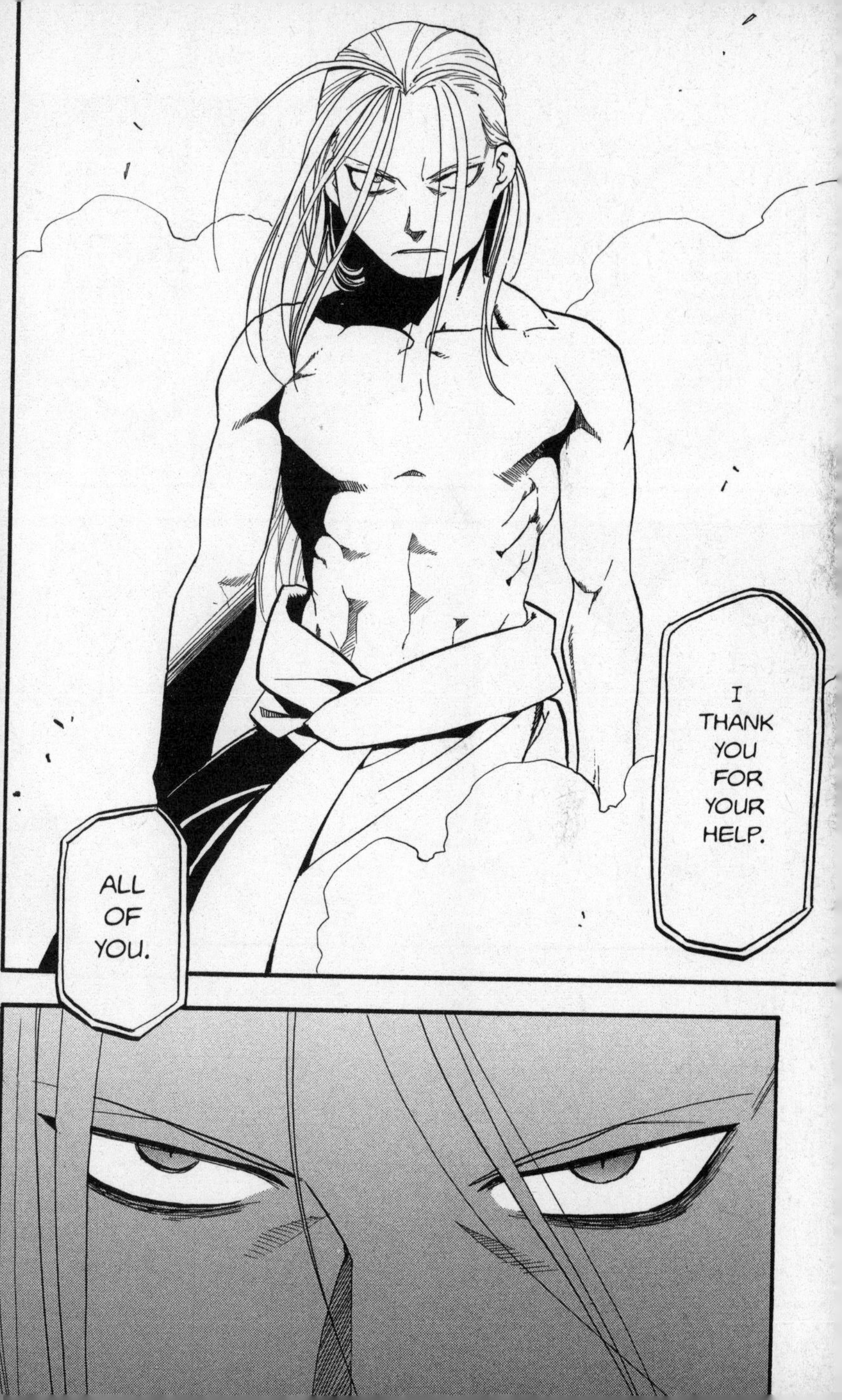
I THANK YOU FOR YOUR HELP.
ALL OF YOU.

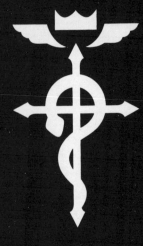

FULLMETAL
ALCHEMIST

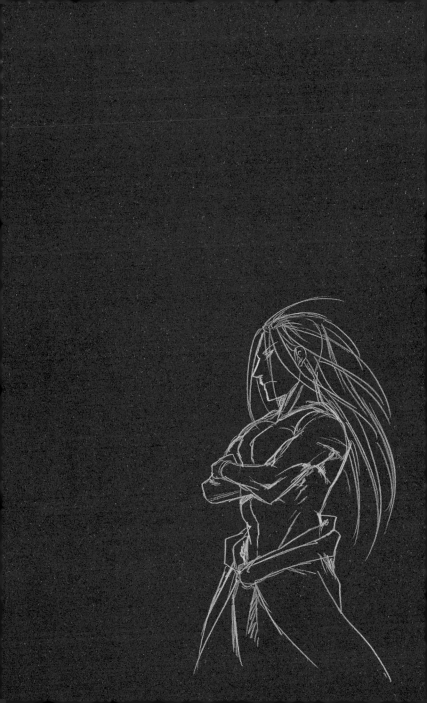

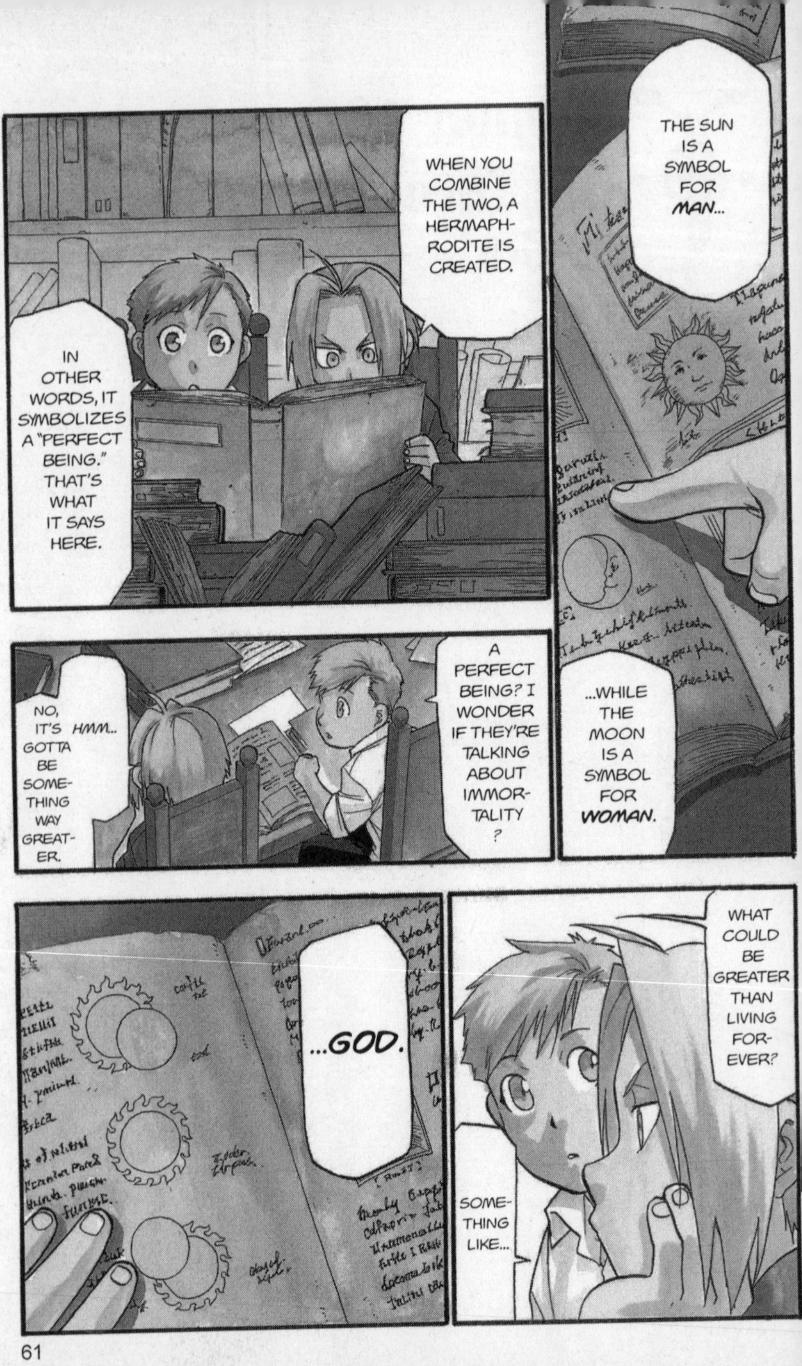

THE SUN IS A SYMBOL FOR MAN...
...WHILE THE MOON IS A SYMBOL FOR WOMAN.
WHEN YOU COMBINE THE TWO, A HERMAPHRODITE IS CREATED.
IN OTHER WORDS, IT SYMBOLIZES A "PERFECT BEING." THAT'S WHAT IT SAYS HERE.
A PERFECT BEING? I WONDER IF THEY'RE TALKING ABOUT IMMORTALITY?
NO, IT'S
HMM...
GOTTA BE SOMETHING WAY GREATER.
WHAT COULD BE GREATER THAN LIVING FOREVER?
SOMETHING LIKE...
...GOD.

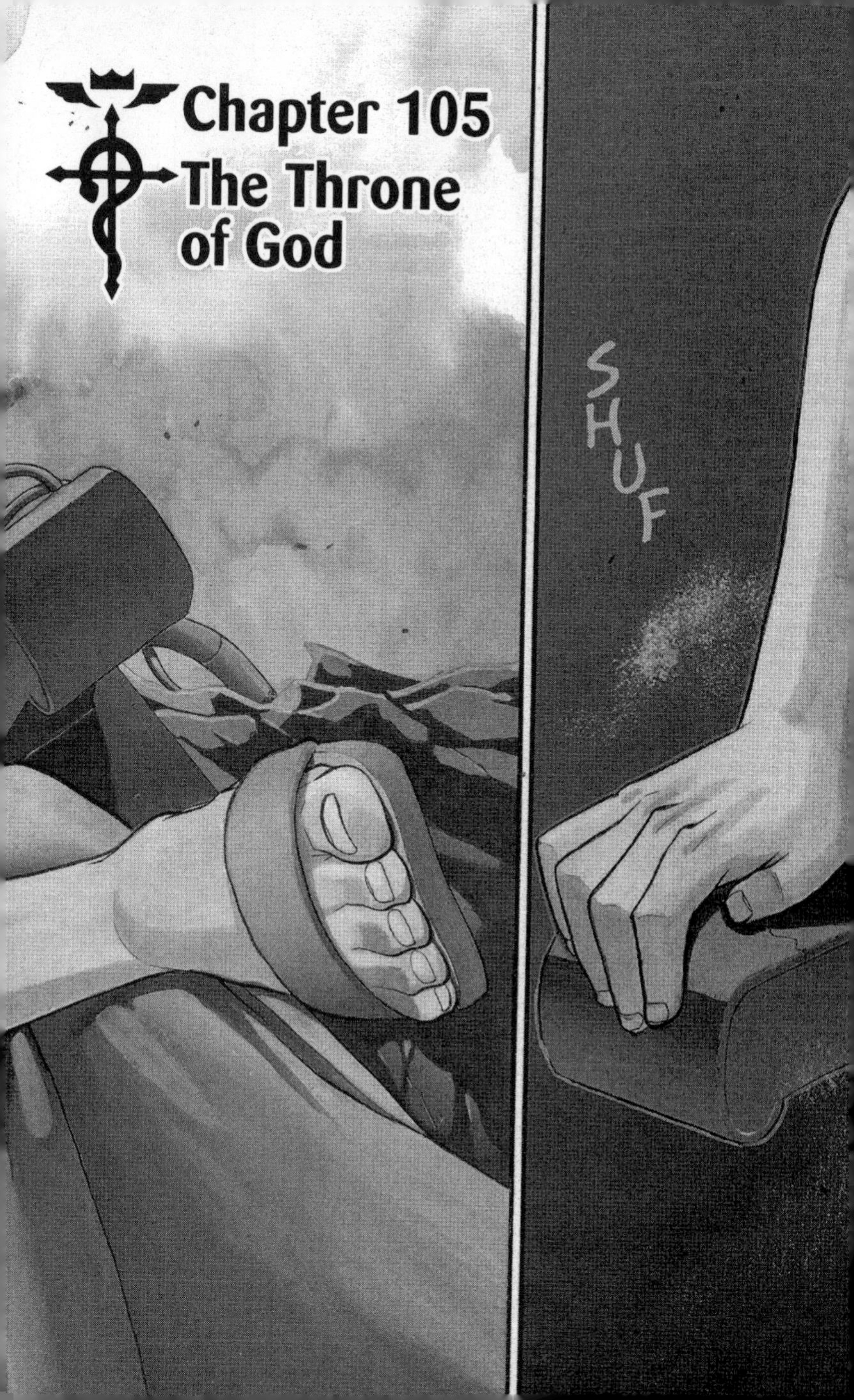
SHUF
Chapter 105
The Throne of God

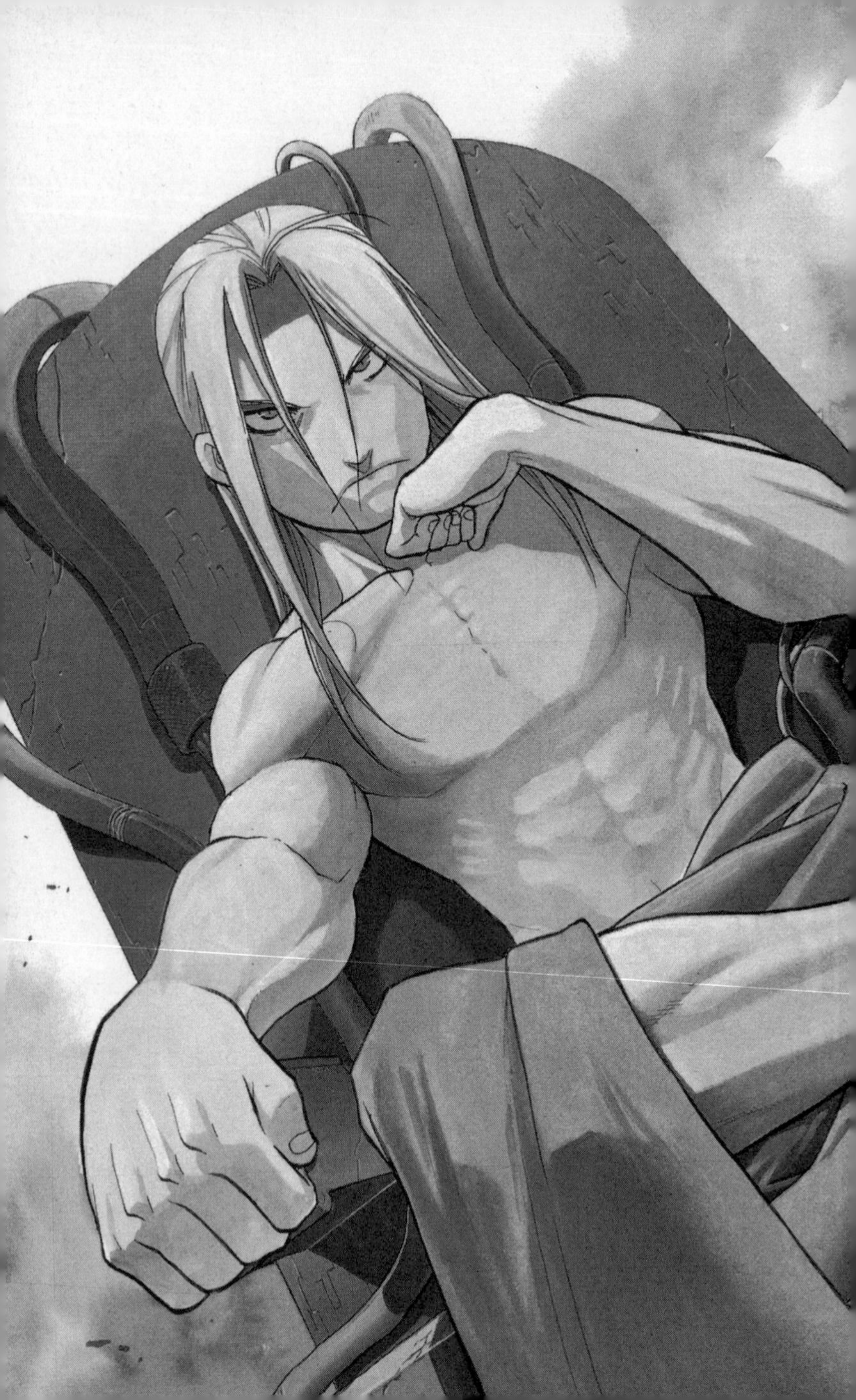

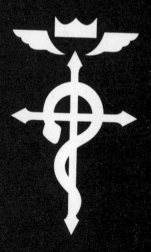

FULLMETAL
ALCHEMIST

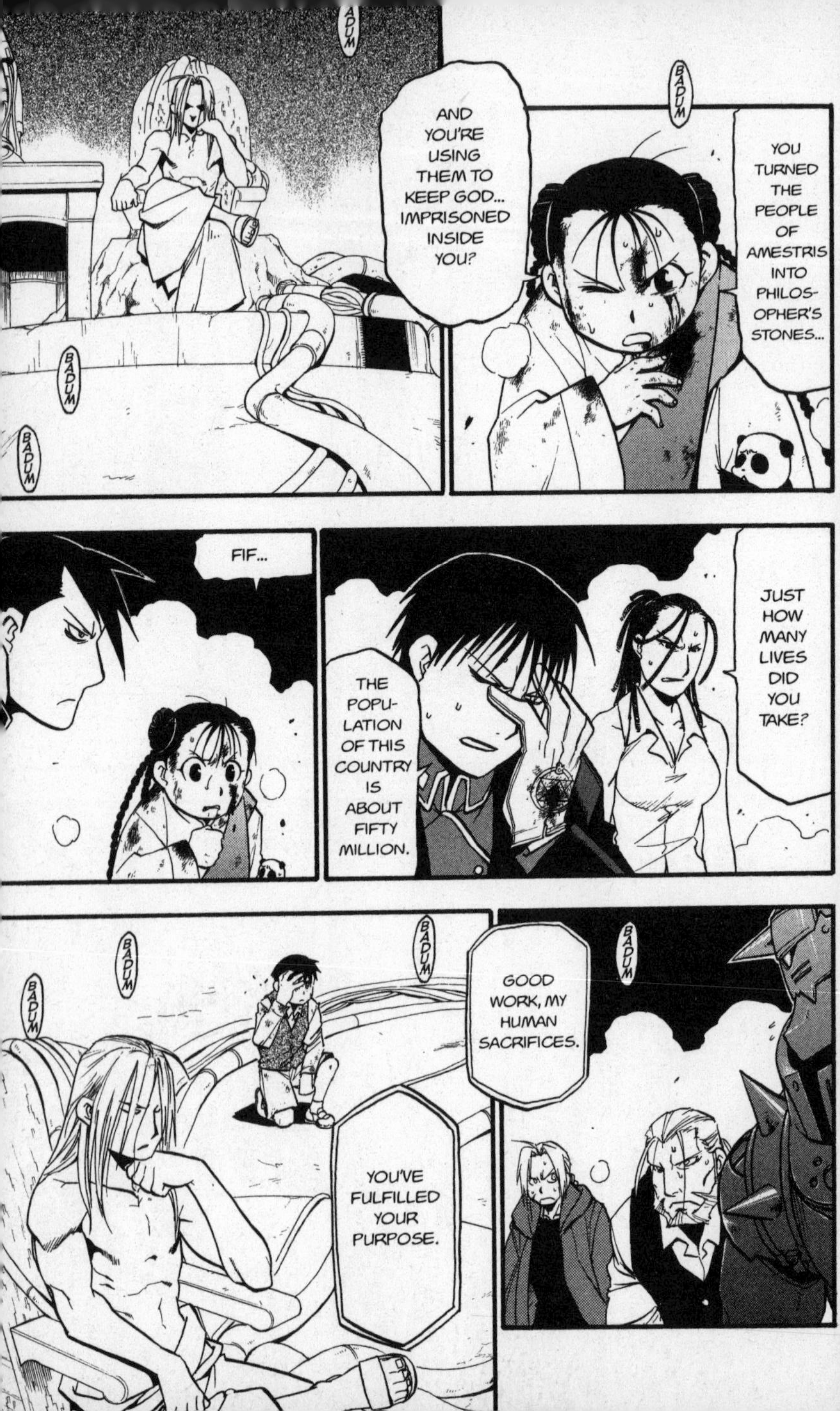
BADUM
YOU TURNED THE PEOPLE OF AMESTRIS INTO PHILOSOPHER'S STONES...
AND YOU'RE USING THEM TO KEEP GOD... IMPRISONED INSIDE YOU?
BADUM
BADUM
BADUM
JUST HOW MANY LIVES DID YOU TAKE?
THE POPULATION OF THIS COUNTRY IS ABOUT FIFTY MILLION.
FIF...
BADUM
GOOD WORK, MY HUMAN SACRIFICES.
BADUM
BADUM
BADUM
YOU'VE FULFILLED YOUR PURPOSE.

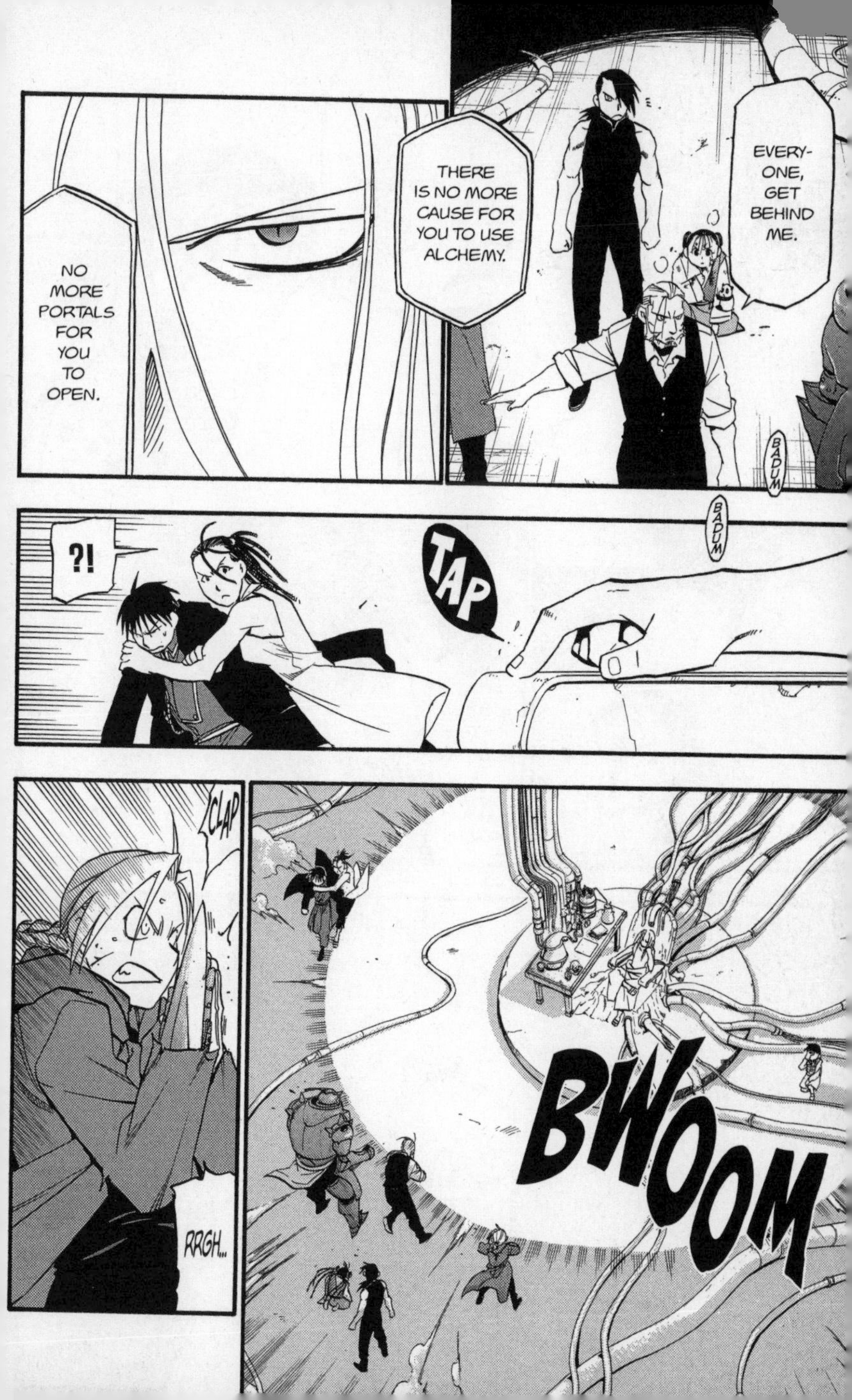
EVERY-ONE, GET BEHIND ME.
BADUM
THERE IS NO MORE CAUSE FOR YOU TO USE ALCHEMY.
NO MORE PORTALS FOR YOU TO OPEN.
BADUM
TAP
?!
BWOOM
CLAP
RRGH...

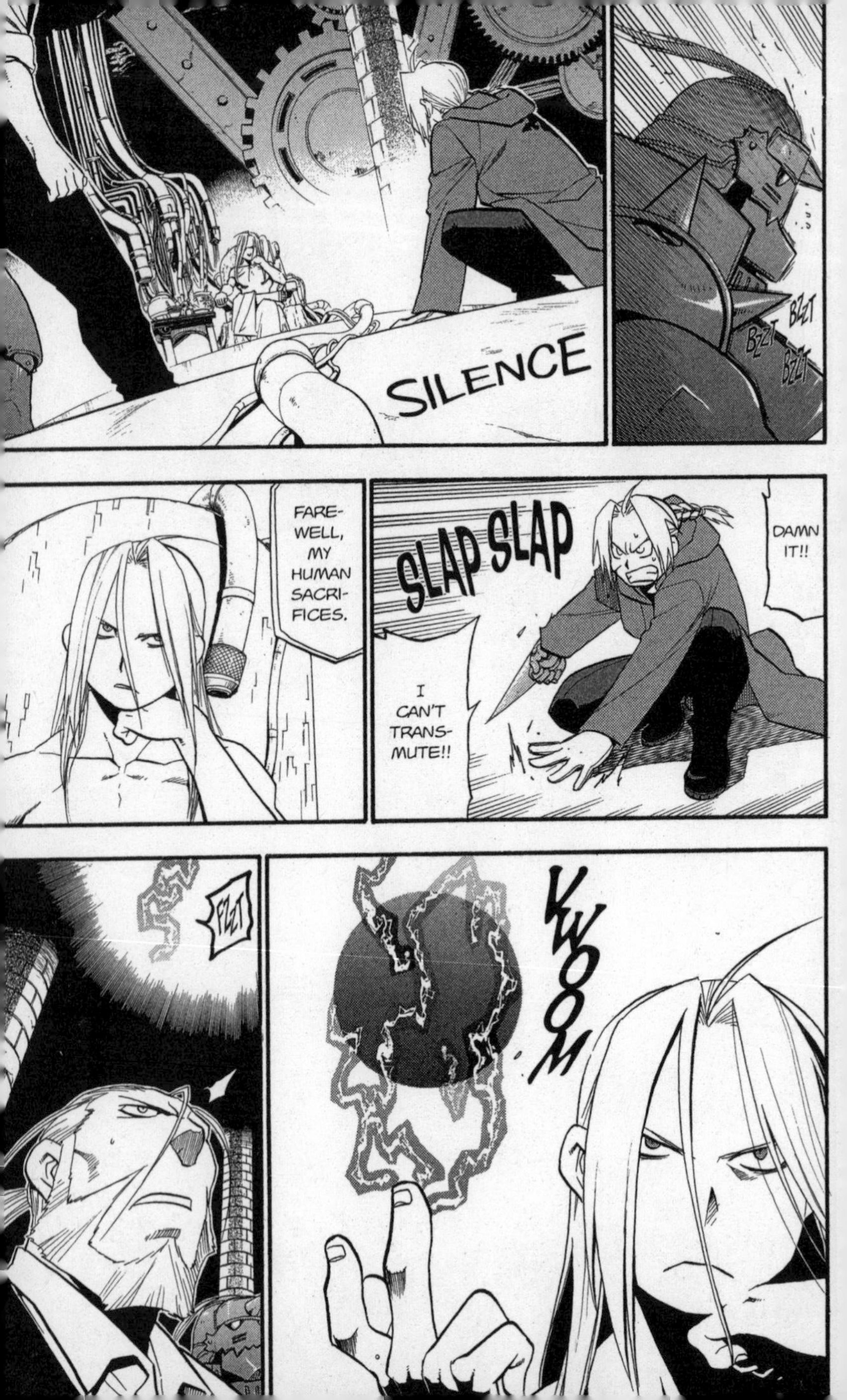
BZZT
BZZT
BZZT
BZZT
SILENCE
DAMN IT!!
SLAP SLAP
I CAN'T TRANSMUTE!!
FAREWELL, MY HUMAN SACRIFICES.
KWOOM
FZZT

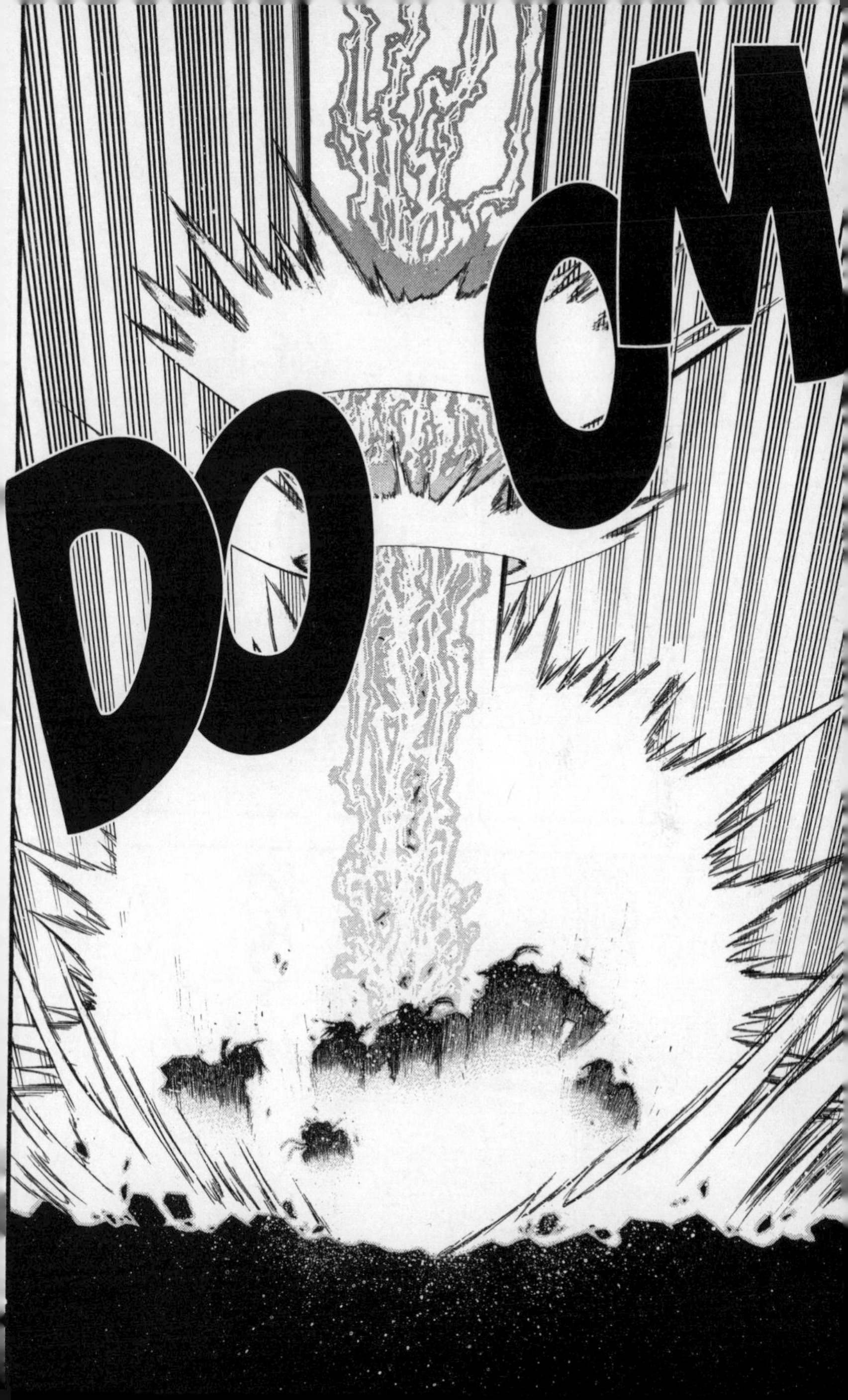
DOOOM

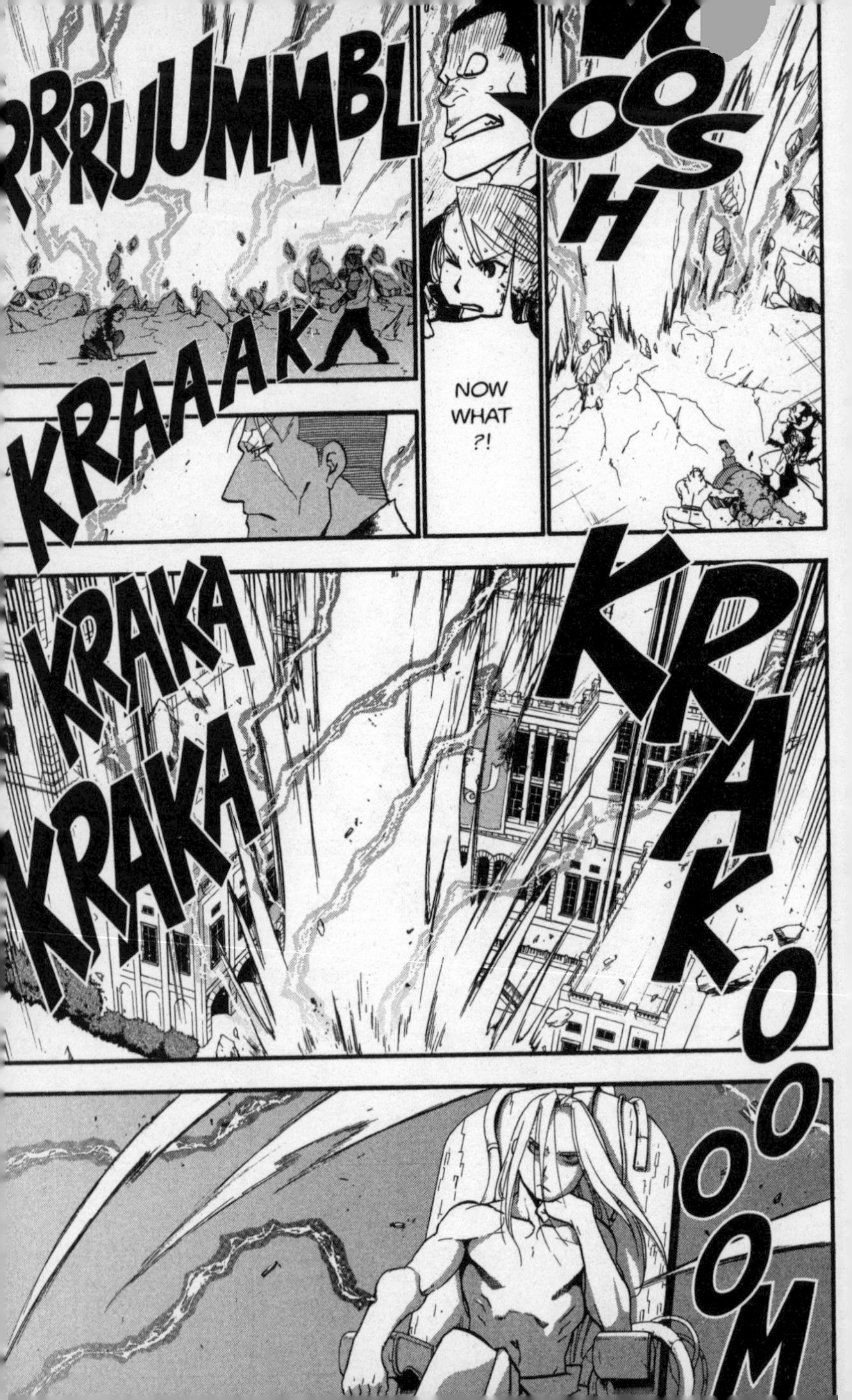
VOOOSH
NOW WHAT ?!
RRRUUMMBL
KRAAAK
KRAKOOOOM
KRAKA KRAKA

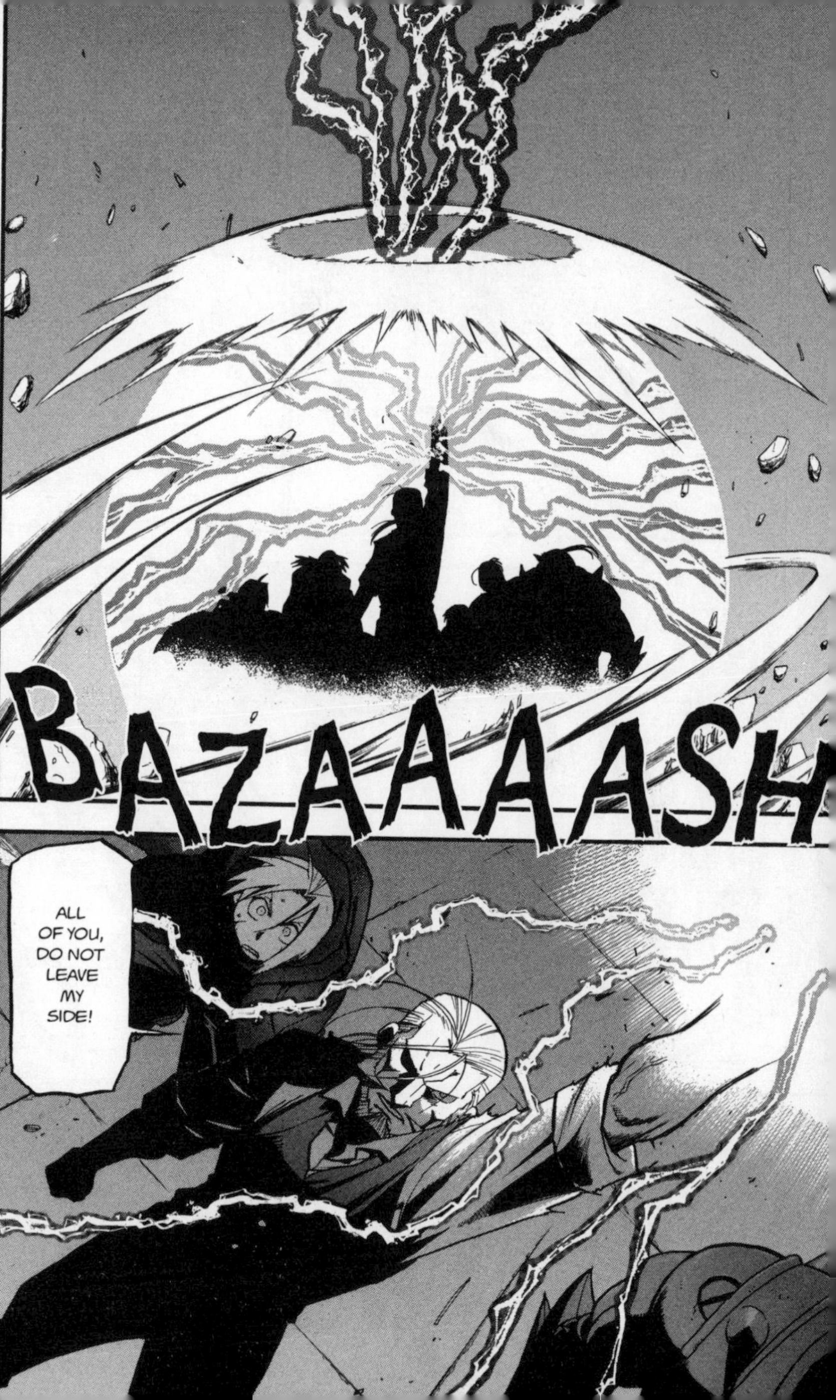
BAZAAAASH
ALL OF YOU, DO NOT LEAVE MY SIDE!

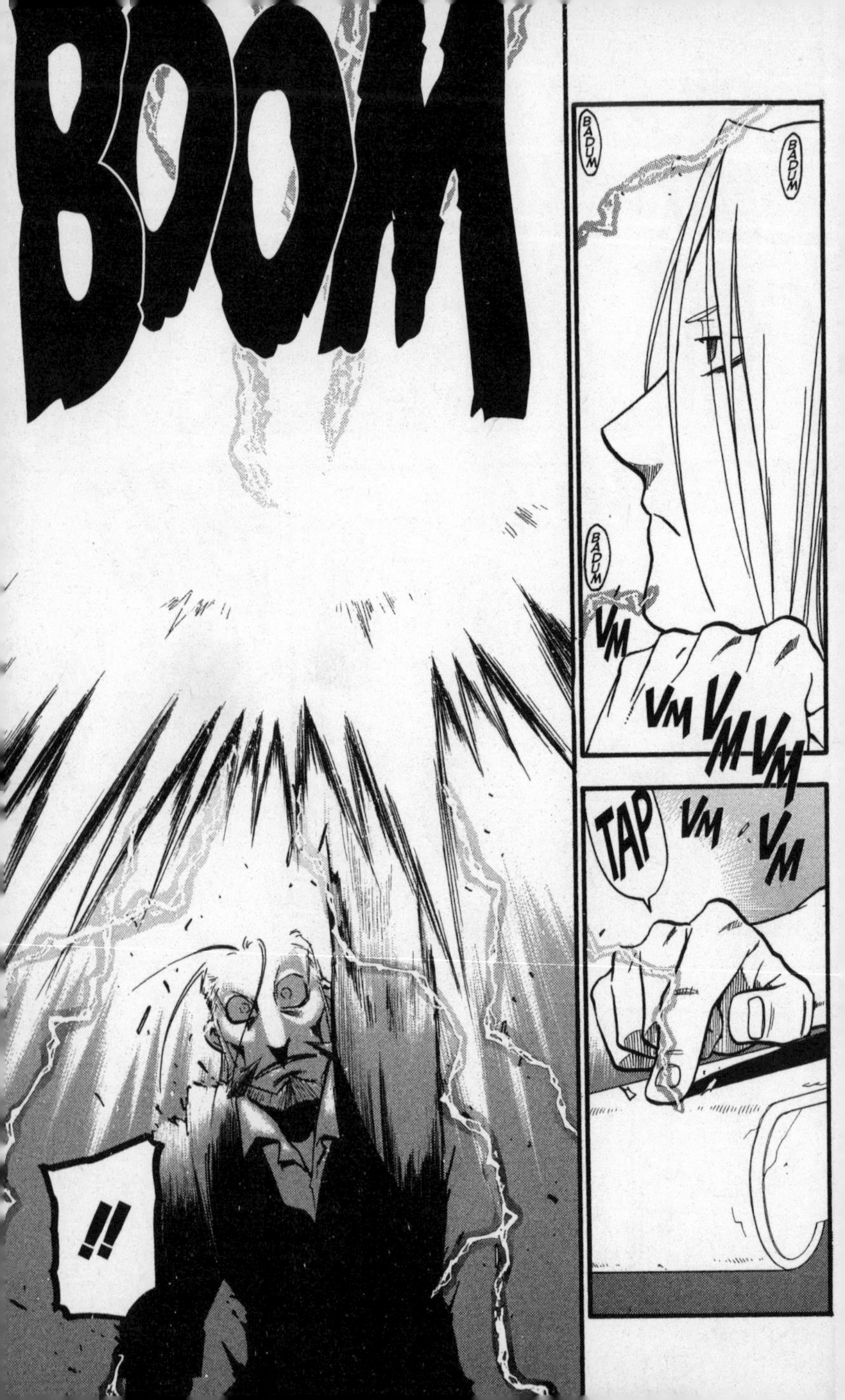
BADUM
BADUM
BADUM
VM
VM VM VM
TAP
VM
VM VM
BOOM
!!

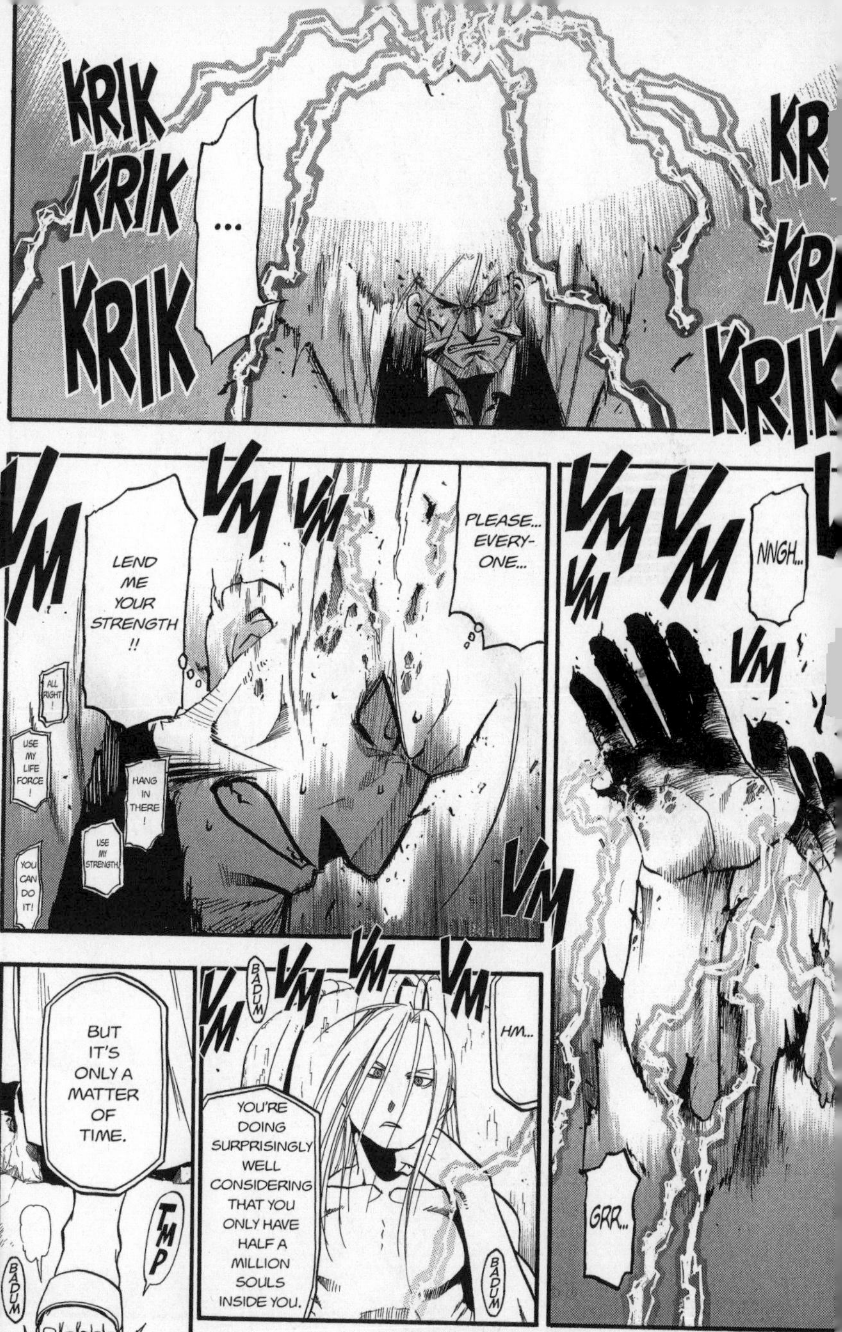
KR
KR
KRIK
...
KRIK
KRIK
KRIK
VM
VM
VM
VM
NNGH...
VM
VM
GRR...
VM
VM
VM
PLEASE... EVERY-ONE...
LEND ME YOUR STRENGTH!!
ALL RIGHT!
USE MY LIFE FORCE!
HANG IN THERE!
USE MY STRENGTH
YOU CAN DO IT!
VM
VM
VM
VM
BADUM
HM...
YOU'RE DOING SURPRISINGLY WELL CONSIDERING THAT YOU ONLY HAVE HALF A MILLION SOULS INSIDE YOU.
BADUM
BUT IT'S ONLY A MATTER OF TIME.
TMP
BADUM

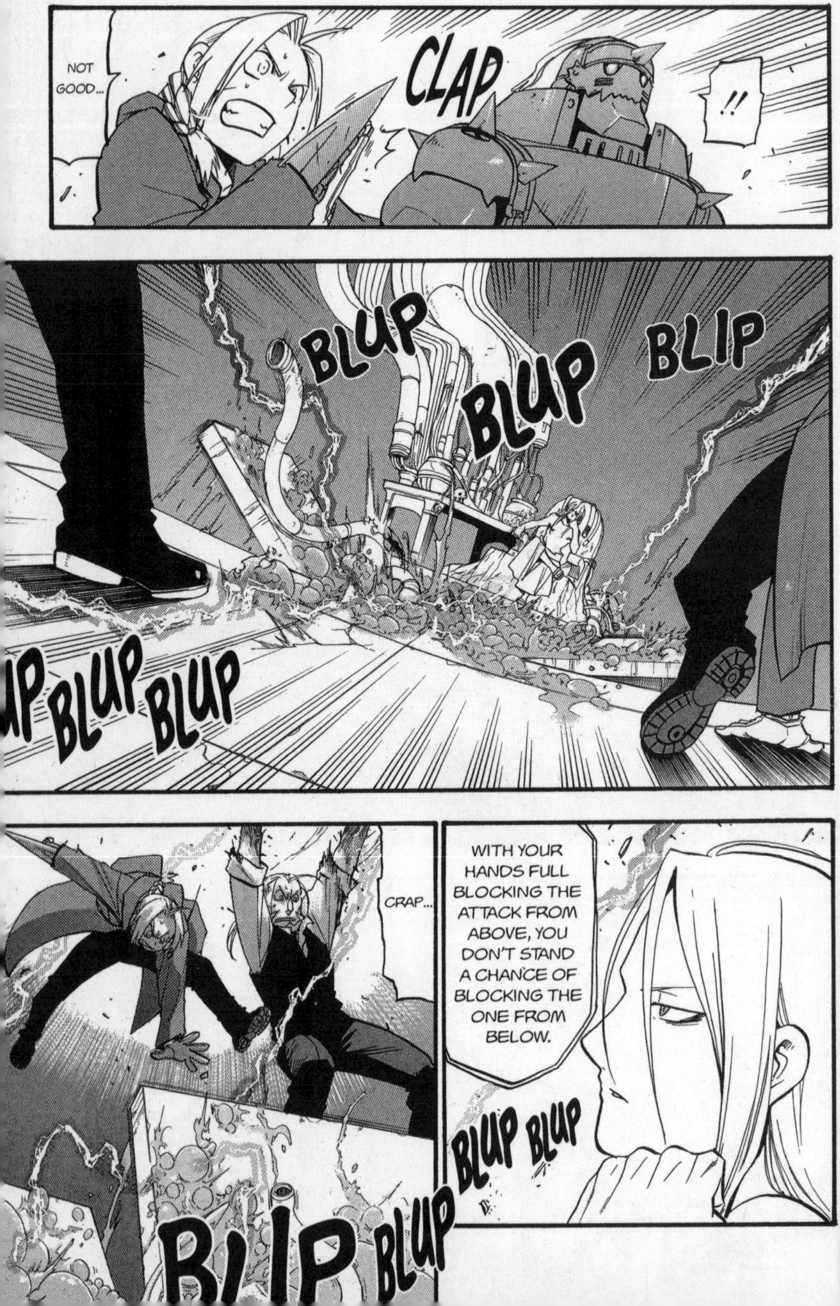
!!
CLAP
NOT GOOD...
BLIP
BLUP
BLUP
BLUP
BLUP
WITH YOUR HANDS FULL BLOCKING THE ATTACK FROM ABOVE, YOU DON'T STAND A CHANCE OF BLOCKING THE ONE FROM BELOW.
BLUP
BLUP
CRAP...
BLUP
BLIP

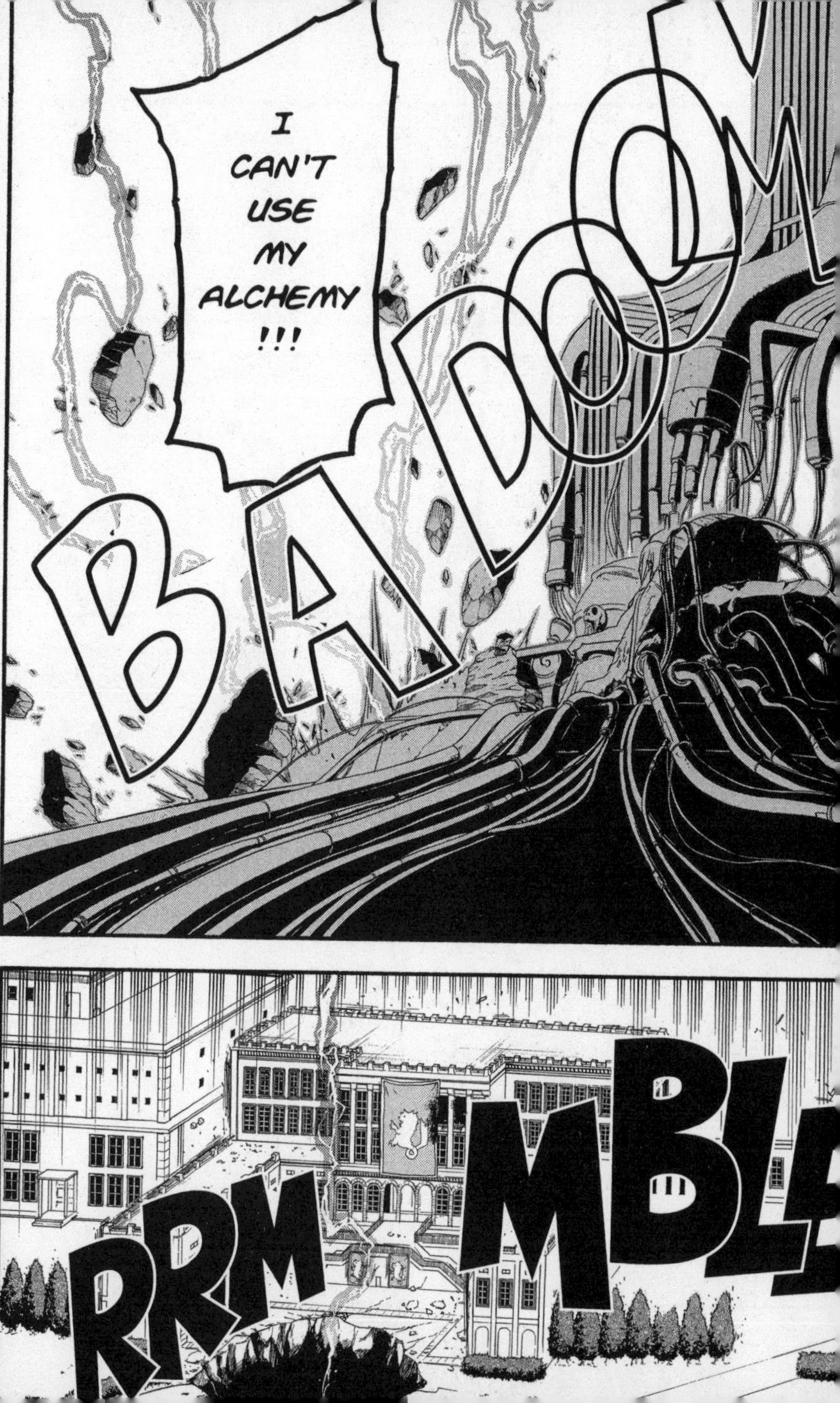
I CAN'T USE MY ALCHEMY !!!
BADOOM
RRMMBL

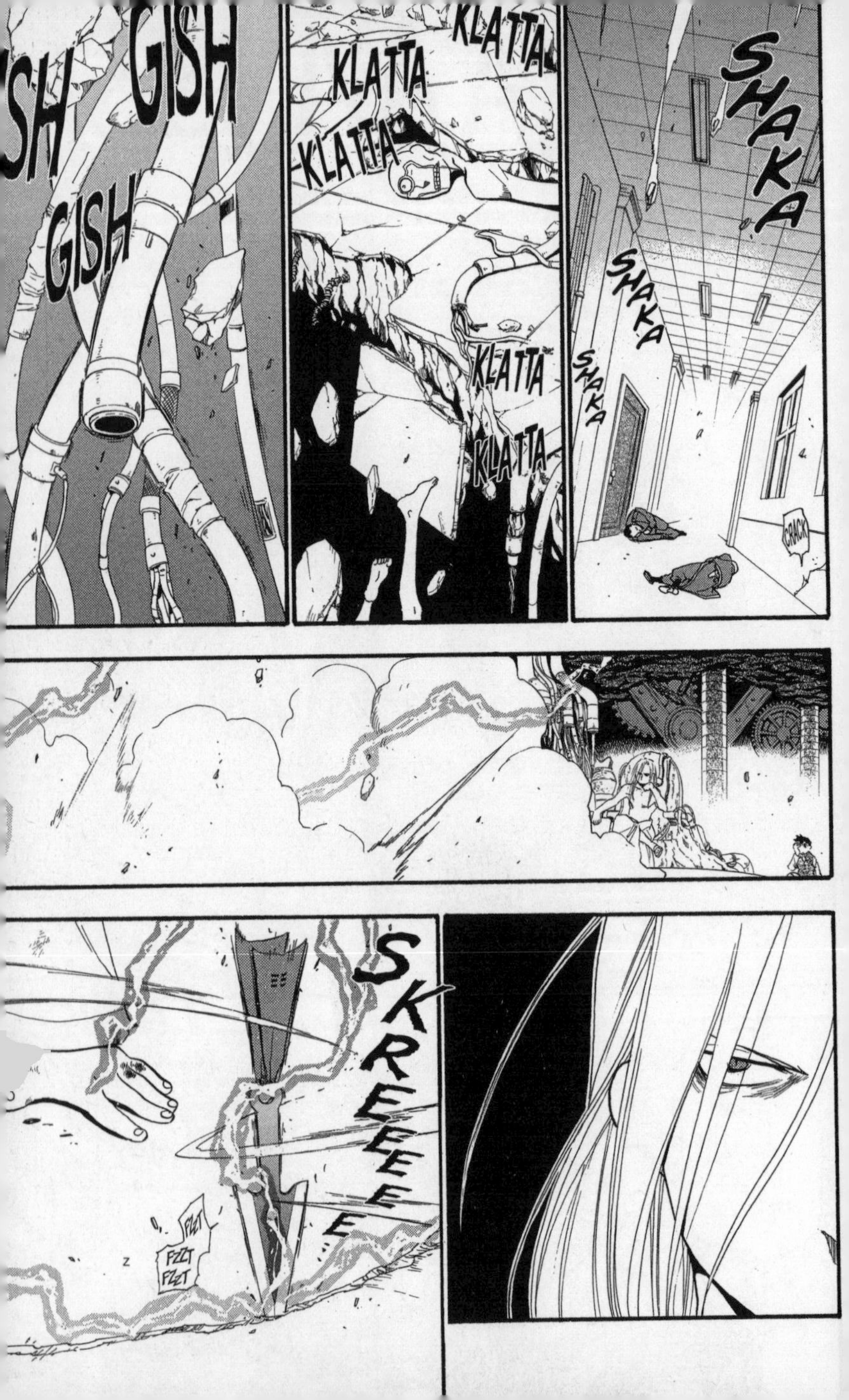
SHAKA
SHAKA
SHAKA
CRACK
KLATTA
KLATTA
KLATTA
KLATTA
KLATTA
GISH
GISH
SKREEEEE
FZZT
FZZT
FZZT

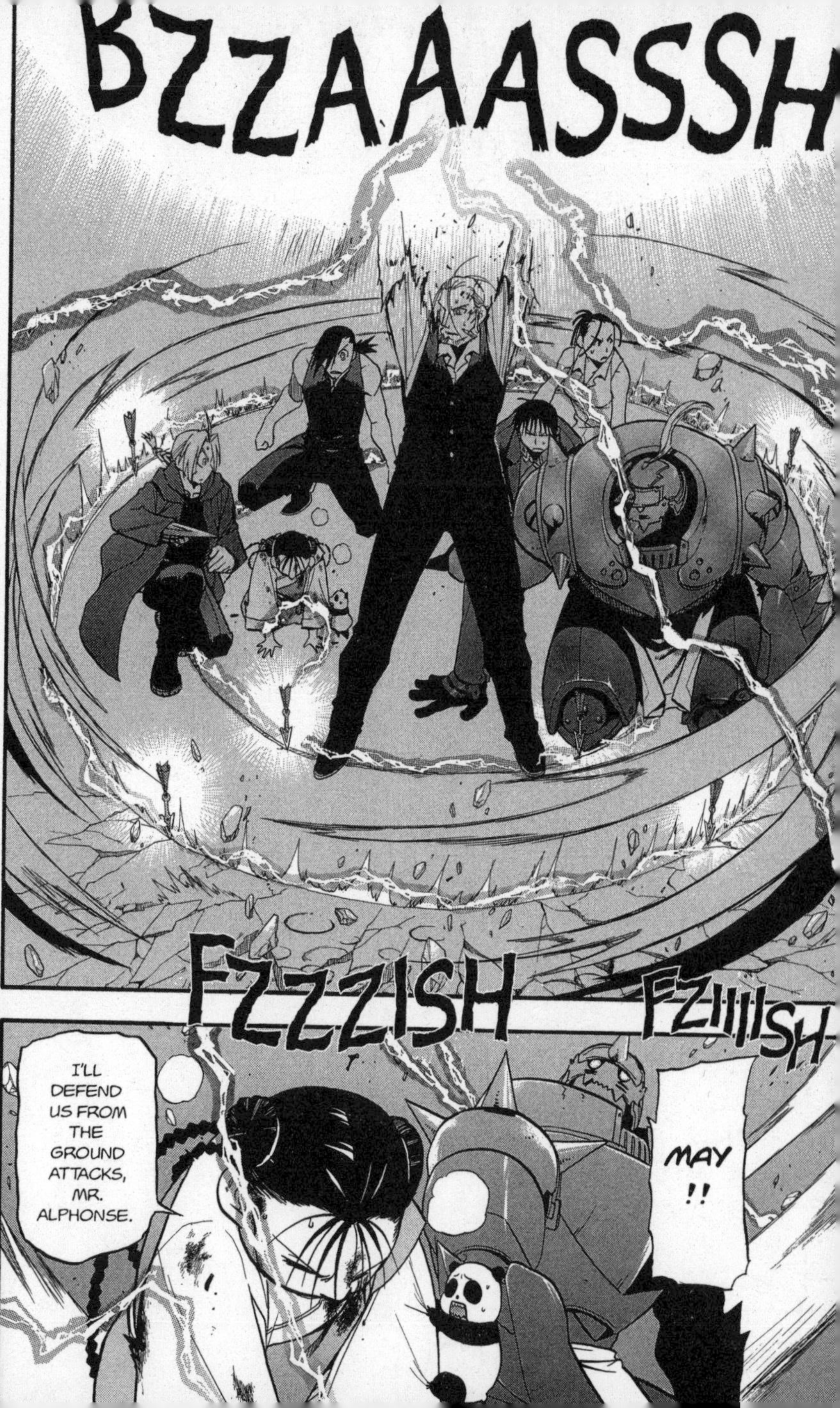
BZZAAASSSH
FZIIIISH
FZZZISH
MAY!!
I'LL DEFEND US FROM THE GROUND ATTACKS, MR. ALPHONSE.

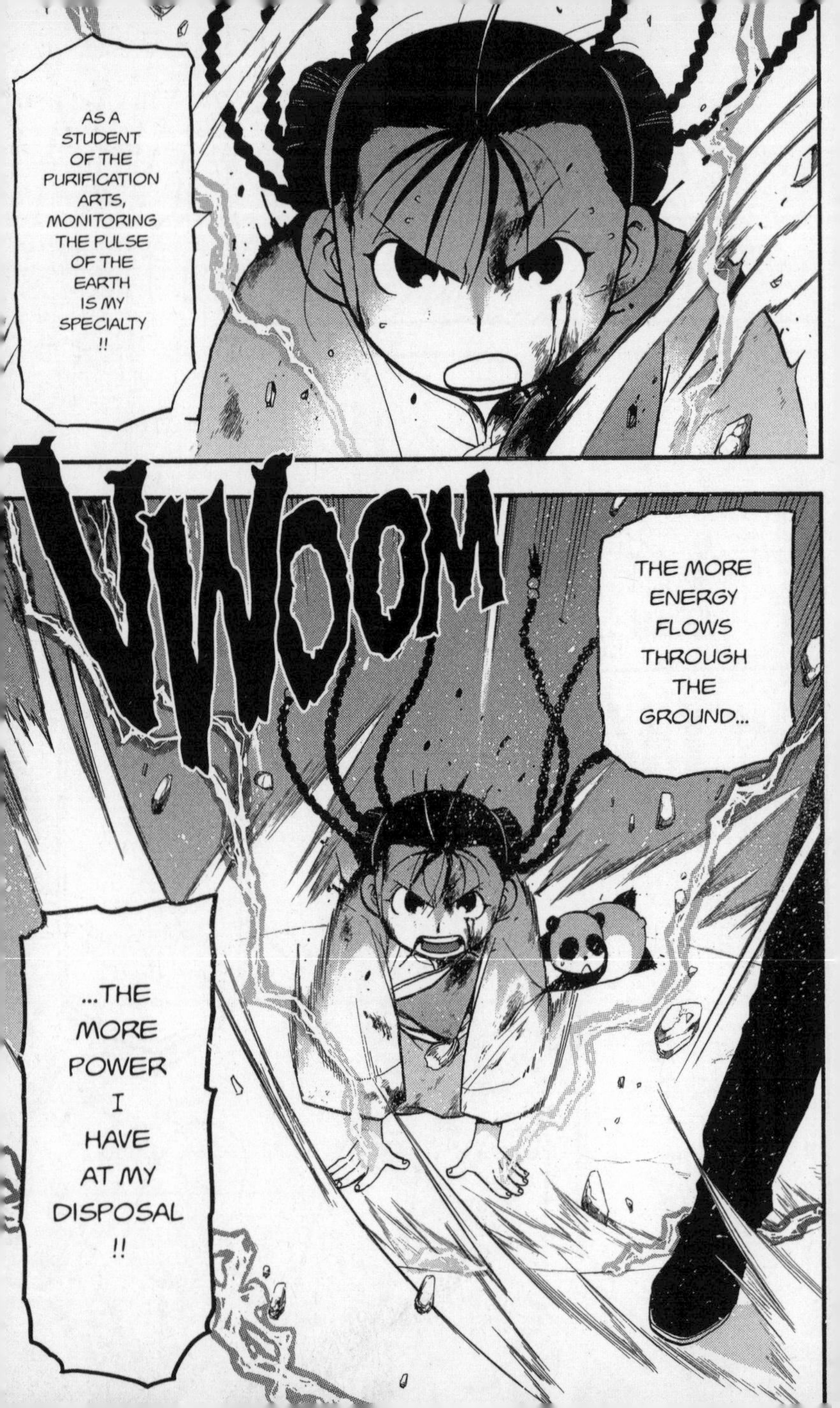
AS A STUDENT OF THE PURIFICATION ARTS, MONITORING THE PULSE OF THE EARTH IS MY SPECIALTY !!
THE MORE ENERGY FLOWS THROUGH THE GROUND...
VWOOM
...THE MORE POWER I HAVE AT MY DISPOSAL !!

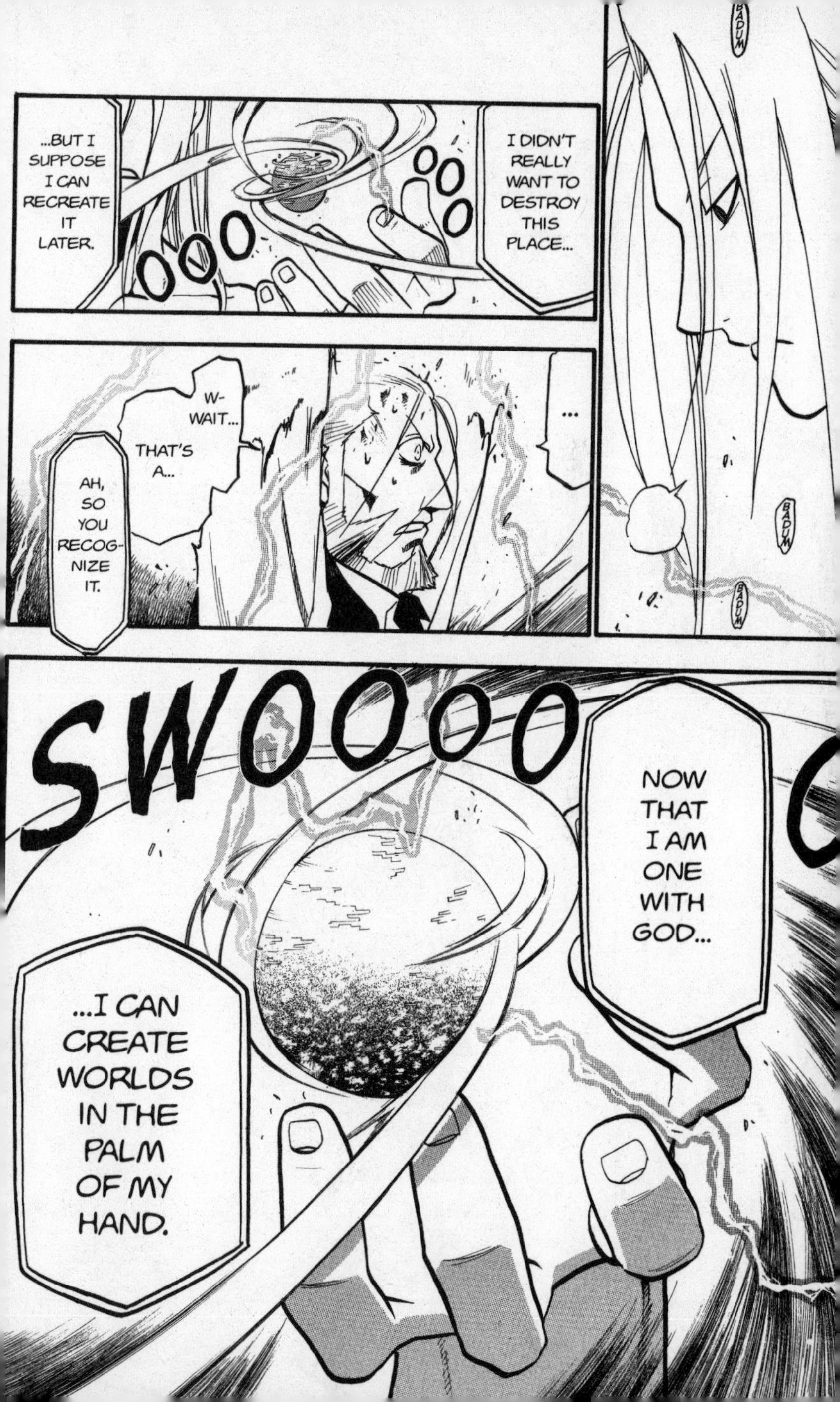
BADUM
BADUM
BADUM
I DIDN'T REALLY WANT TO DESTROY THIS PLACE...
OOO
...BUT I SUPPOSE I CAN RECREATE IT LATER.
OOO
...
W- WAIT... THAT'S A...
AH, SO YOU RECOGNIZE IT.
SWOOOO
NOW THAT I AM ONE WITH GOD...
...I CAN CREATE WORLDS IN THE PALM OF MY HAND.

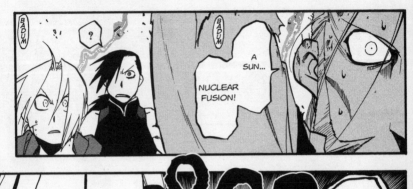

? BADUM BADUM

A SUN...

NUCLEAR FUSION!

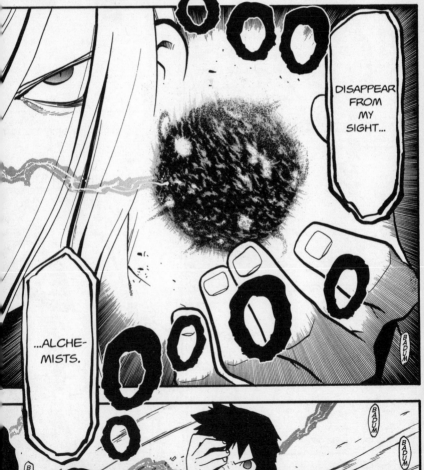

DISAPPEAR FROM MY SIGHT...

...ALCHE-MISTS.

BADUM

BADUM

BADUM

BADUM

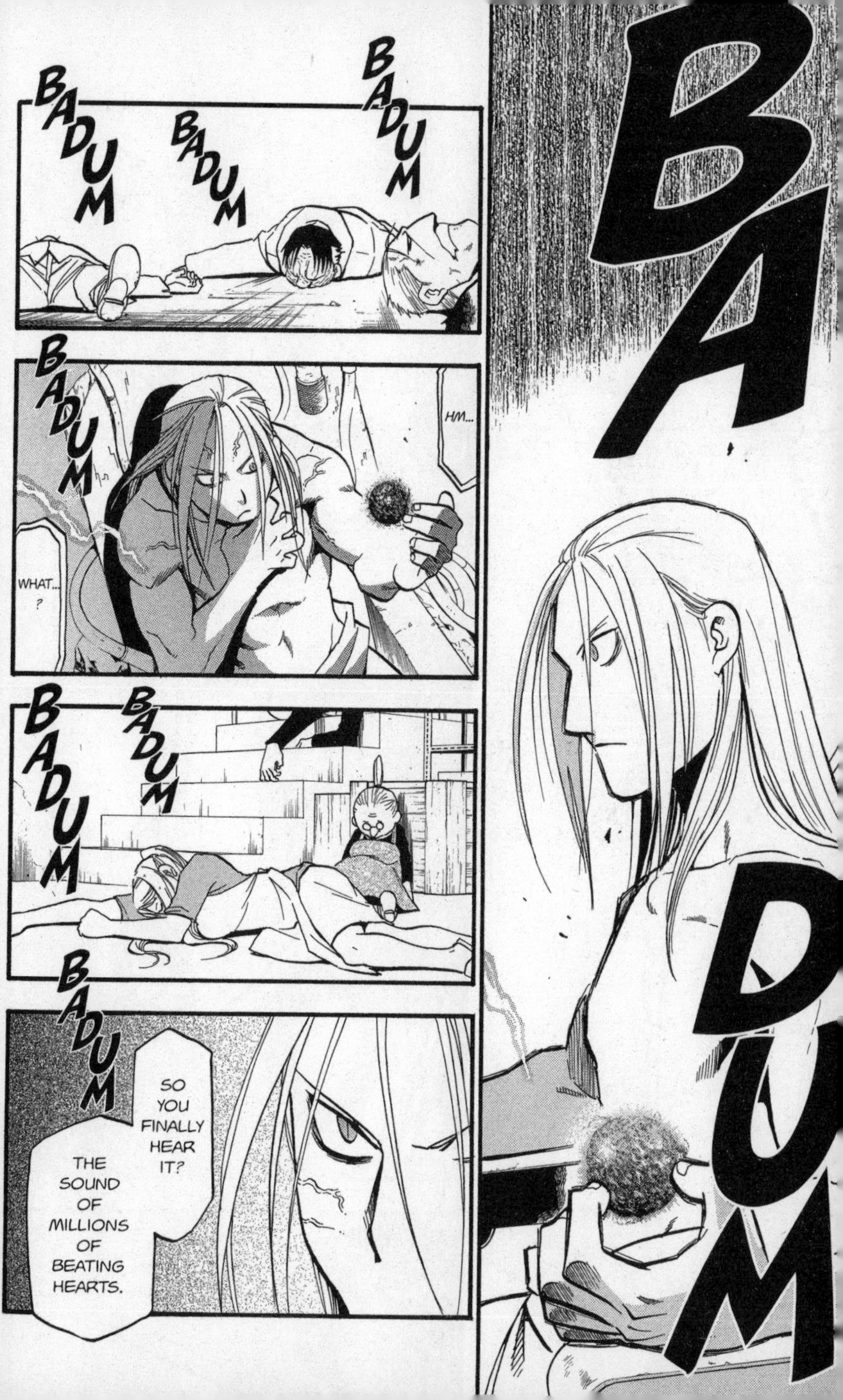
BA-DUM
BADUM
BADUM
BADUM
HM...
BADUM
WHAT...?
BADUM
BADUM
BADUM
SO YOU FINALLY HEAR IT?
THE SOUND OF MILLIONS OF BEATING HEARTS.

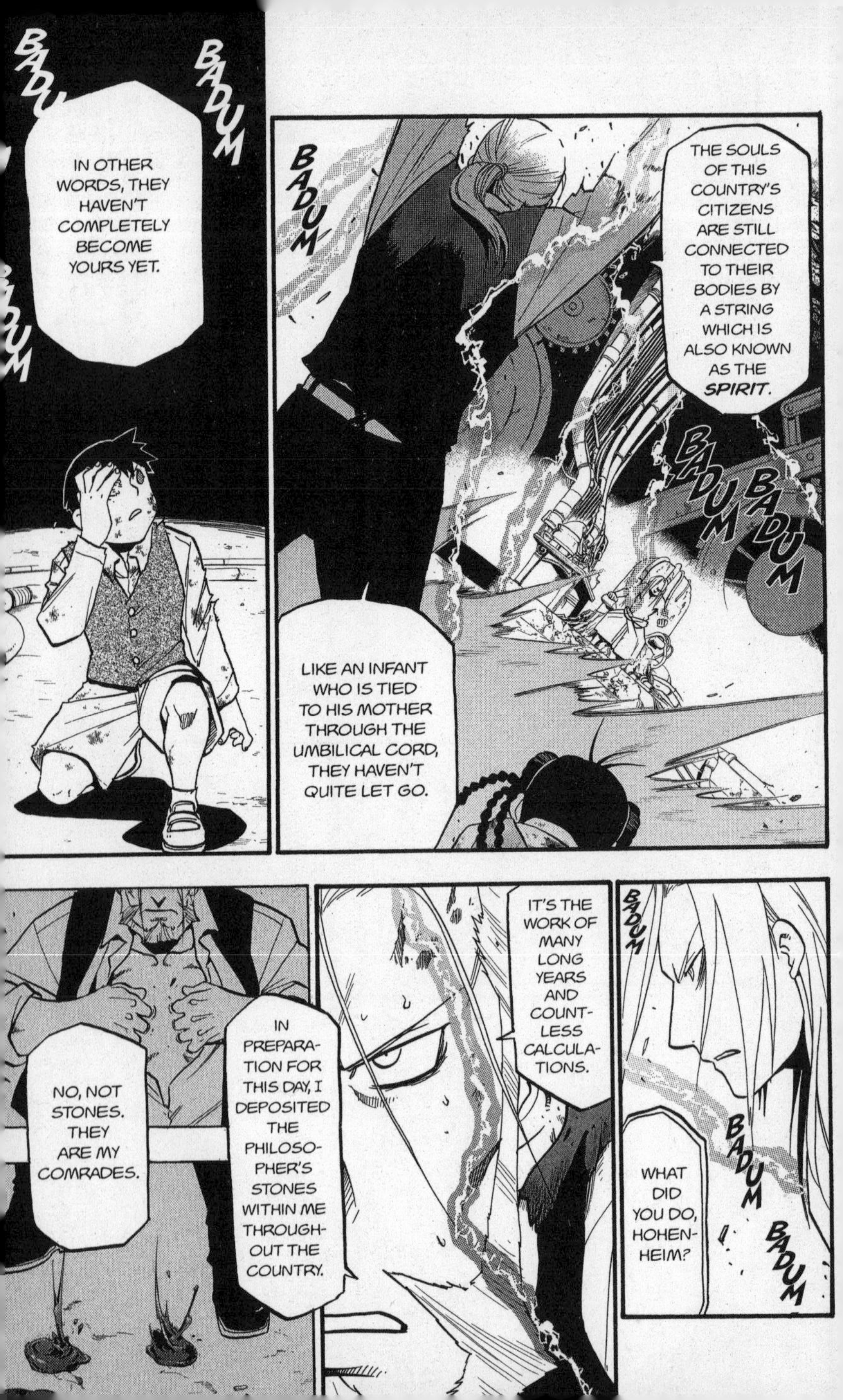
THE SOULS OF THIS COUNTRY'S CITIZENS ARE STILL CONNECTED TO THEIR BODIES BY A STRING WHICH IS ALSO KNOWN AS THE *SPIRIT*.
BADUM
BADUM BADUM
LIKE AN INFANT WHO IS TIED TO HIS MOTHER THROUGH THE UMBILICAL CORD, THEY HAVEN'T QUITE LET GO.
BADUM
BADUM
IN OTHER WORDS, THEY HAVEN'T COMPLETELY BECOME YOURS YET.
BADUM
WHAT DID YOU DO, HOHENHEIM?
BADUM
BADUM
IT'S THE WORK OF MANY LONG YEARS AND COUNT-LESS CALCULA-TIONS.
IN PREPARA-TION FOR THIS DAY, I DEPOSITED THE PHILOSO-PHER'S STONES WITHIN ME THROUGH-OUT THE COUNTRY.
NO, NOT STONES. THEY ARE MY COMRADES.

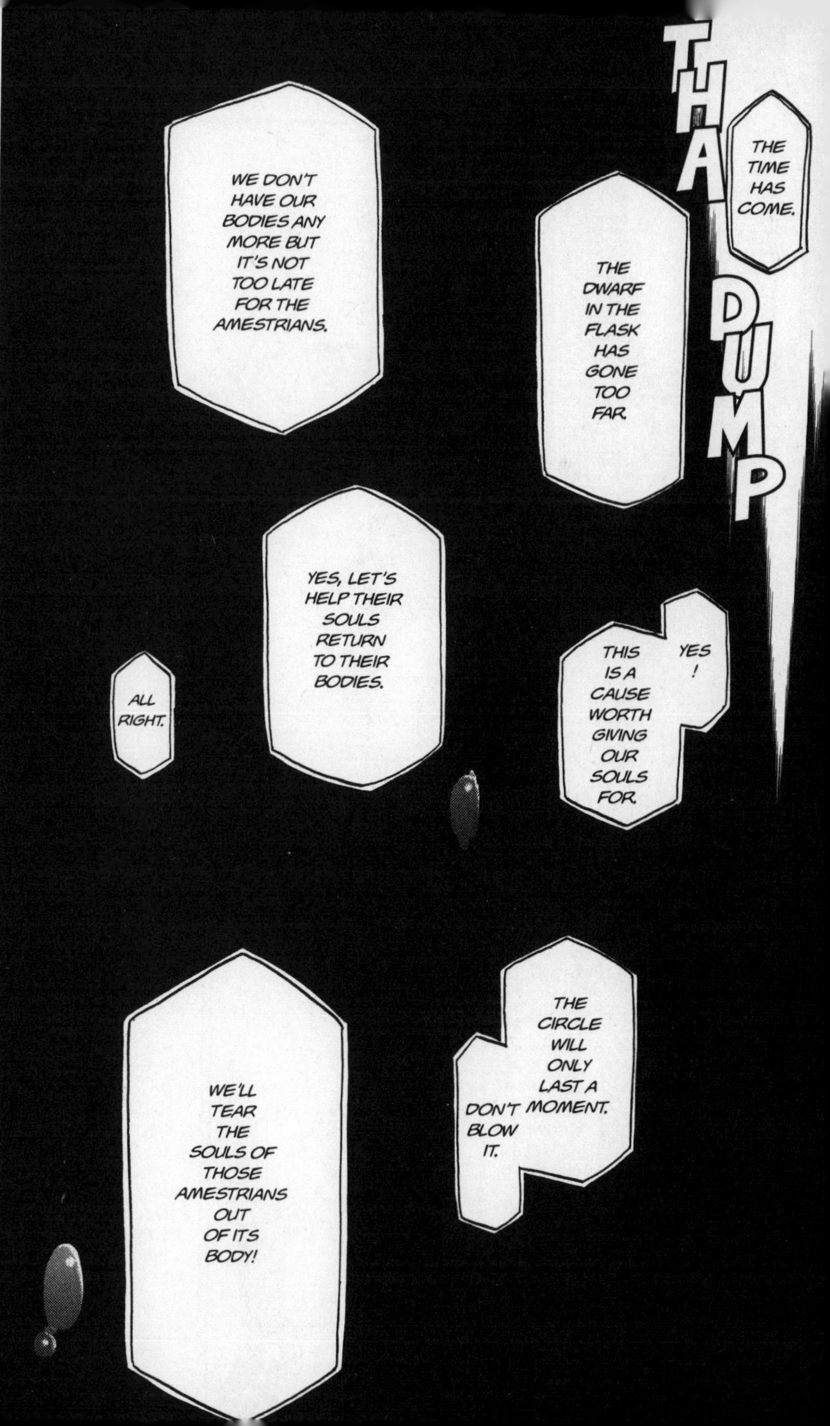
THA-DUMP
THE TIME HAS COME.
THE DWARF IN THE FLASK HAS GONE TOO FAR.
WE DON'T HAVE OUR BODIES ANY MORE BUT IT'S NOT TOO LATE FOR THE AMESTRIANS.
YES!
THIS IS A CAUSE WORTH GIVING OUR SOULS FOR.
YES, LET'S HELP THEIR SOULS RETURN TO THEIR BODIES.
ALL RIGHT.
THE CIRCLE WILL ONLY LAST A MOMENT.
DON'T BLOW IT.
WE'LL TEAR THE SOULS OF THOSE AMESTRIANS OUT OF ITS BODY!

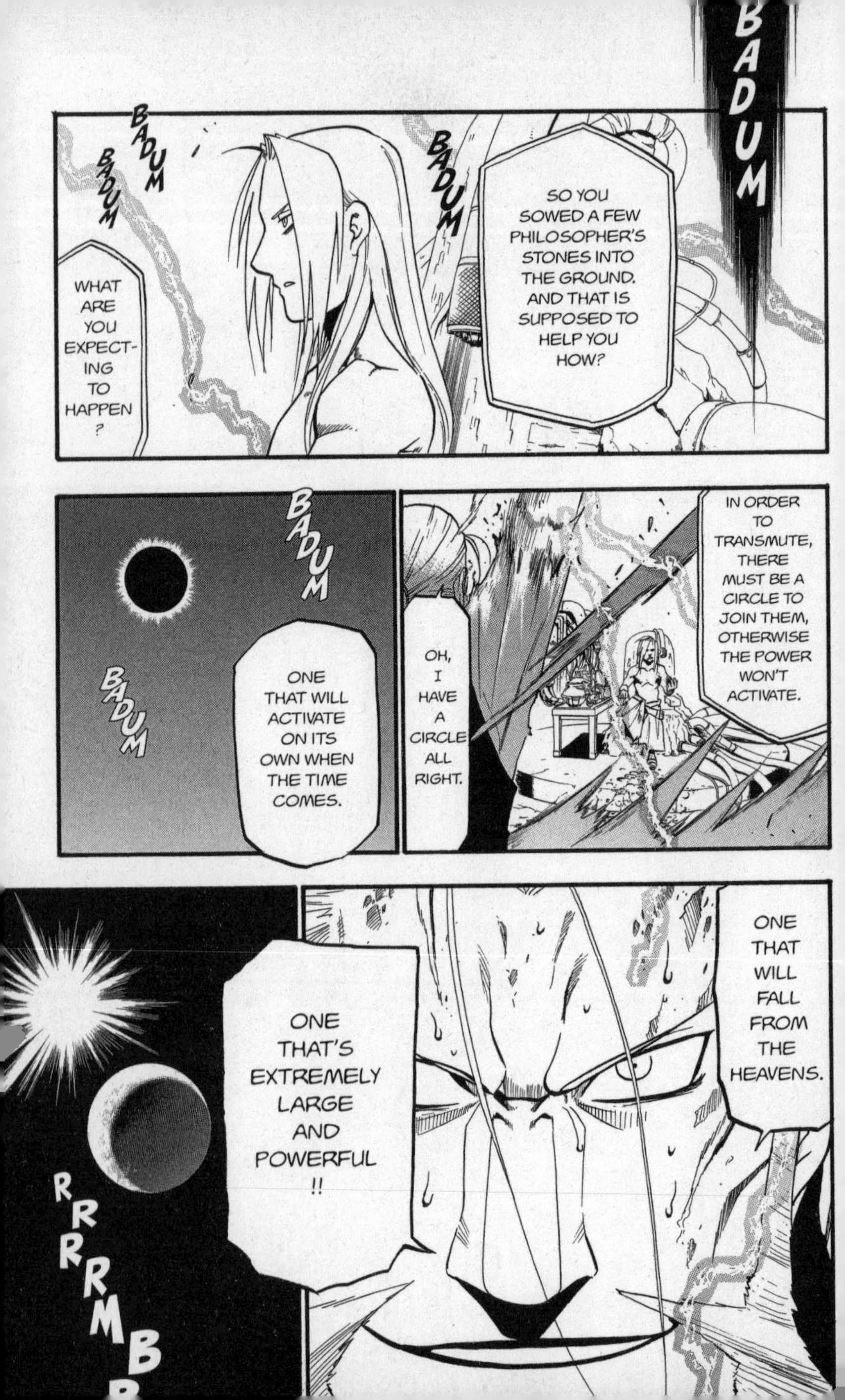
BADUM
BADUM
SO YOU SOWED A FEW PHILOSOPHER'S STONES INTO THE GROUND. AND THAT IS SUPPOSED TO HELP YOU HOW?
BADUM
BADUM
WHAT ARE YOU EXPECTING TO HAPPEN?
IN ORDER TO TRANSMUTE, THERE MUST BE A CIRCLE TO JOIN THEM, OTHERWISE THE POWER WON'T ACTIVATE.
OH, I HAVE A CIRCLE ALL RIGHT.
BADUM
ONE THAT WILL ACTIVATE ON ITS OWN WHEN THE TIME COMES.
BADUM
ONE THAT WILL FALL FROM THE HEAVENS.
ONE THAT'S EXTREMELY LARGE AND POWERFUL!!
RRRRMB

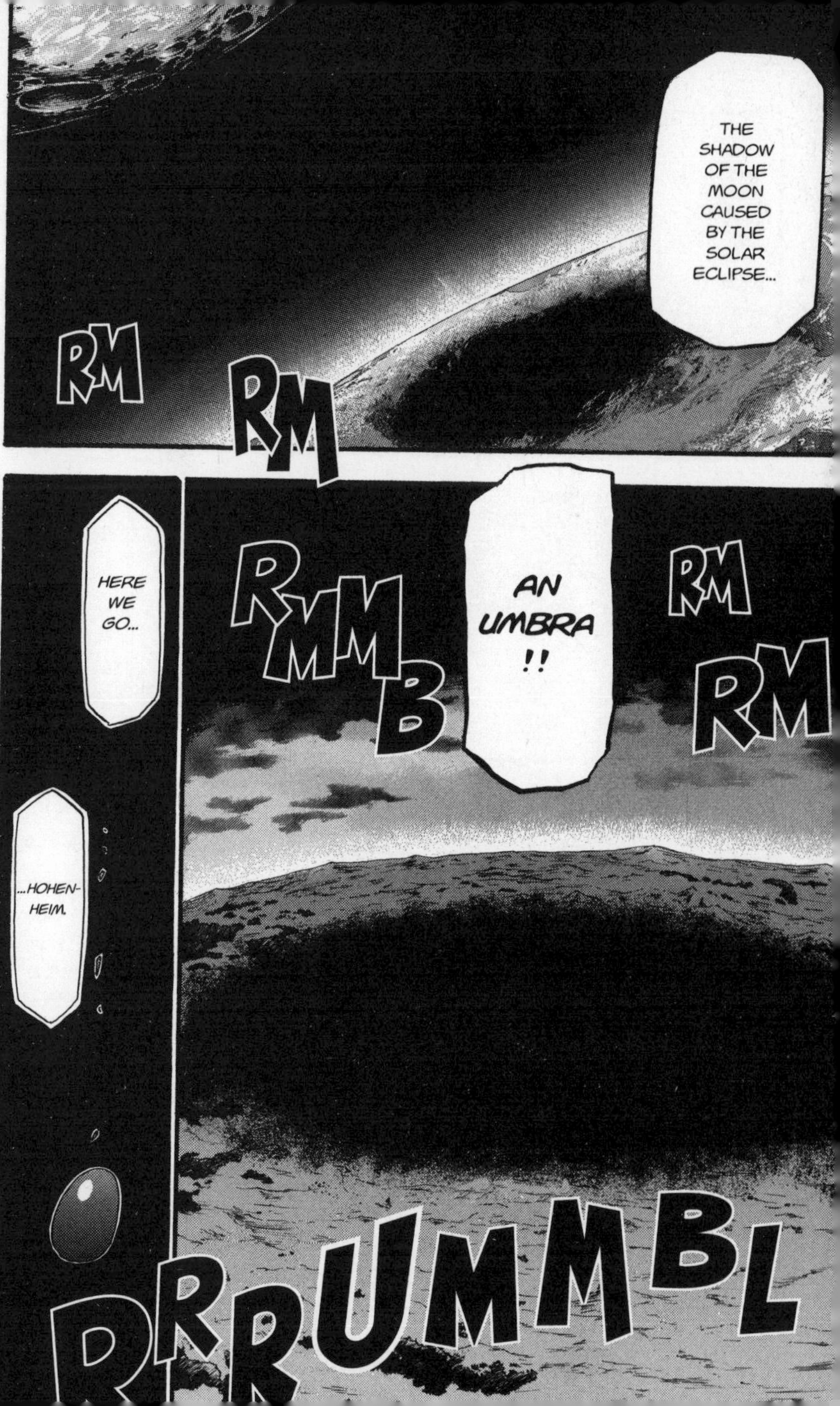
THE SHADOW OF THE MOON CAUSED BY THE SOLAR ECLIPSE...
RM
RM
RM
RM
AN UMBRA!!
RMMMB
HERE WE GO...
...HOHEN-HEIM.
DRRUMMBL

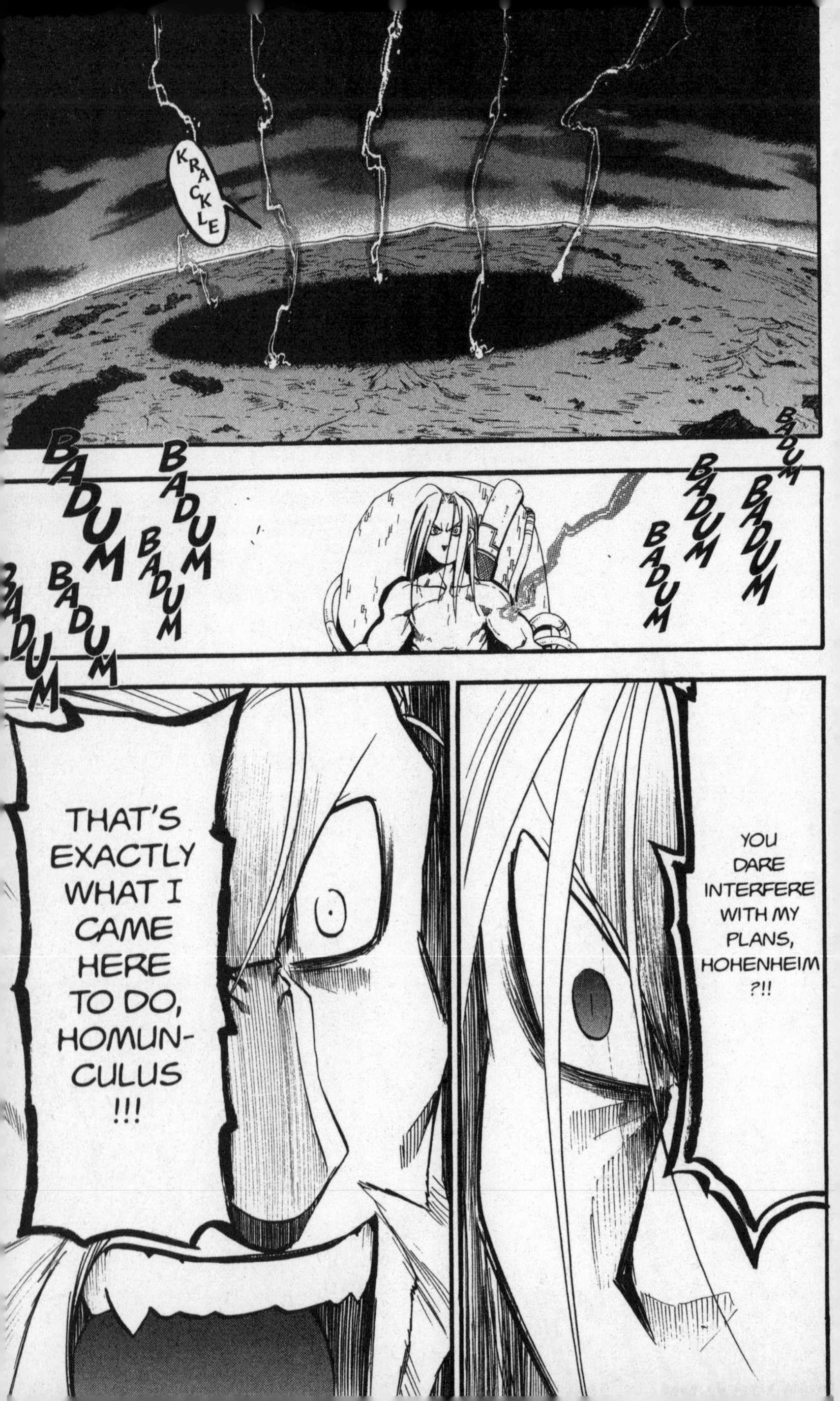
KRACKLE
BADUM
BADUM
BADUM
BADUM
BADUM
BADUM
BADUM
BADUM
BADUM
YOU DARE INTERFERE WITH MY PLANS, HOHENHEIM ?!!
THAT'S EXACTLY WHAT I CAME HERE TO DO, HOMUNCULUS !!!

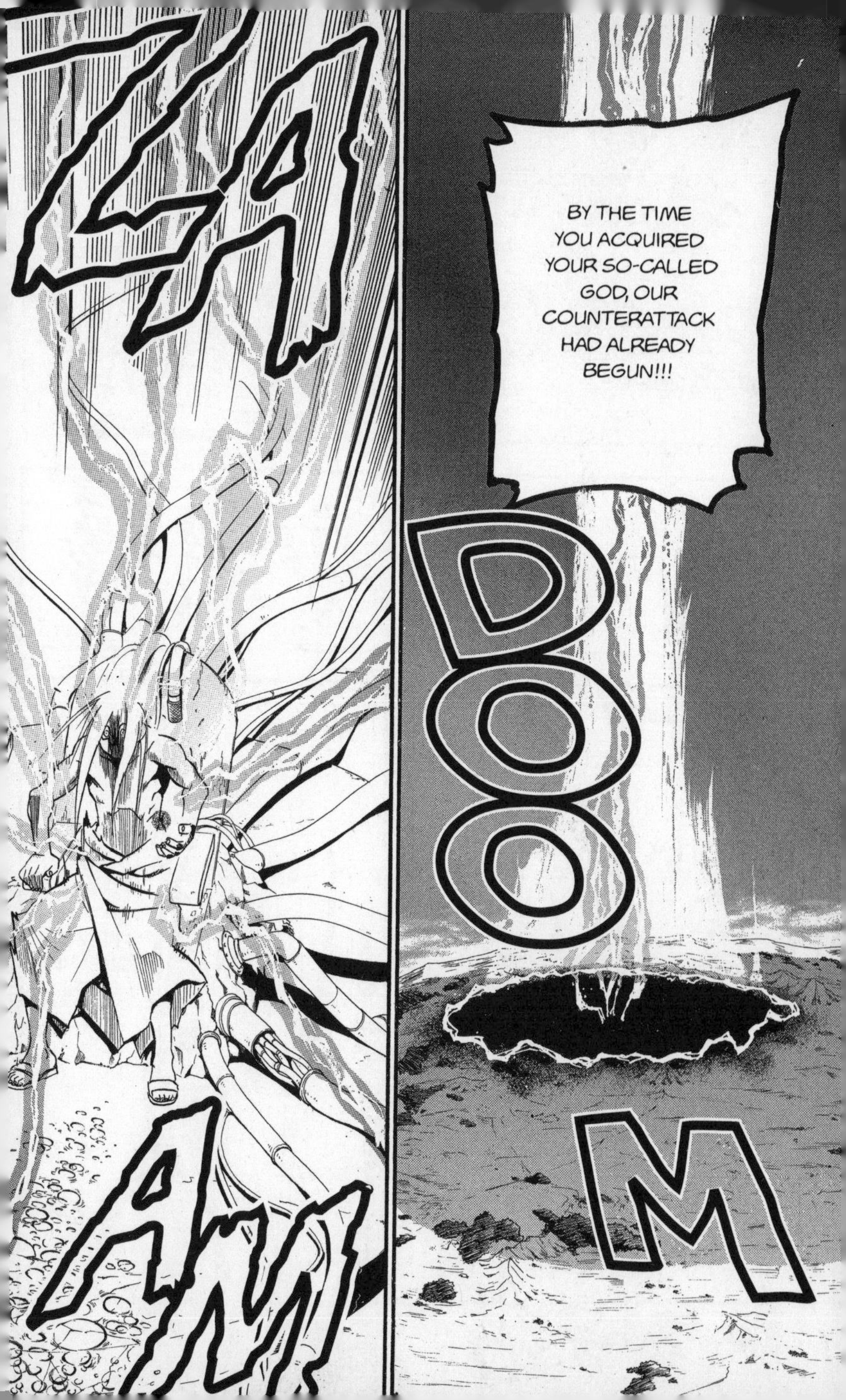
BY THE TIME YOU ACQUIRED YOUR SO-CALLED GOD, OUR COUNTERATTACK HAD ALREADY BEGUN!!!
DOO
M
ZA
AM

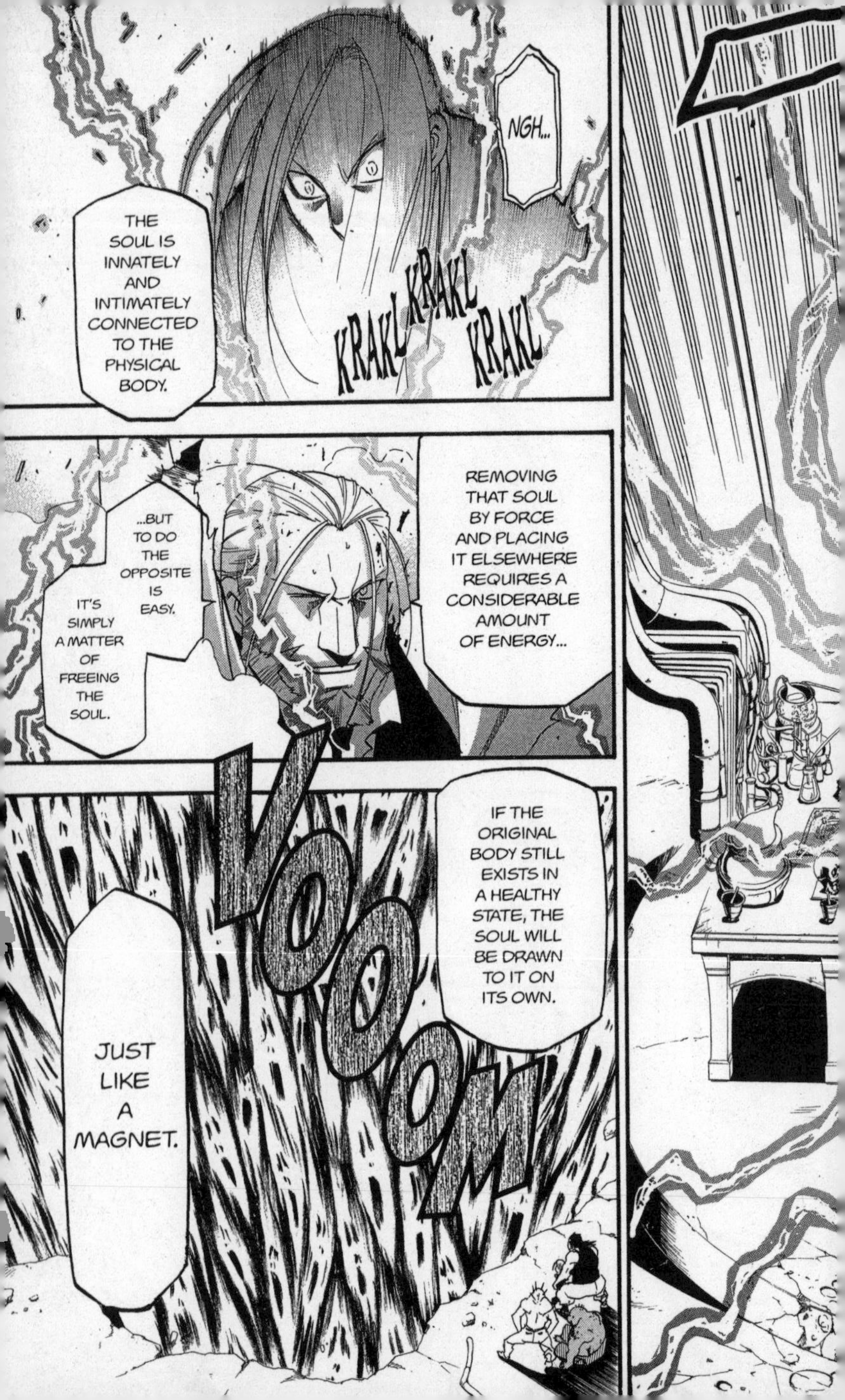
NGH...
KRAKL KRAKL KRAKL
THE SOUL IS INNATELY AND INTIMATELY CONNECTED TO THE PHYSICAL BODY.
REMOVING THAT SOUL BY FORCE AND PLACING IT ELSEWHERE REQUIRES A CONSIDERABLE AMOUNT OF ENERGY...
...BUT TO DO THE OPPOSITE IS EASY.
IT'S SIMPLY A MATTER OF FREEING THE SOUL.
VOOOOM
IF THE ORIGINAL BODY STILL EXISTS IN A HEALTHY STATE, THE SOUL WILL BE DRAWN TO IT ON ITS OWN.
JUST LIKE A MAGNET.

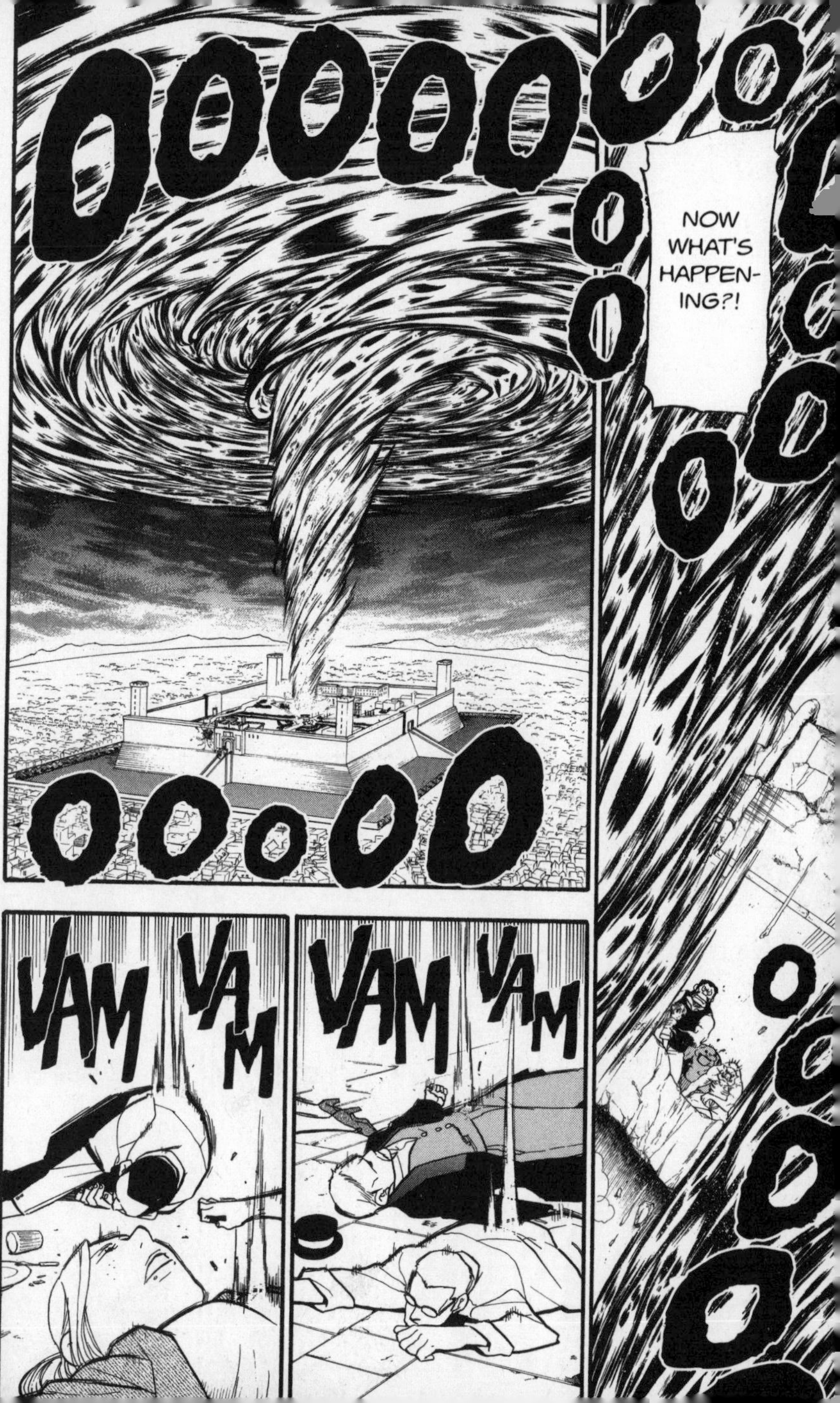
NOW WHAT'S HAPPEN-ING?!
OOOOOOOOOOOO
OOOOOO
VAM VAM
VAM VAM

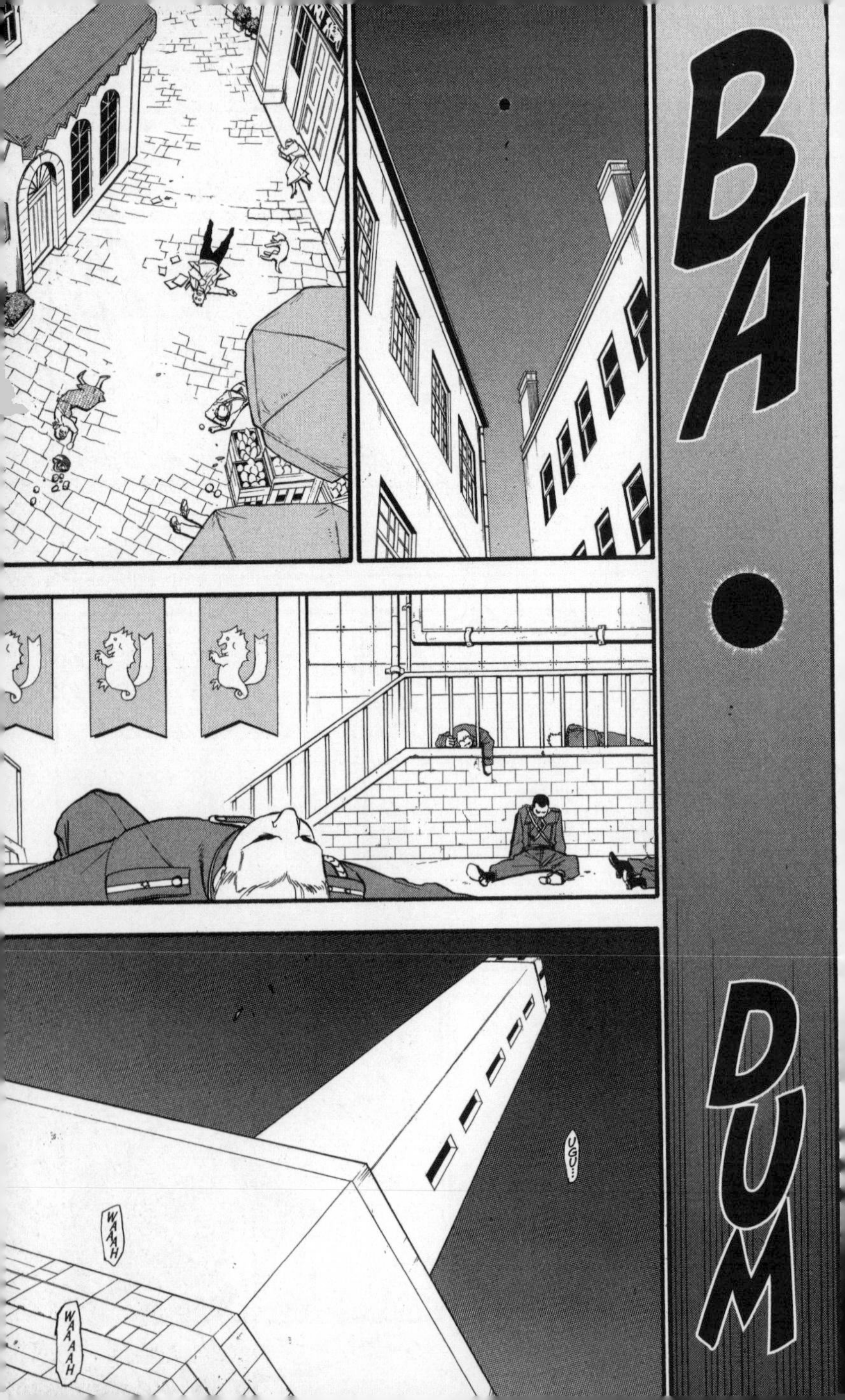
BA • DUM
UGU...
WAAAH
WAAAAH

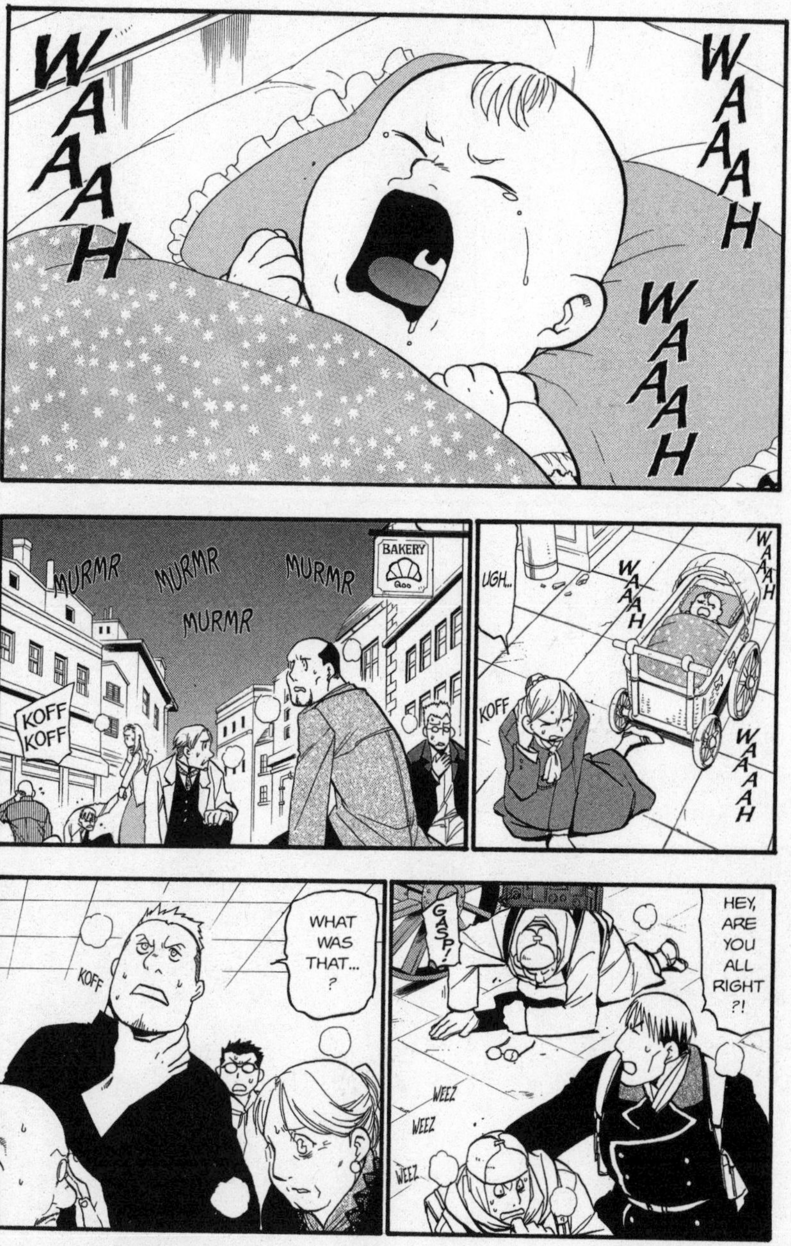
WAAAH
WAAAH
WAAAH
WAAAH
WAAAH
UGH...
KOFF
WAAAAAH
BAKERY
MURMR
MURMR
MURMR
MURMR
KOFF KOFF
HEY, ARE YOU ALL RIGHT?!
GASP!
WEEZ
WEEZ
WEEZ
WHAT WAS THAT...?
KOFF

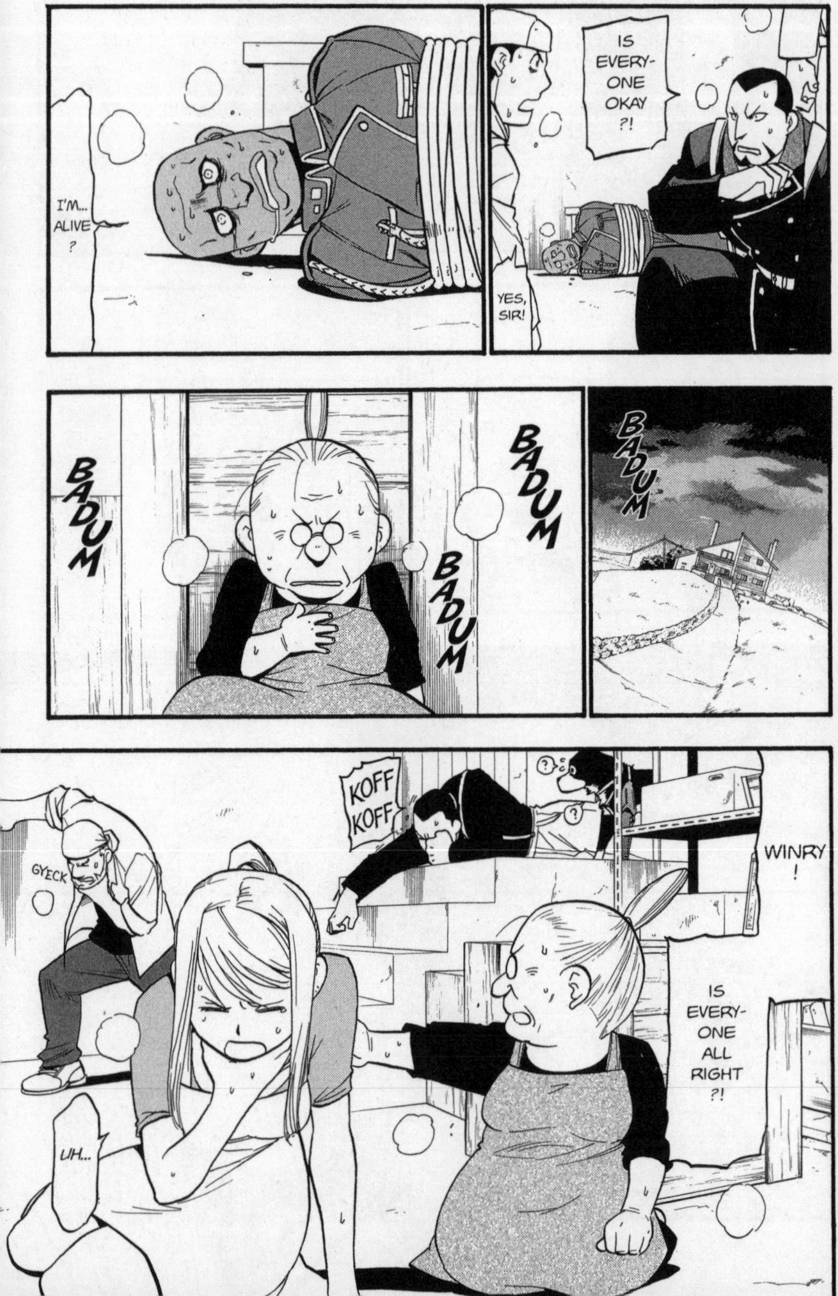
IS EVERY-ONE OKAY ?!
YES, SIR!
I'M... ALIVE ?
BADUM
BADUM
BADUM
BADUM
WINRY !
IS EVERY-ONE ALL RIGHT ?!
KOFF KOFF
GYECK
UH...

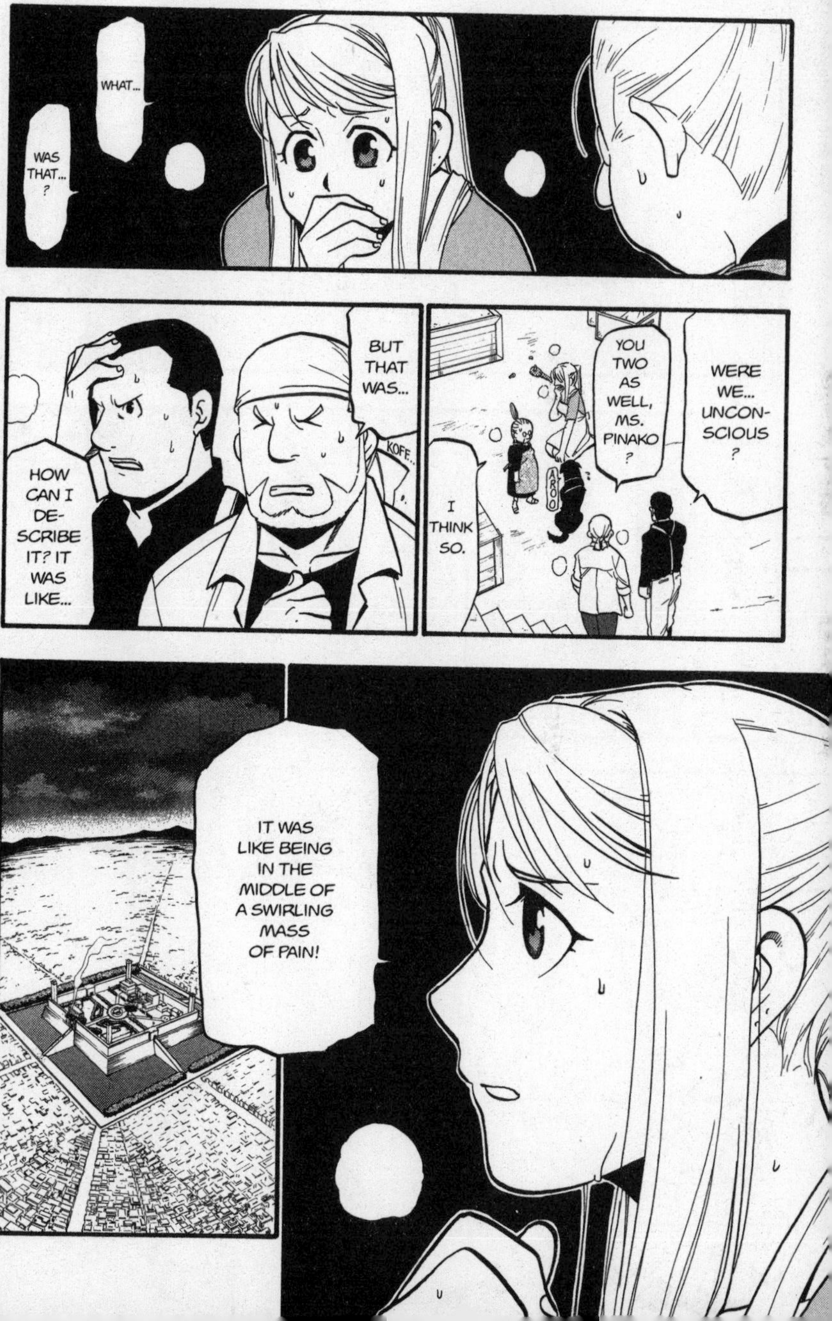
WHAT...
WAS THAT...?
WERE WE... UNCON-SCIOUS?
YOU TWO AS WELL, MS. PINAKO?
AROO
I THINK SO.
BUT THAT WAS...
KOFF...
HOW CAN I DE-SCRIBE IT? IT WAS LIKE...
IT WAS LIKE BEING IN THE MIDDLE OF A SWIRLING MASS OF PAIN!

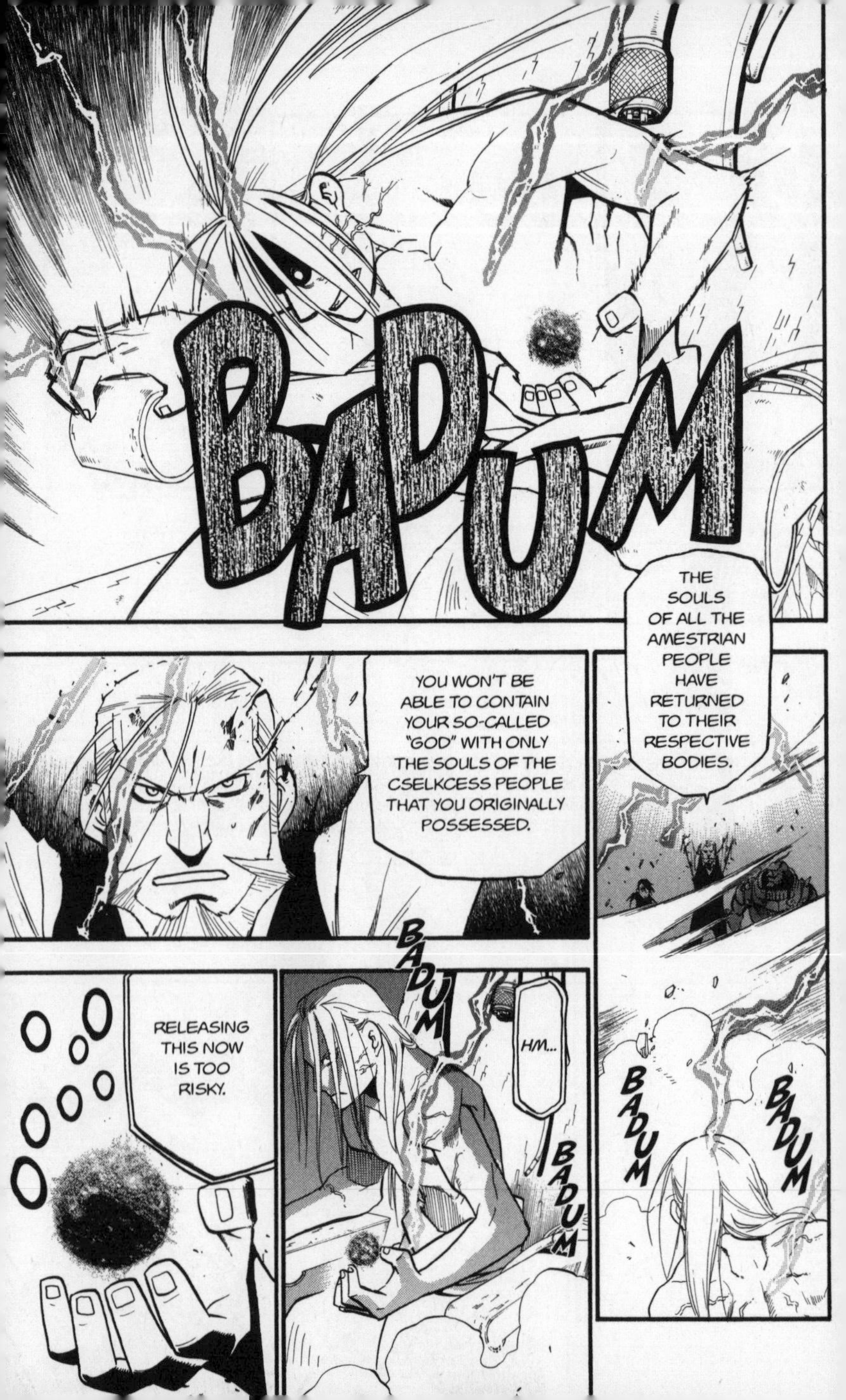
BADUM
THE SOULS OF ALL THE AMESTRIAN PEOPLE HAVE RETURNED TO THEIR RESPECTIVE BODIES.
YOU WON'T BE ABLE TO CONTAIN YOUR SO-CALLED "GOD" WITH ONLY THE SOULS OF THE CSELKCESS PEOPLE THAT YOU ORIGINALLY POSSESSED.
BADUM
BADUM
BADUM
HM...
BADUM
RELEASING THIS NOW IS TOO RISKY.

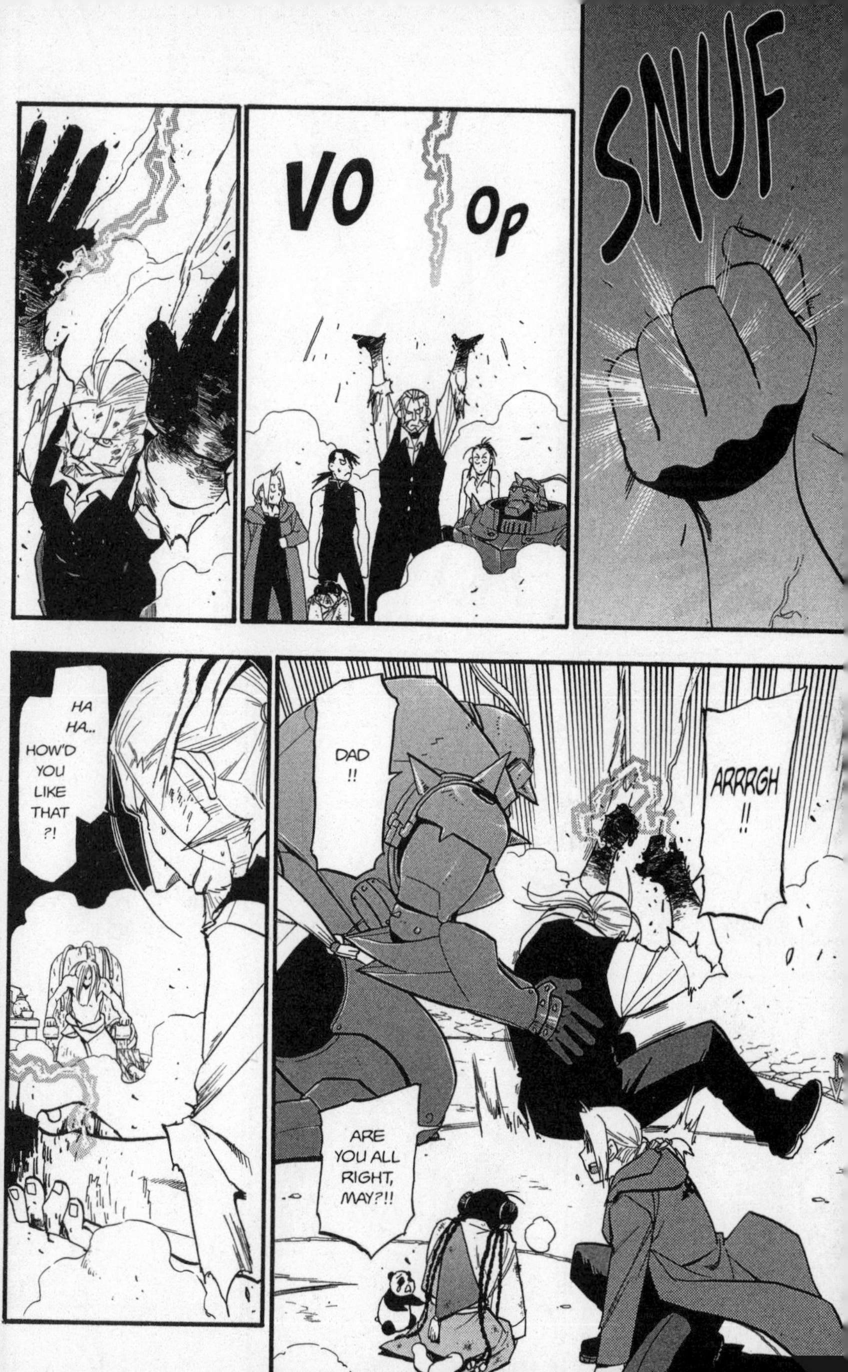
SNUF
VO OP
ARRRGH !!
DAD !!
ARE YOU ALL RIGHT, MAY?!!
HA HA... HOW'D YOU LIKE THAT ?!

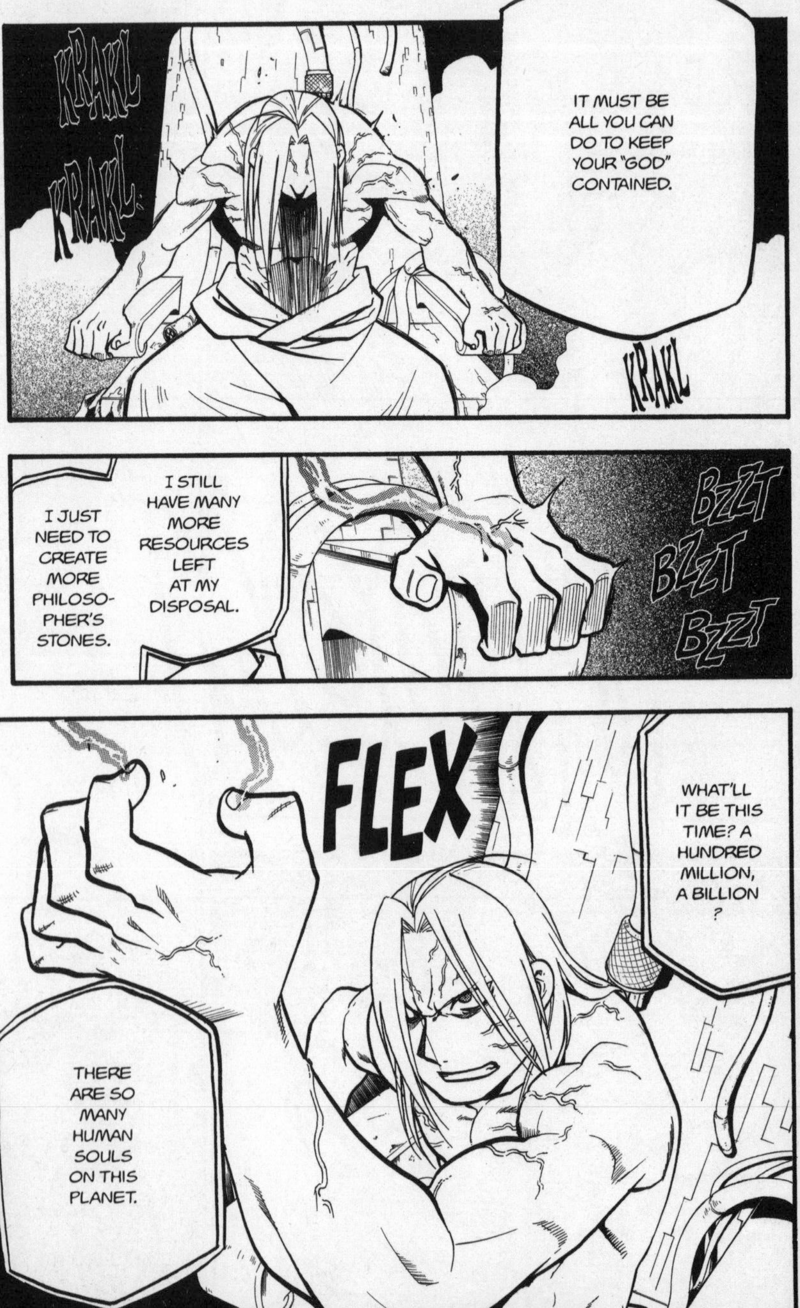
IT MUST BE ALL YOU CAN DO TO KEEP YOUR "GOD" CONTAINED.
KRAKL
KRAKL
KRAKL
BZZT BZZT BZZT
I STILL HAVE MANY MORE RESOURCES LEFT AT MY DISPOSAL.
I JUST NEED TO CREATE MORE PHILOSO-PHER'S STONES.
WHAT'LL IT BE THIS TIME? A HUNDRED MILLION, A BILLION?
FLEX
THERE ARE SO MANY HUMAN SOULS ON THIS PLANET.

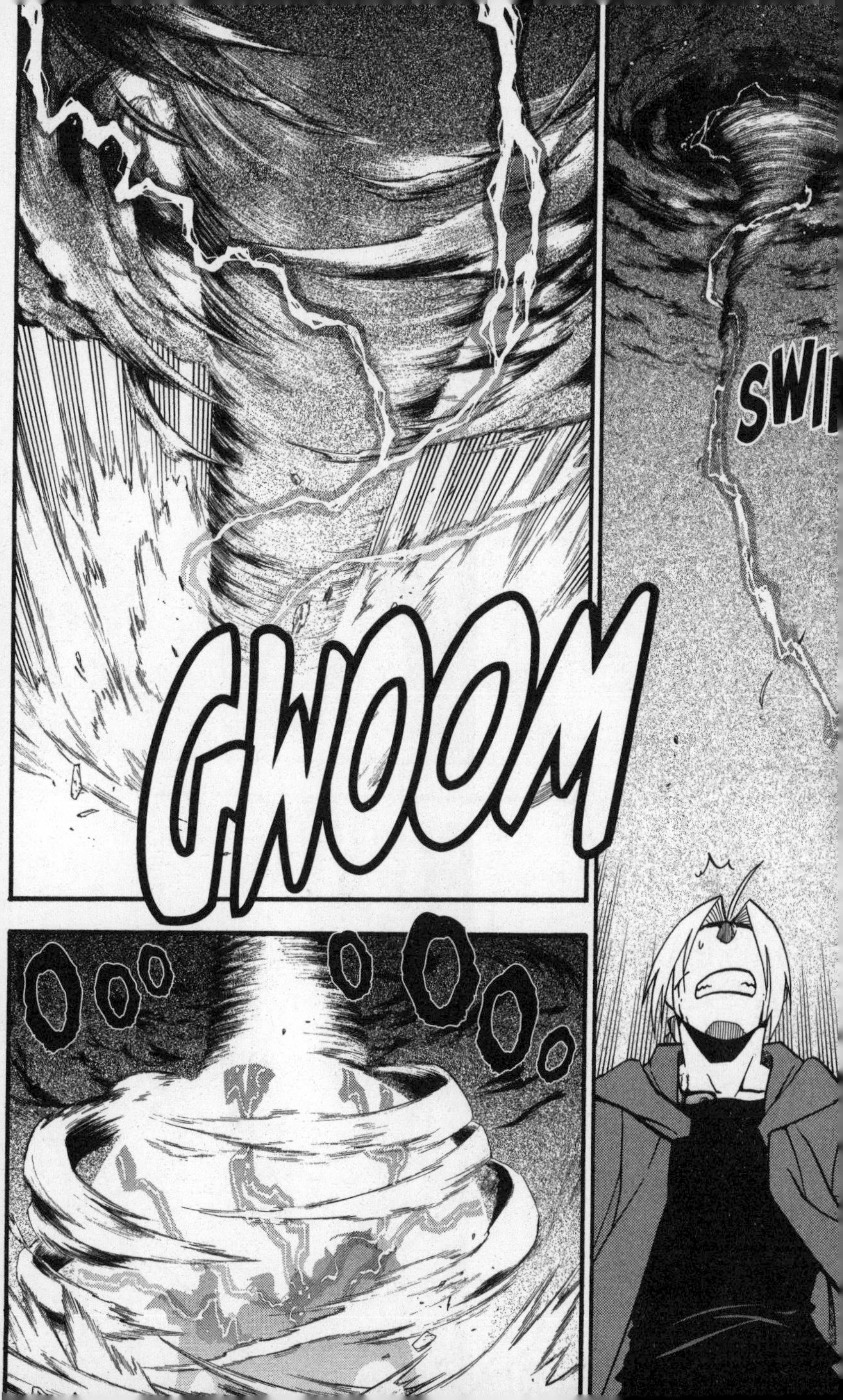
SWI
GWOOM
OOO
OOOO

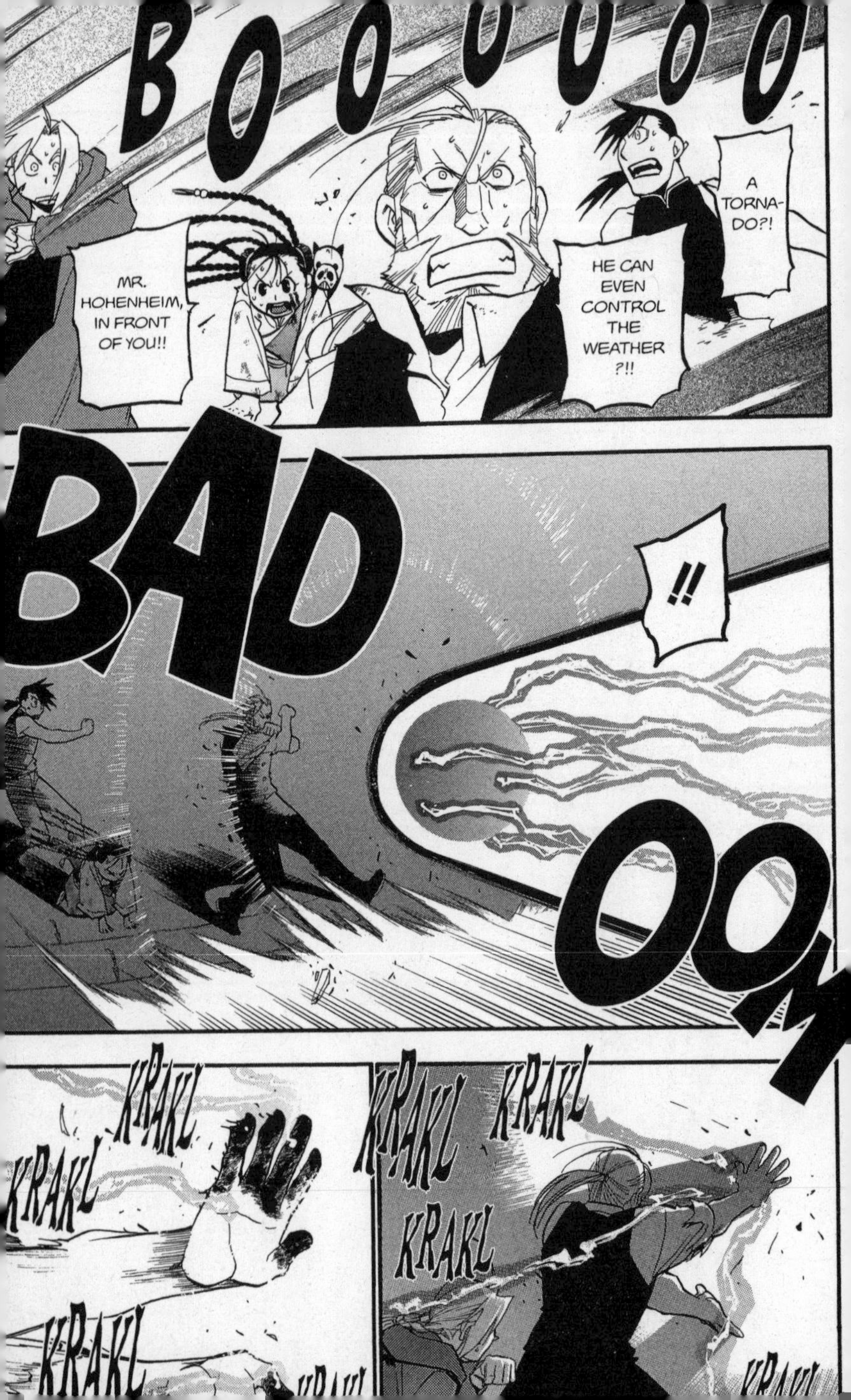
BOOOOOOO
A TORNADO?!
HE CAN EVEN CONTROL THE WEATHER?!!
MR. HOHENHEIM, IN FRONT OF YOU!!
BADOOM
!!
KRAKL
KRAKL
KRAKL
KRAKL
KRAKL
KRAKL

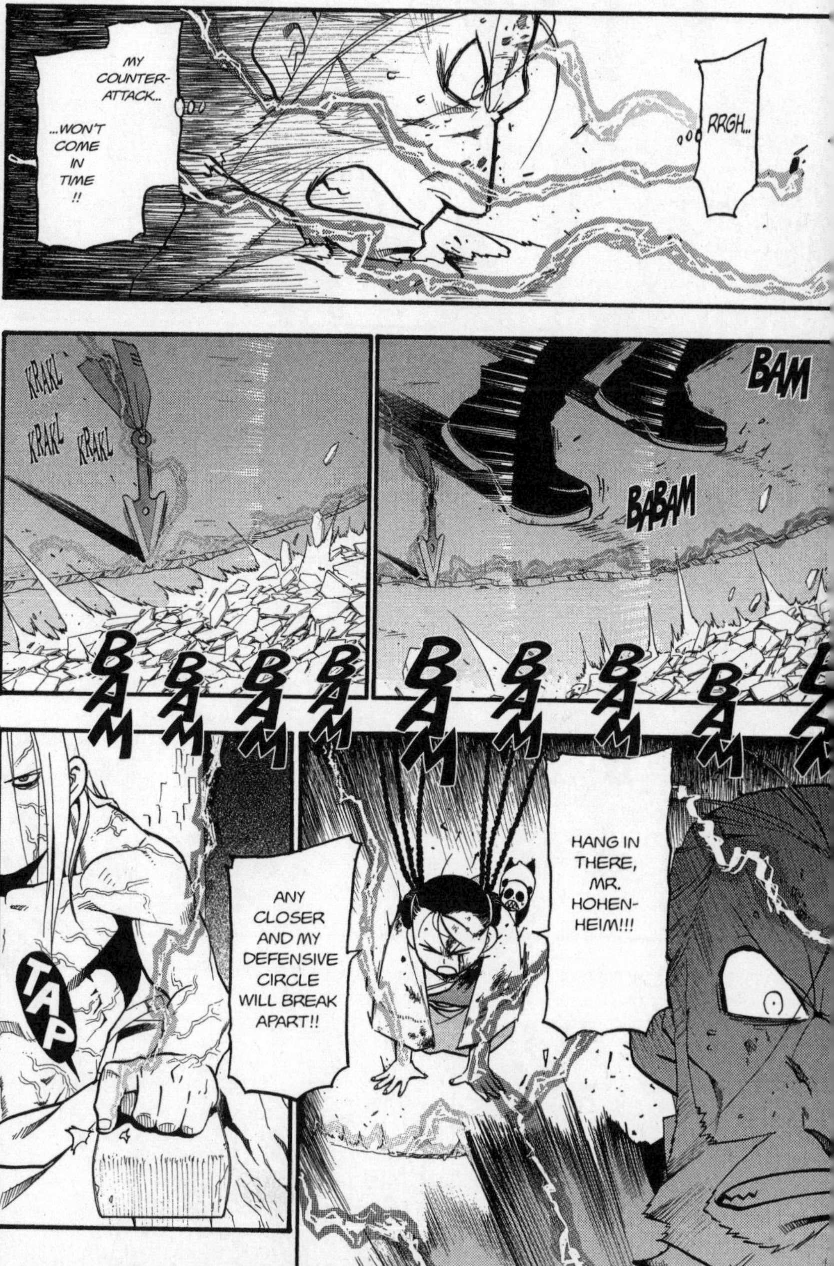
RRGH...
MY COUNTER-ATTACK...
...WON'T COME IN TIME!!
BAM
BABAM
KRAKL
KRAKL
KRAKL
BAM BAM BAM BAM BAM BAM BAM BAM
HANG IN THERE, MR. HOHENHEIM!!!
ANY CLOSER AND MY DEFENSIVE CIRCLE WILL BREAK APART!!
TAP

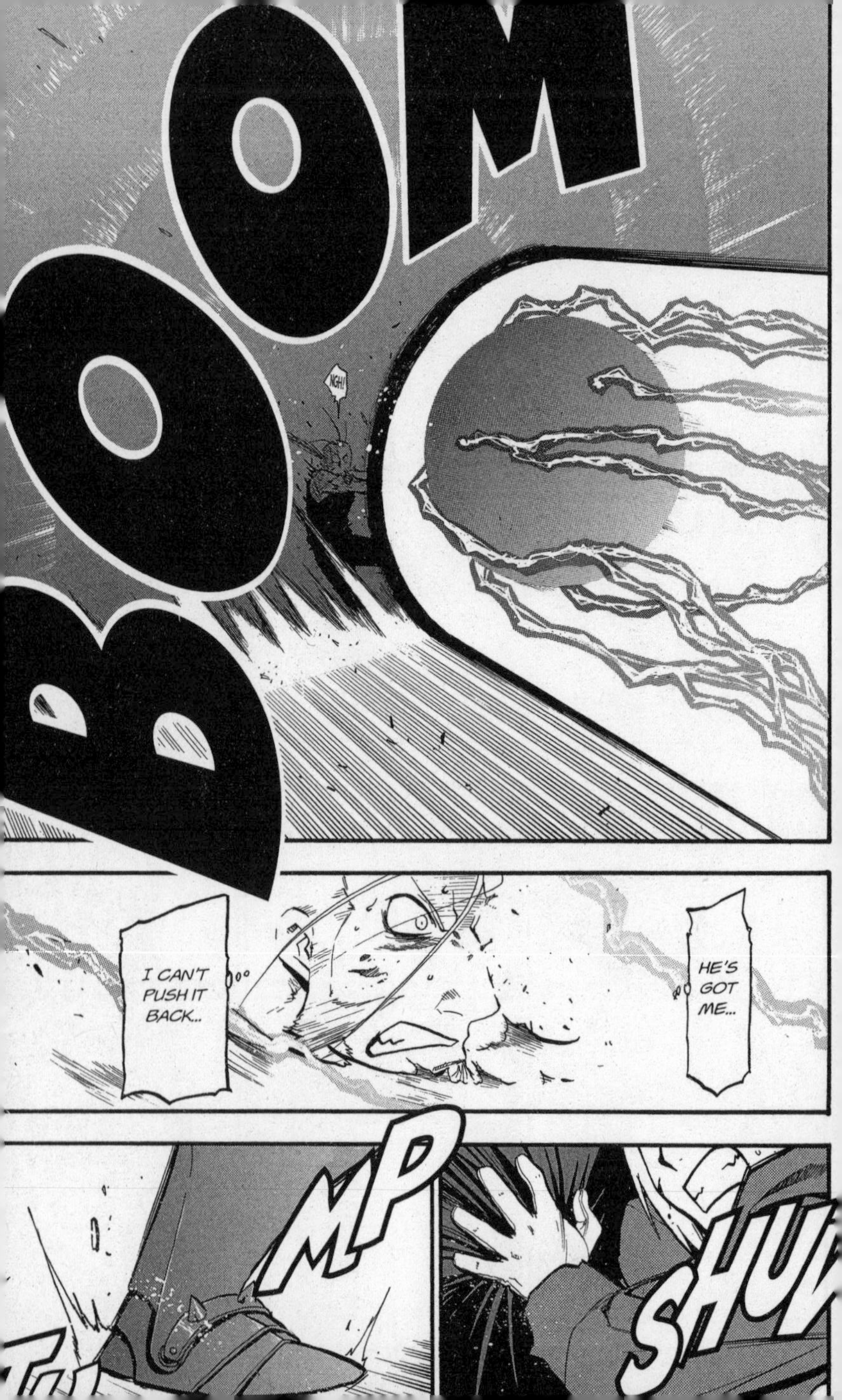
BOOM
NGH!
HE'S GOT ME...
I CAN'T PUSH IT BACK...
SHUV
MP

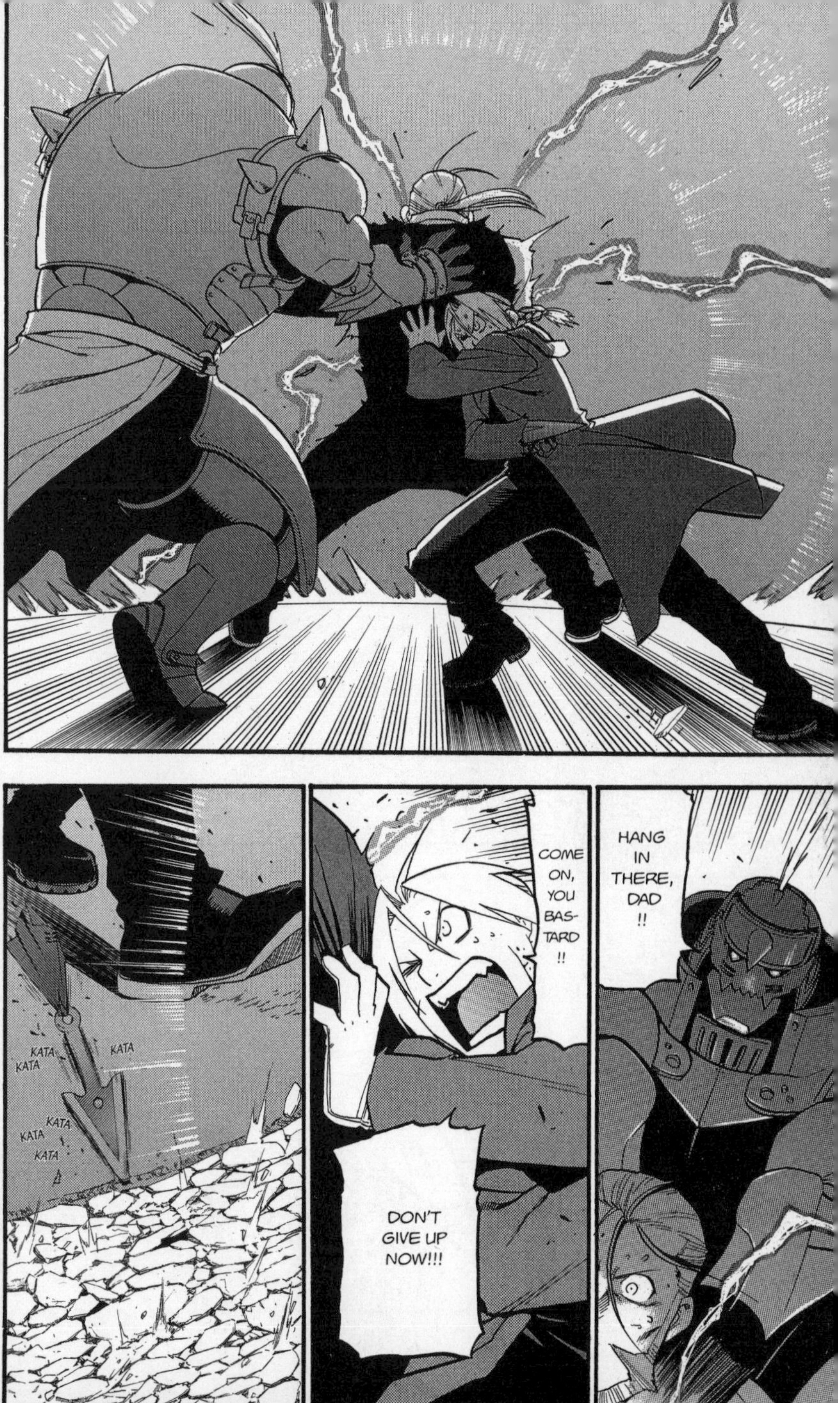
HANG IN THERE, DAD!!
COME ON, YOU BAS-TARD!!
DON'T GIVE UP NOW!!!
KATA
KATA KATA
KATA KATA KATA

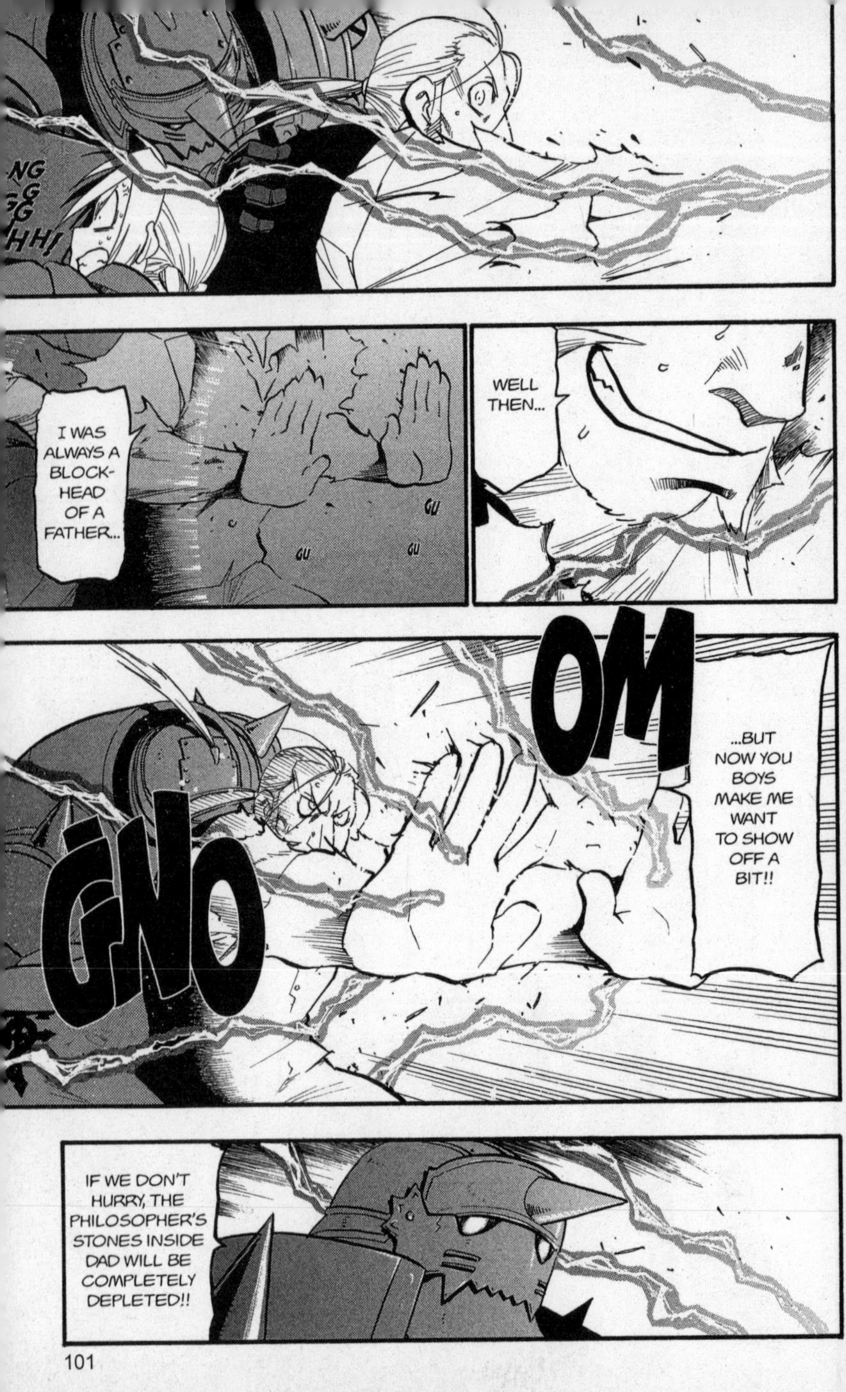

NGGGHH!
WELL THEN...
I WAS ALWAYS A BLOCKHEAD OF A FATHER...
GU
GU
GU
OM
...BUT NOW YOU BOYS MAKE ME WANT TO SHOW OFF A BIT!!
GNO
IF WE DON'T HURRY, THE PHILOSOPHER'S STONES INSIDE DAD WILL BE COMPLETELY DEPLETED!!

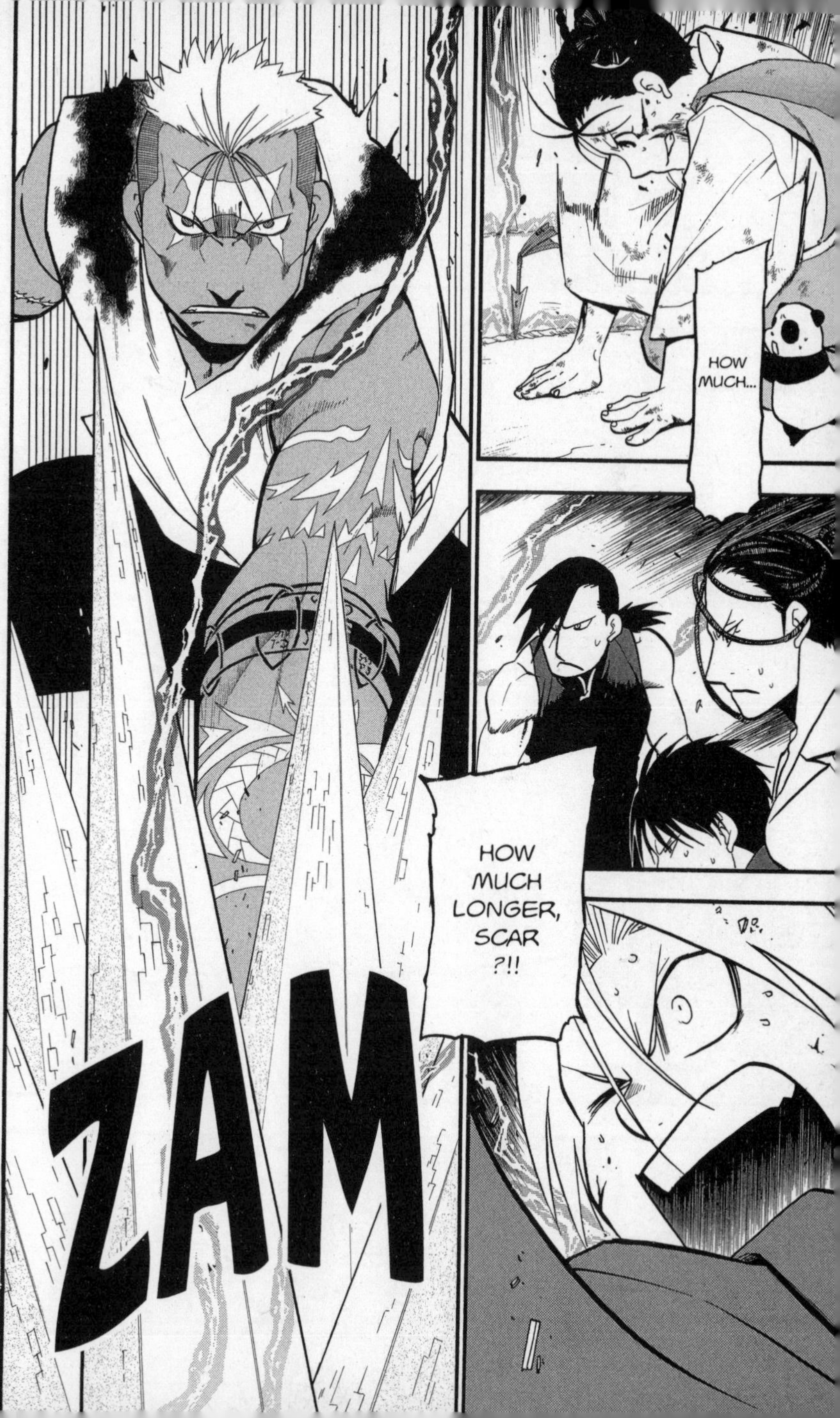
HOW MUCH...
HOW MUCH LONGER, SCAR ?!!
ZAM

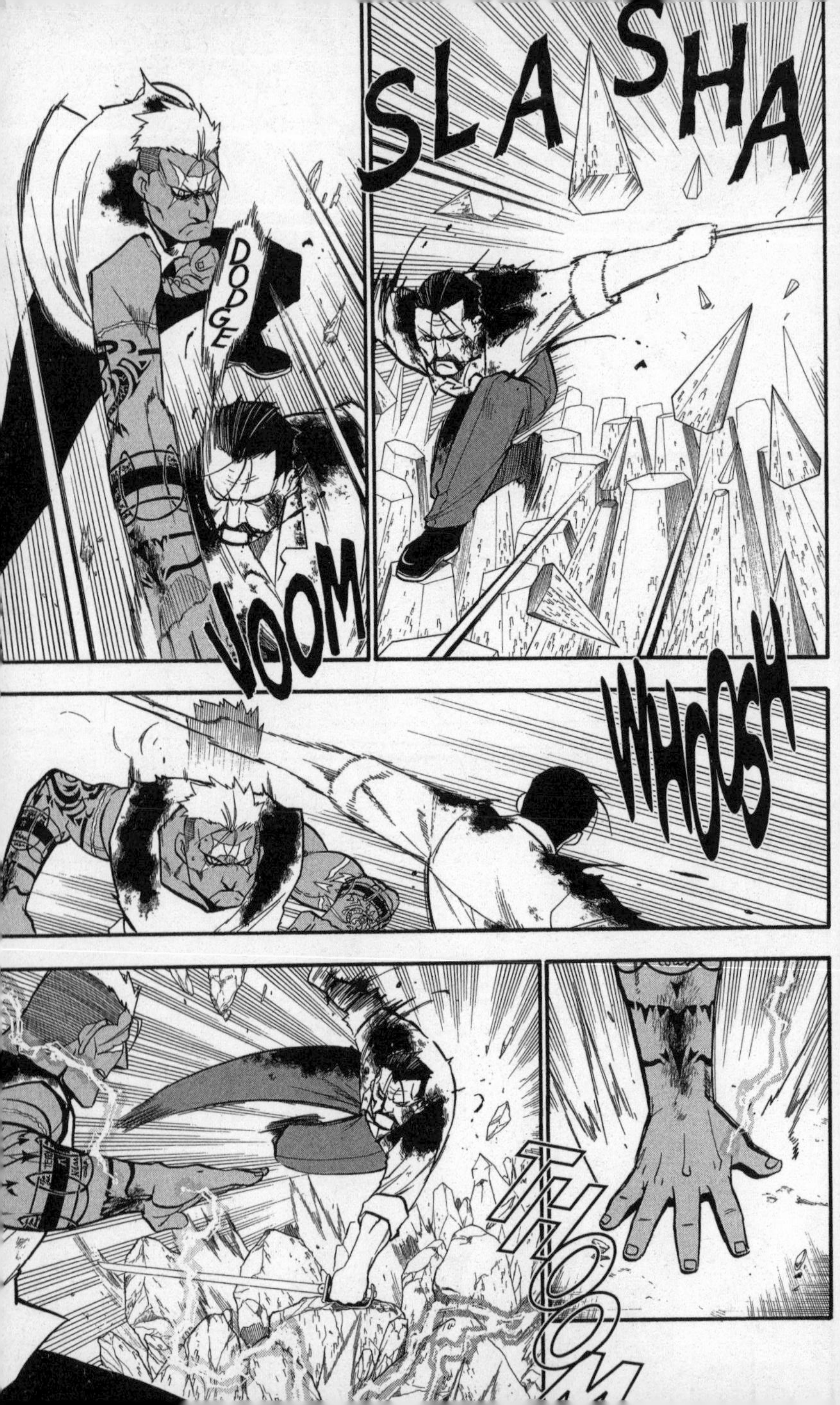
SLASHA
DODGE
VOOM
WHOOSH
THOOM

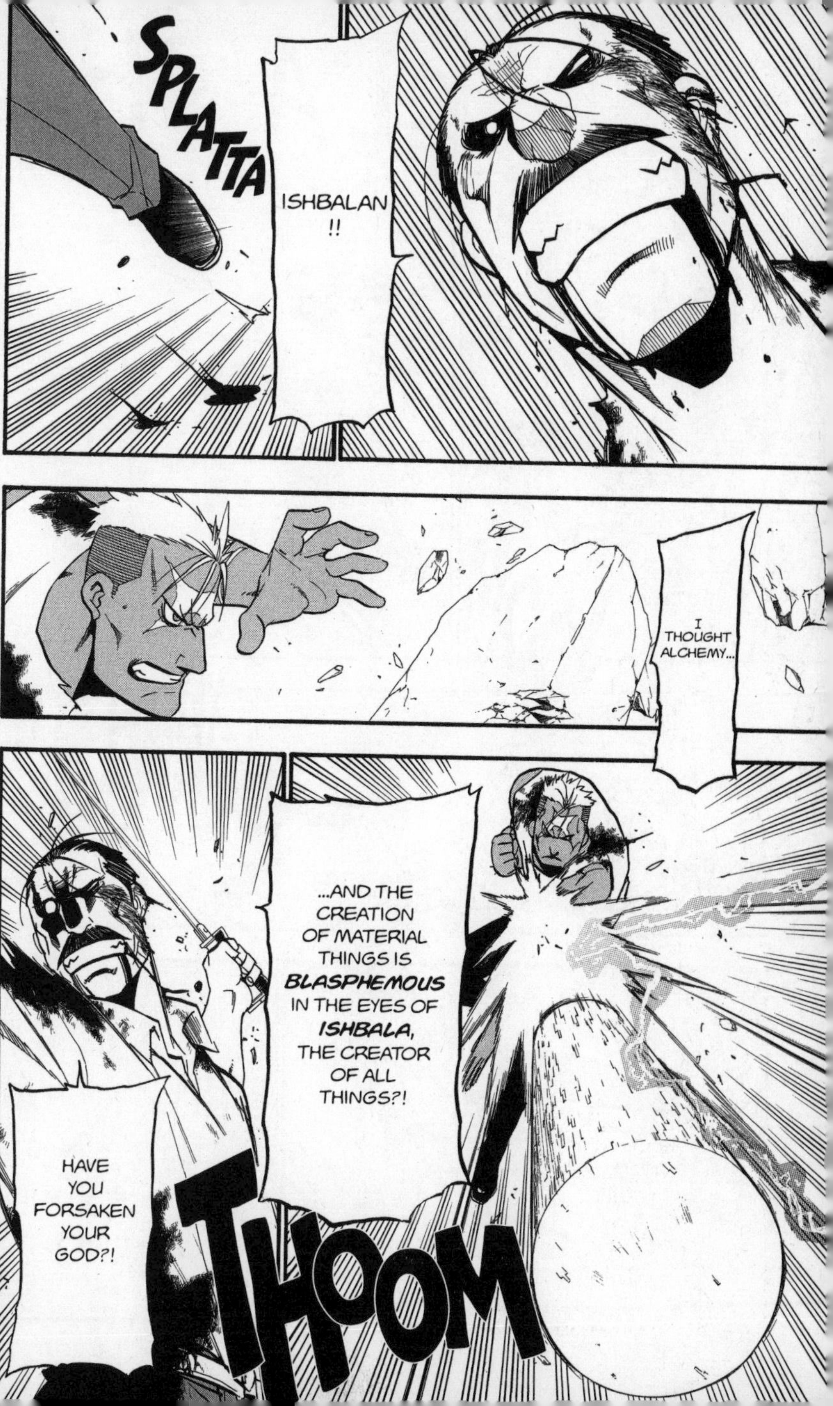
ISHBALAN !!
SPLATTA
I THOUGHT ALCHEMY...
...AND THE CREATION OF MATERIAL THINGS IS BLASPHEMOUS IN THE EYES OF ISHBALA, THE CREATOR OF ALL THINGS?!
THOOM
HAVE YOU FORSAKEN YOUR GOD?!

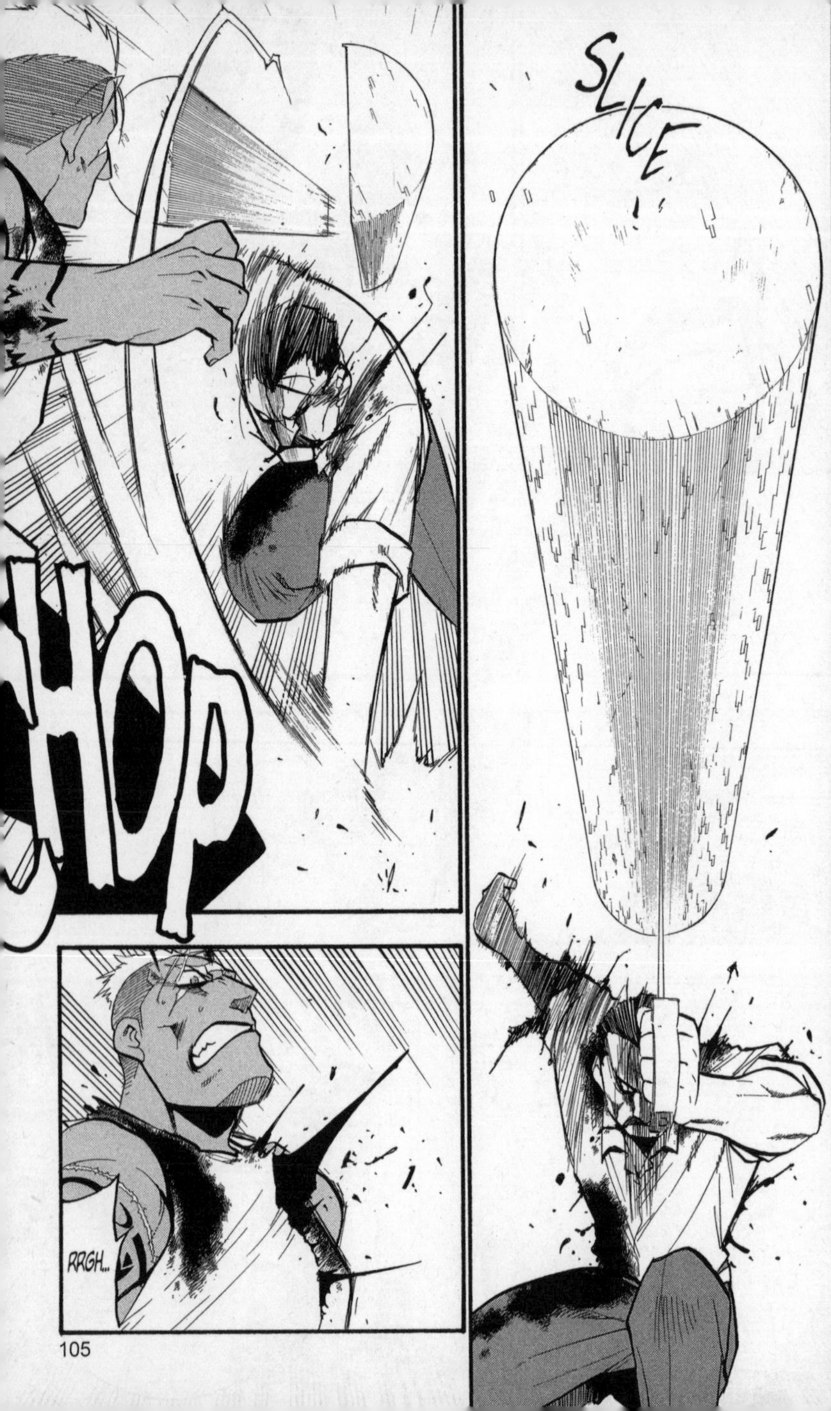
SLICE
HOP
RRGH...

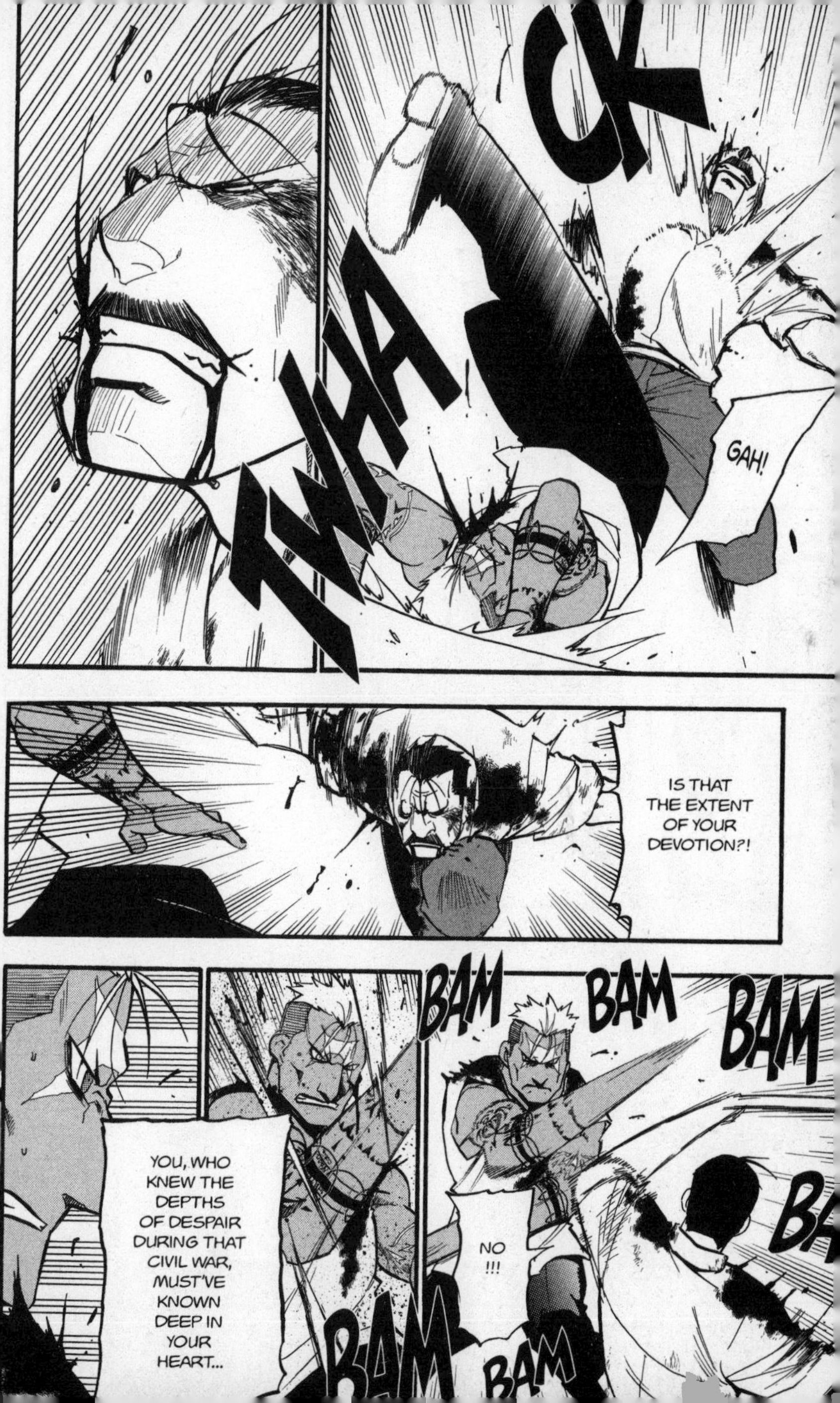
TWHACK
GAH!
IS THAT THE EXTENT OF YOUR DEVOTION?!
BAM BAM BAM
NO !!!
BAM BAM
YOU, WHO KNEW THE DEPTHS OF DESPAIR DURING THAT CIVIL WAR, MUST'VE KNOWN DEEP IN YOUR HEART...

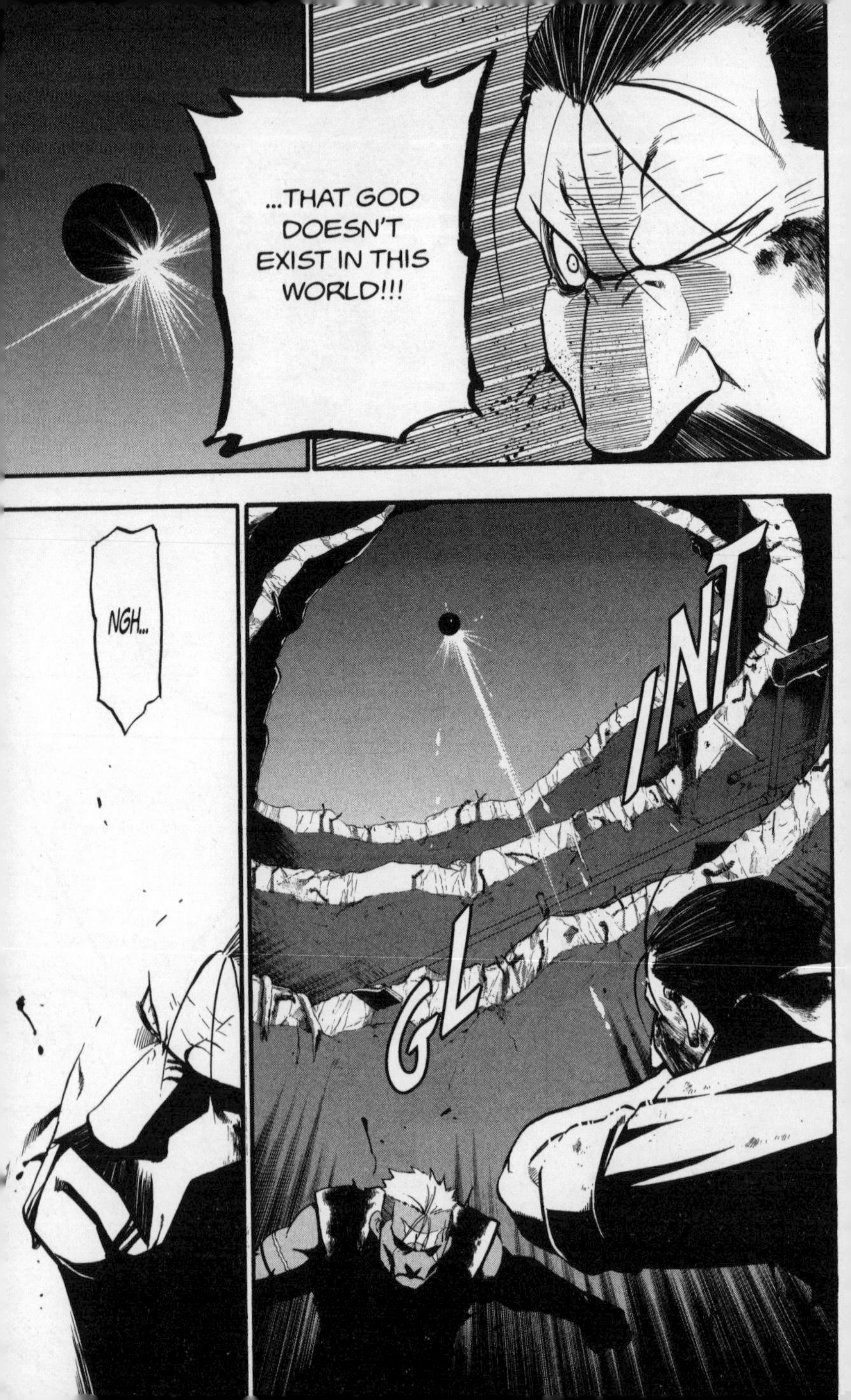
...THAT GOD DOESN'T EXIST IN THIS WORLD!!!
GLINT
NGH...

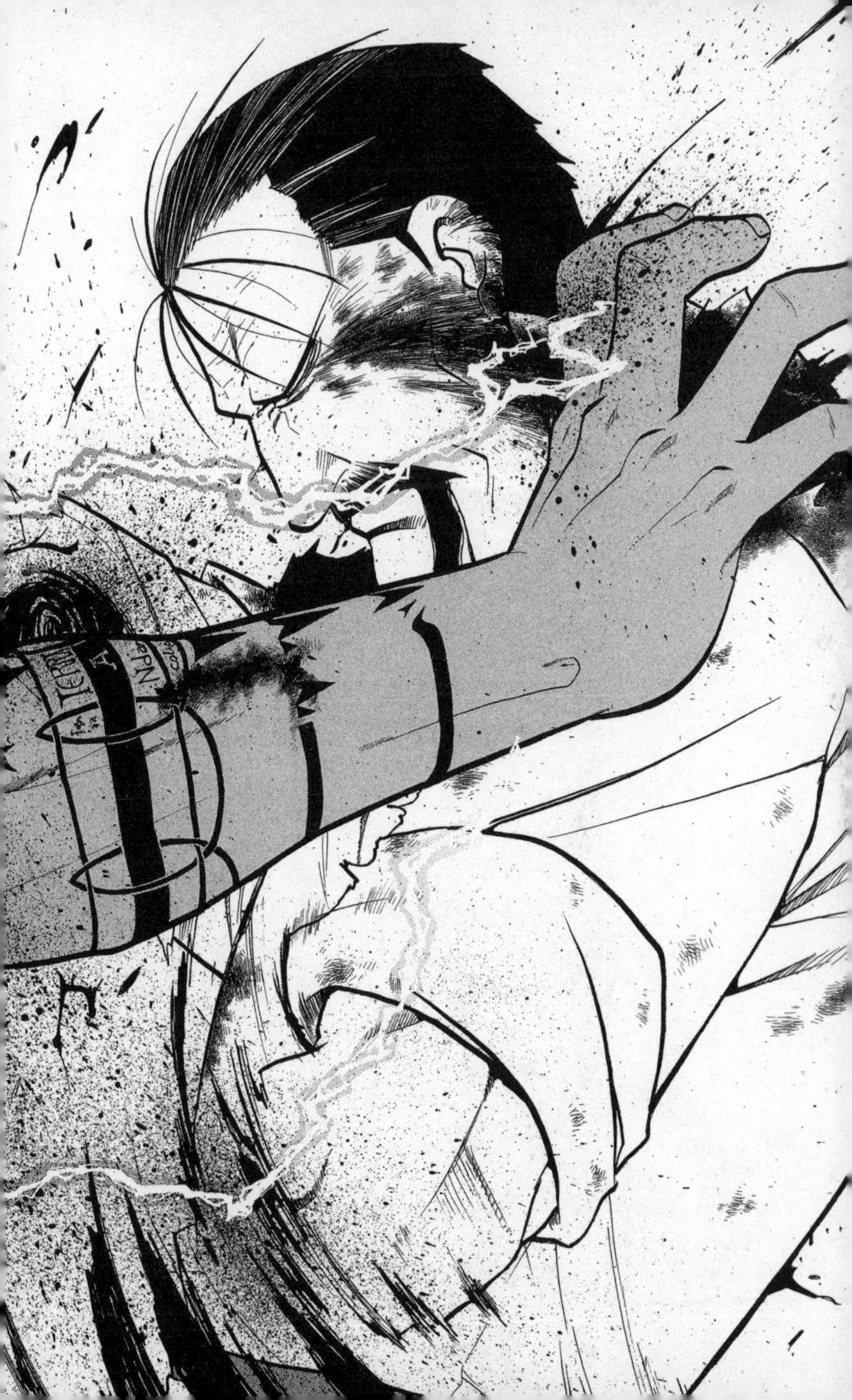

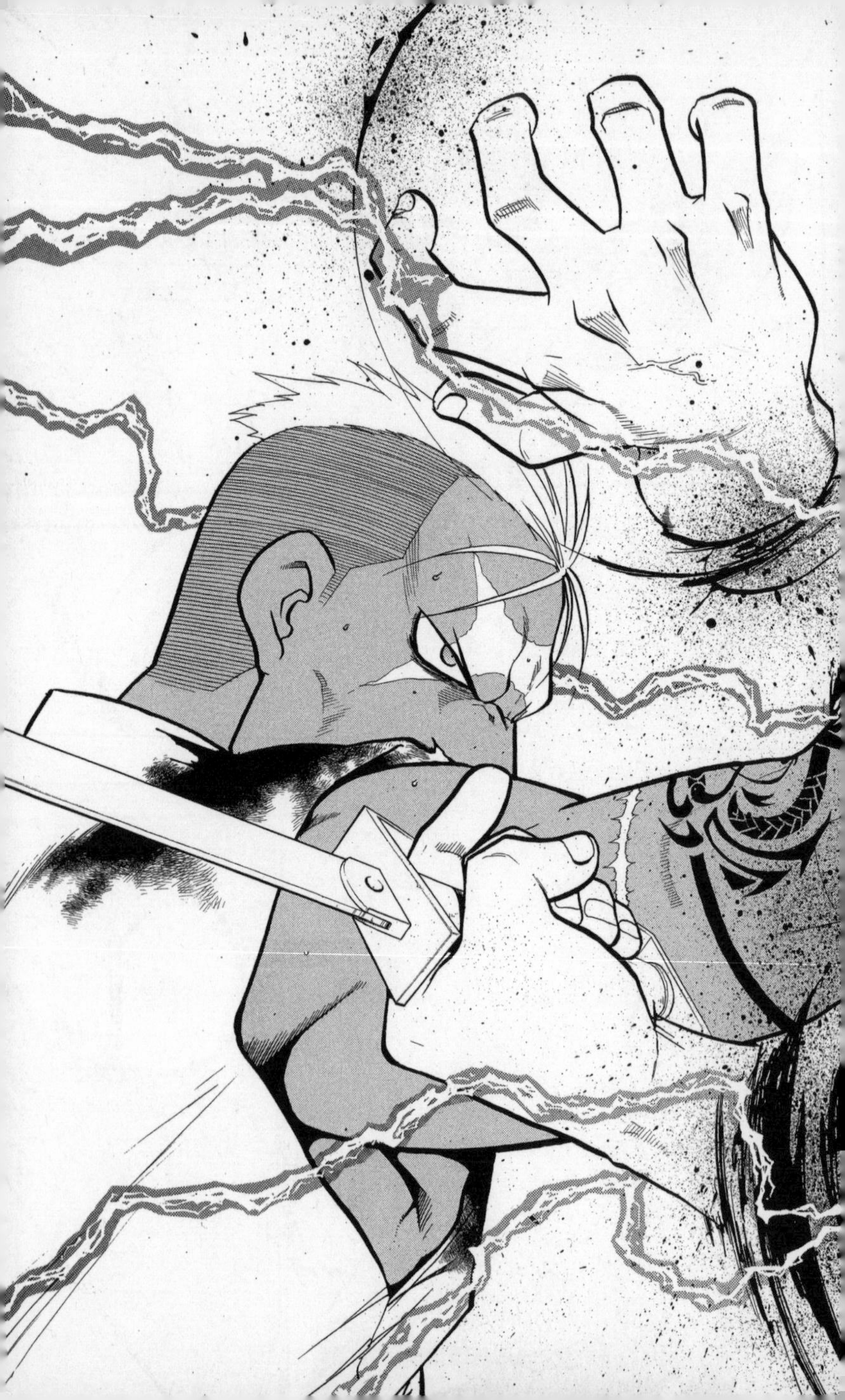

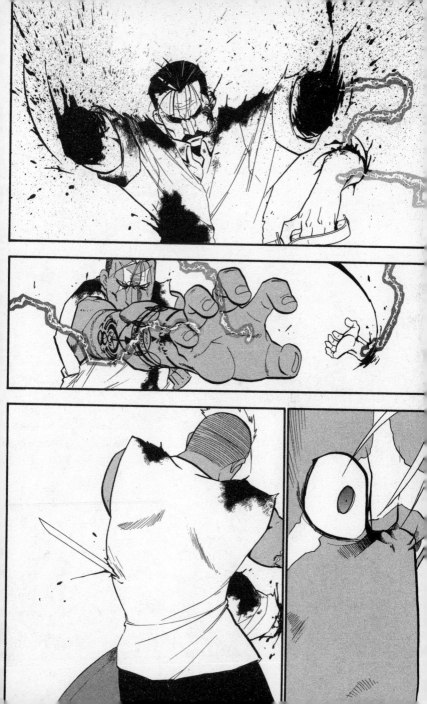

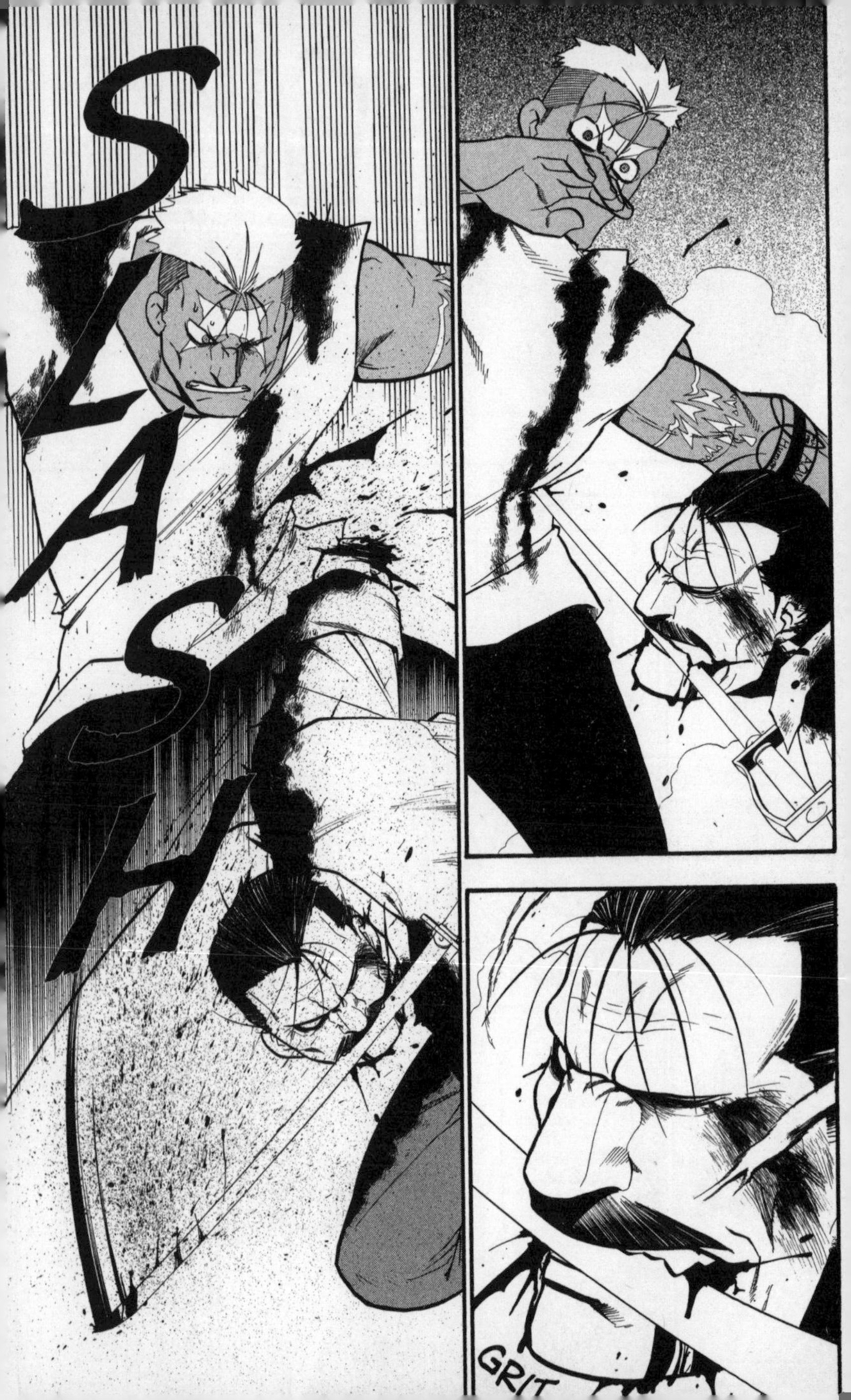
SLASH
GRIT

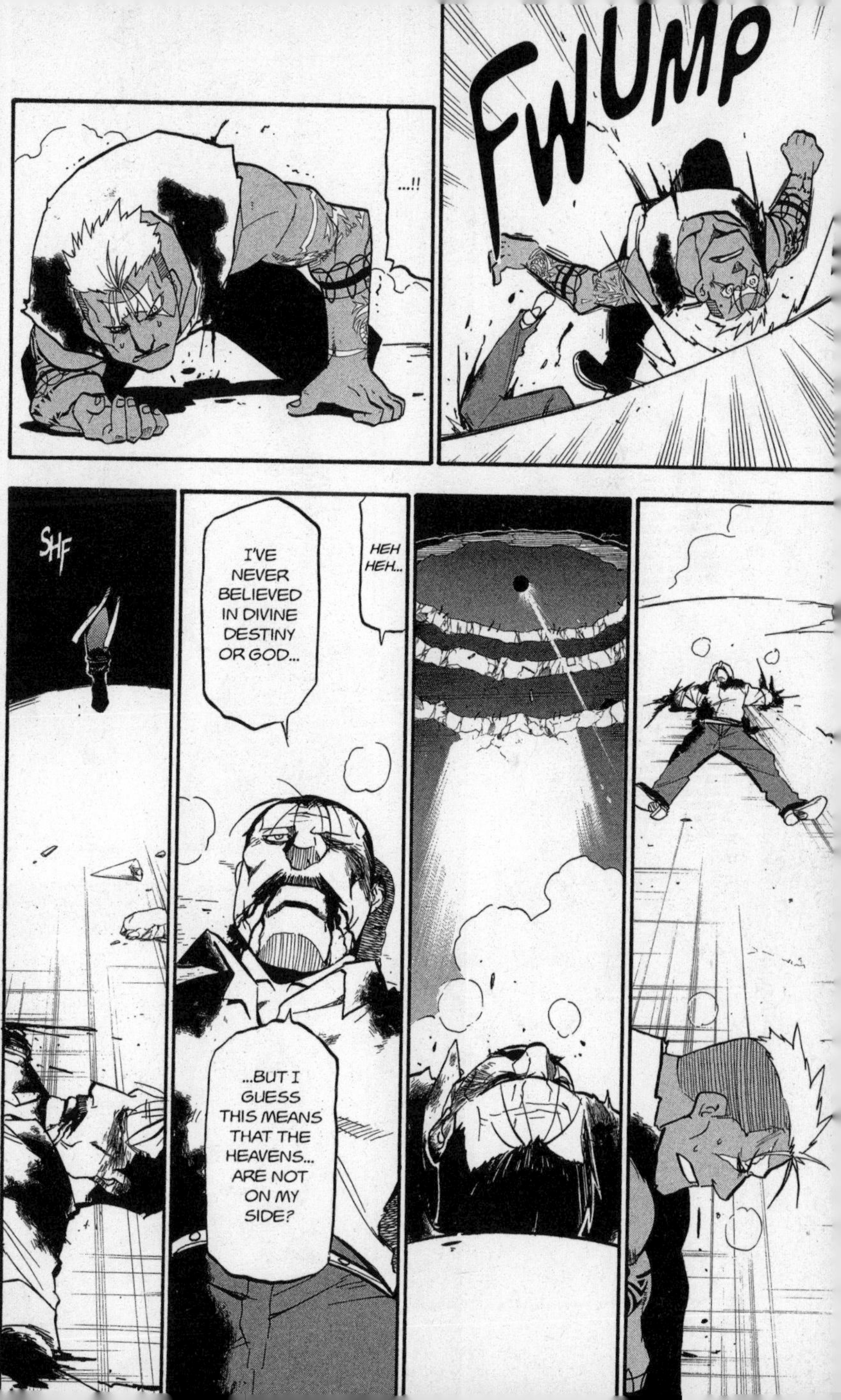
FWUMP
...!!
HEH HEH...
I'VE NEVER BELIEVED IN DIVINE DESTINY OR GOD...
...BUT I GUESS THIS MEANS THAT THE HEAVENS... ARE NOT ON MY SIDE?
SHF

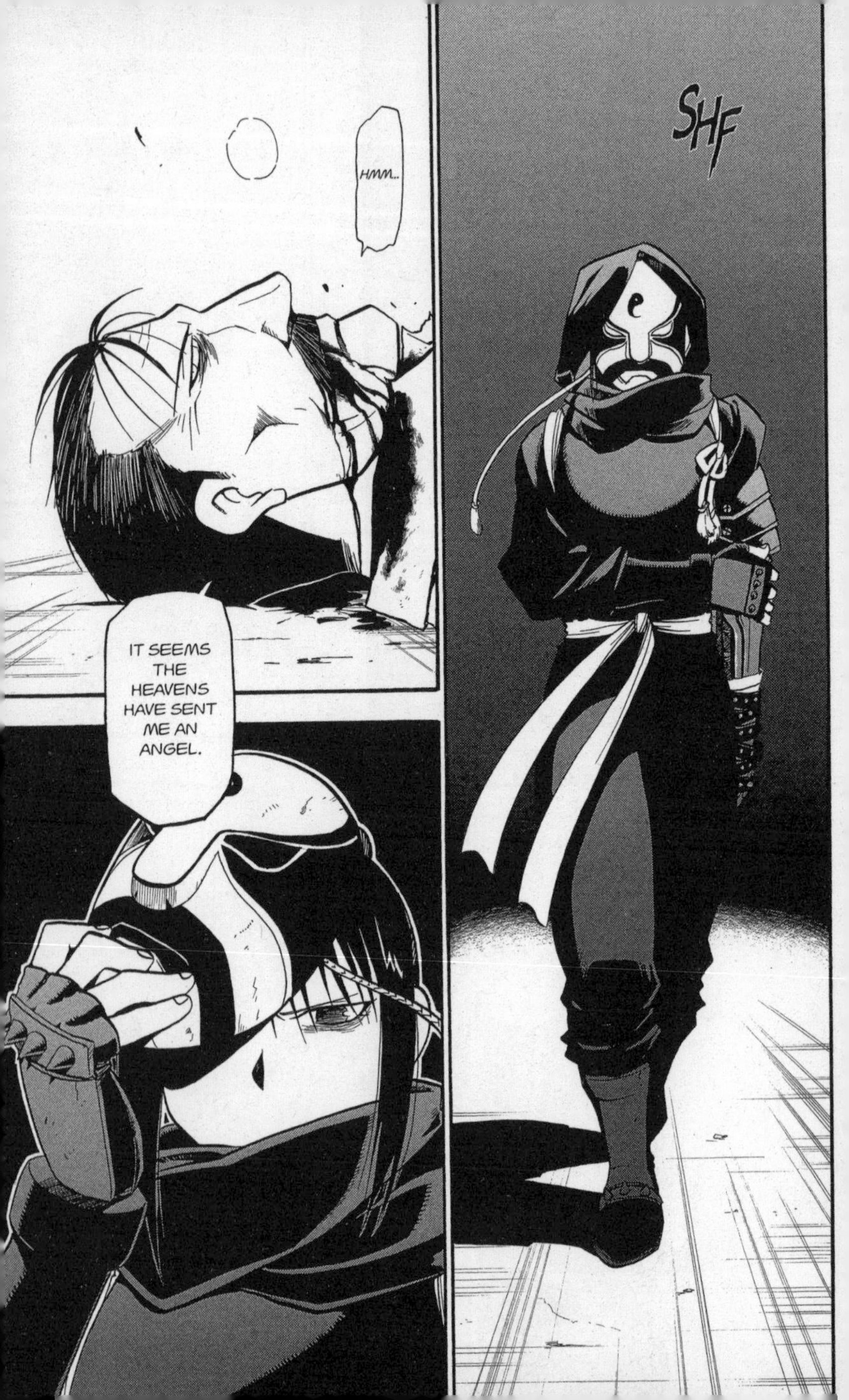
SHF
HMM..
IT SEEMS THE HEAVENS HAVE SENT ME AN ANGEL.

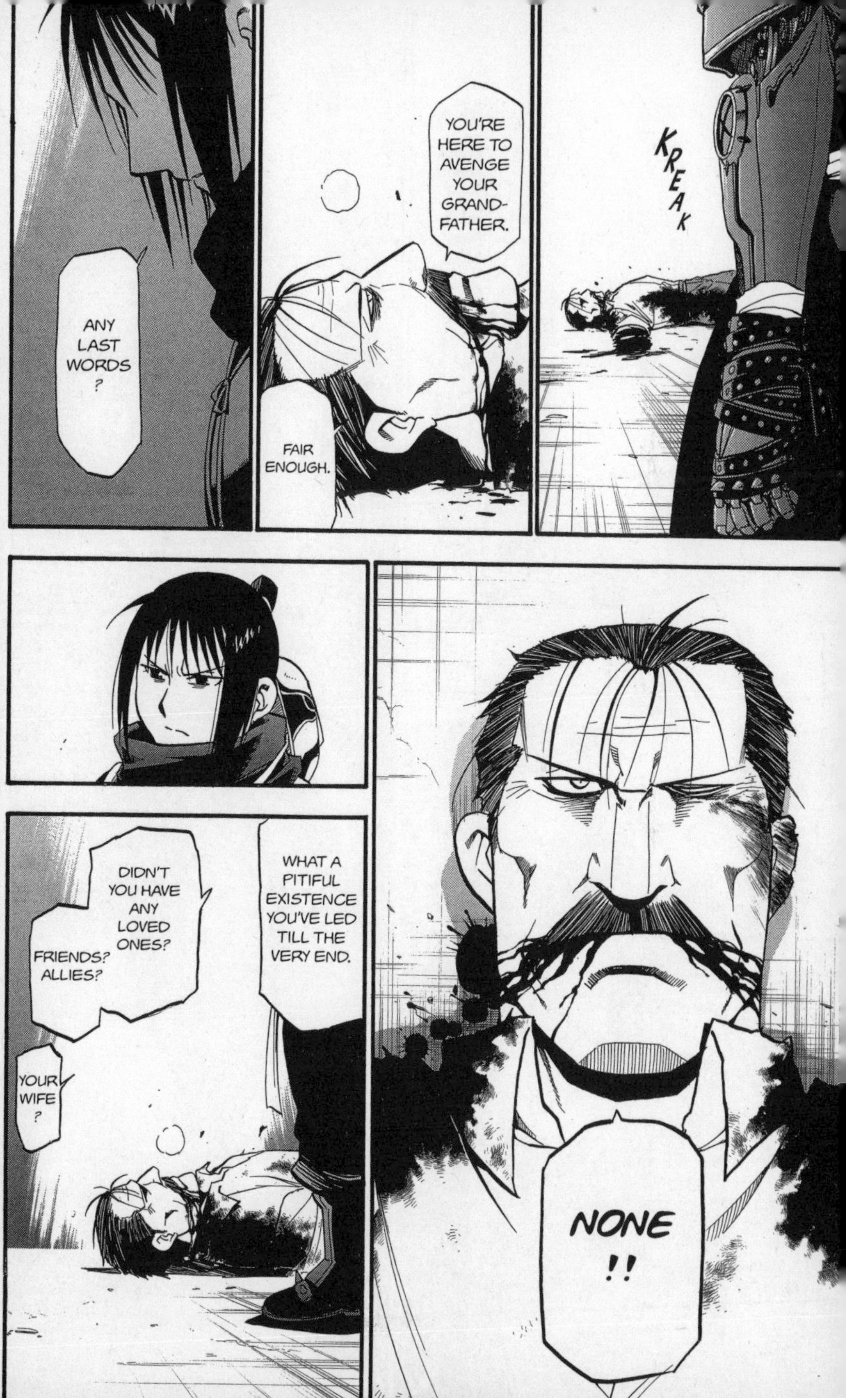
KREAK
YOU'RE HERE TO AVENGE YOUR GRAND-FATHER.
FAIR ENOUGH.
ANY LAST WORDS ?
NONE !!
WHAT A PITIFUL EXISTENCE YOU'VE LED TILL THE VERY END.
DIDN'T YOU HAVE ANY LOVED ONES? FRIENDS? ALLIES?
YOUR WIFE ?

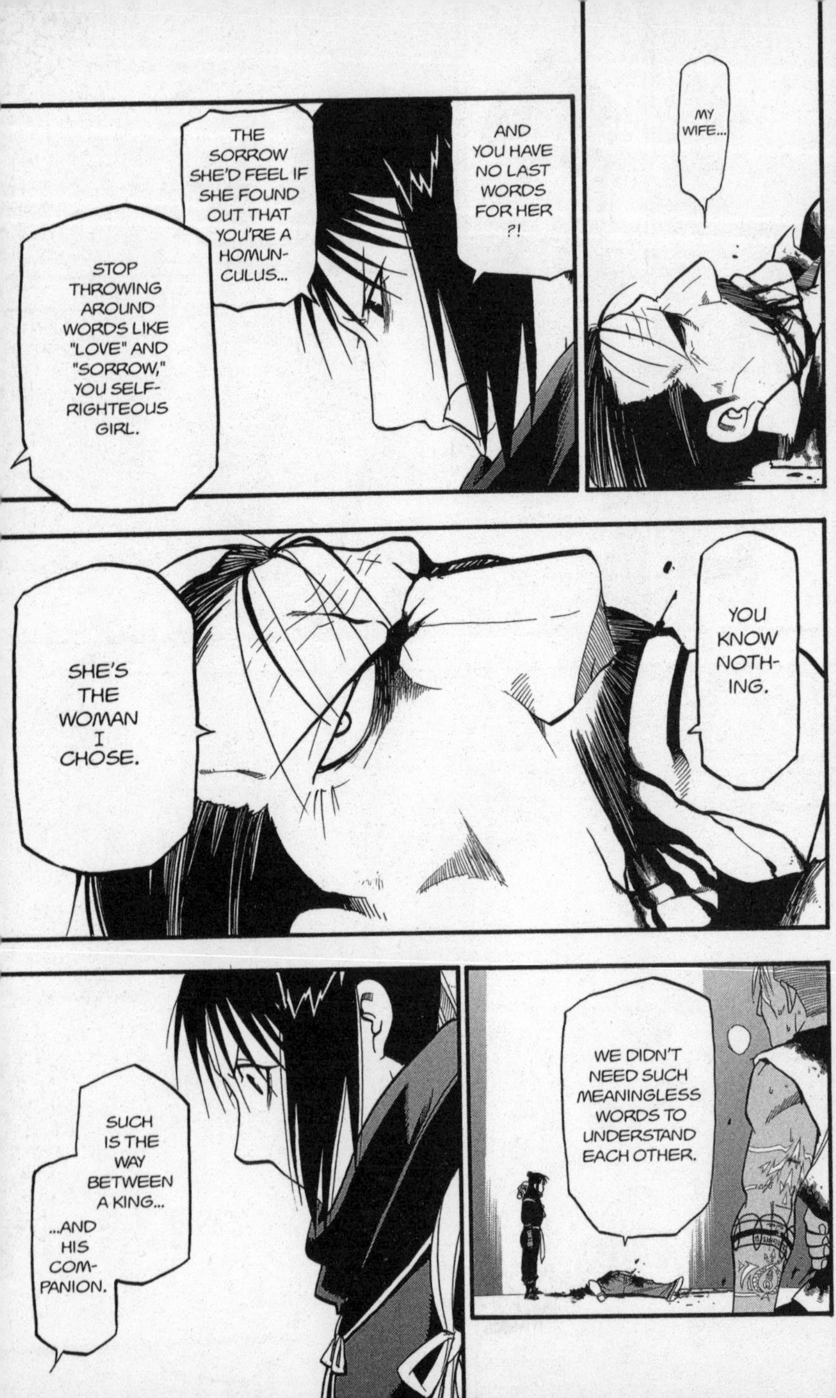
MY WIFE...
AND YOU HAVE NO LAST WORDS FOR HER ?!
THE SORROW SHE'D FEEL IF SHE FOUND OUT THAT YOU'RE A HOMUNCULUS...
STOP THROWING AROUND WORDS LIKE "LOVE" AND "SORROW," YOU SELF-RIGHTEOUS GIRL.
YOU KNOW NOTHING.
SHE'S THE WOMAN I CHOSE.
WE DIDN'T NEED SUCH MEANINGLESS WORDS TO UNDERSTAND EACH OTHER.
SUCH IS THE WAY BETWEEN A KING...
...AND HIS COMPANION.

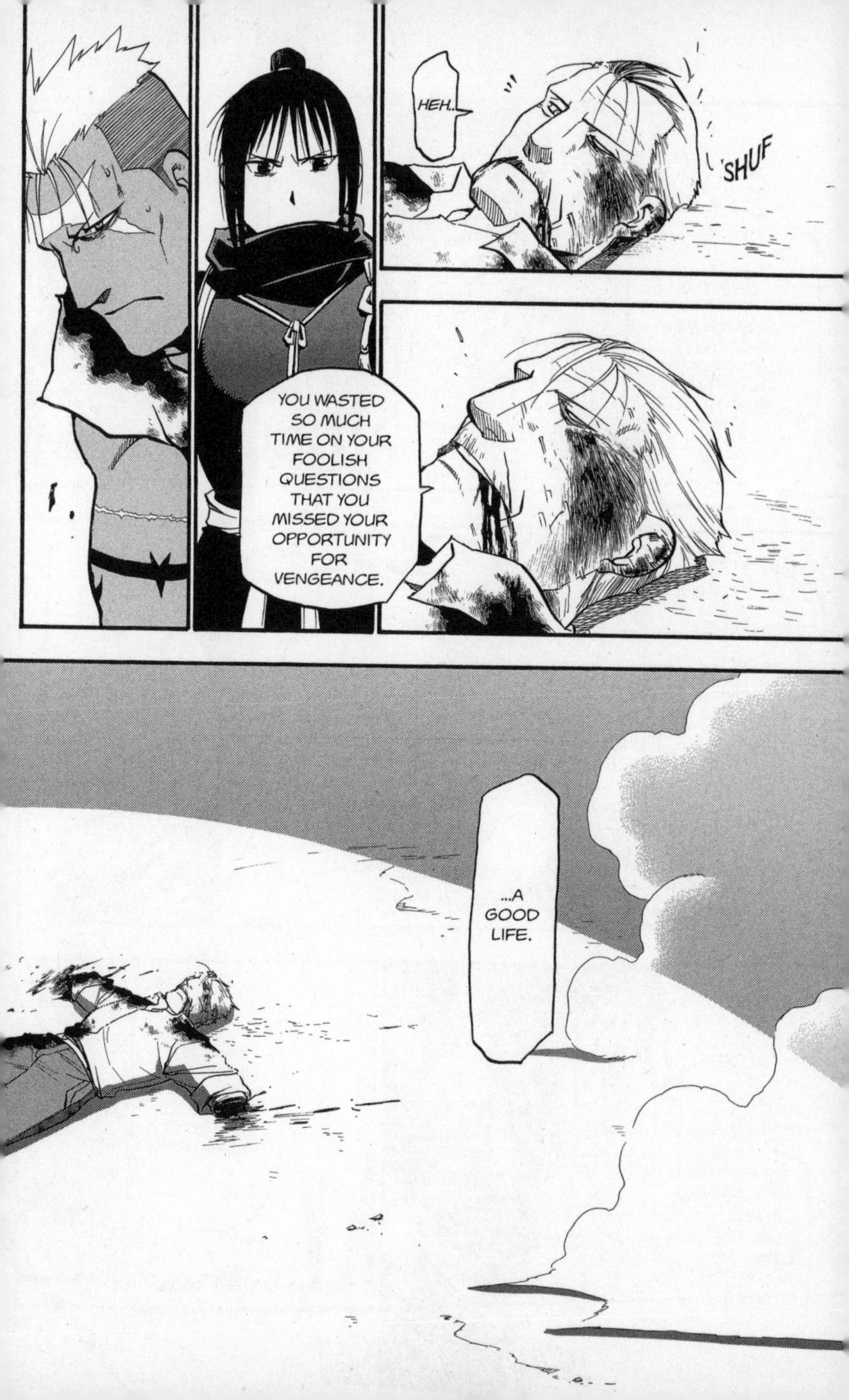
HEH...
SHUF
YOU WASTED SO MUCH TIME ON YOUR FOOLISH QUESTIONS THAT YOU MISSED YOUR OPPORTUNITY FOR VENGEANCE.
...A GOOD LIFE.

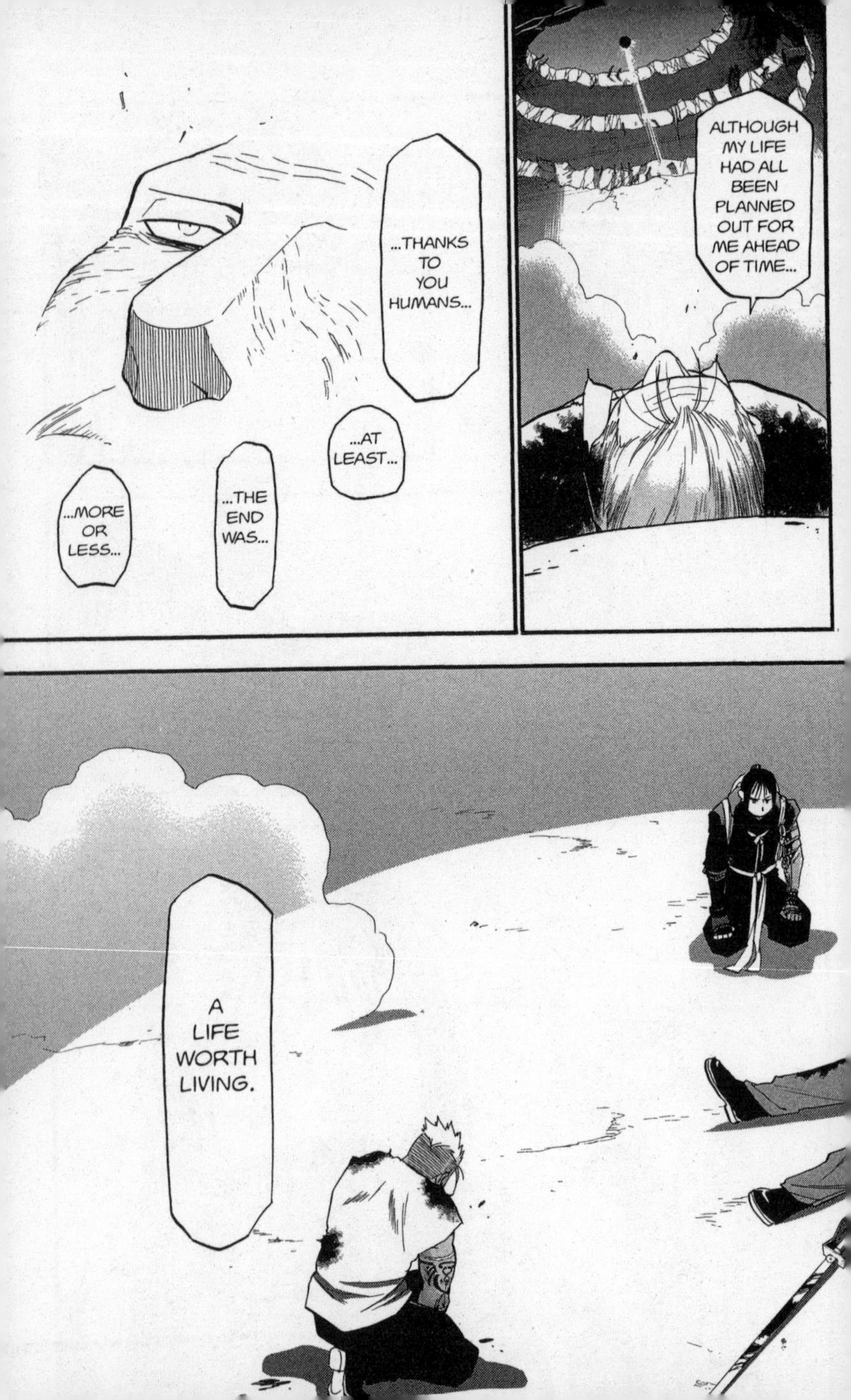
ALTHOUGH MY LIFE HAD ALL BEEN PLANNED OUT FOR ME AHEAD OF TIME...
...THANKS TO YOU HUMANS...
...AT LEAST...
...THE END WAS...
...MORE OR LESS...
A LIFE WORTH LIVING.

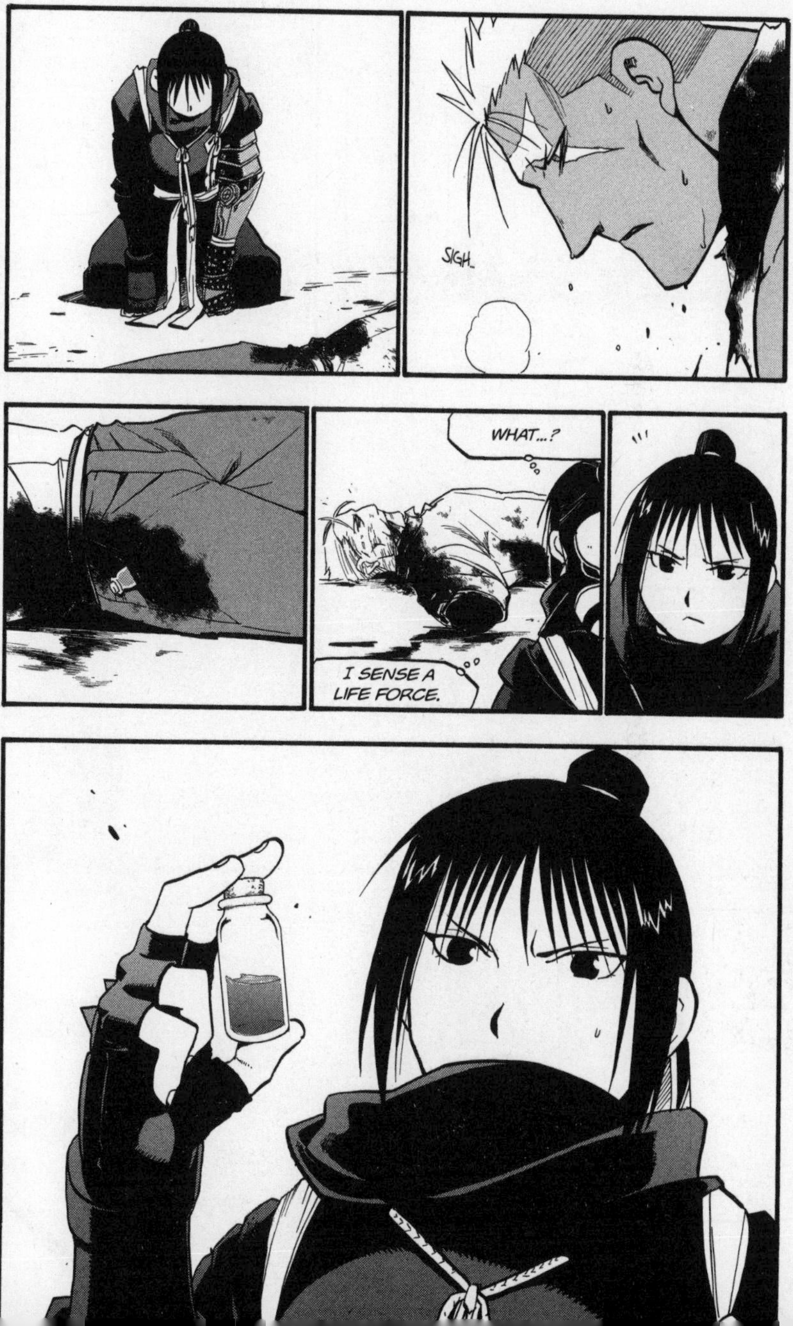

SIGH...
WHAT...?
I SENSE A LIFE FORCE.

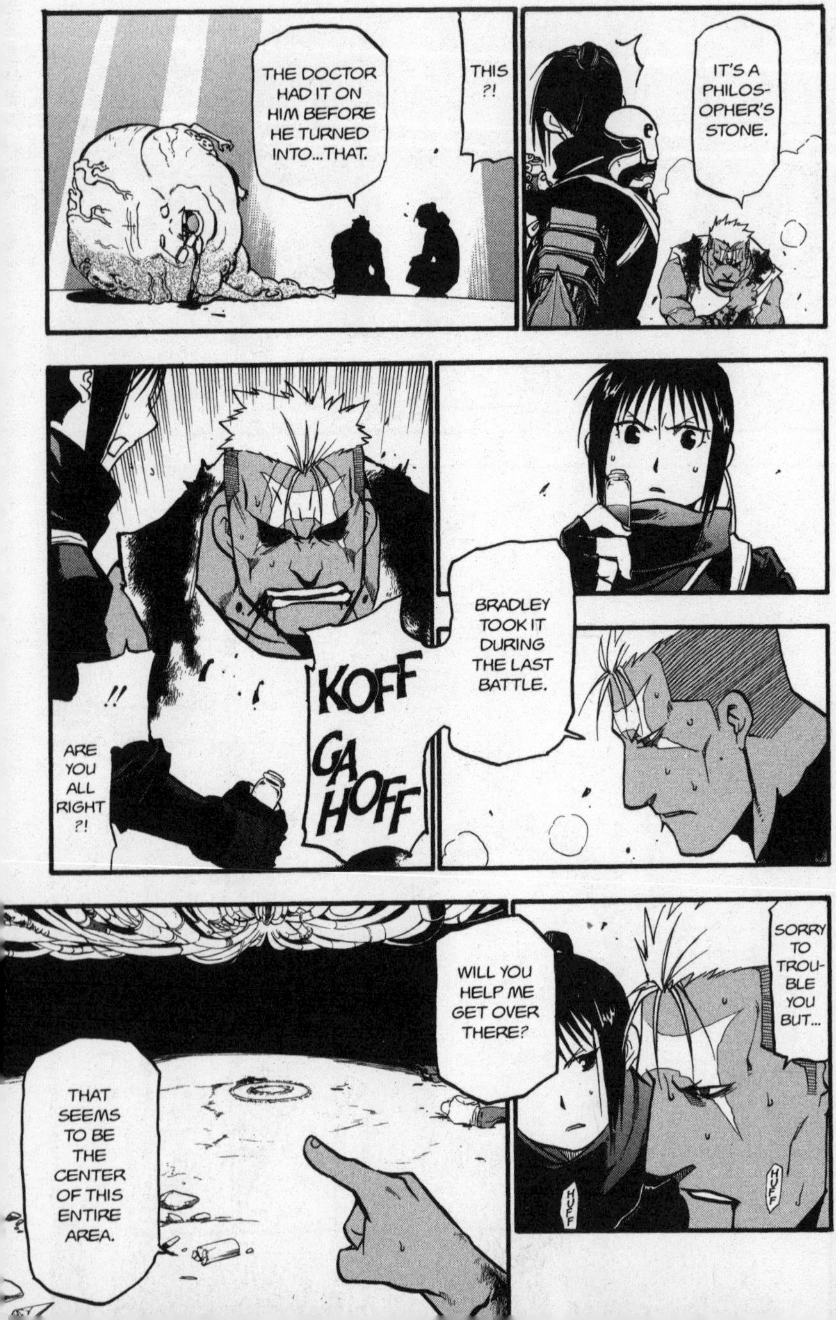
IT'S A PHILOSOPHER'S STONE.
THIS ?!
THE DOCTOR HAD IT ON HIM BEFORE HE TURNED INTO...THAT.
BRADLEY TOOK IT DURING THE LAST BATTLE.
KOFF
GAHOFF
!!
ARE YOU ALL RIGHT ?!
SORRY TO TROUBLE YOU BUT...
WILL YOU HELP ME GET OVER THERE?
HUFF
HUFF
THAT SEEMS TO BE THE CENTER OF THIS ENTIRE AREA.

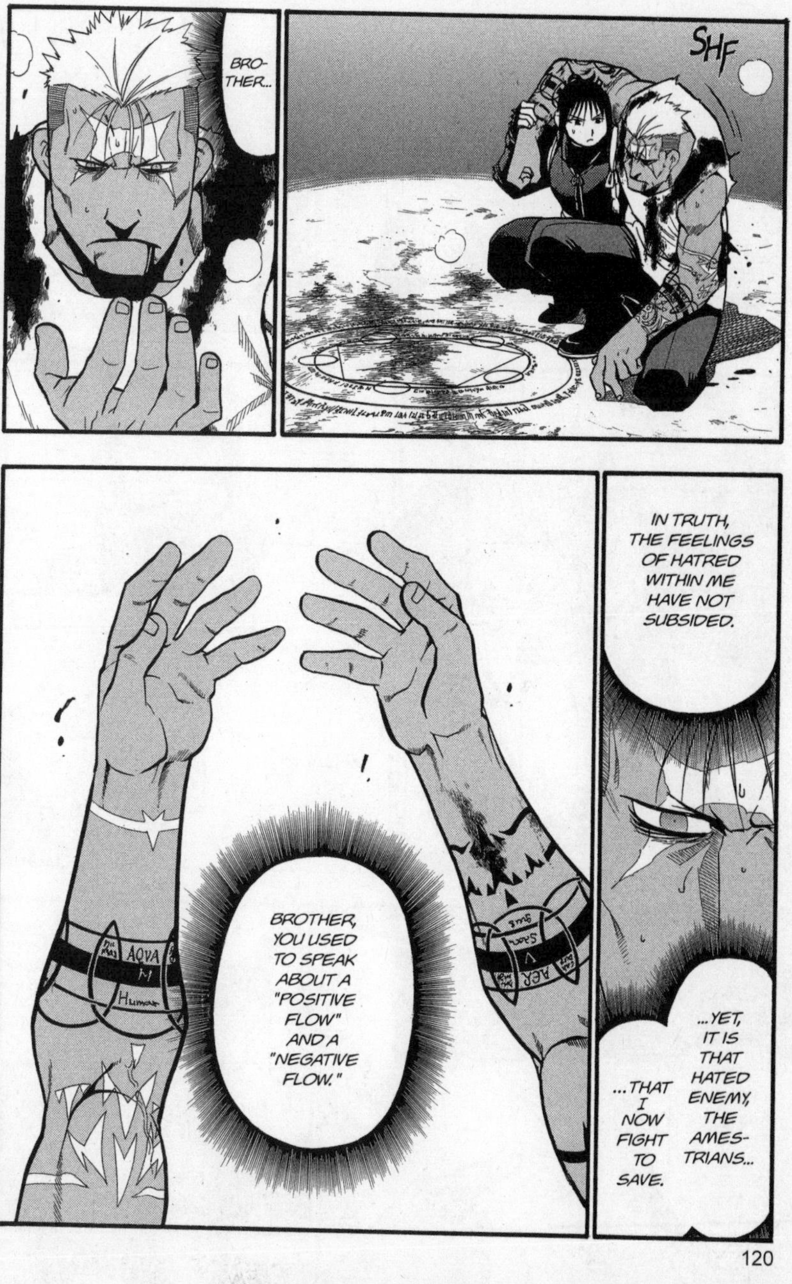
SHF
BROTHER...
IN TRUTH, THE FEELINGS OF HATRED WITHIN ME HAVE NOT SUBSIDED.
...YET, IT IS THAT HATED ENEMY, THE AMESTRIANS...
...THAT I NOW FIGHT TO SAVE.
BROTHER, YOU USED TO SPEAK ABOUT A "POSITIVE FLOW" AND A "NEGATIVE FLOW."

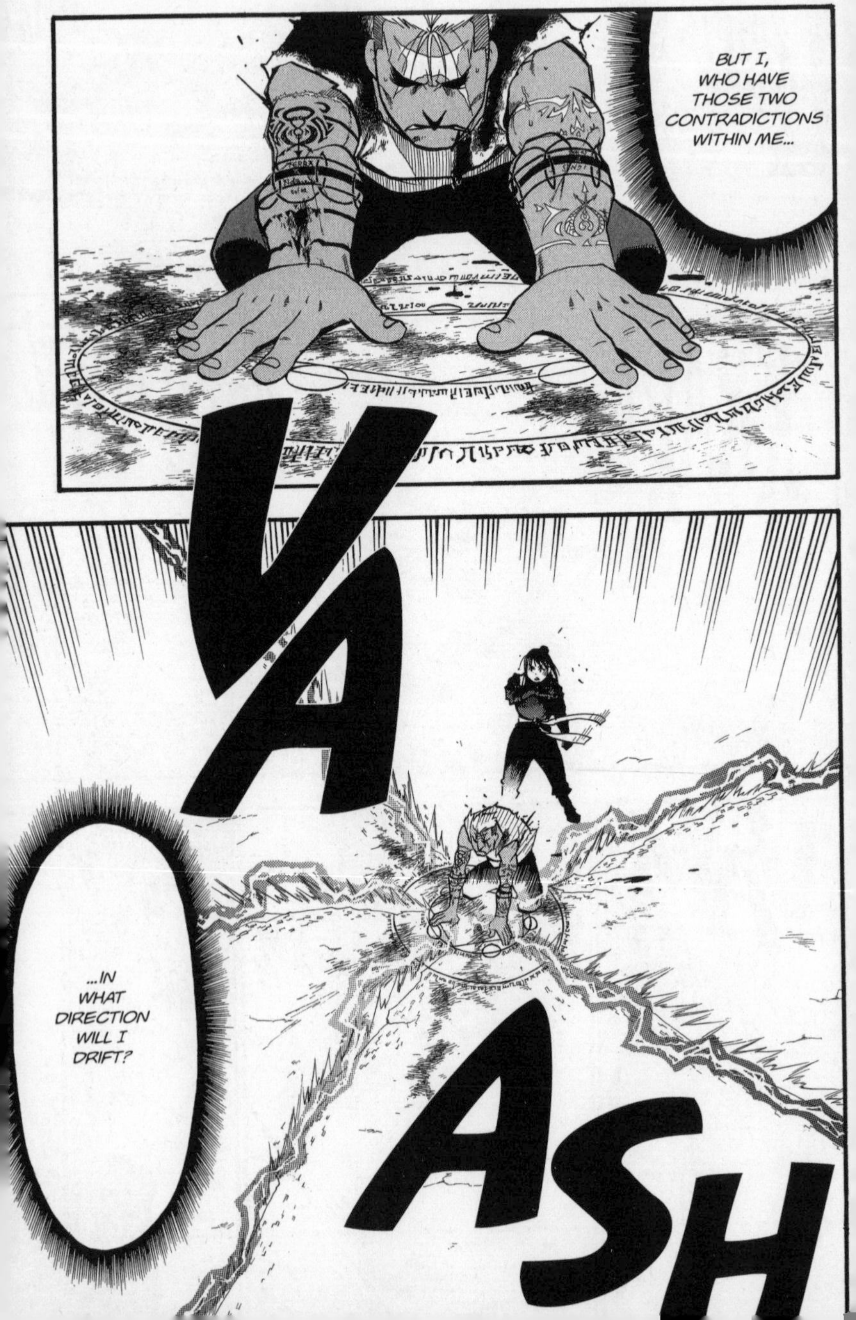
BUT I, WHO HAVE THOSE TWO CONTRADICTIONS WITHIN ME...
VA
...IN WHAT DIRECTION WILL I DRIFT?
ASH

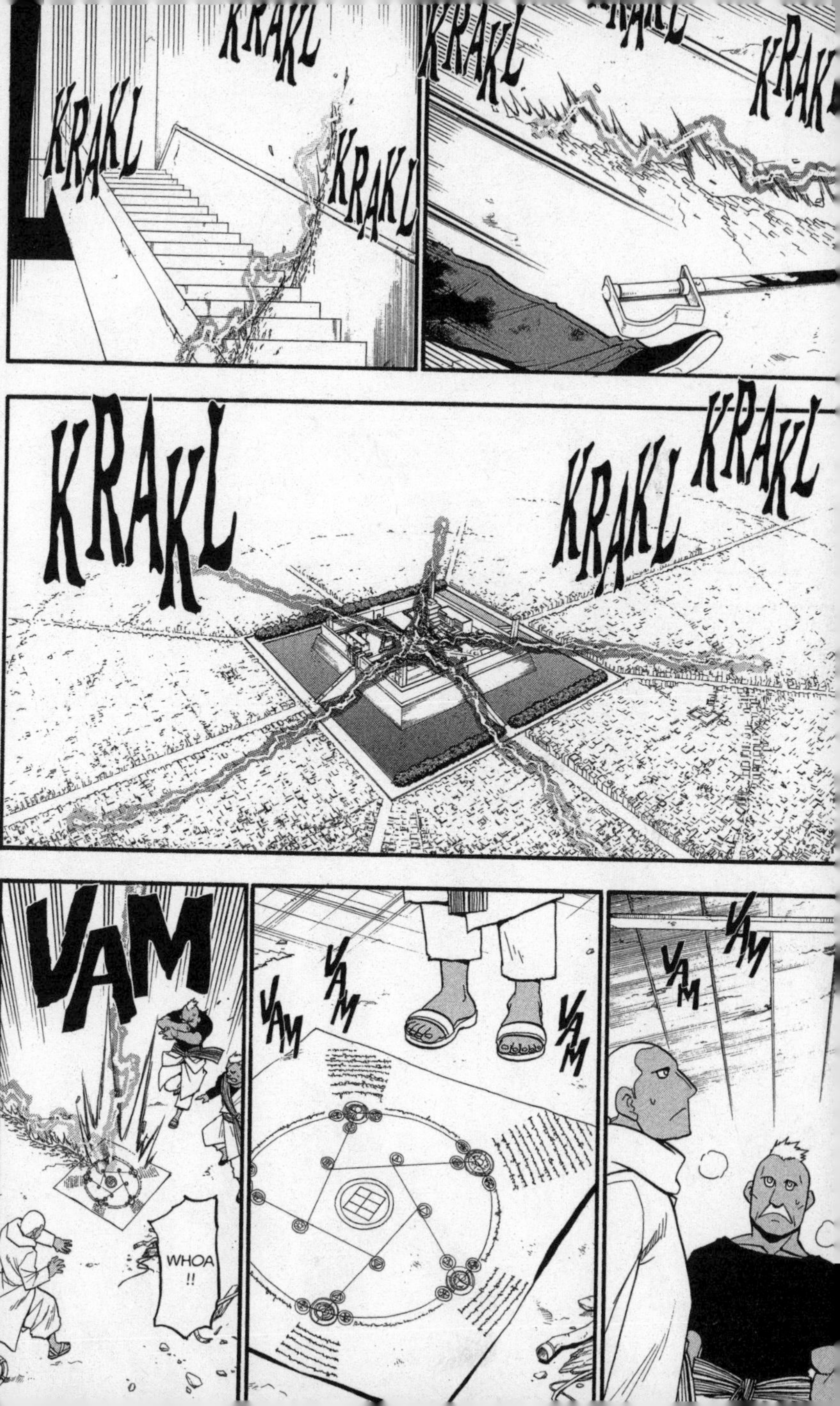
KRAKL
KRAKL
KRAKL
KRAKL
KRAKL
KRAKL
KRAKL
KRAKL
VAM
VAM
VAM
VAM
VAM
VAM
WHOA !!

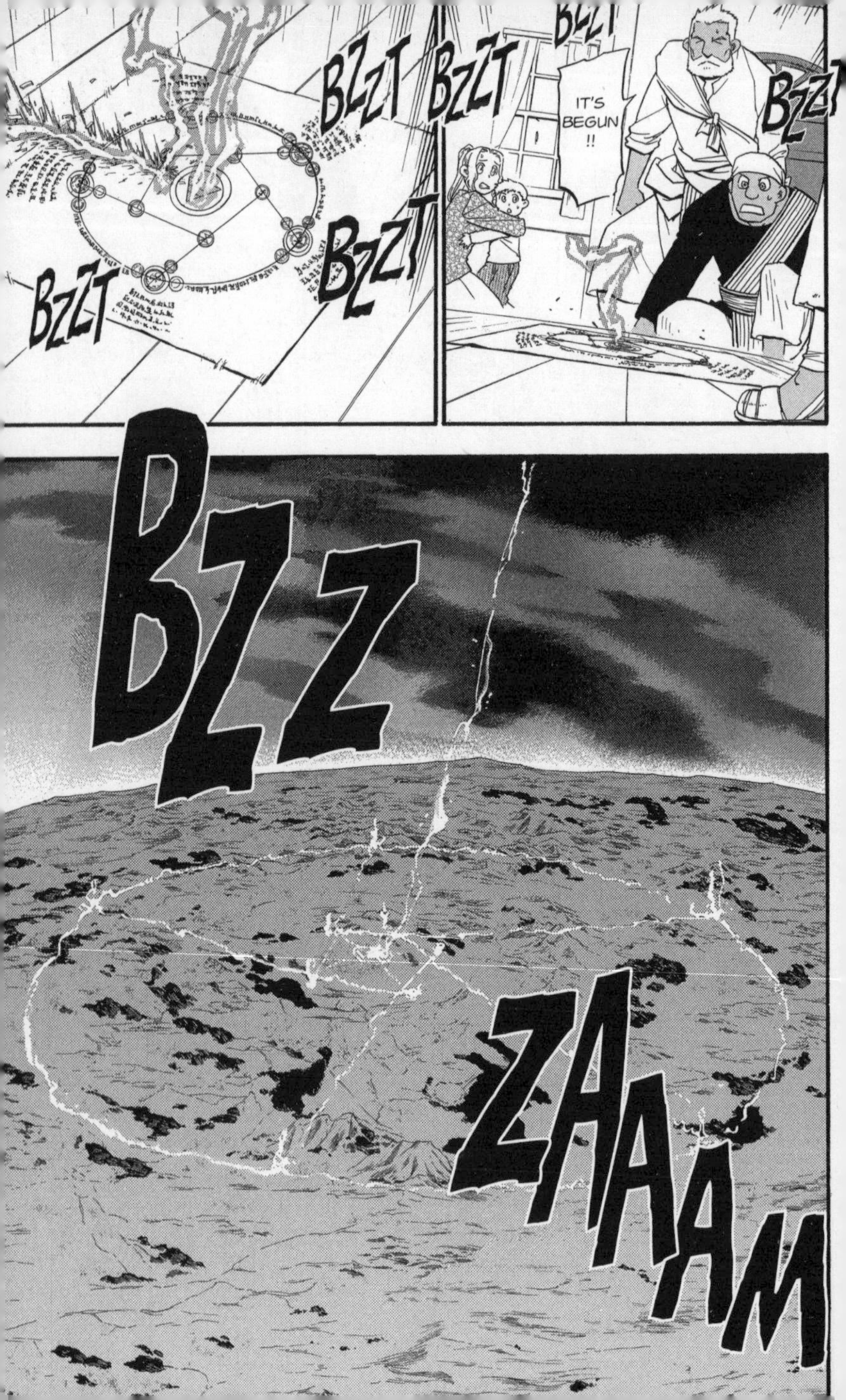
BZZT
BZZT
IT'S BEGUN !!
BZZT
BZZT
BZZT
BZZT
BZZT
BZZ
ZAAAM

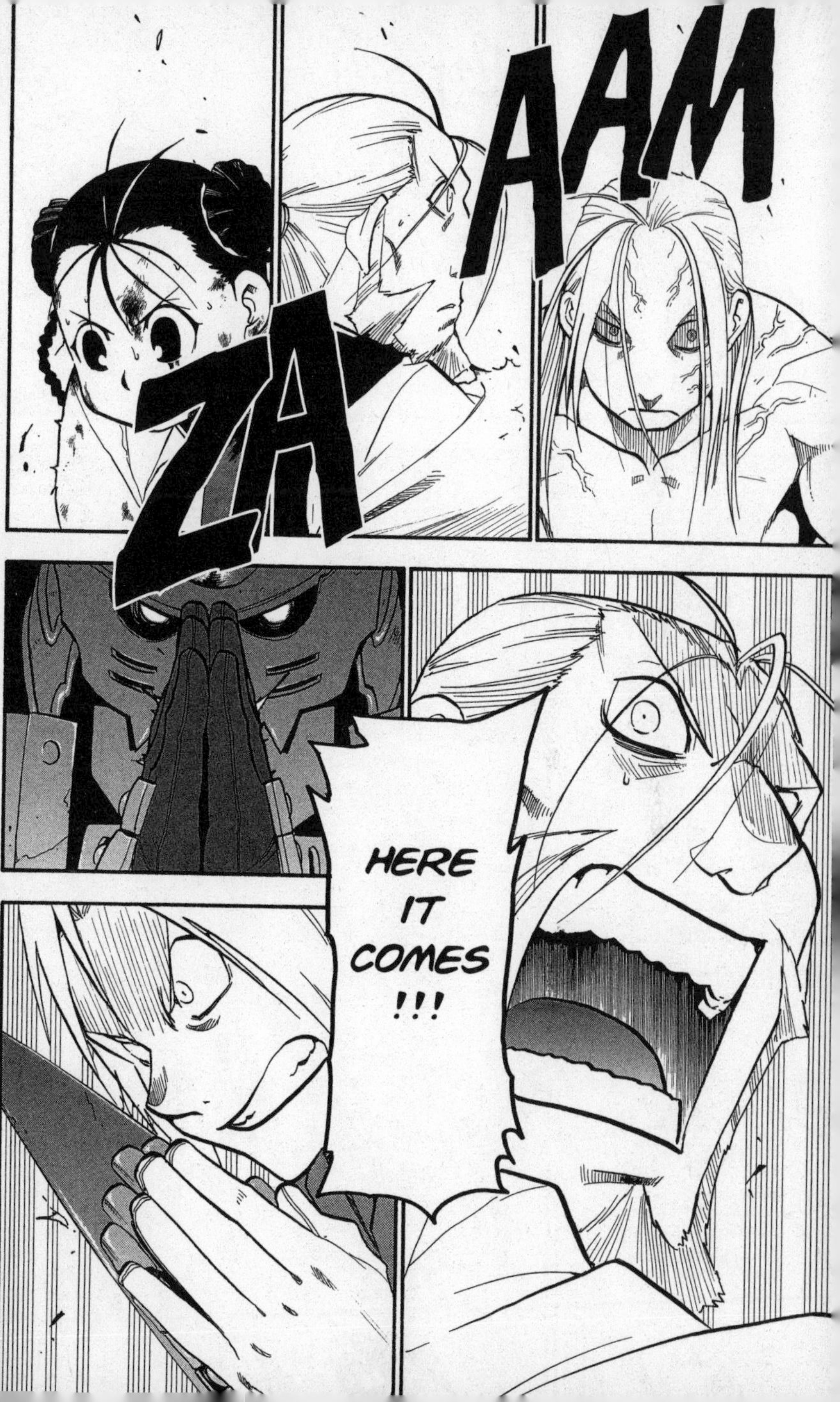
ZA AAM
HERE IT COMES!!!

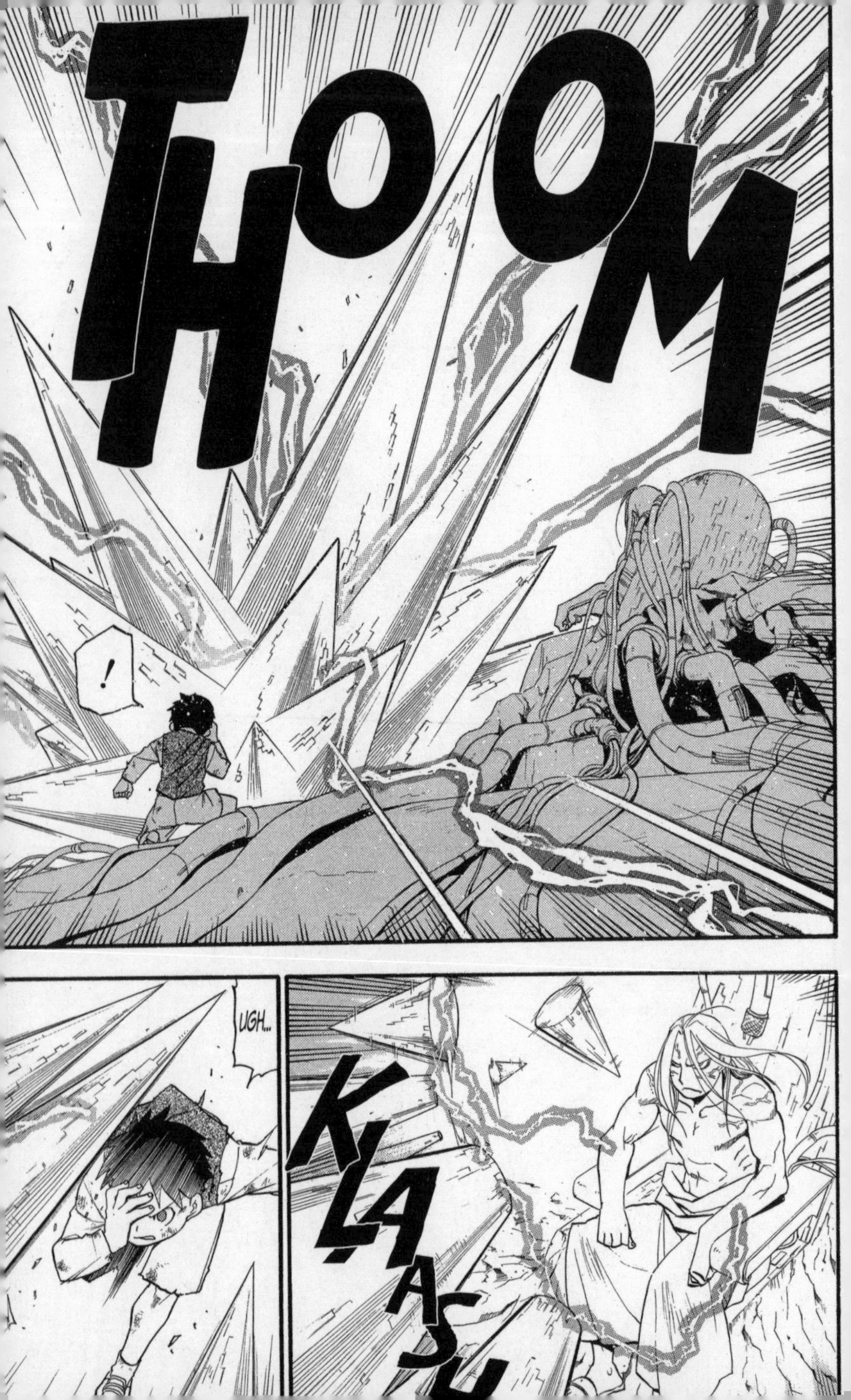
THOOM
!
KLAS
UGH...

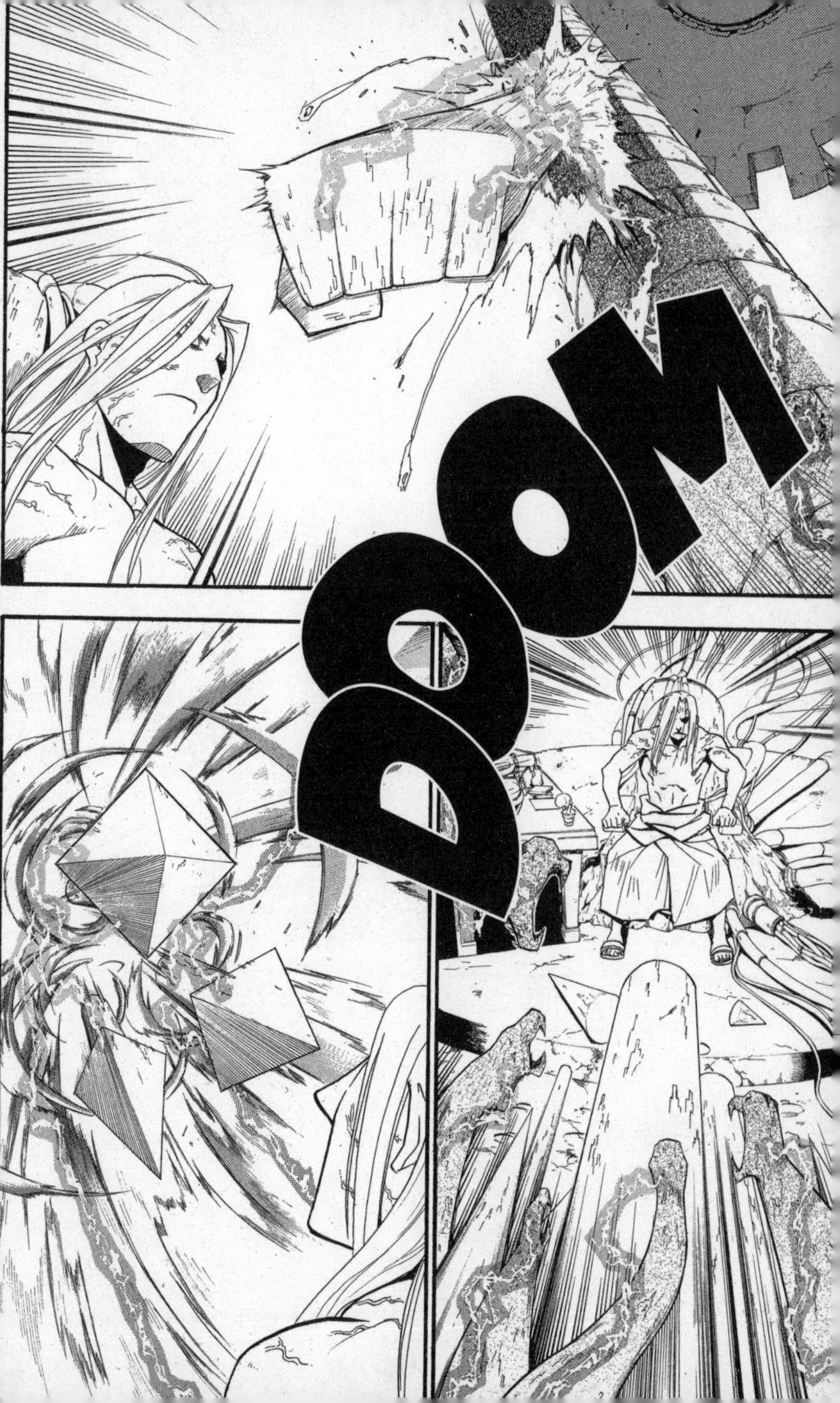
DOOM

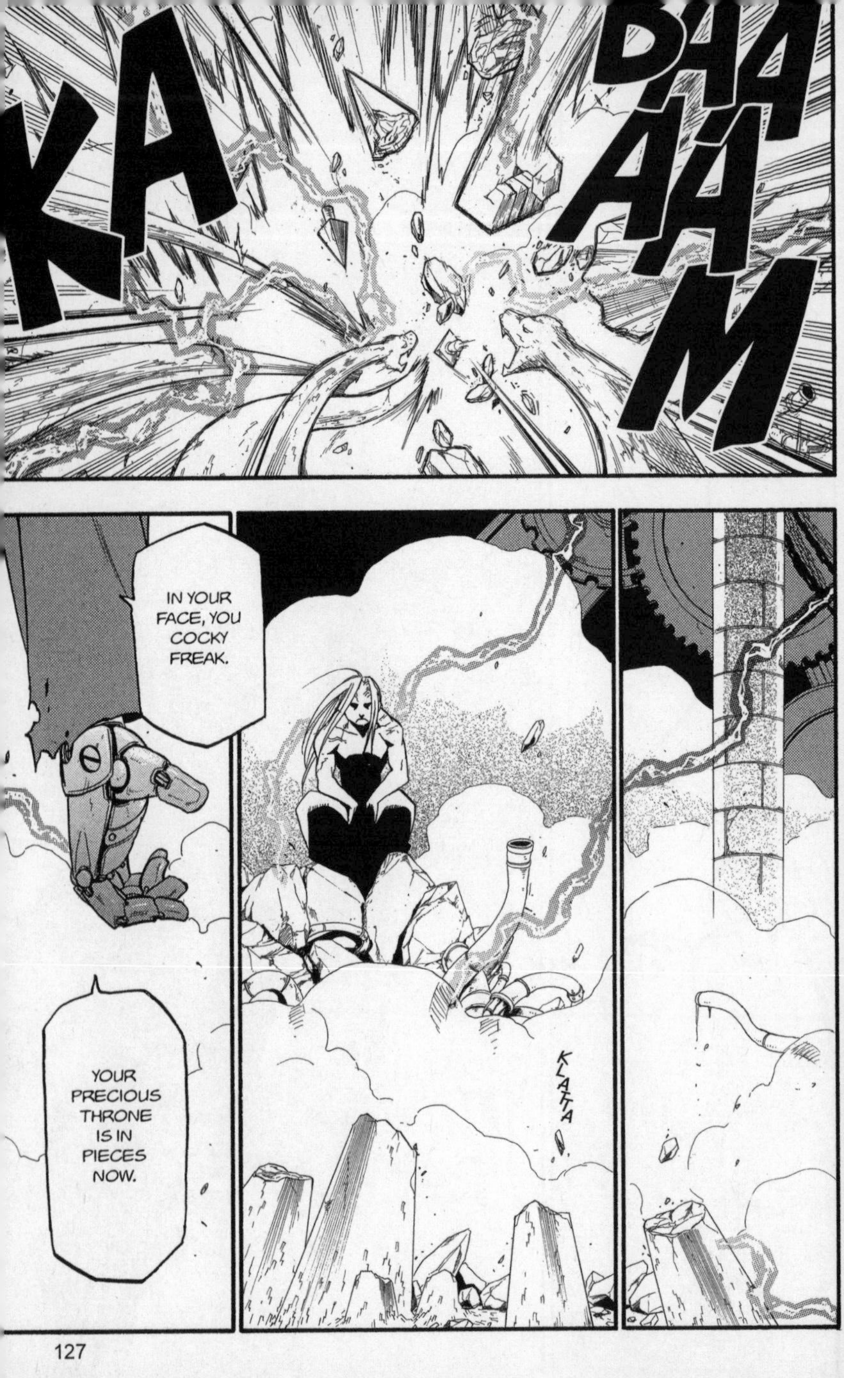
KA
DAAAAAM
KLATTA
IN YOUR FACE, YOU COCKY FREAK.
YOUR PRECIOUS THRONE IS IN PIECES NOW.

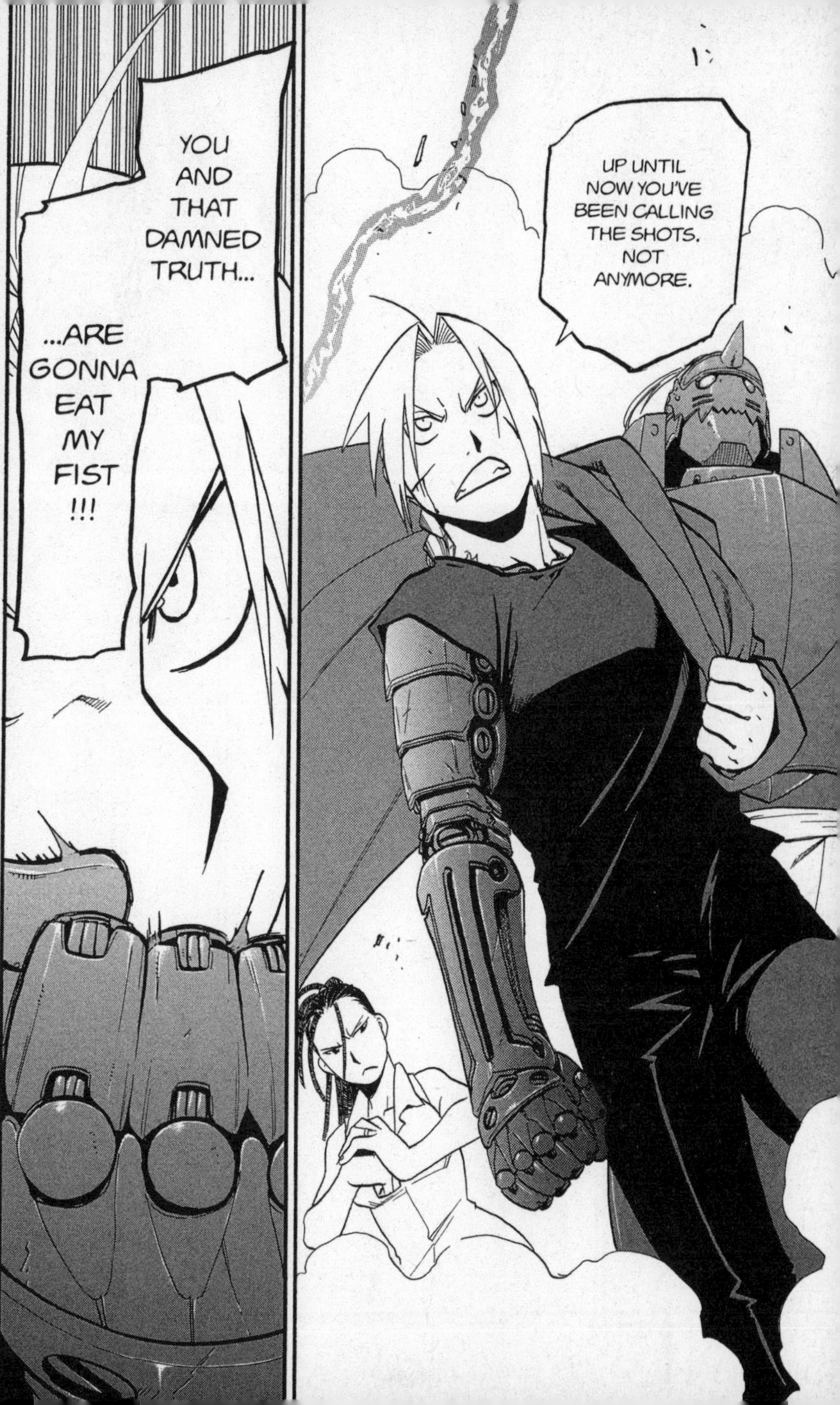
UP UNTIL NOW YOU'VE BEEN CALLING THE SHOTS. NOT ANYMORE.
YOU AND THAT DAMNED TRUTH...
...ARE GONNA EAT MY FIST!!!

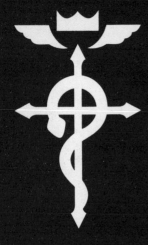

FULLMETAL
ALCHEMIST

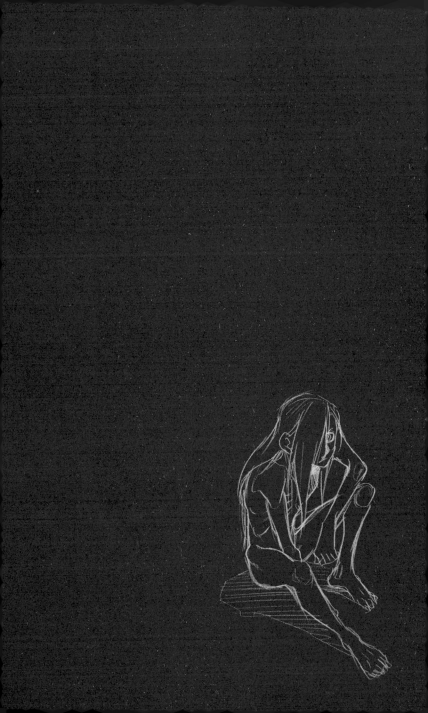

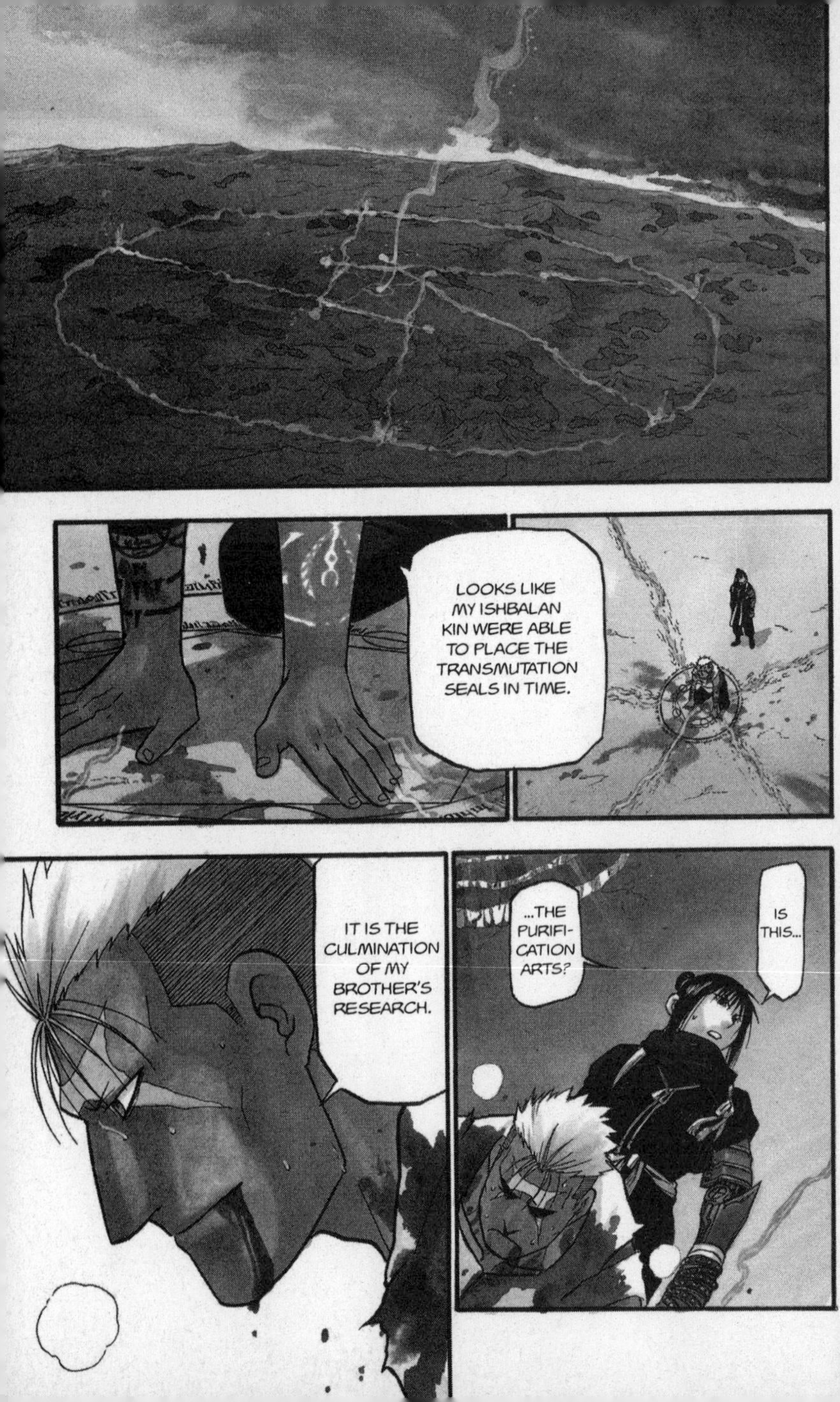
LOOKS LIKE MY ISHBALAN KIN WERE ABLE TO PLACE THE TRANSMUTATION SEALS IN TIME.
IS THIS...
...THE PURIFICATION ARTS?
IT IS THE CULMINATION OF MY BROTHER'S RESEARCH.

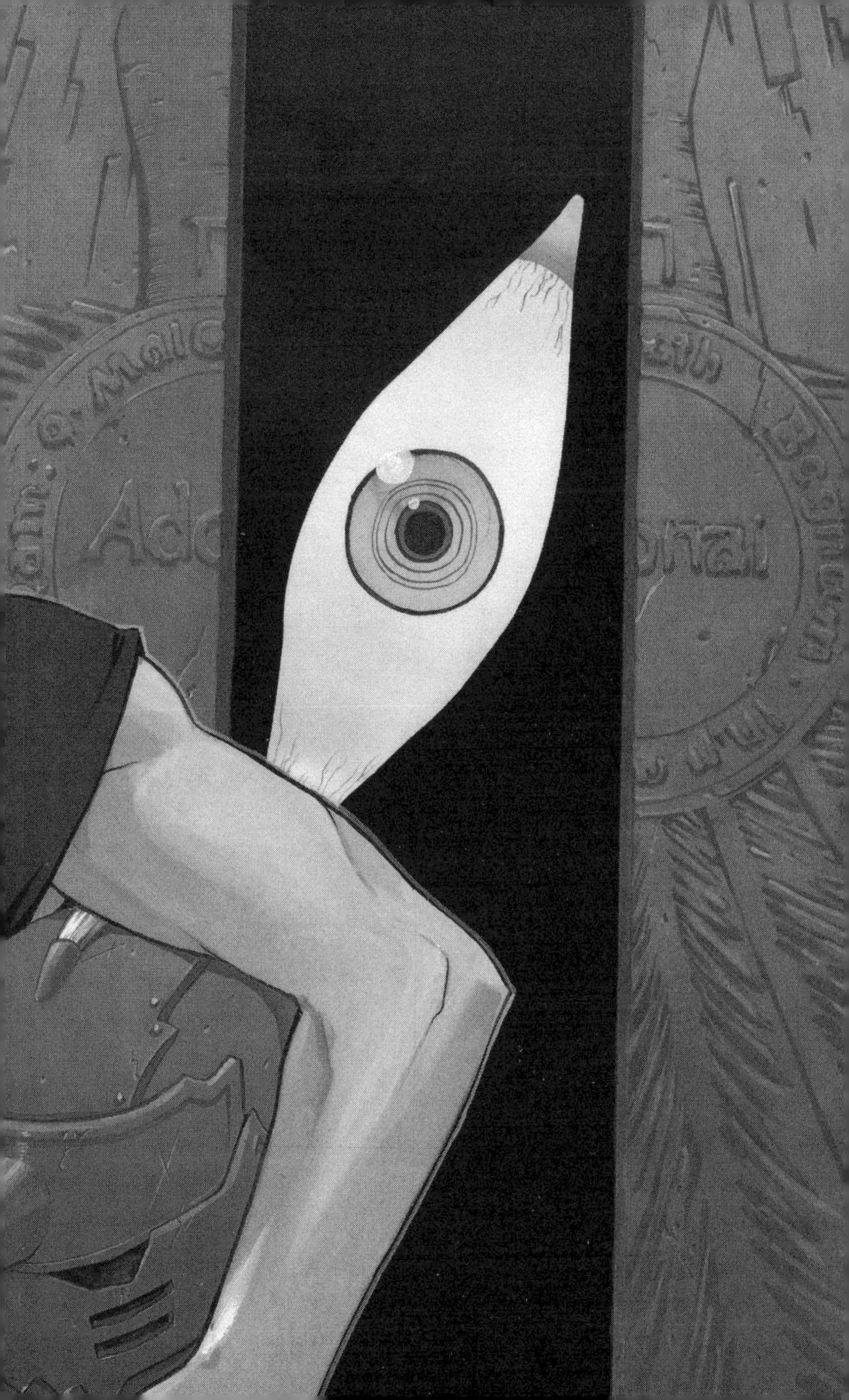
Ado
onai

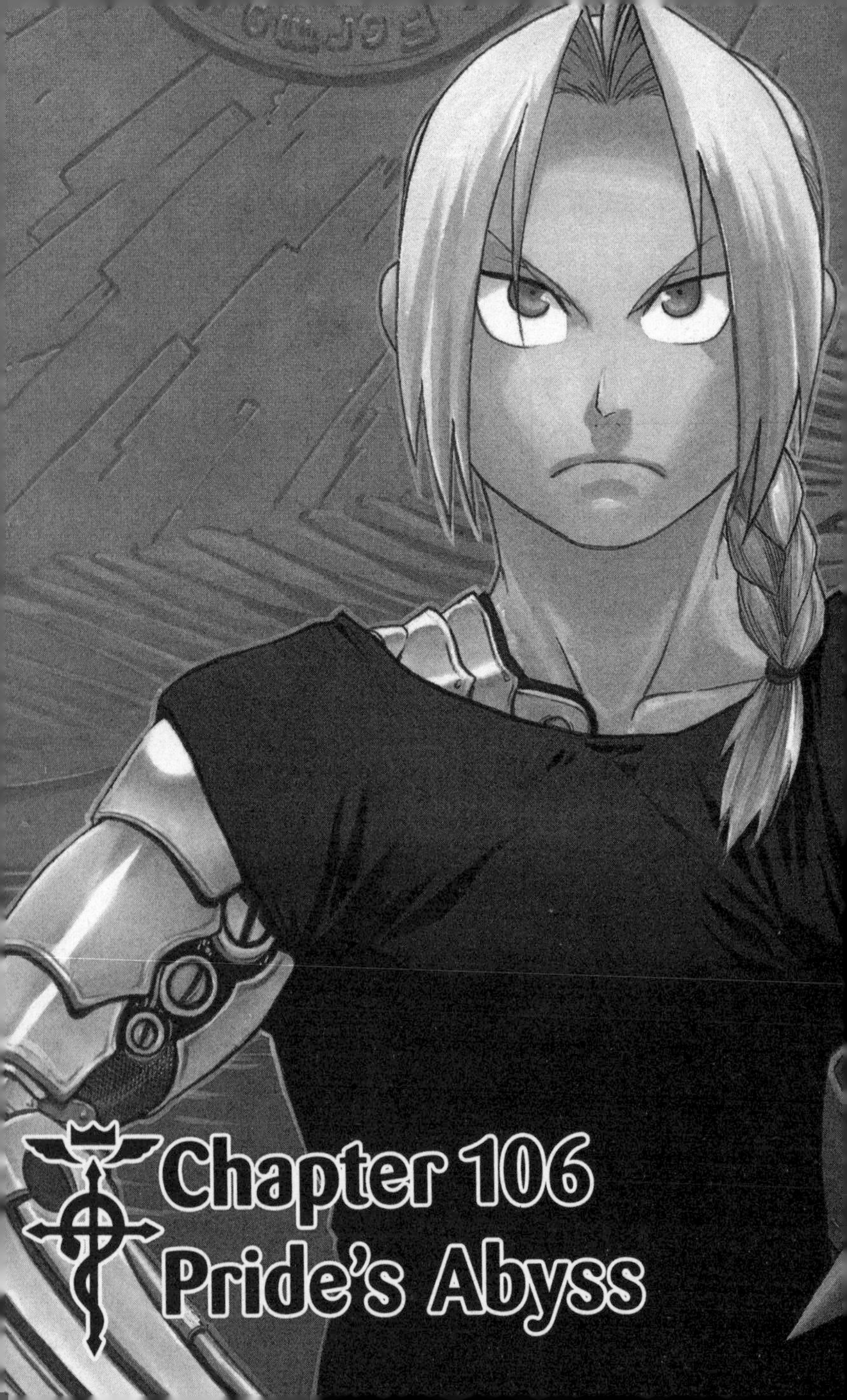
Chapter 106
Pride's Abyss

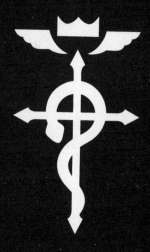

FULLMETAL
ALCHEMIST

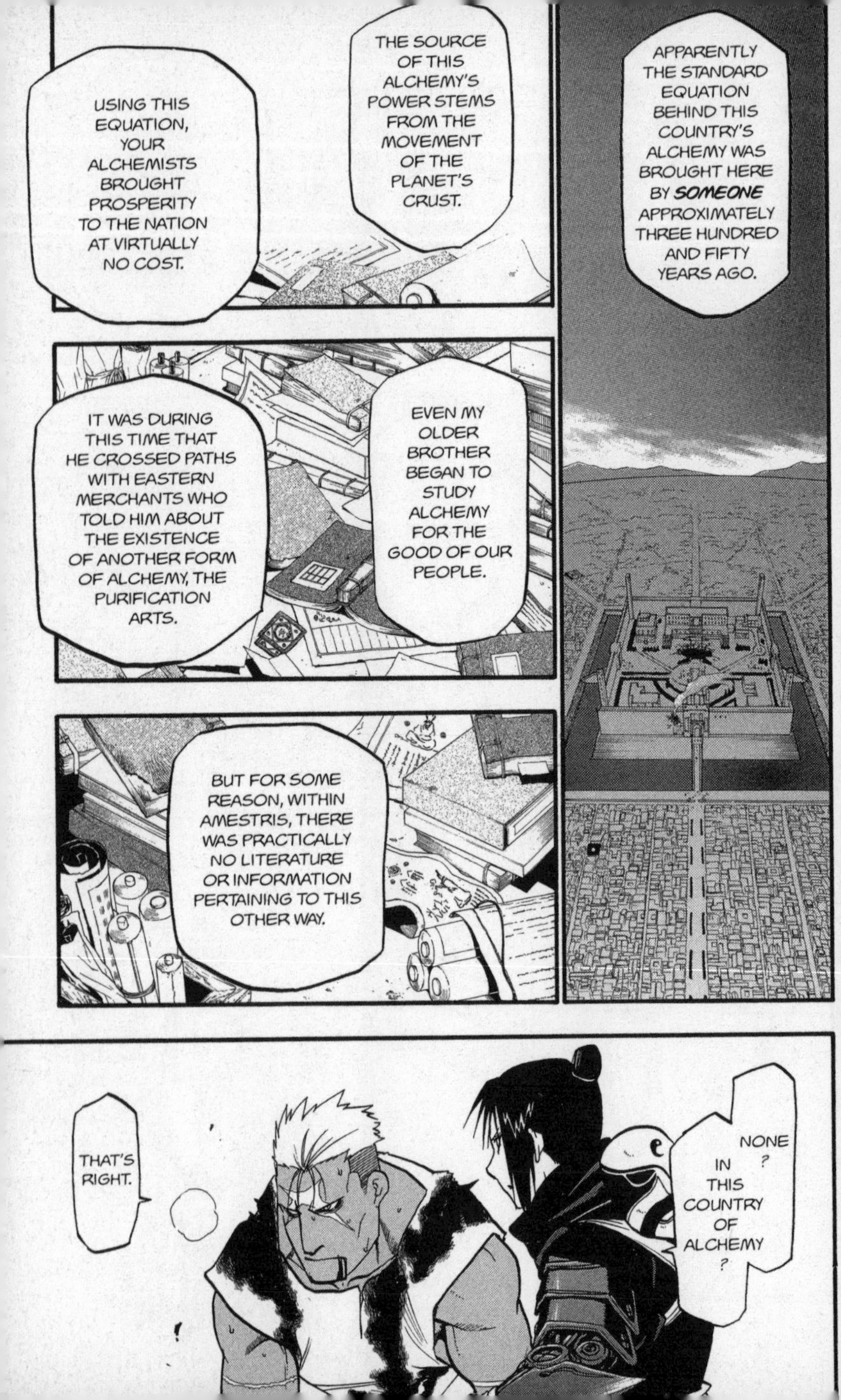
APPARENTLY THE STANDARD EQUATION BEHIND THIS COUNTRY'S ALCHEMY WAS BROUGHT HERE BY ***SOMEONE*** APPROXIMATELY THREE HUNDRED AND FIFTY YEARS AGO.
THE SOURCE OF THIS ALCHEMY'S POWER STEMS FROM THE MOVEMENT OF THE PLANET'S CRUST.
USING THIS EQUATION, YOUR ALCHEMISTS BROUGHT PROSPERITY TO THE NATION AT VIRTUALLY NO COST.
EVEN MY OLDER BROTHER BEGAN TO STUDY ALCHEMY FOR THE GOOD OF OUR PEOPLE.
IT WAS DURING THIS TIME THAT HE CROSSED PATHS WITH EASTERN MERCHANTS WHO TOLD HIM ABOUT THE EXISTENCE OF ANOTHER FORM OF ALCHEMY, THE PURIFICATION ARTS.
BUT FOR SOME REASON, WITHIN AMESTRIS, THERE WAS PRACTICALLY NO LITERATURE OR INFORMATION PERTAINING TO THIS OTHER WAY.
NONE? IN THIS COUNTRY OF ALCHEMY?
THAT'S RIGHT.

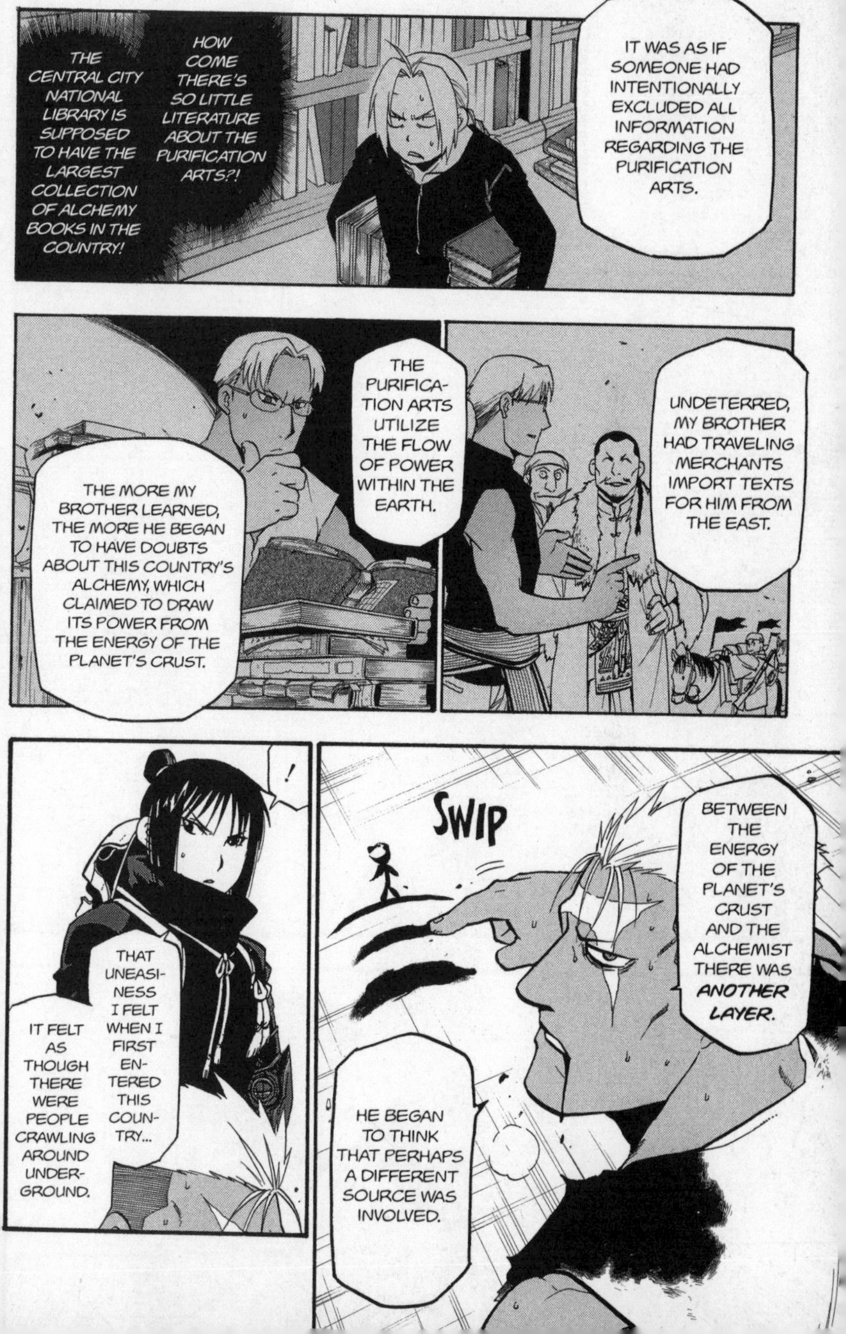
IT WAS AS IF SOMEONE HAD INTENTIONALLY EXCLUDED ALL INFORMATION REGARDING THE PURIFICATION ARTS.
HOW COME THERE'S SO LITTLE LITERATURE ABOUT THE PURIFICATION ARTS?!
THE CENTRAL CITY NATIONAL LIBRARY IS SUPPOSED TO HAVE THE LARGEST COLLECTION OF ALCHEMY BOOKS IN THE COUNTRY!
UNDETERRED, MY BROTHER HAD TRAVELING MERCHANTS IMPORT TEXTS FOR HIM FROM THE EAST.
THE PURIFICATION ARTS UTILIZE THE FLOW OF POWER WITHIN THE EARTH.
THE MORE MY BROTHER LEARNED, THE MORE HE BEGAN TO HAVE DOUBTS ABOUT THIS COUNTRY'S ALCHEMY, WHICH CLAIMED TO DRAW ITS POWER FROM THE ENERGY OF THE PLANET'S CRUST.
SWIP
BETWEEN THE ENERGY OF THE PLANET'S CRUST AND THE ALCHEMIST THERE WAS ANOTHER LAYER.
HE BEGAN TO THINK THAT PERHAPS A DIFFERENT SOURCE WAS INVOLVED.
!
THAT UNEASINESS I FELT WHEN I FIRST ENTERED THIS COUNTRY...
IT FELT AS THOUGH THERE WERE PEOPLE CRAWLING AROUND UNDERGROUND.

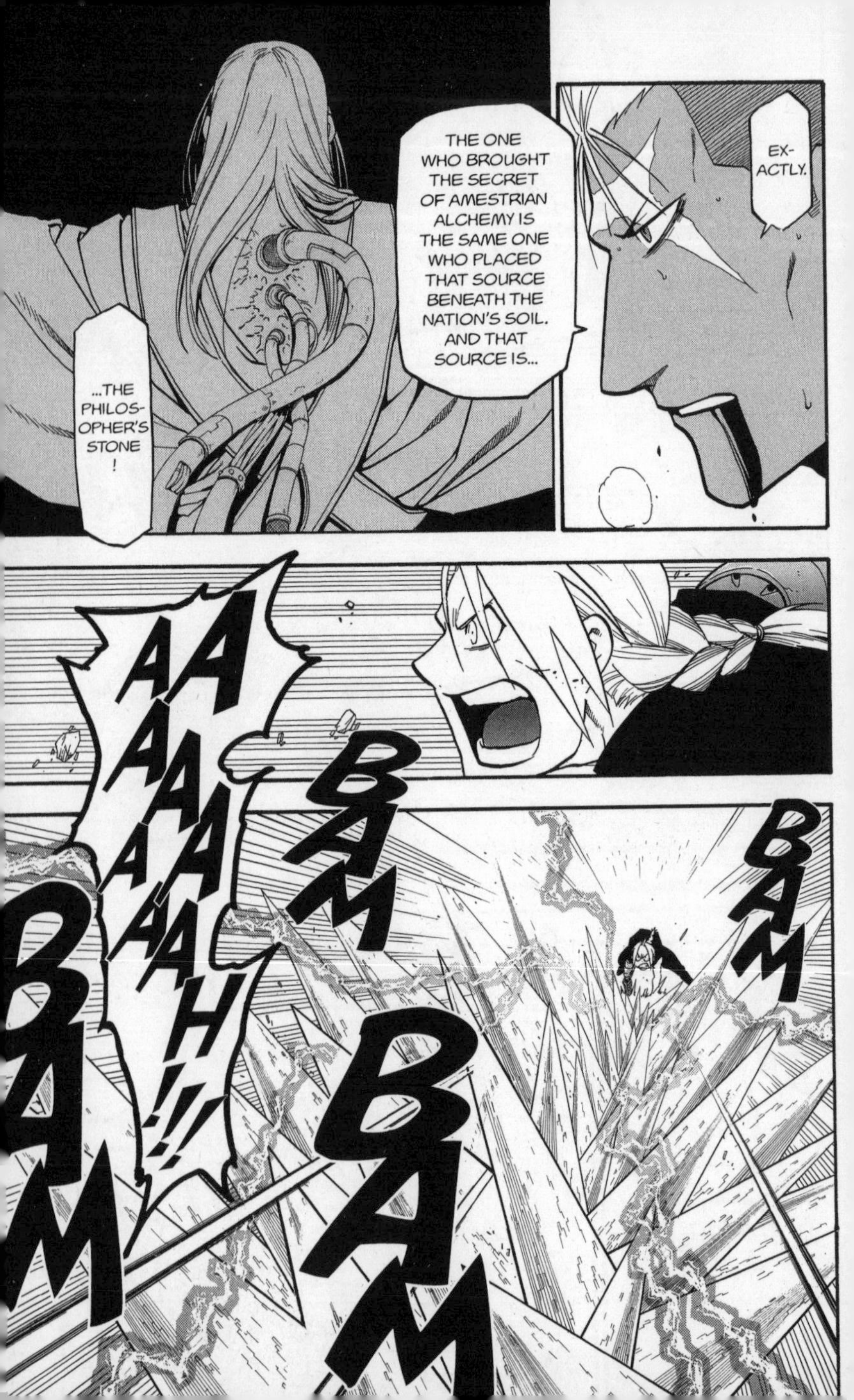
THE ONE WHO BROUGHT THE SECRET OF AMESTRIAN ALCHEMY IS THE SAME ONE WHO PLACED THAT SOURCE BENEATH THE NATION'S SOIL. AND THAT SOURCE IS...
...THE PHILOSOPHER'S STONE!
EX-ACTLY.
AAAAAAAAH!!!!
BAM
BAM
BAM
BAM

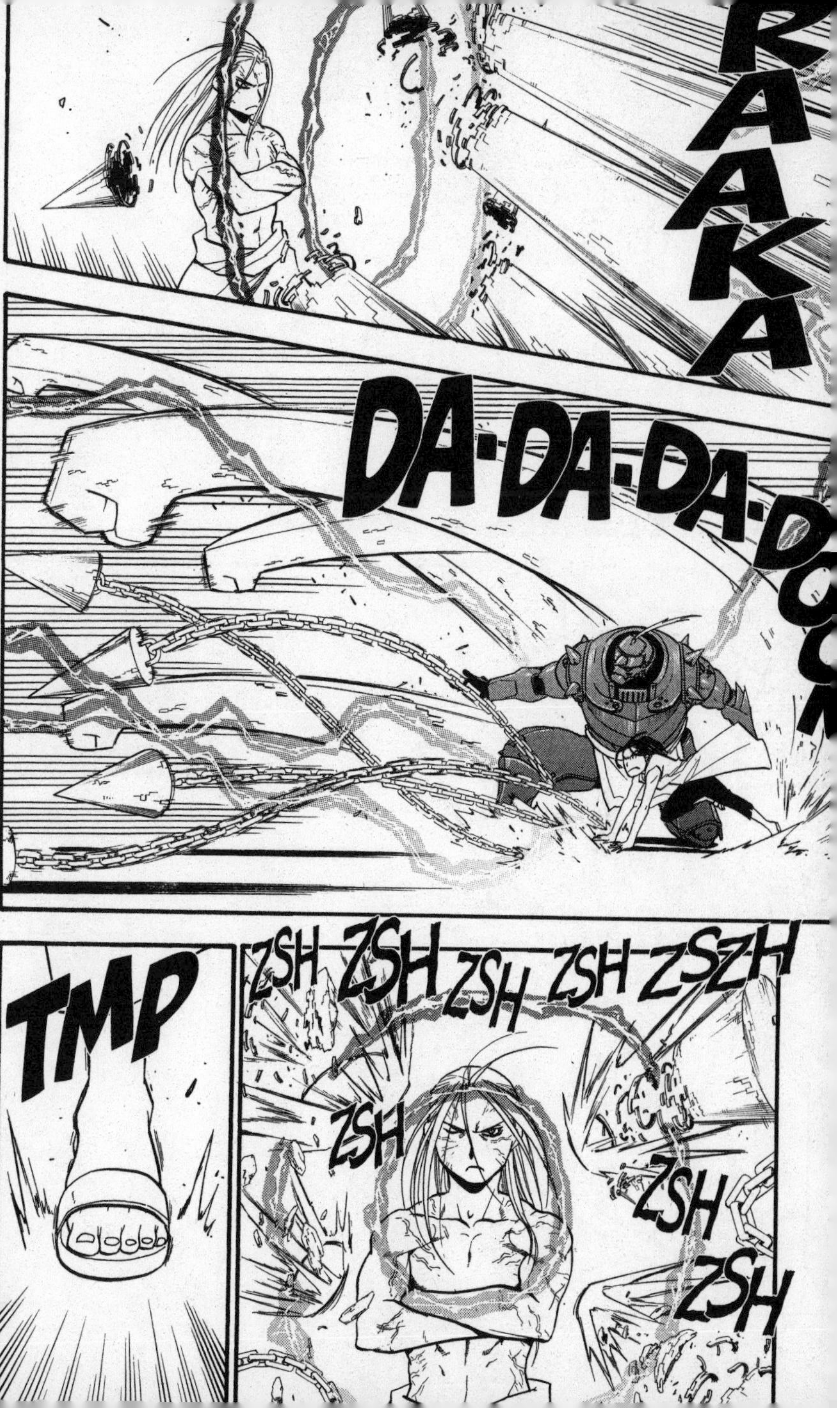
RAKAKA
DA-DA-DA-DOOM
ZSH ZSH ZSH ZSH ZSZH
ZSH
ZSH
ZSH
TMP

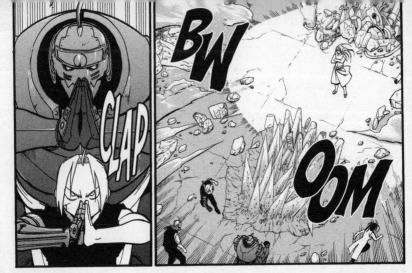

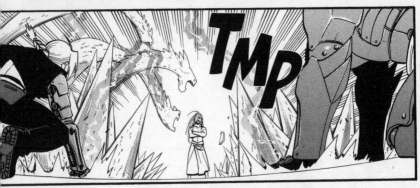

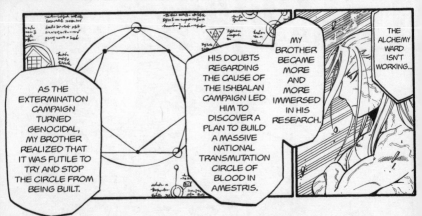

THE ALCHEMY WARD ISN'T WORKING...

MY BROTHER BECAME MORE AND MORE IMMERSED IN HIS RESEARCH.

HIS DOUBTS REGARDING THE CAUSE OF THE ISHBALAN CAMPAIGN LED HIM TO DISCOVER A PLAN TO BUILD A MASSIVE NATIONAL TRANSMUTATION CIRCLE OF BLOOD IN AMESTRIS.

AS THE EXTERMINATION CAMPAIGN TURNED GENOCIDAL, MY BROTHER REALIZED THAT IT WAS FUTILE TO TRY AND STOP THE CIRCLE FROM BEING BUILT.

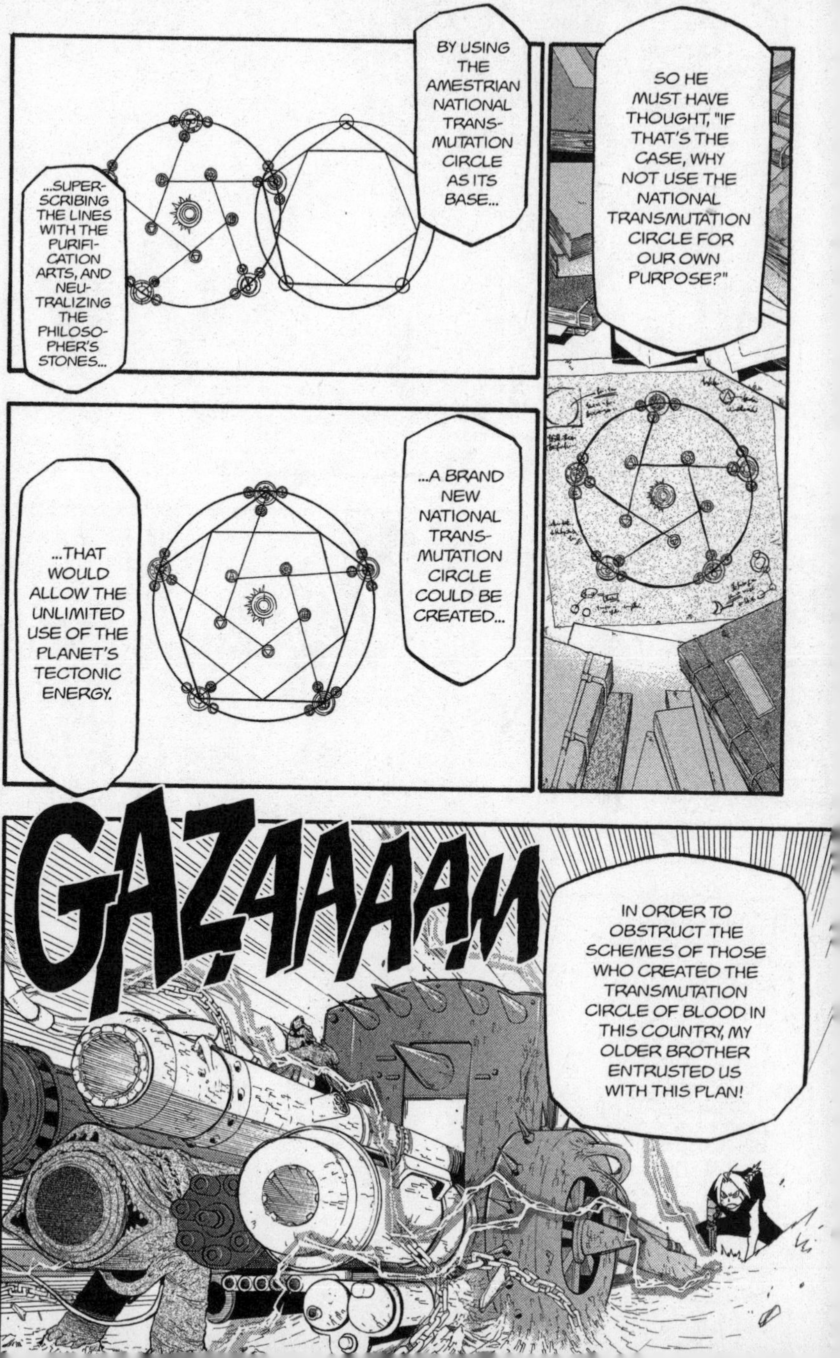
SO HE MUST HAVE THOUGHT, "IF THAT'S THE CASE, WHY NOT USE THE NATIONAL TRANSMUTATION CIRCLE FOR OUR OWN PURPOSE?"
BY USING THE AMESTRIAN NATIONAL TRANS-MUTATION CIRCLE AS ITS BASE...
...SUPER-SCRIBING THE LINES WITH THE PURIFI-CATION ARTS, AND NEU-TRALIZING THE PHILOSO-PHER'S STONES...
...A BRAND NEW NATIONAL TRANS-MUTATION CIRCLE COULD BE CREATED...
...THAT WOULD ALLOW THE UNLIMITED USE OF THE PLANET'S TECTONIC ENERGY.
GAZAAAAM
IN ORDER TO OBSTRUCT THE SCHEMES OF THOSE WHO CREATED THE TRANSMUTATION CIRCLE OF BLOOD IN THIS COUNTRY, MY OLDER BROTHER ENTRUSTED US WITH THIS PLAN!

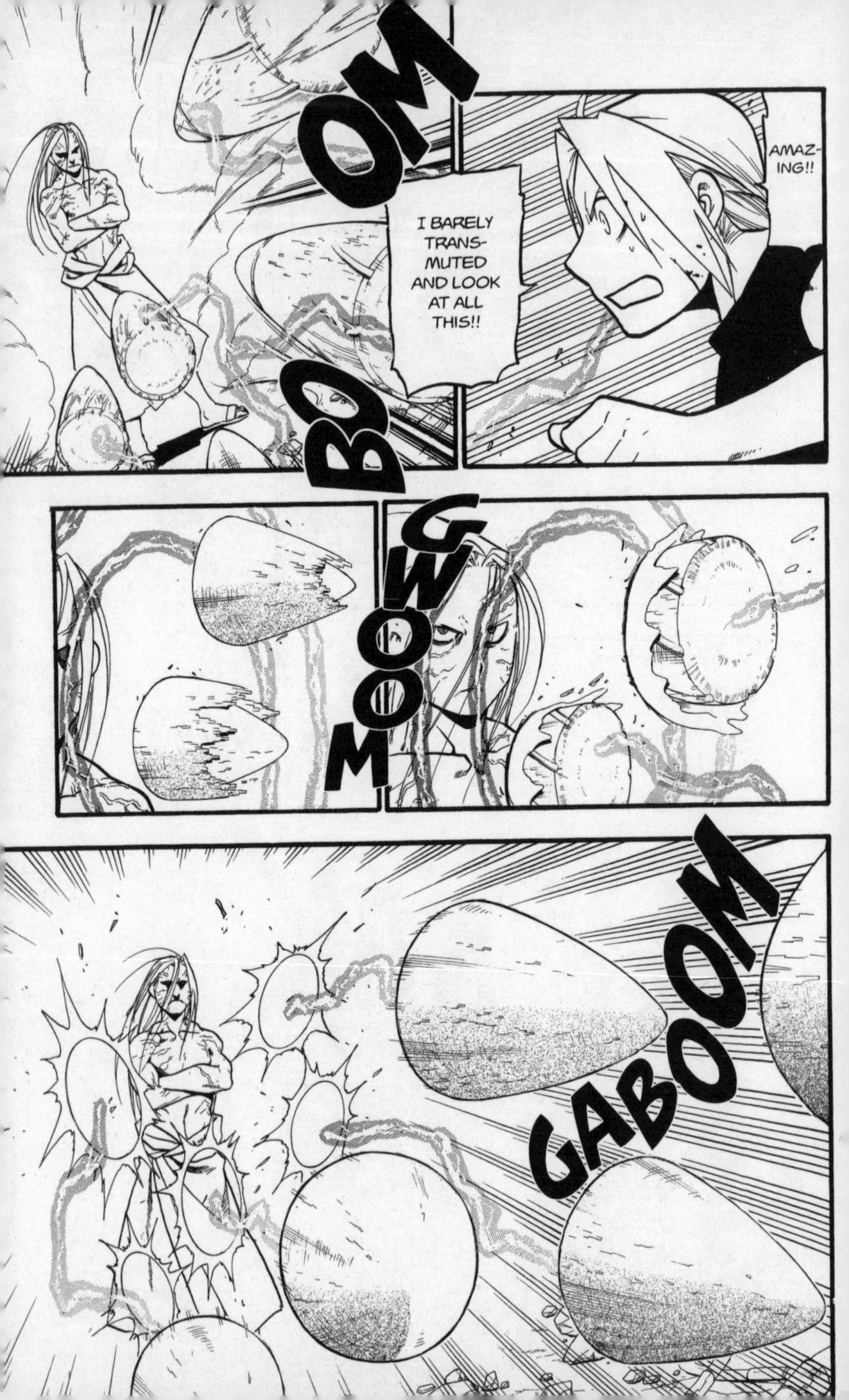
AMAZ-ING!!
I BARELY TRANS-MUTED AND LOOK AT ALL THIS!!
BOOM
GWOOM
GABOOM

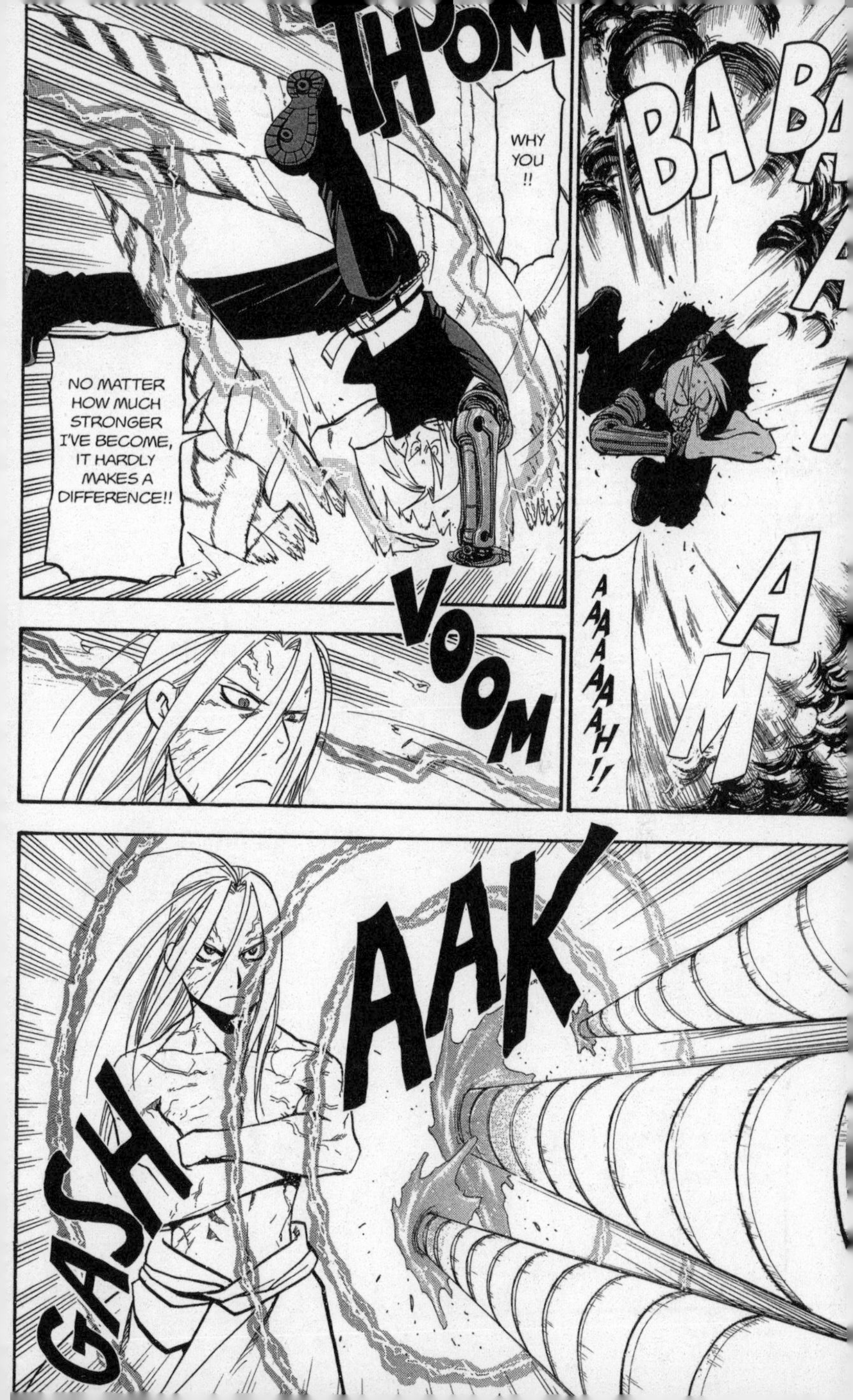

BABAAAAM
AAAAAAAH!!
THOOM
WHY YOU !!
NO MATTER HOW MUCH STRONGER I'VE BECOME, IT HARDLY MAKES A DIFFERENCE!!
VOOM
GASH
AAK

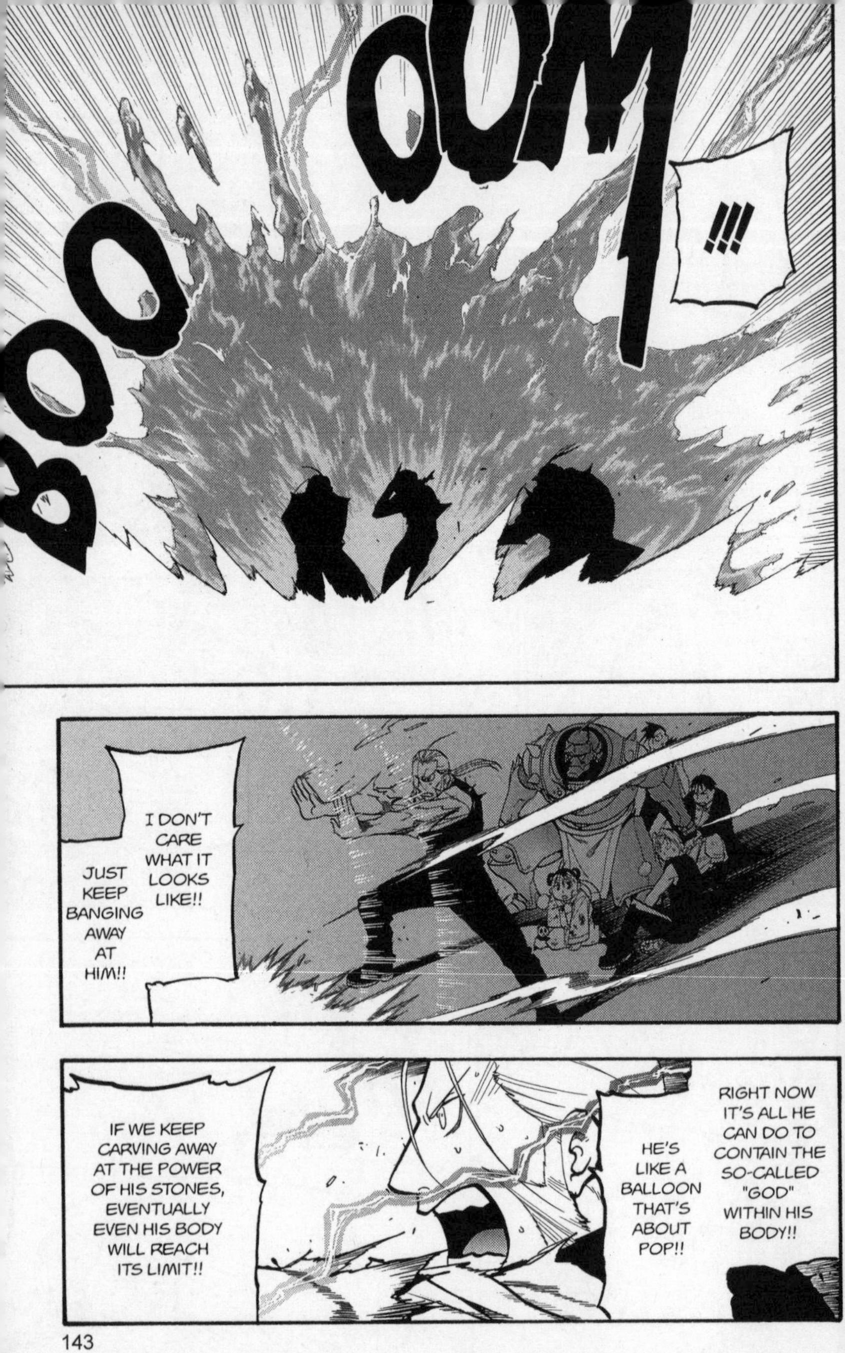
BOOOOM
!!!
I DON'T CARE WHAT IT LOOKS LIKE!!
JUST KEEP BANGING AWAY AT HIM!!
RIGHT NOW IT'S ALL HE CAN DO TO CONTAIN THE SO-CALLED "GOD" WITHIN HIS BODY!!
HE'S LIKE A BALLOON THAT'S ABOUT POP!!
IF WE KEEP CARVING AWAY AT THE POWER OF HIS STONES, EVENTUALLY EVEN HIS BODY WILL REACH ITS LIMIT!!

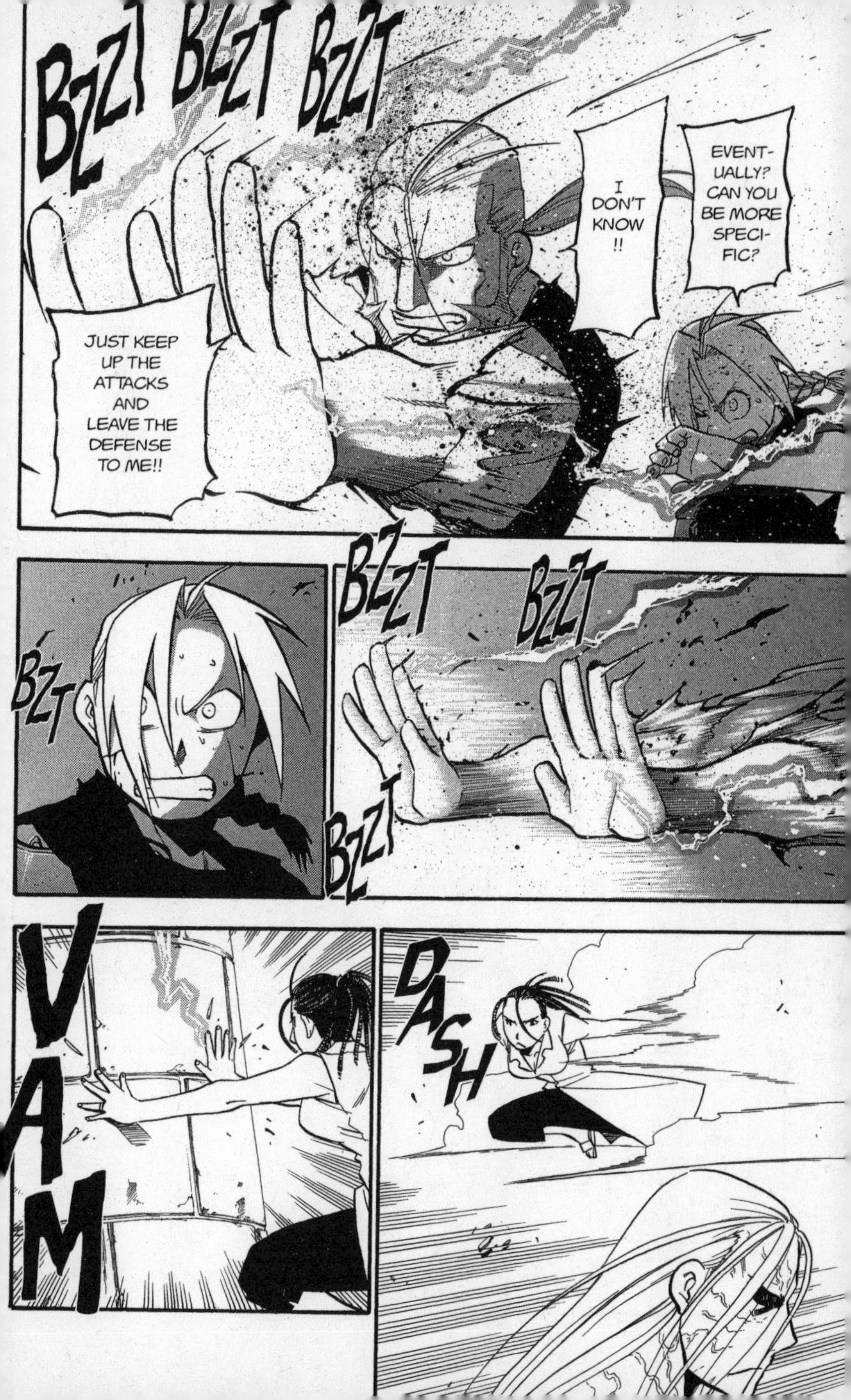
EVENT-UALLY? CAN YOU BE MORE SPECI-FIC?
I DON'T KNOW!!
BZZT BZZT BZZT
JUST KEEP UP THE ATTACKS AND LEAVE THE DEFENSE TO ME!!
BZZT
BZZT
BZZT
BZT
DASH
VAM

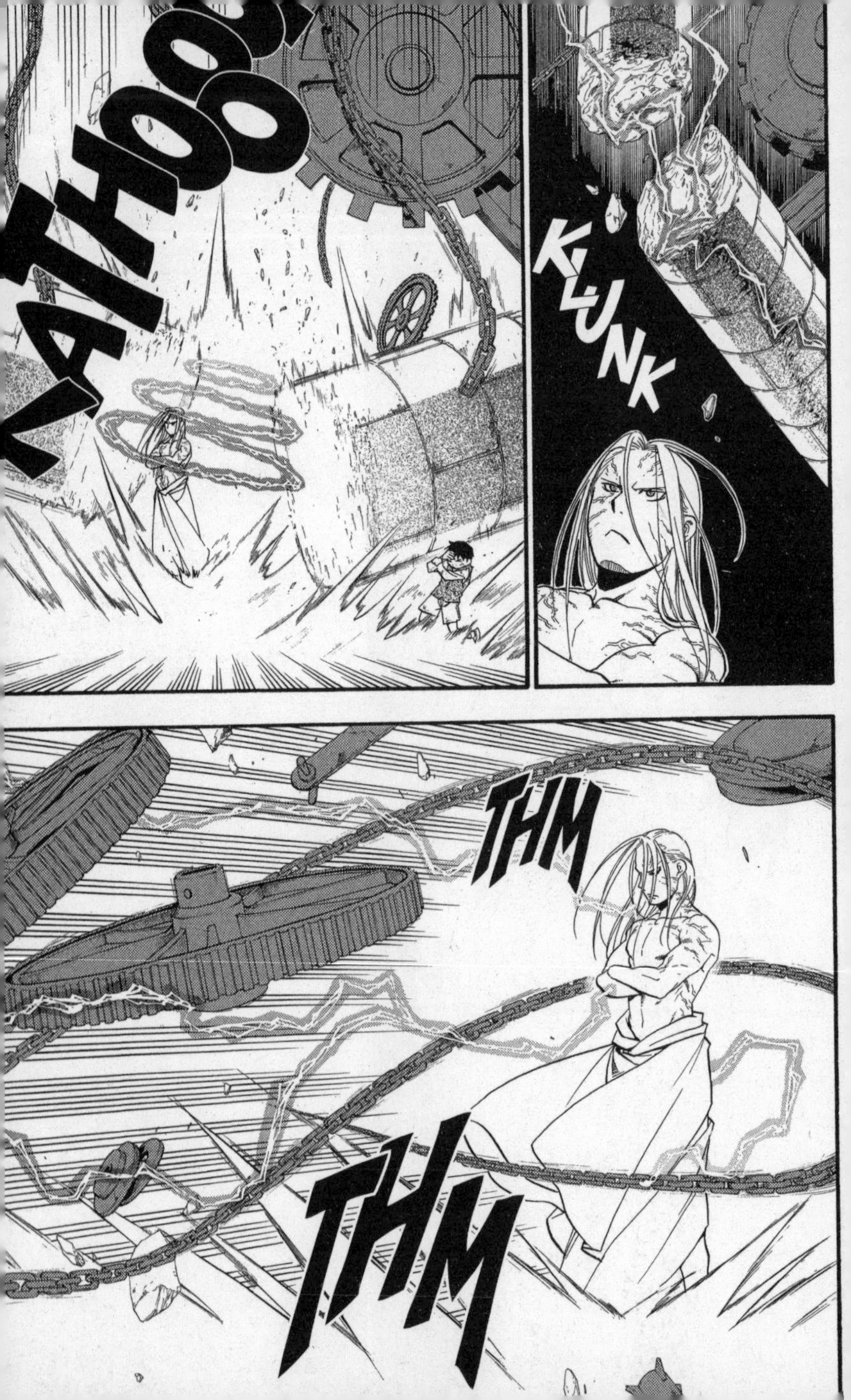
KLUNK
VATHOOS
THM
THM

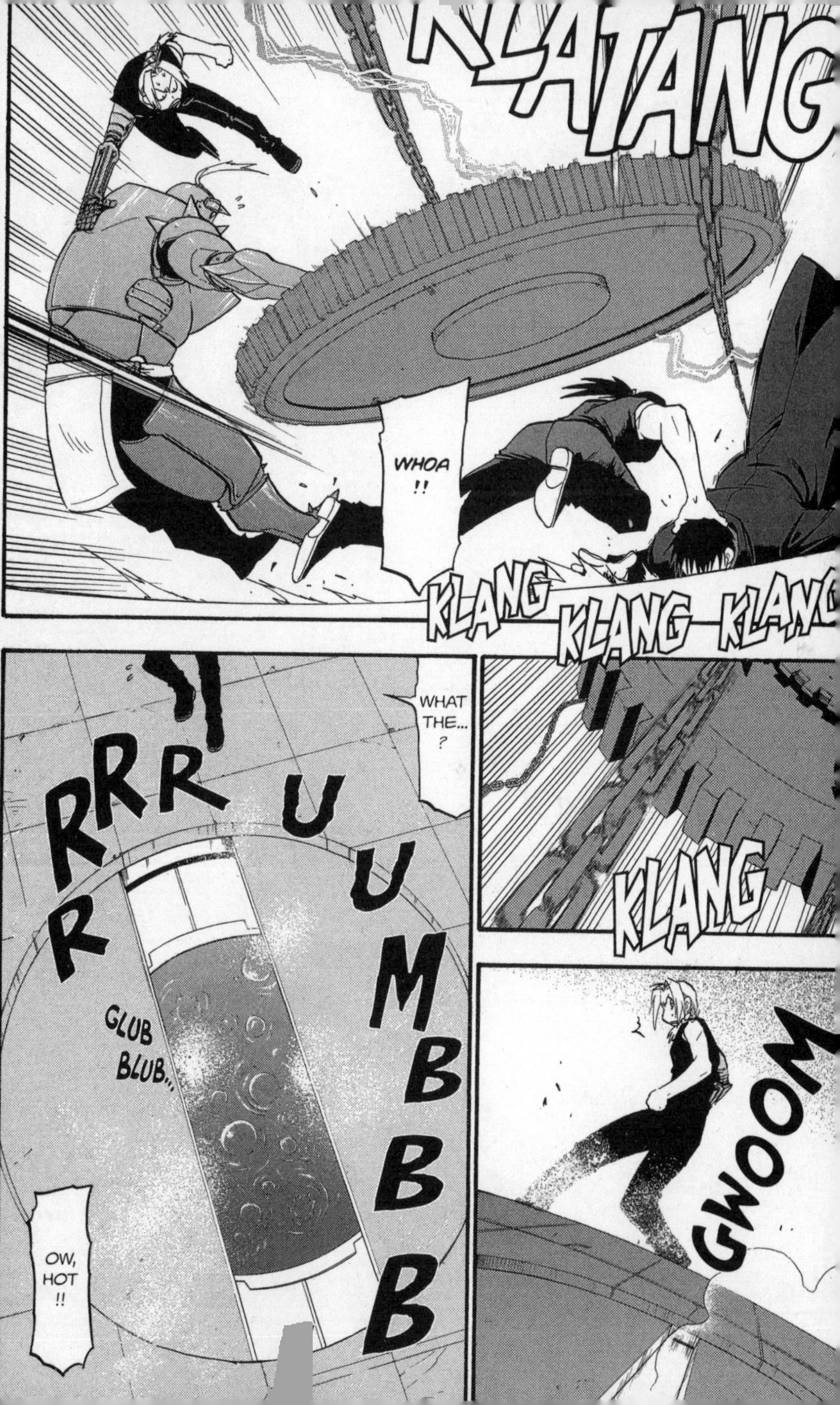
KLATANG
WHOA!!
KLANG KLANG KLANG
KLANG
GWOOM
WHAT THE...?
RRRRUMBBB
GLUB BLUB...
OW, HOT!!

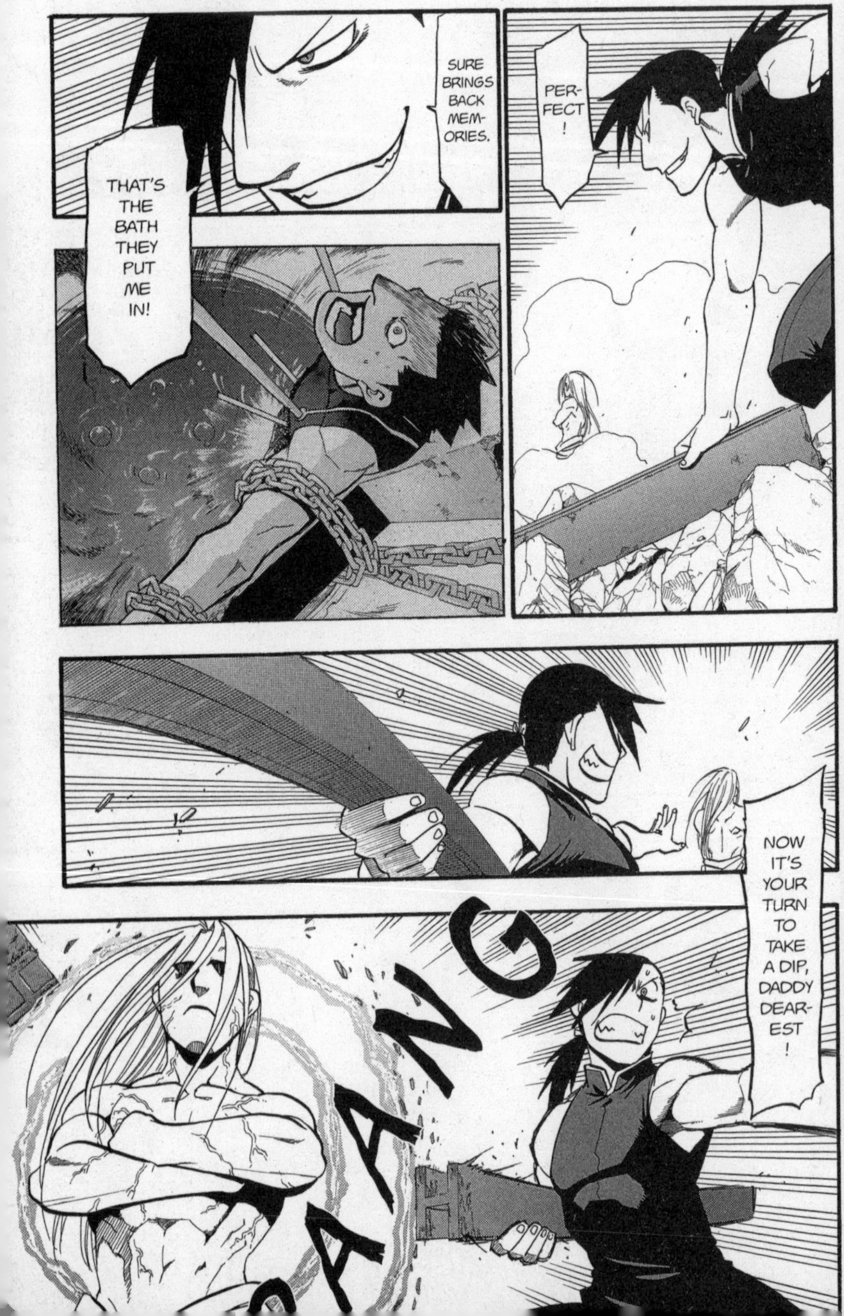
PER-FECT!
SURE BRINGS BACK MEM-ORIES.
THAT'S THE BATH THEY PUT ME IN!
NOW IT'S YOUR TURN TO TAKE A DIP, DADDY DEAR-EST!
AANG

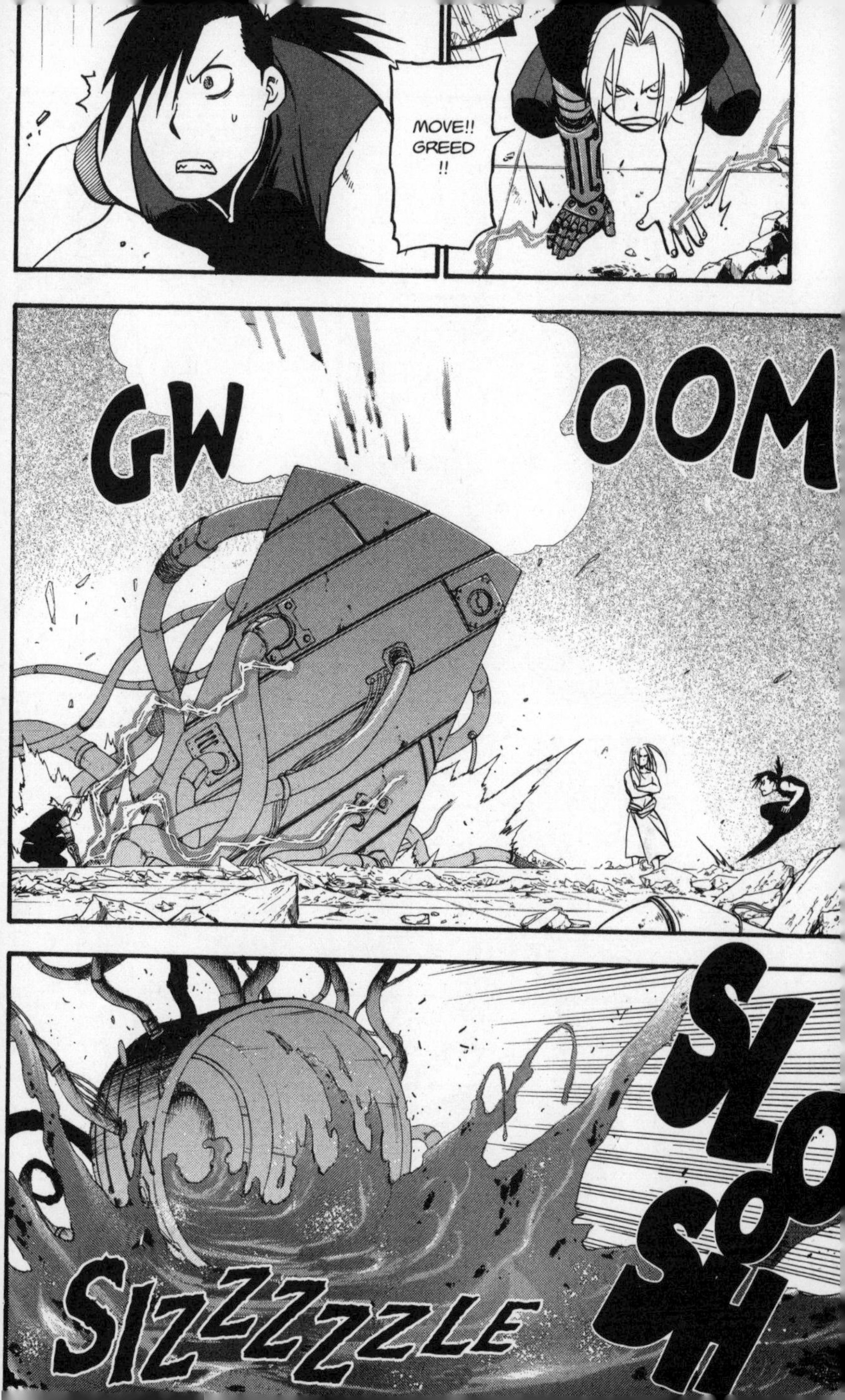
MOVE!! GREED !!
GW OOM
SLOSH
SIZZZZZLE

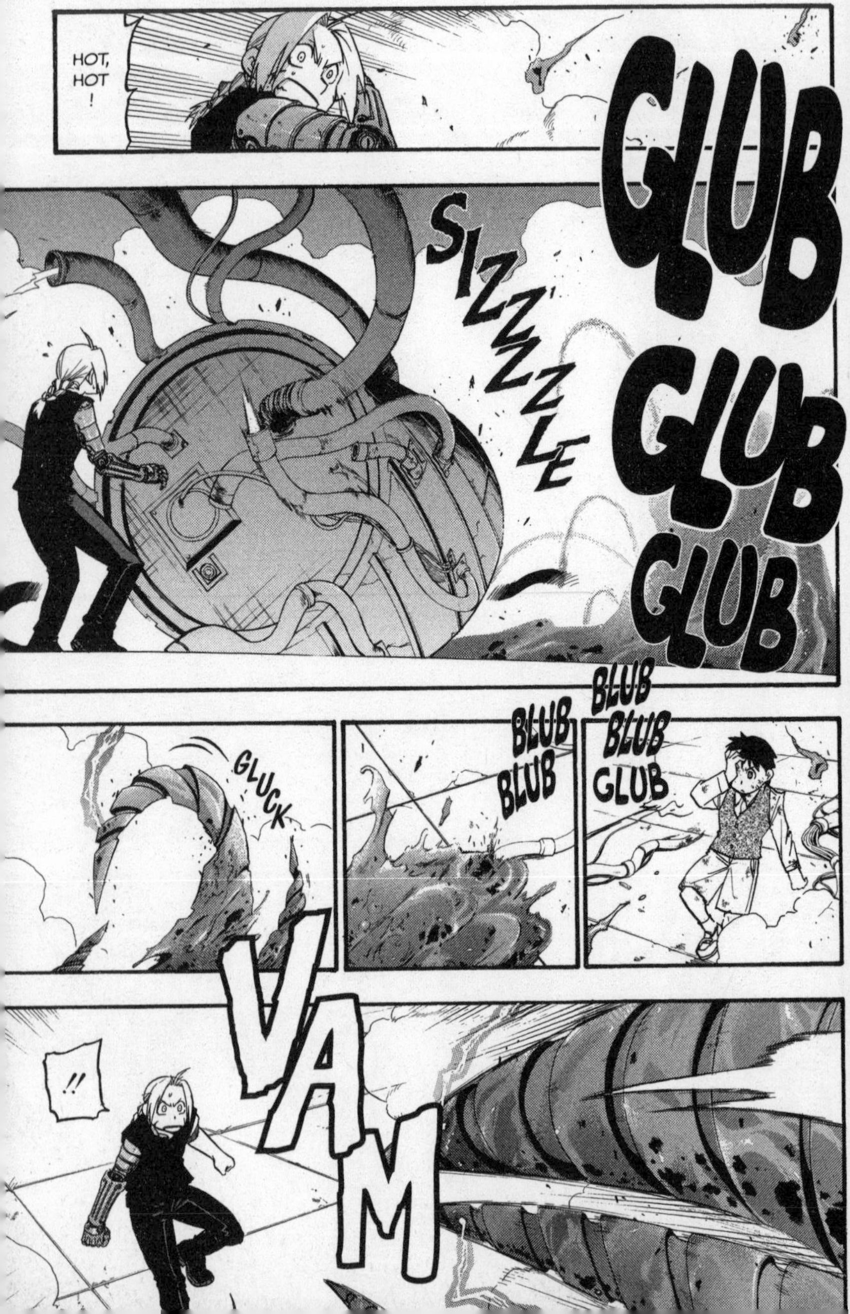

GLUB GLUB GLUB
HOT, HOT!
SIZZZZZLE
BLUB BLUB GLUB
BLUB BLUB
GLUCK
VAM
!!

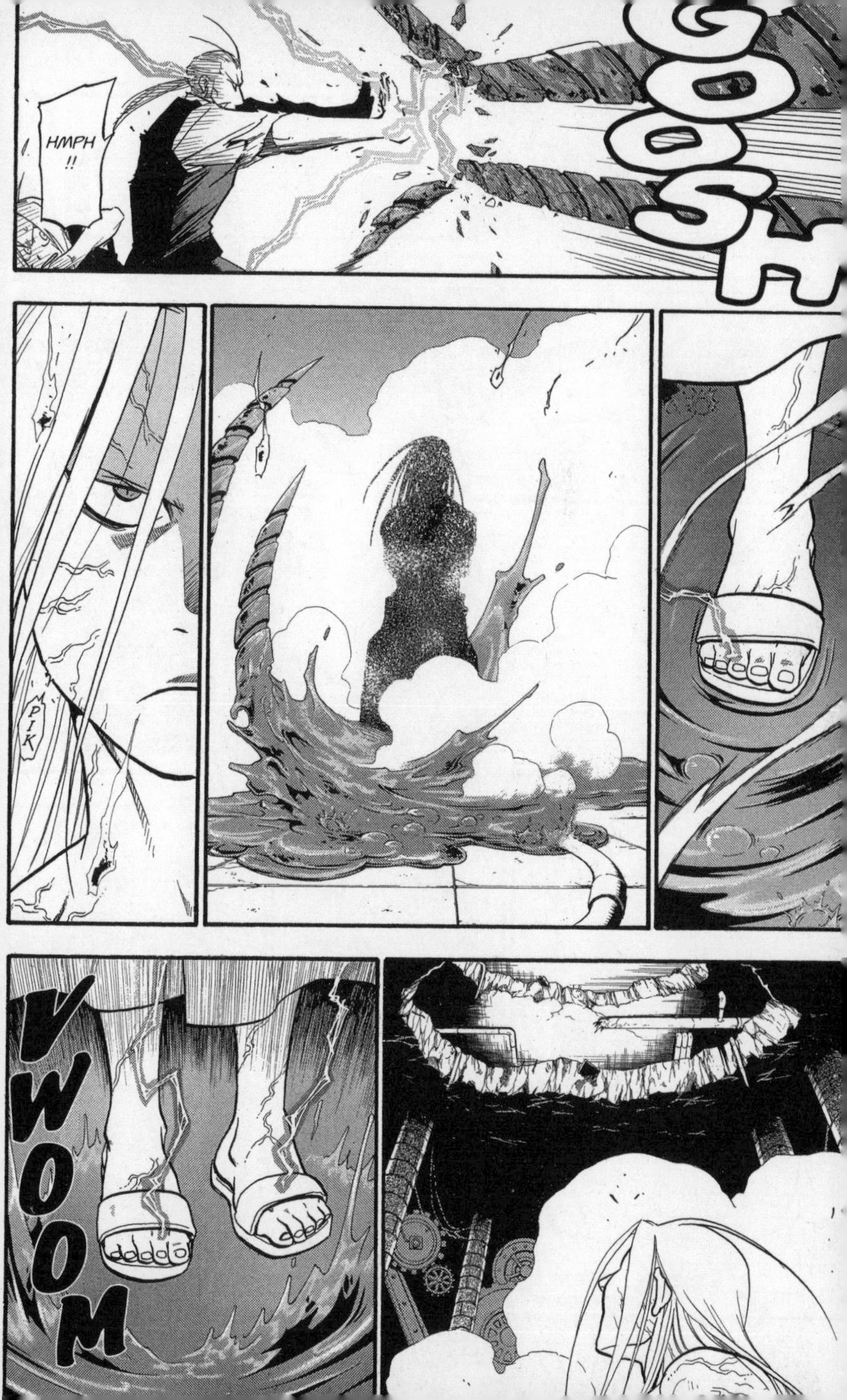
GOOSH
HMPH !!
PIK
VWOOM

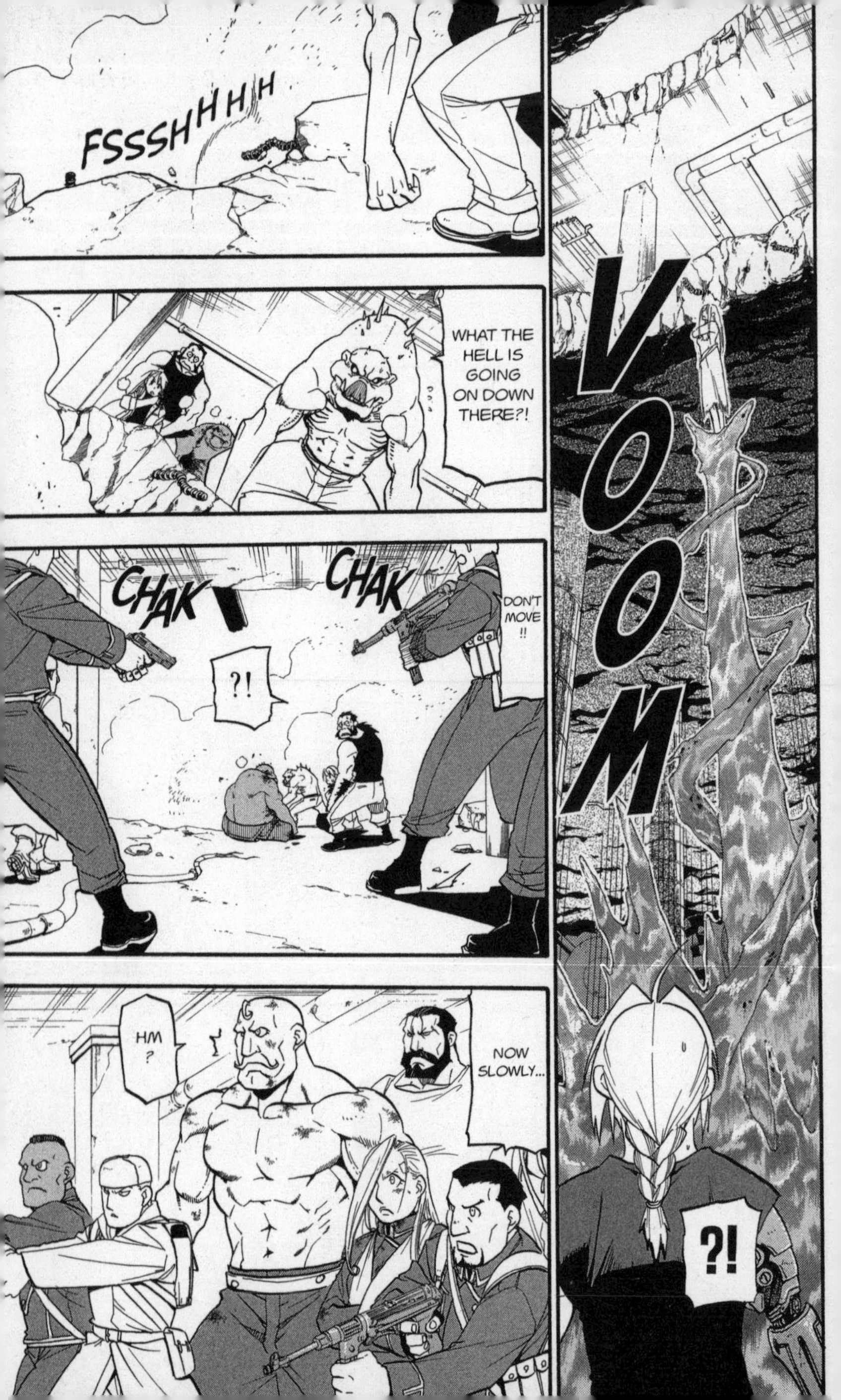
VOOOM
?!
FSSSHHHHH
WHAT THE HELL IS GOING ON DOWN THERE?!
DON'T MOVE!!
CHAK
CHAK
?!
NOW SLOWLY...
HM ?

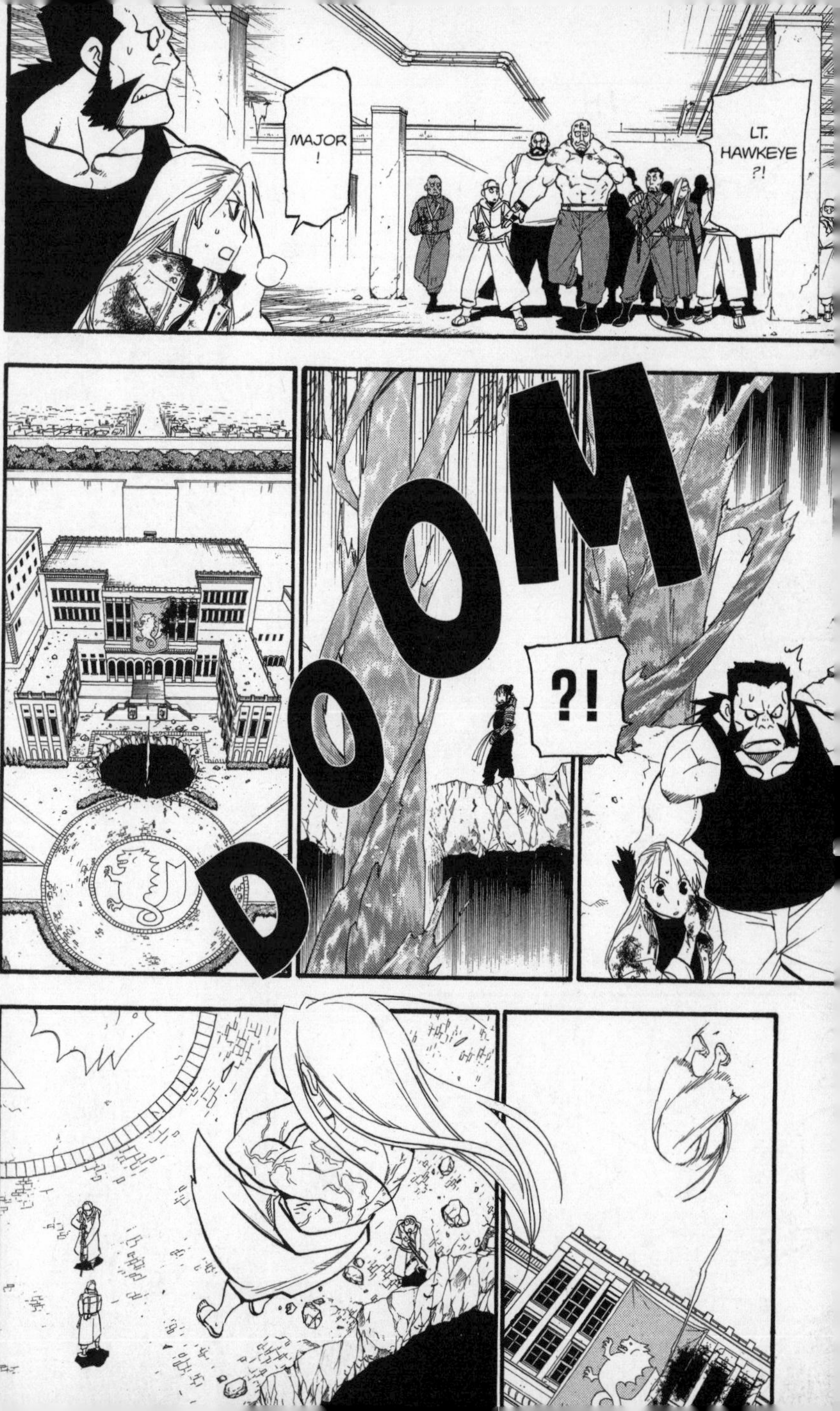
LT. HAWKEYE ?!
MAJOR !
DOOM
?!

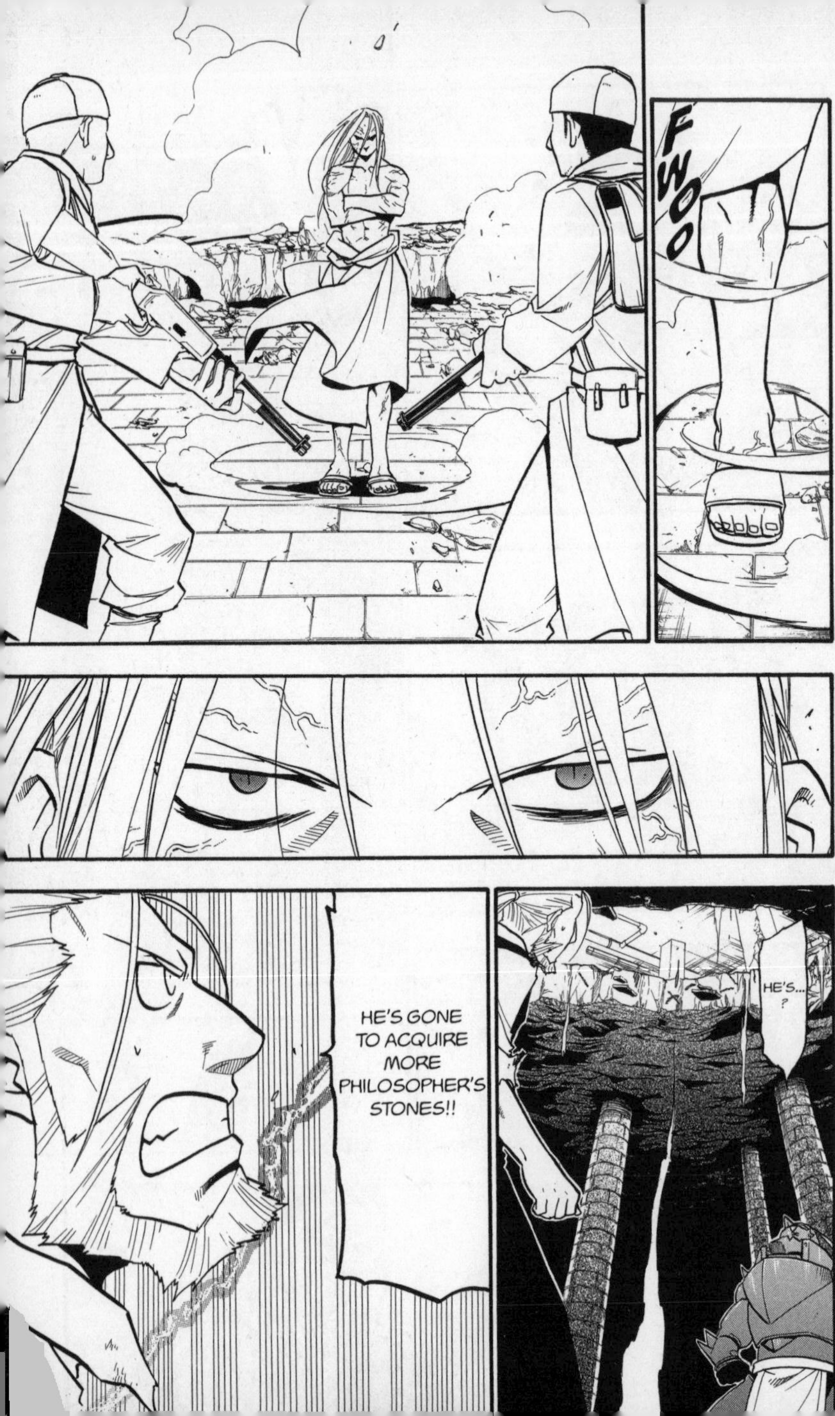
FWOO
HE'S...?
HE'S GONE TO ACQUIRE MORE PHILOSOPHER'S STONES!!

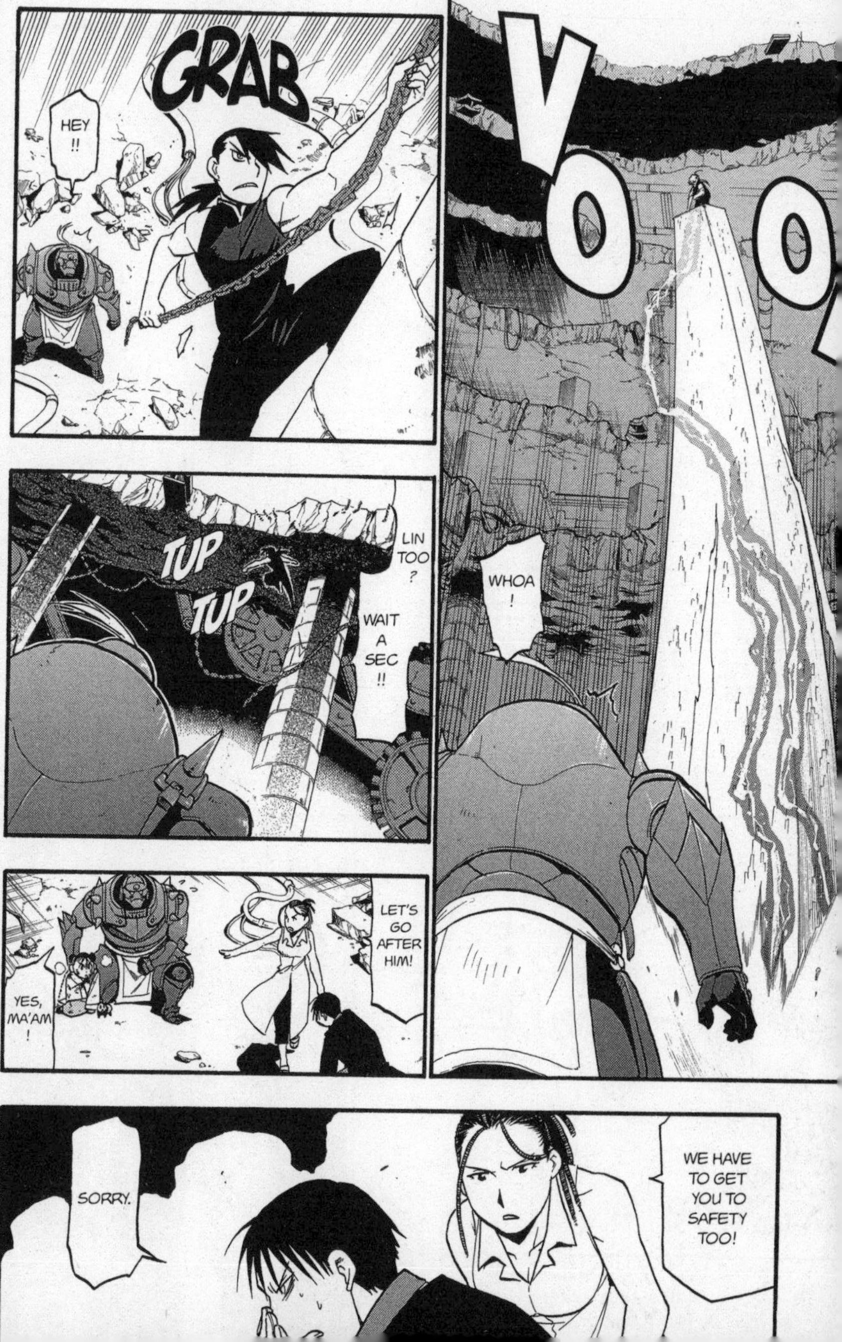
VOO
WHOA!
GRAB
HEY!!
LIN TOO?
TUP
TUP
WAIT A SEC!!
LET'S GO AFTER HIM!
YES, MA'AM!
WE HAVE TO GET YOU TO SAFETY TOO!
SORRY.

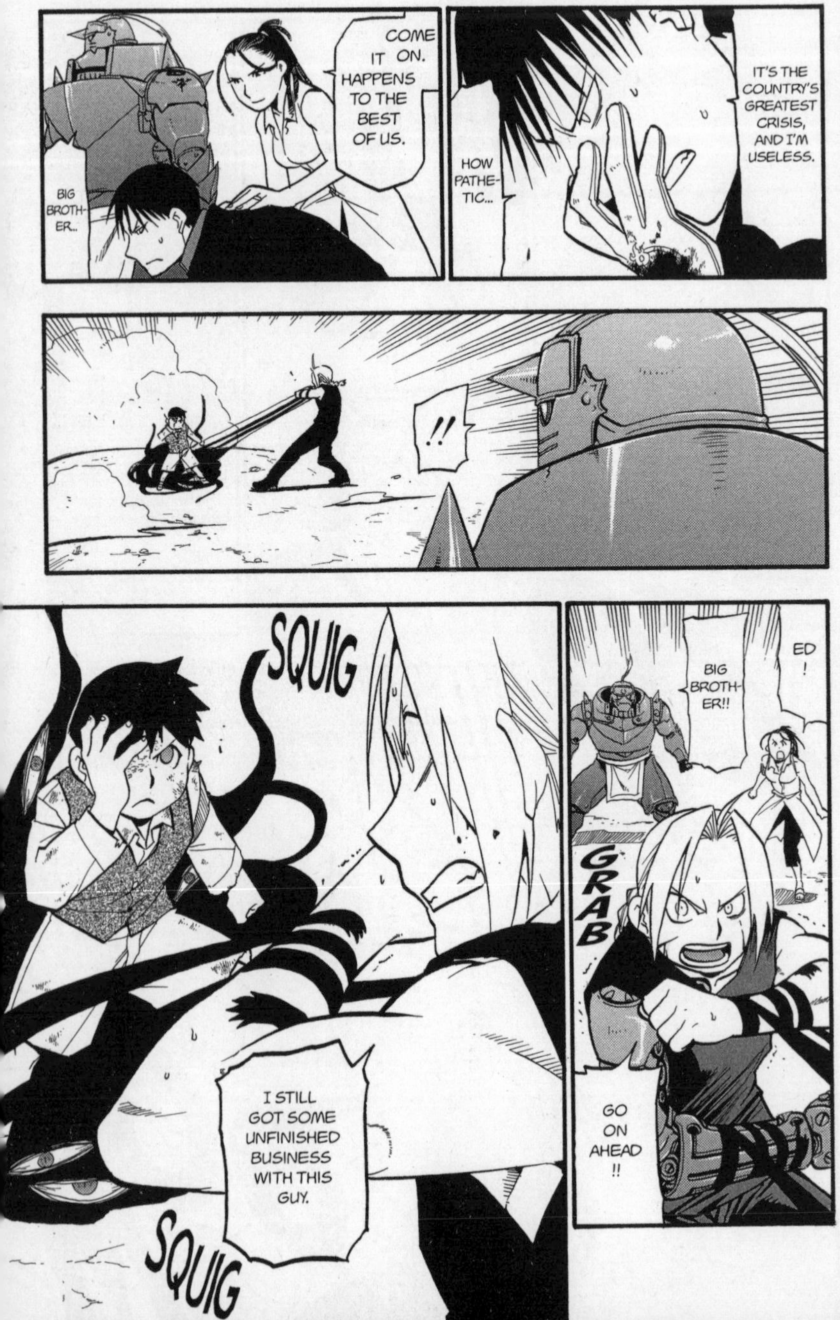
IT'S THE COUNTRY'S GREATEST CRISIS, AND I'M USELESS.
HOW PATHETIC...
COME ON. IT HAPPENS TO THE BEST OF US.
BIG BROTHER...
!!
ED!
BIG BROTHER!!
GRAB
GO ON AHEAD!!
SQUIG
I STILL GOT SOME UNFINISHED BUSINESS WITH THIS GUY.
SQUIG

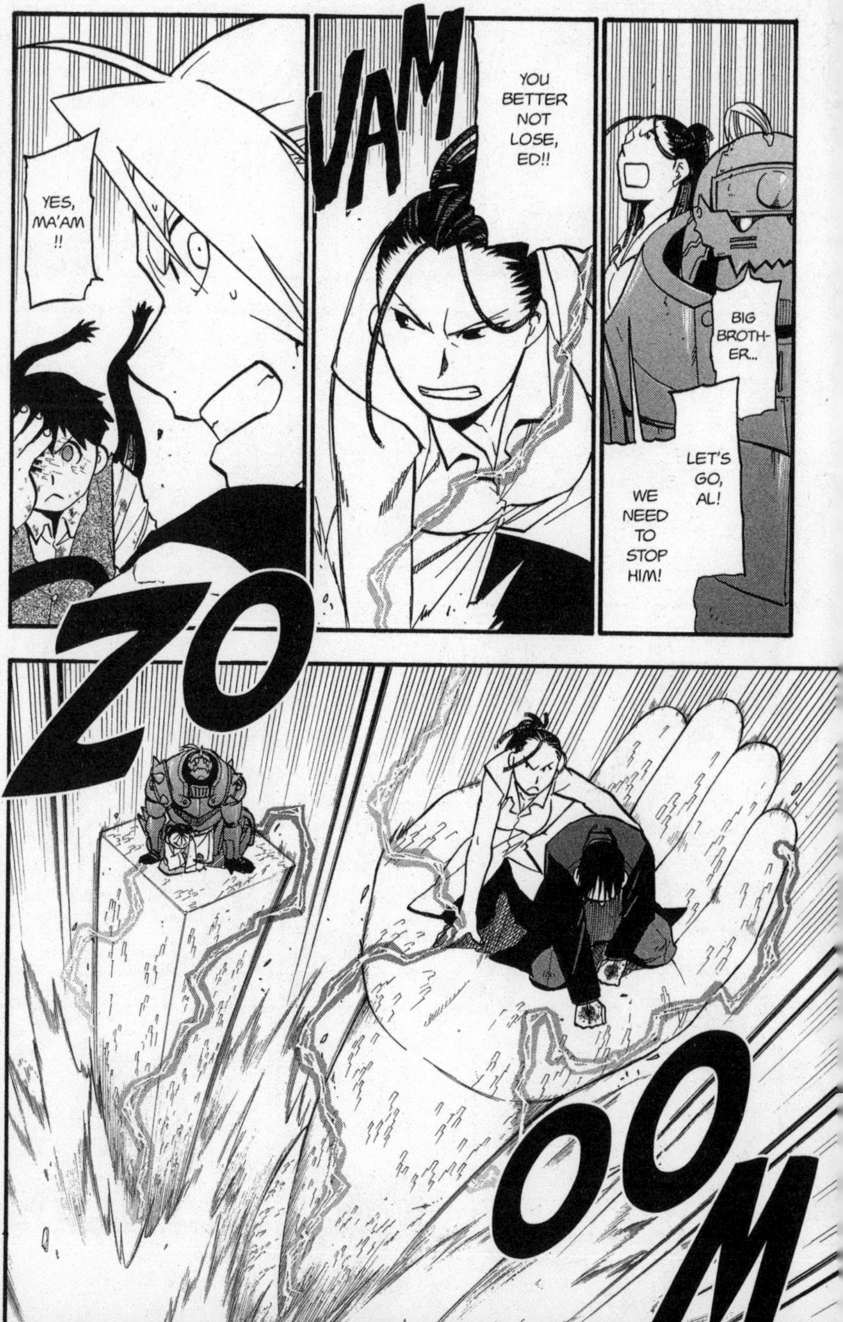
BIG BROTHER...
LET'S GO, AL!
WE NEED TO STOP HIM!
VAM
YOU BETTER NOT LOSE, ED!!
YES, MA'AM!!
ZO
OOM

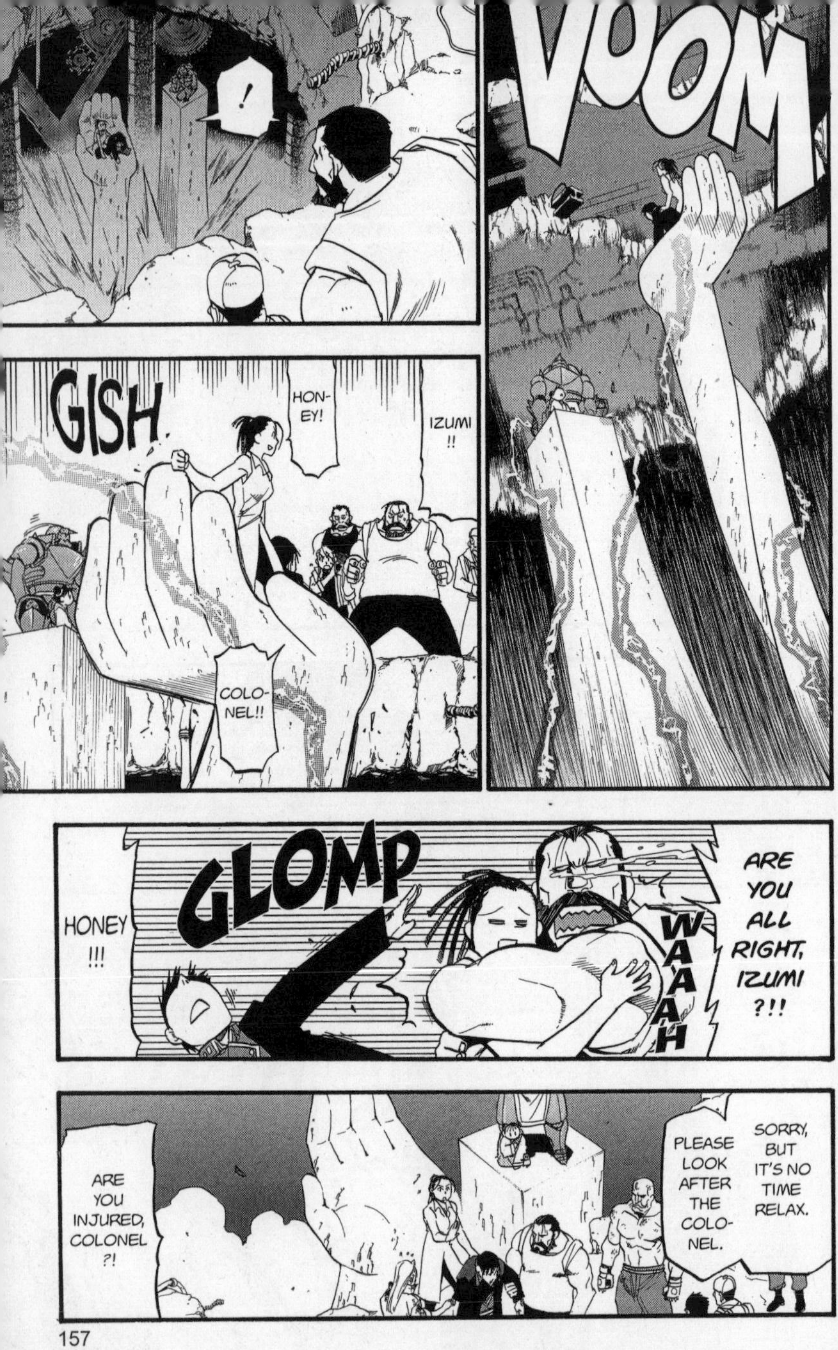
VOOM
!
IZUMI !!
HONEY!
GISH
COLONEL!!
ARE YOU ALL RIGHT, IZUMI ?!!
WAAAH
GLOMP
HONEY !!!
SORRY, BUT IT'S NO TIME RELAX.
PLEASE LOOK AFTER THE COLONEL.
ARE YOU INJURED, COLONEL ?!

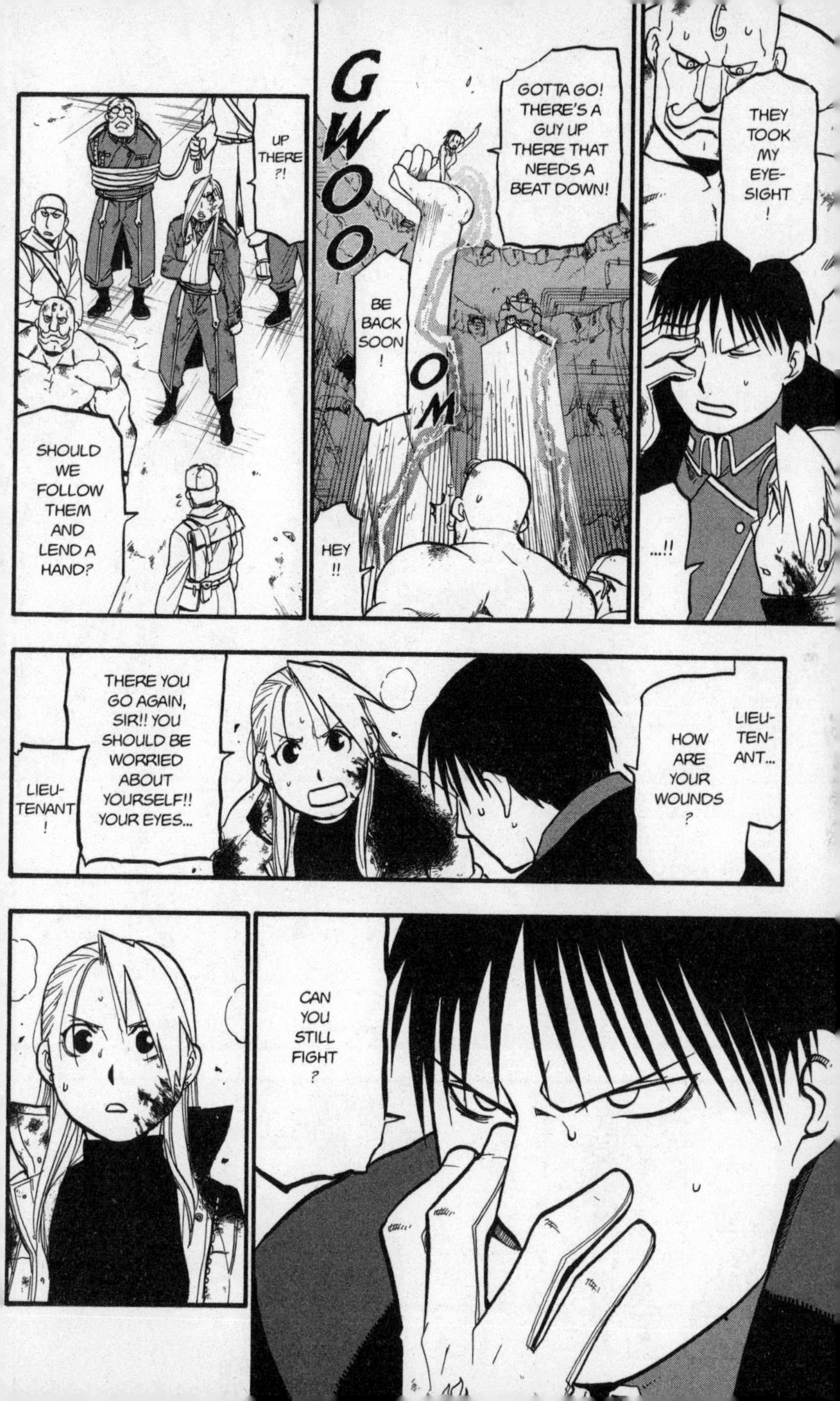
THEY TOOK MY EYE-SIGHT!
...!!
GWOOOM
GOTTA GO! THERE'S A GUY UP THERE THAT NEEDS A BEAT DOWN!
BE BACK SOON!
HEY!!
UP THERE?!
SHOULD WE FOLLOW THEM AND LEND A HAND?
LIEU-TENANT...
HOW ARE YOUR WOUNDS?
THERE YOU GO AGAIN, SIR!! YOU SHOULD BE WORRIED ABOUT YOURSELF!! YOUR EYES...
LIEU-TENANT!
CAN YOU STILL FIGHT?

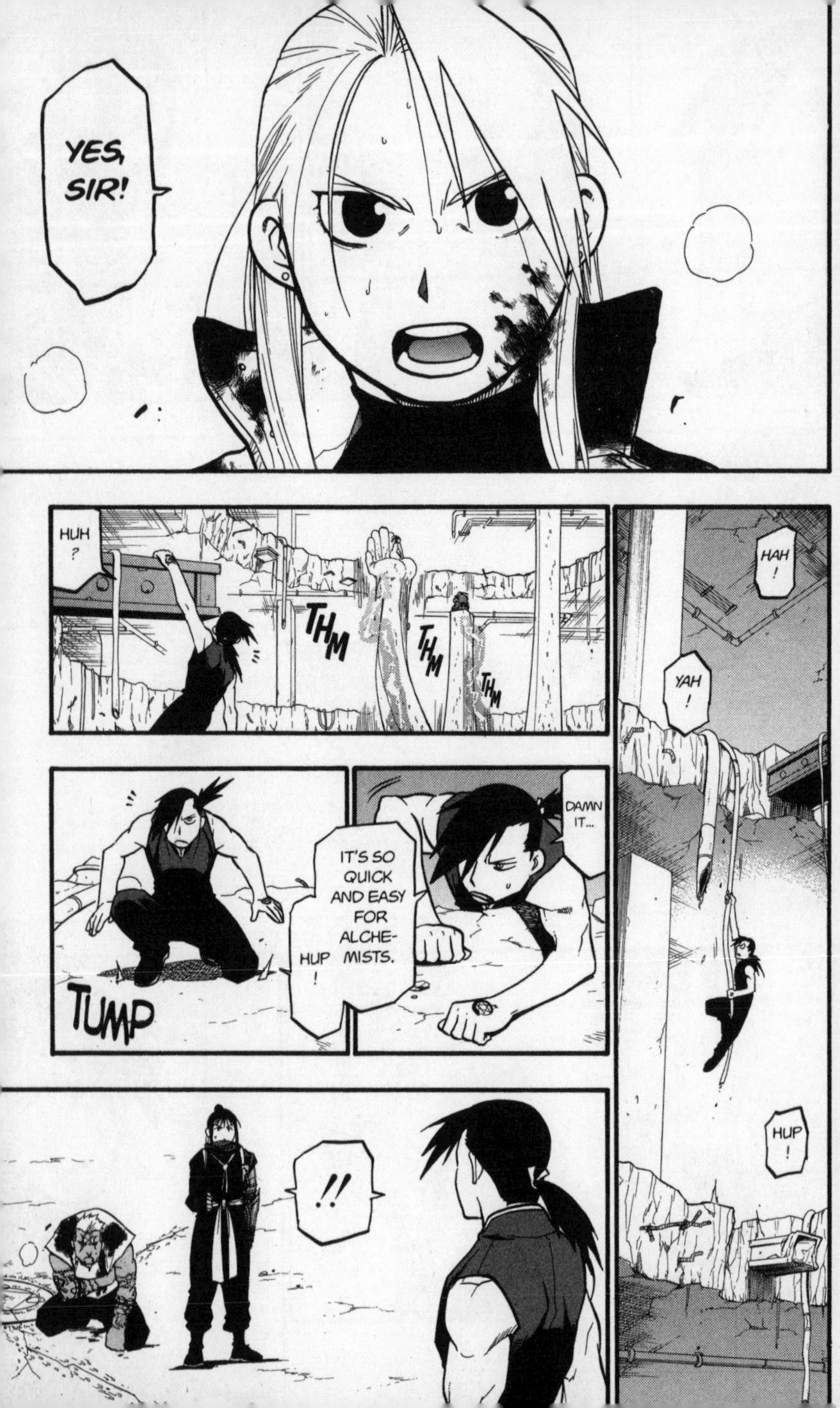
YES, SIR!
HAH!
YAH!
HUP!
HUH?
THM
THM
THM
DAMN IT...
IT'S SO QUICK AND EASY FOR ALCHEMISTS.
HUP!
TUMP
!!

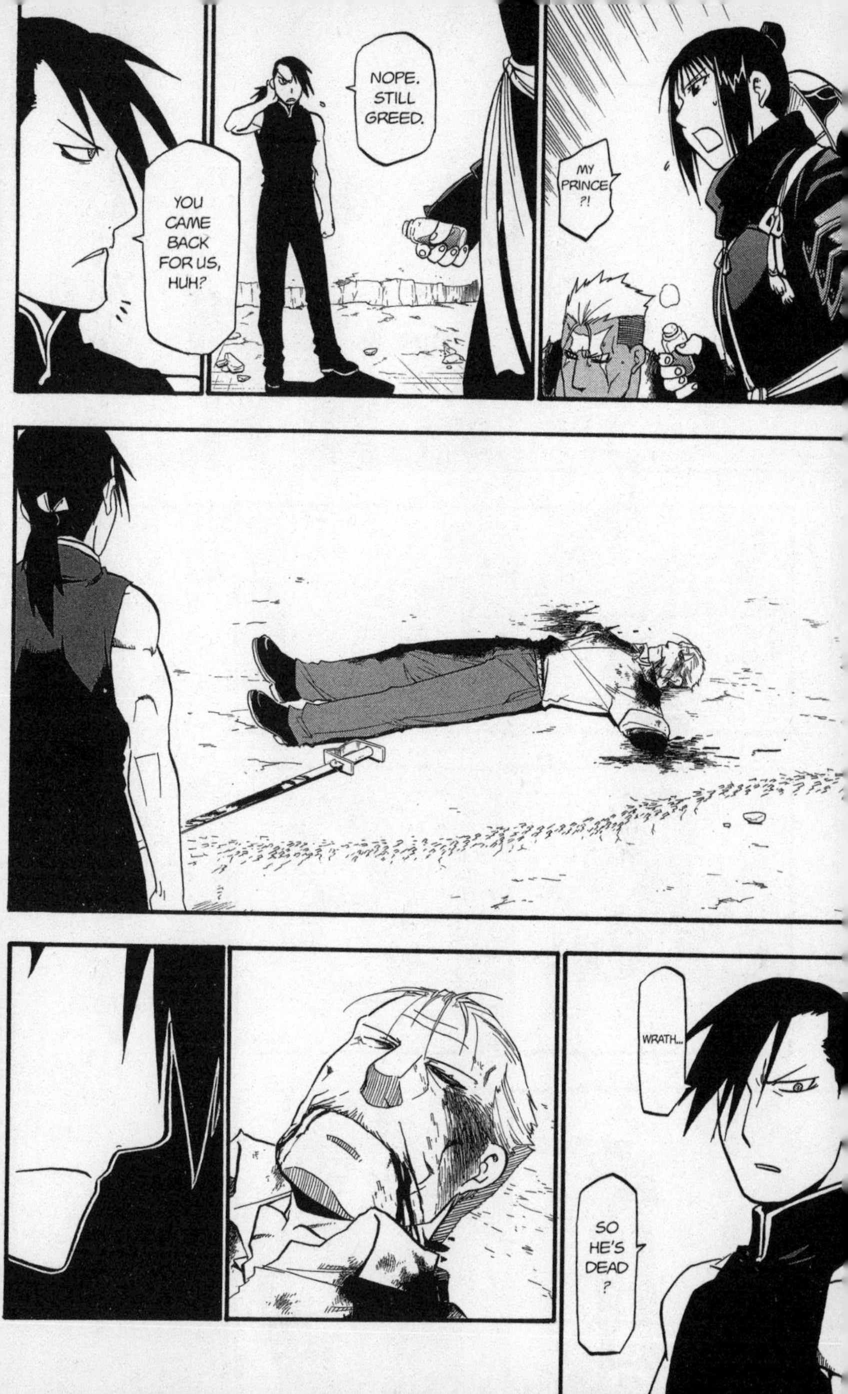
MY PRINCE?!
NOPE. STILL GREED.
YOU CAME BACK FOR US, HUH?
WRATH...
SO HE'S DEAD?

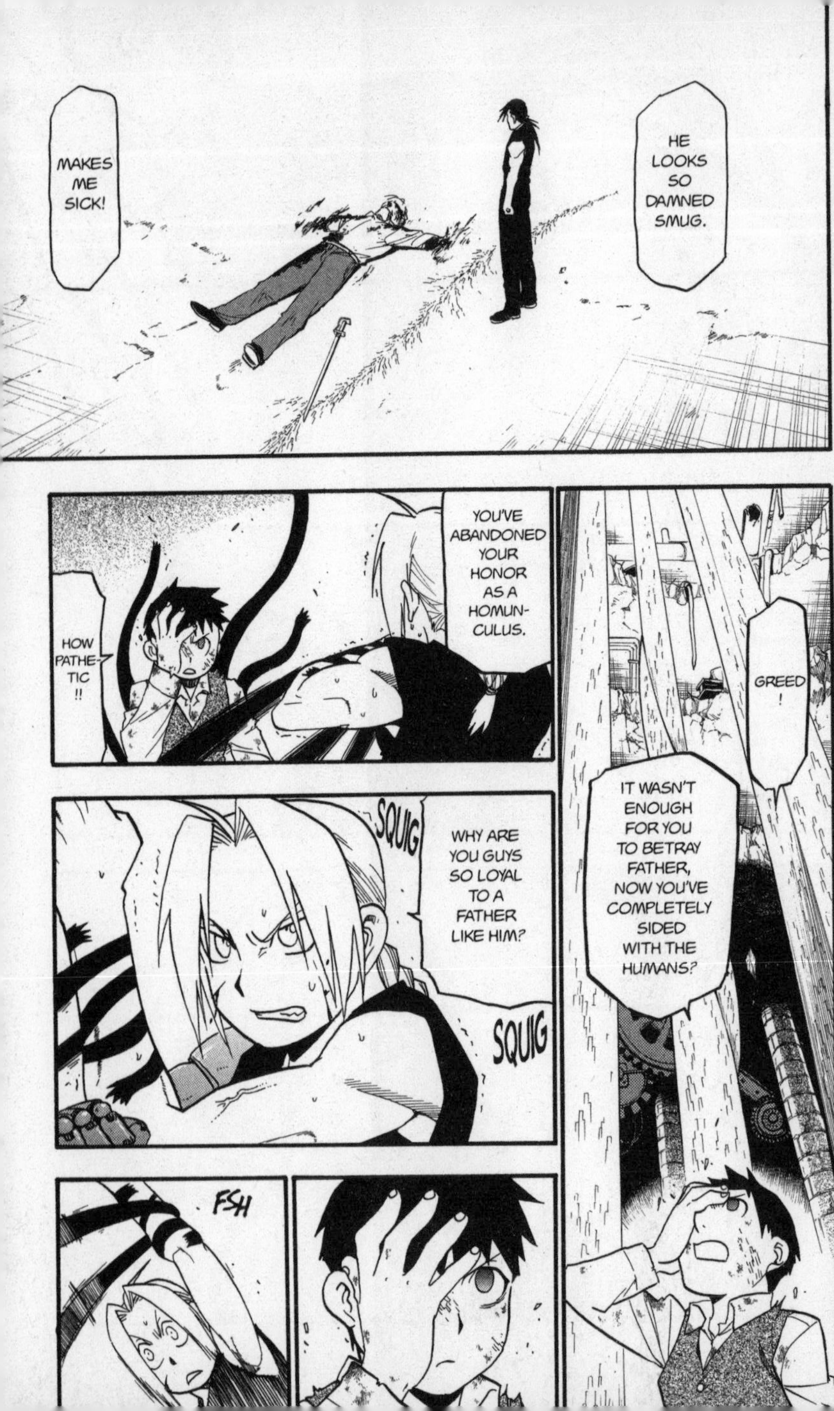
HE LOOKS SO DAMNED SMUG.
MAKES ME SICK!
GREED!
IT WASN'T ENOUGH FOR YOU TO BETRAY FATHER, NOW YOU'VE COMPLETELY SIDED WITH THE HUMANS?
YOU'VE ABANDONED YOUR HONOR AS A HOMUN-CULUS.
HOW PATHE-TIC!!
SQUIG
WHY ARE YOU GUYS SO LOYAL TO A FATHER LIKE HIM?
SQUIG
FSH

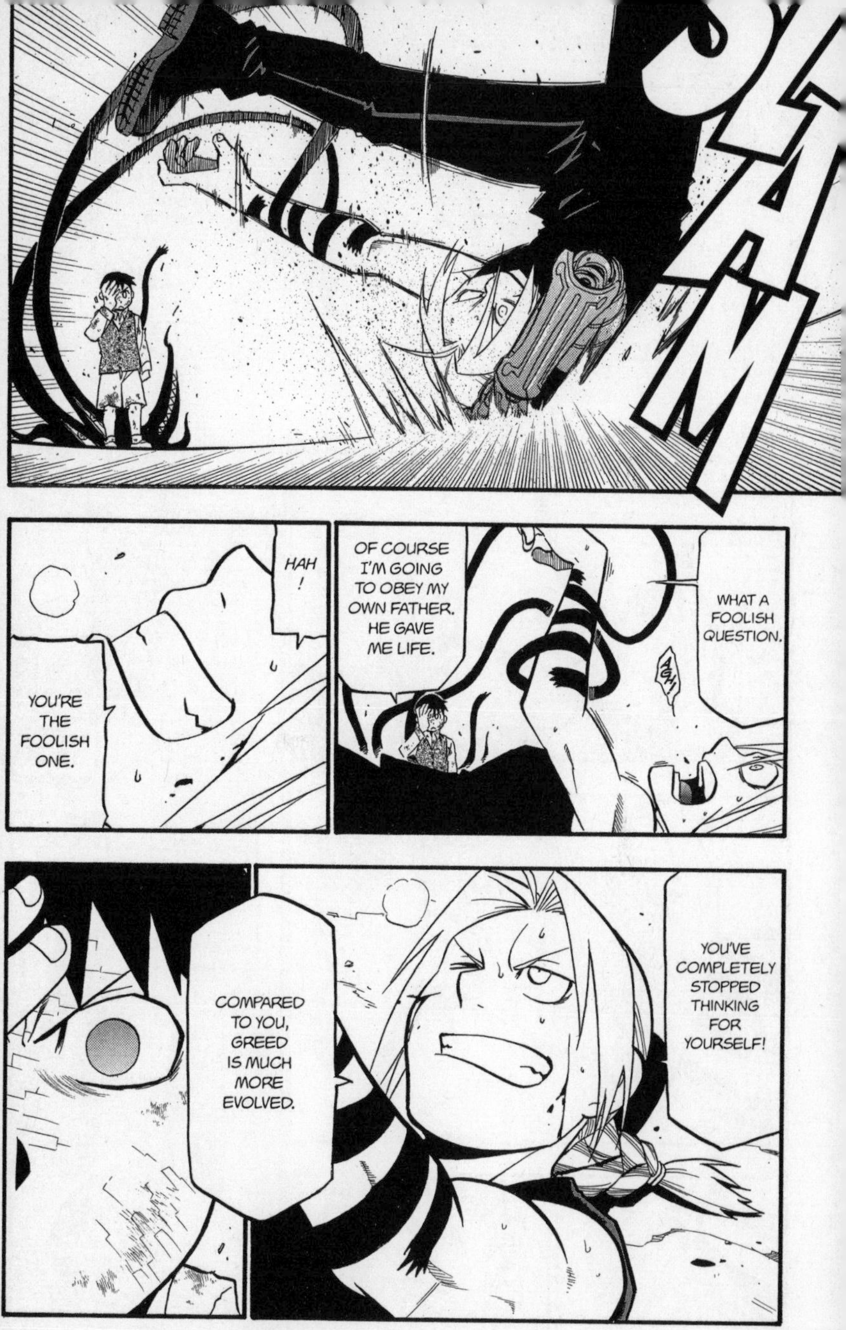
SLAM
WHAT A FOOLISH QUESTION.
AGH!
OF COURSE I'M GOING TO OBEY MY OWN FATHER. HE GAVE ME LIFE.
HAH!
YOU'RE THE FOOLISH ONE.
YOU'VE COMPLETELY STOPPED THINKING FOR YOURSELF!
COMPARED TO YOU, GREED IS MUCH MORE EVOLVED.

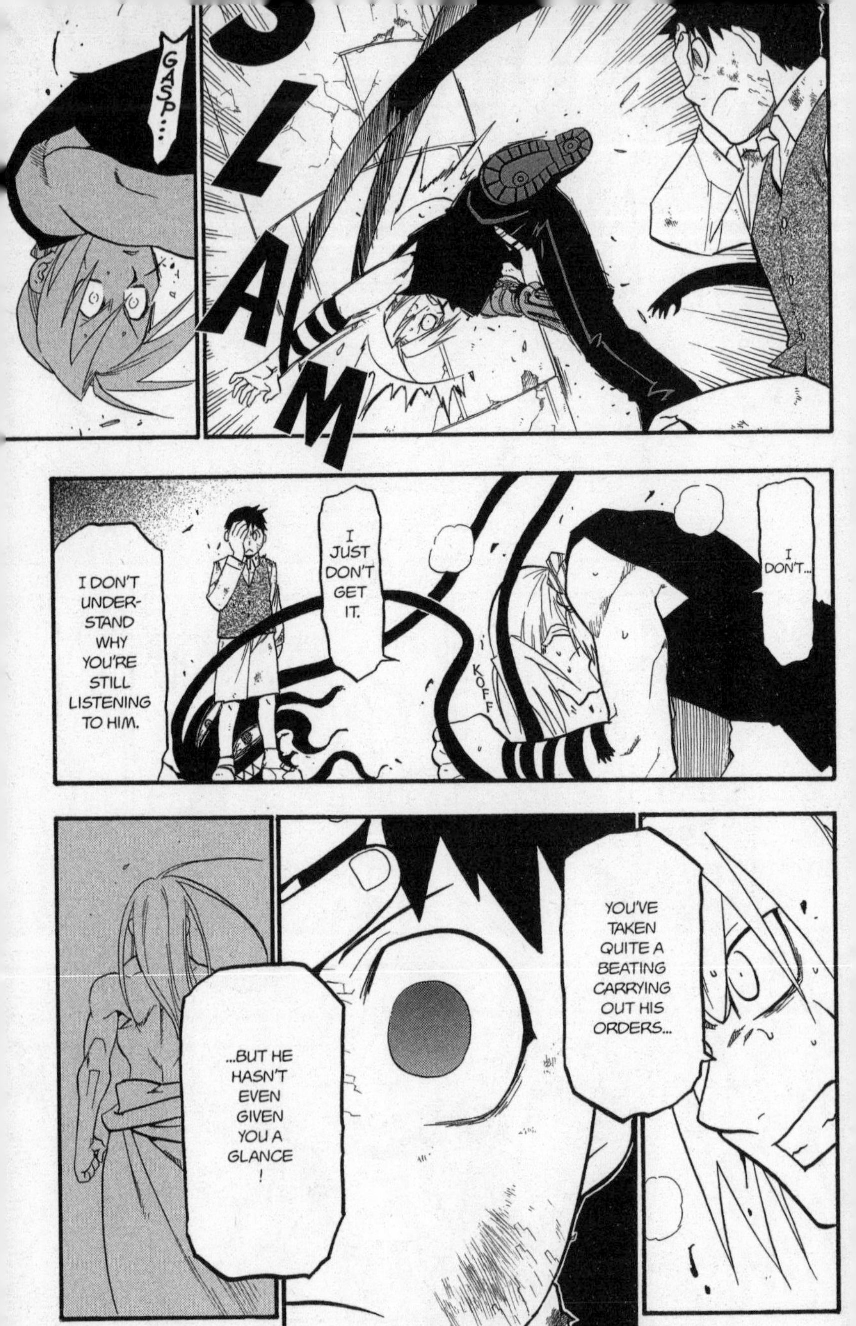
SLAM
GASP...
I DON'T...
I JUST DON'T GET IT.
KOFF
I DON'T UNDERSTAND WHY YOU'RE STILL LISTENING TO HIM.
YOU'VE TAKEN QUITE A BEATING CARRYING OUT HIS ORDERS...
...BUT HE HASN'T EVEN GIVEN YOU A GLANCE!

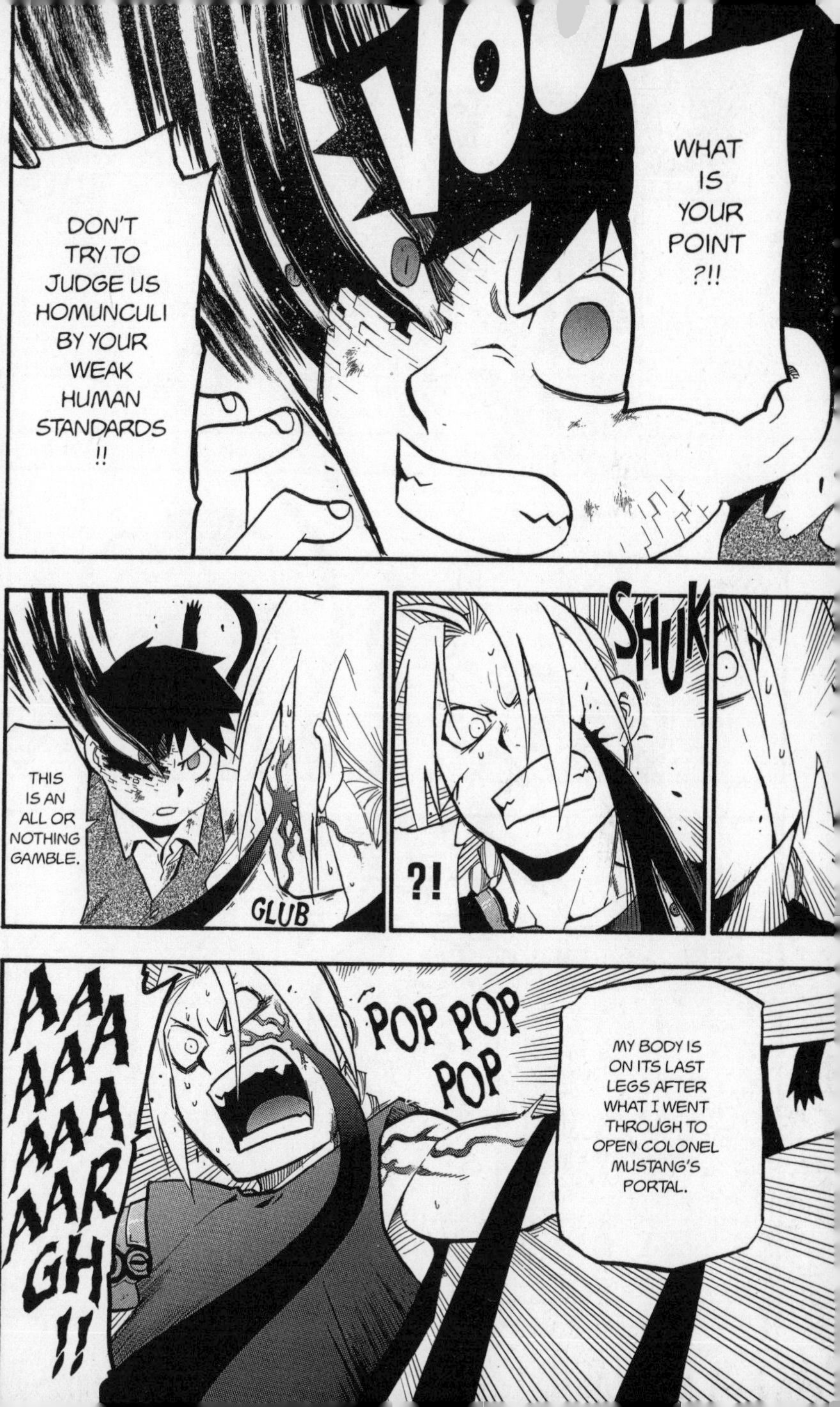
WHAT IS YOUR POINT ?!!
DON'T TRY TO JUDGE US HOMUNCULI BY YOUR WEAK HUMAN STANDARDS !!
SHUK
?!
THIS IS AN ALL OR NOTHING GAMBLE.
GLUB
MY BODY IS ON ITS LAST LEGS AFTER WHAT I WENT THROUGH TO OPEN COLONEL MUSTANG'S PORTAL.
POP POP POP
AAAAAAAAAAARGH !!

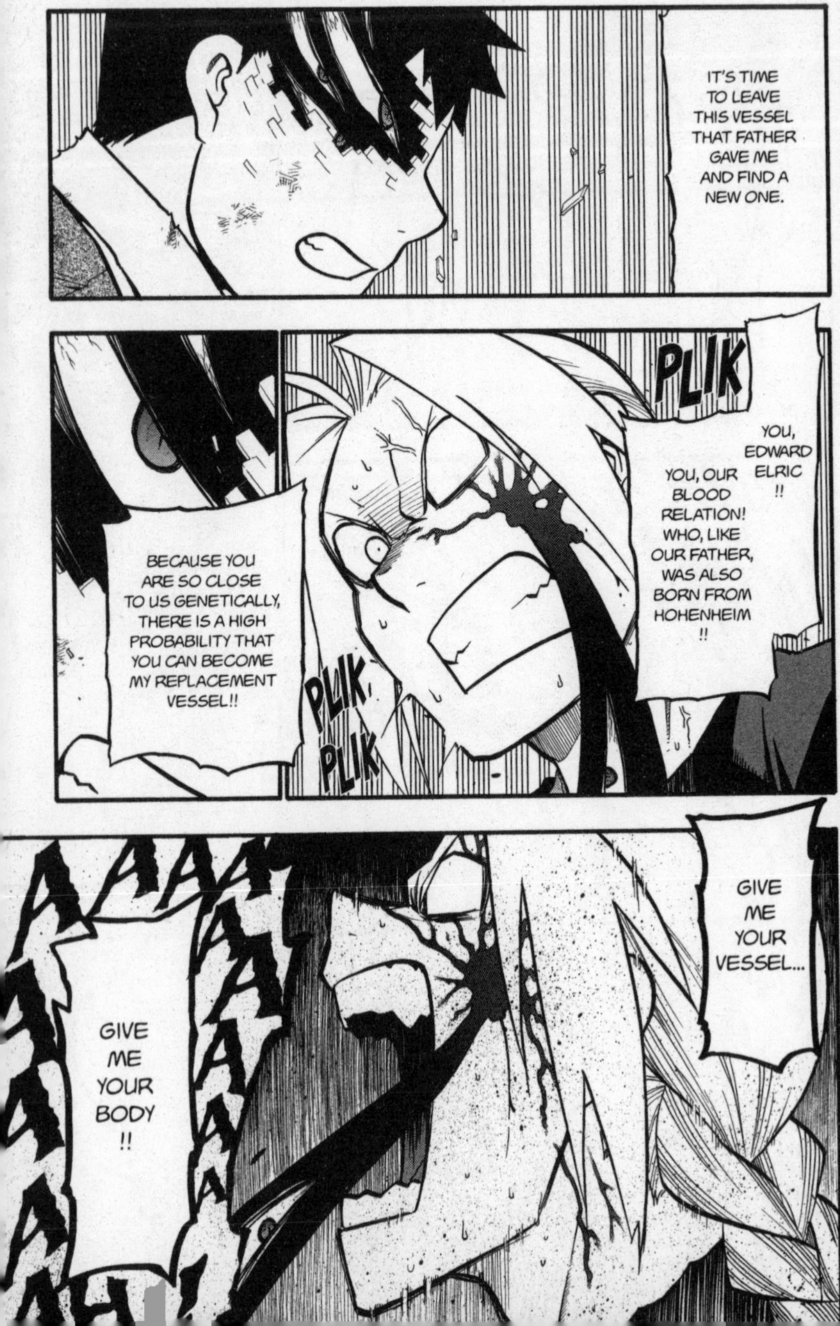
IT'S TIME TO LEAVE THIS VESSEL THAT FATHER GAVE ME AND FIND A NEW ONE.
PLIK
YOU, EDWARD ELRIC !!
YOU, OUR BLOOD RELATION! WHO, LIKE OUR FATHER, WAS ALSO BORN FROM HOHENHEIM !!
PLIK PLIK
BECAUSE YOU ARE SO CLOSE TO US GENETICALLY, THERE IS A HIGH PROBABILITY THAT YOU CAN BECOME MY REPLACEMENT VESSEL!!
GIVE ME YOUR VESSEL...
GIVE ME YOUR BODY !!

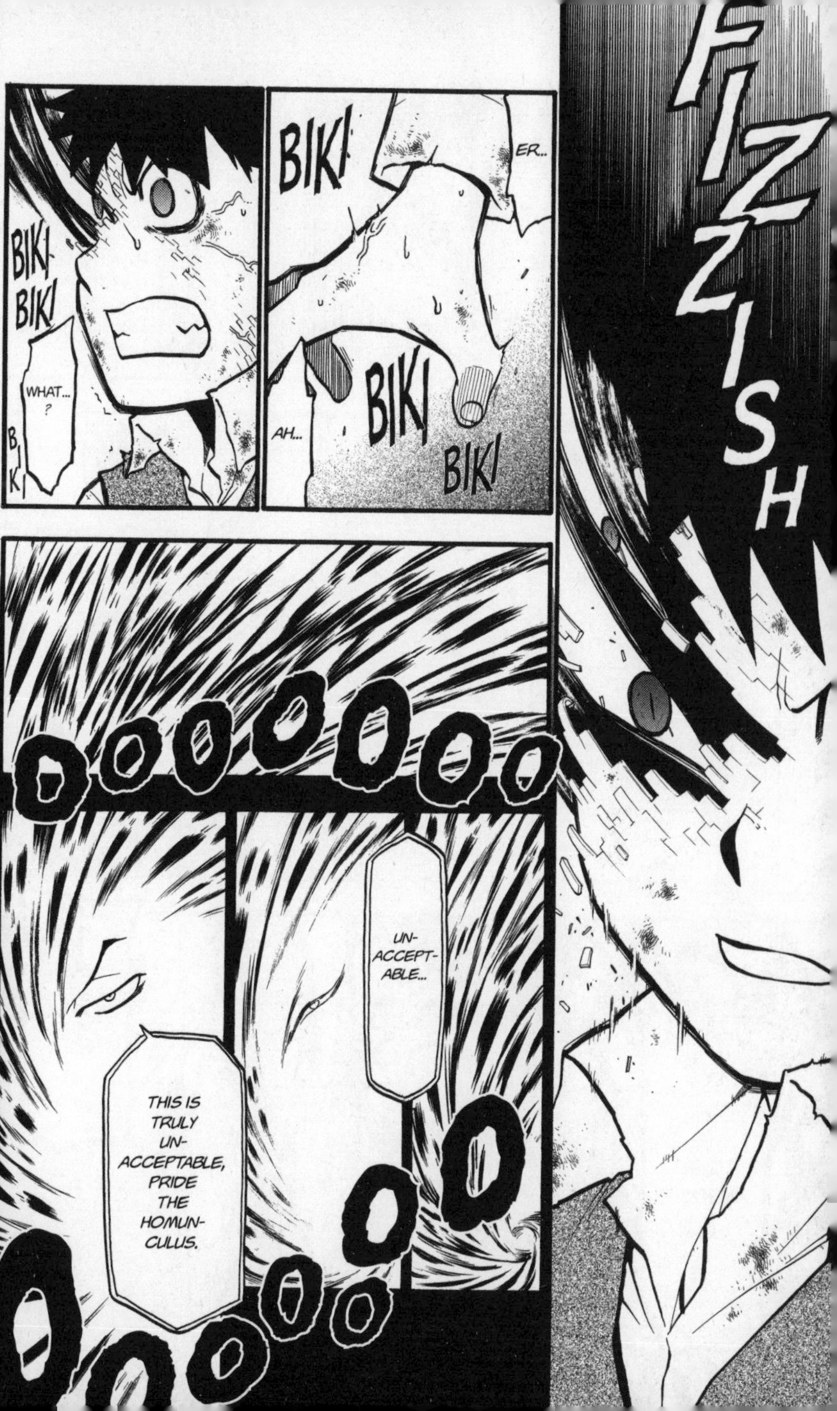
FIZZISH
BIKI
ER...
BIKI
BIKI
AH...
BIKI BIKI
WHAT...?
BIKI
UN-ACCEPTABLE...
THIS IS TRULY UNACCEPTABLE, PRIDE THE HOMUNCULUS.

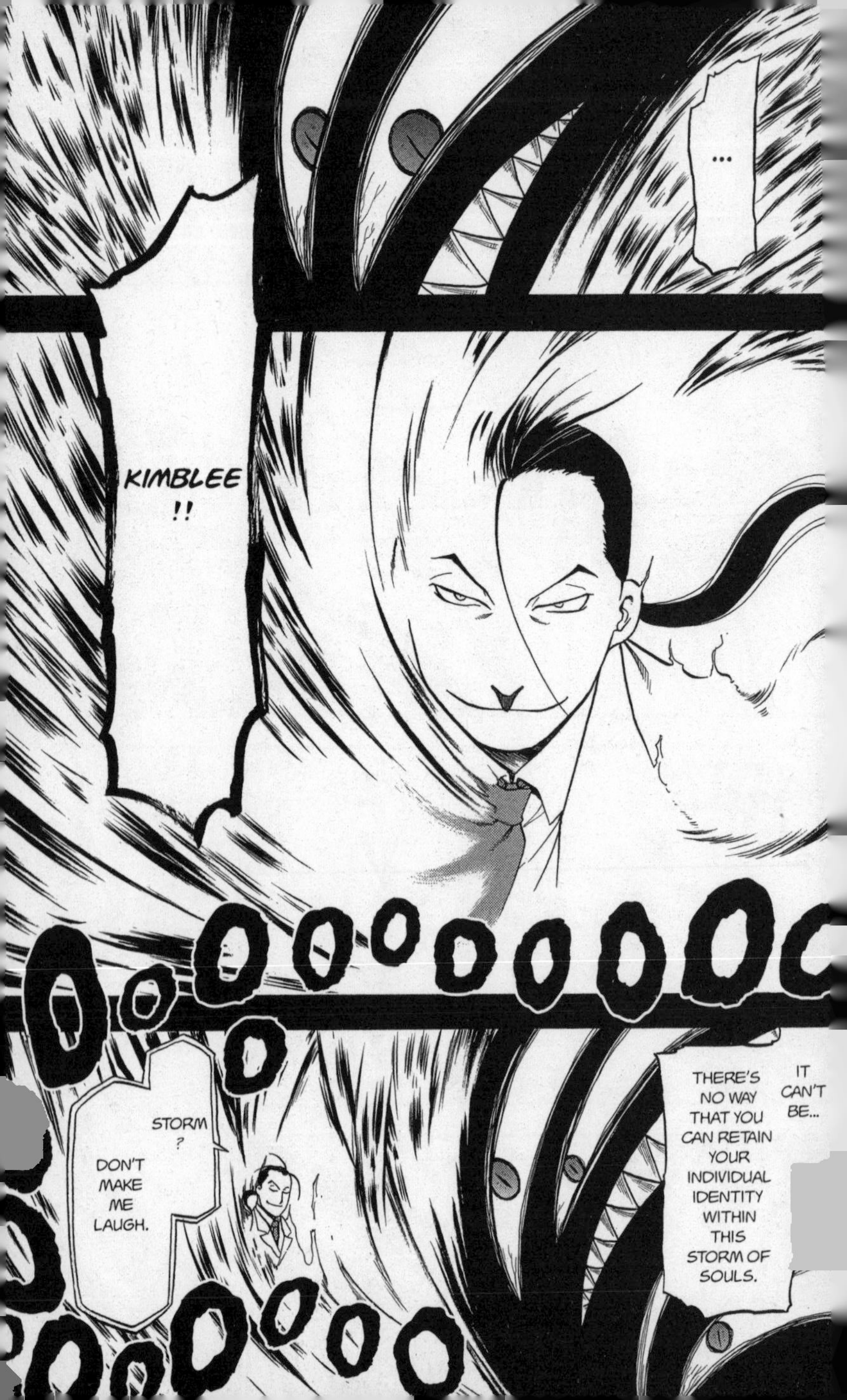
...
KIMBLEE!!
IT CAN'T BE...
THERE'S NO WAY THAT YOU CAN RETAIN YOUR INDIVIDUAL IDENTITY WITHIN THIS STORM OF SOULS.
STORM?
DON'T MAKE ME LAUGH.

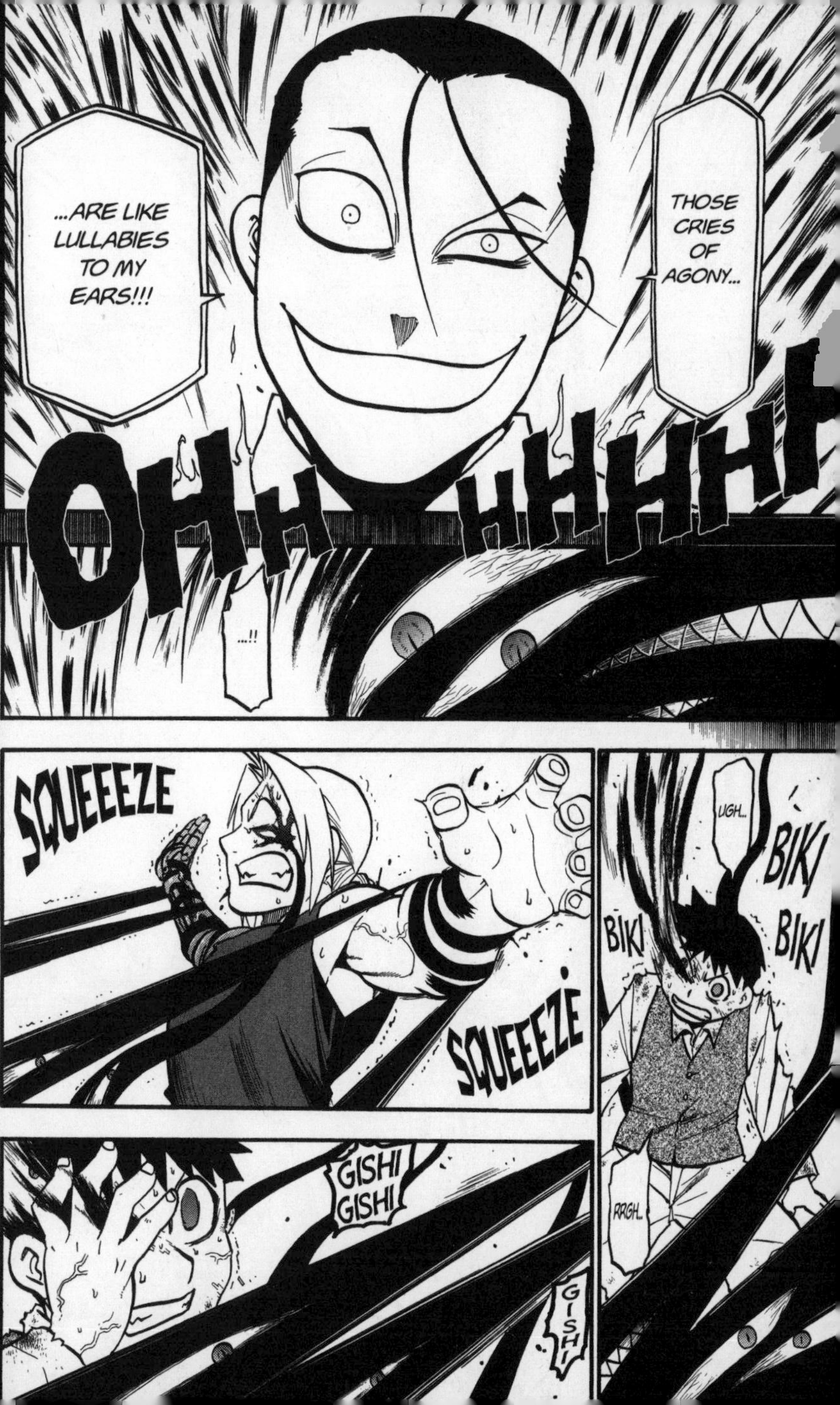
THOSE CRIES OF AGONY...
...ARE LIKE LULLABIES TO MY EARS!!!
OHH HHHHH
...!!
UGH..
BIKI
BIKI
BIKI
RRGH..
SQUEEEZE
SQUEEEZE
GISHI GISHI
GISHI

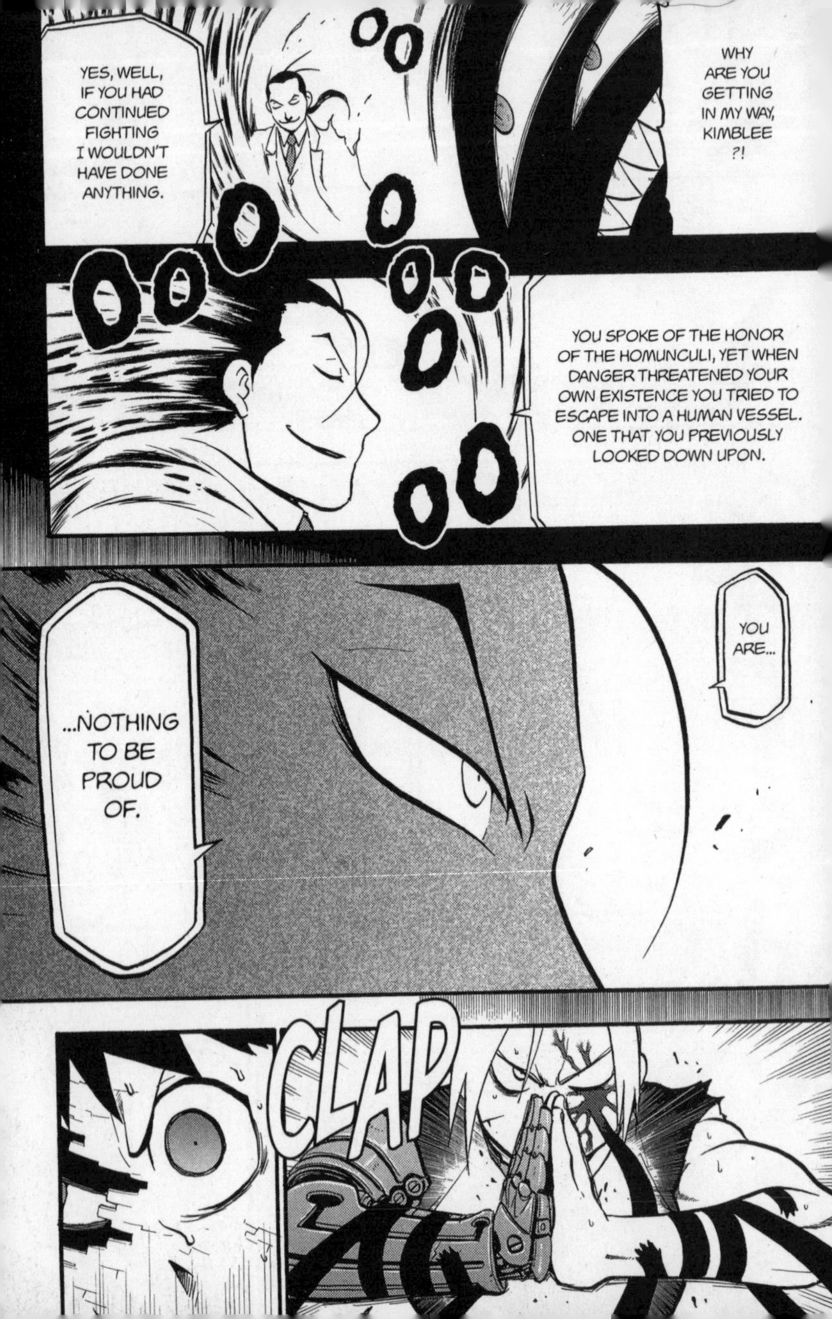
WHY ARE YOU GETTING IN MY WAY, KIMBLEE ?!
YES, WELL, IF YOU HAD CONTINUED FIGHTING I WOULDN'T HAVE DONE ANYTHING.
YOU SPOKE OF THE HONOR OF THE HOMUNCULI, YET WHEN DANGER THREATENED YOUR OWN EXISTENCE YOU TRIED TO ESCAPE INTO A HUMAN VESSEL. ONE THAT YOU PREVIOUSLY LOOKED DOWN UPON.
YOU ARE...
...NOTHING TO BE PROUD OF.
CLAP

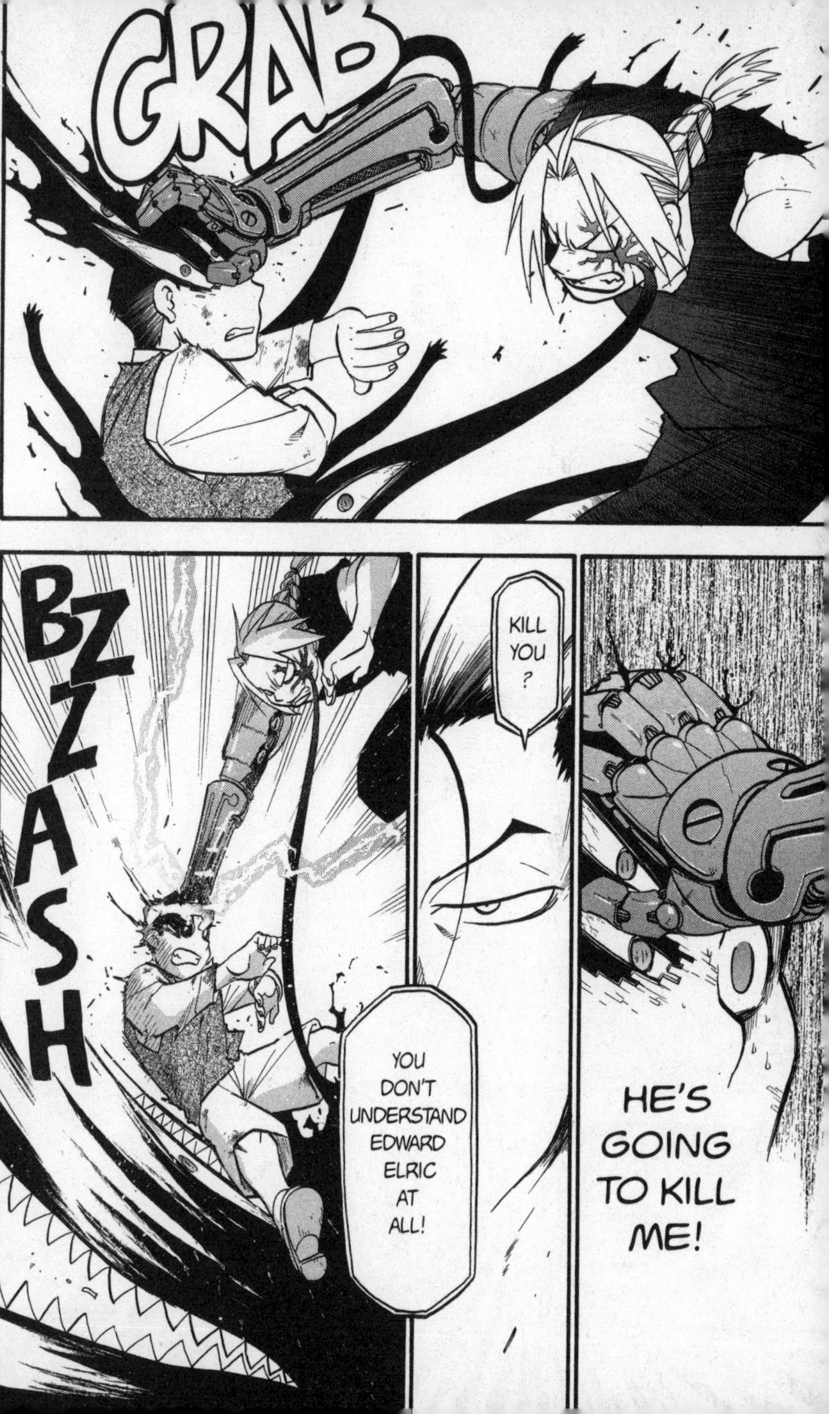
GRAB
HE'S GOING TO KILL ME!
KILL YOU ?
YOU DON'T UNDERSTAND EDWARD ELRIC AT ALL!
BZZASH

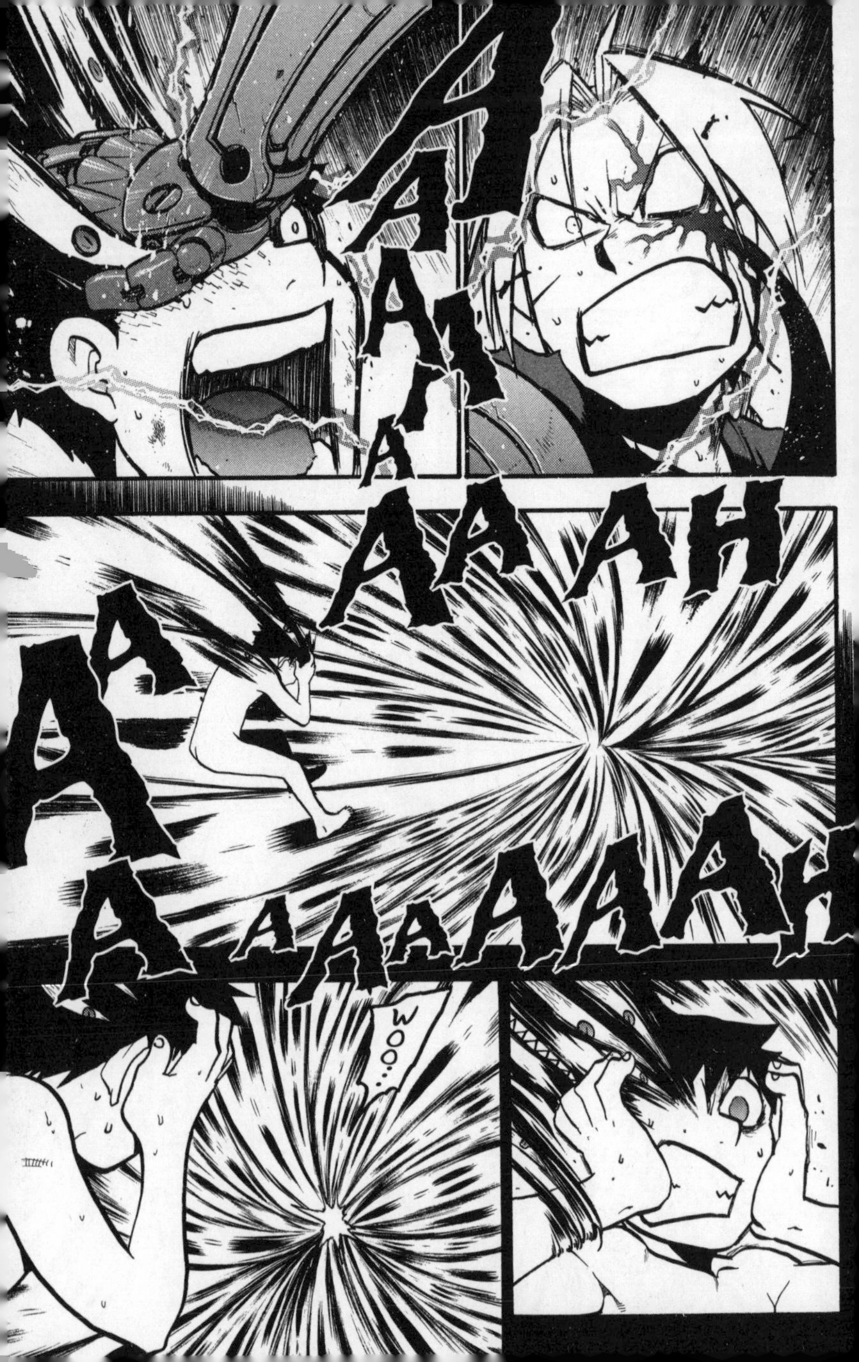
AAA
AAAH
AAAA
AAAAAAAH
WOO...

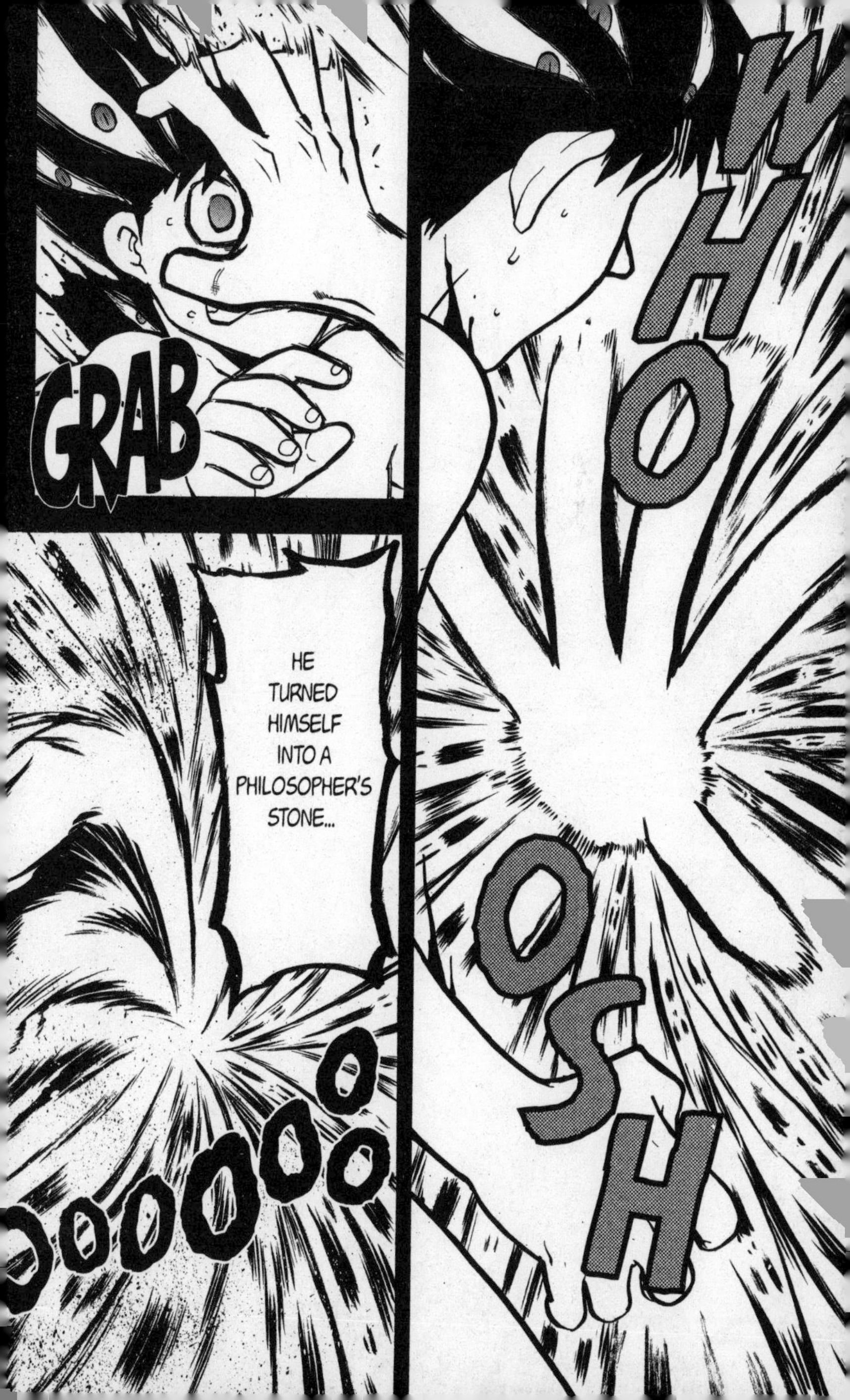
WHOOSH
GRAB
HE TURNED HIMSELF INTO A PHILOSOPHER'S STONE...
OOOOOOOOO

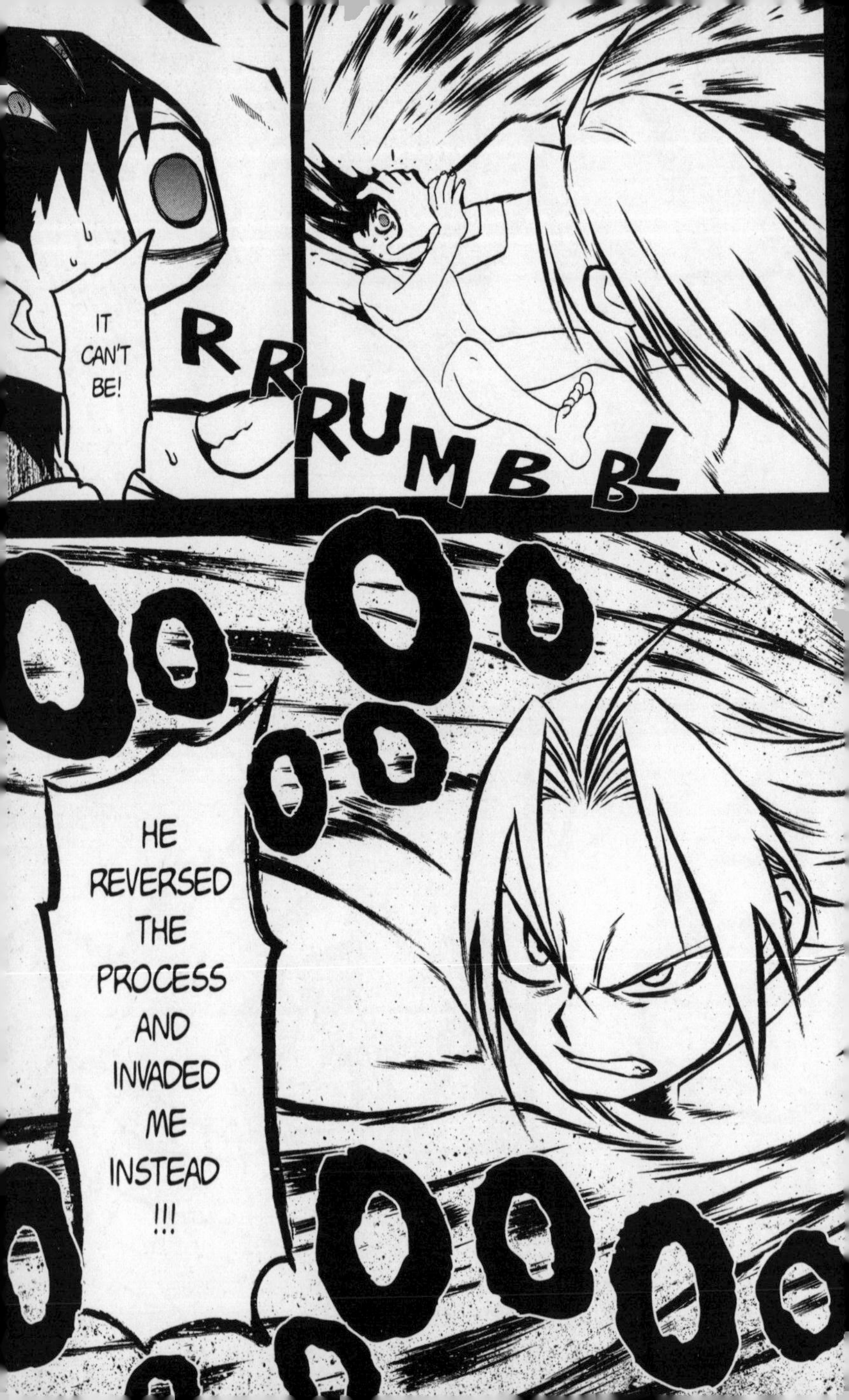
RRRUMBBL
IT CAN'T BE!
OOOOOO
HE REVERSED THE PROCESS AND INVADED ME INSTEAD!!!
OOOOOO

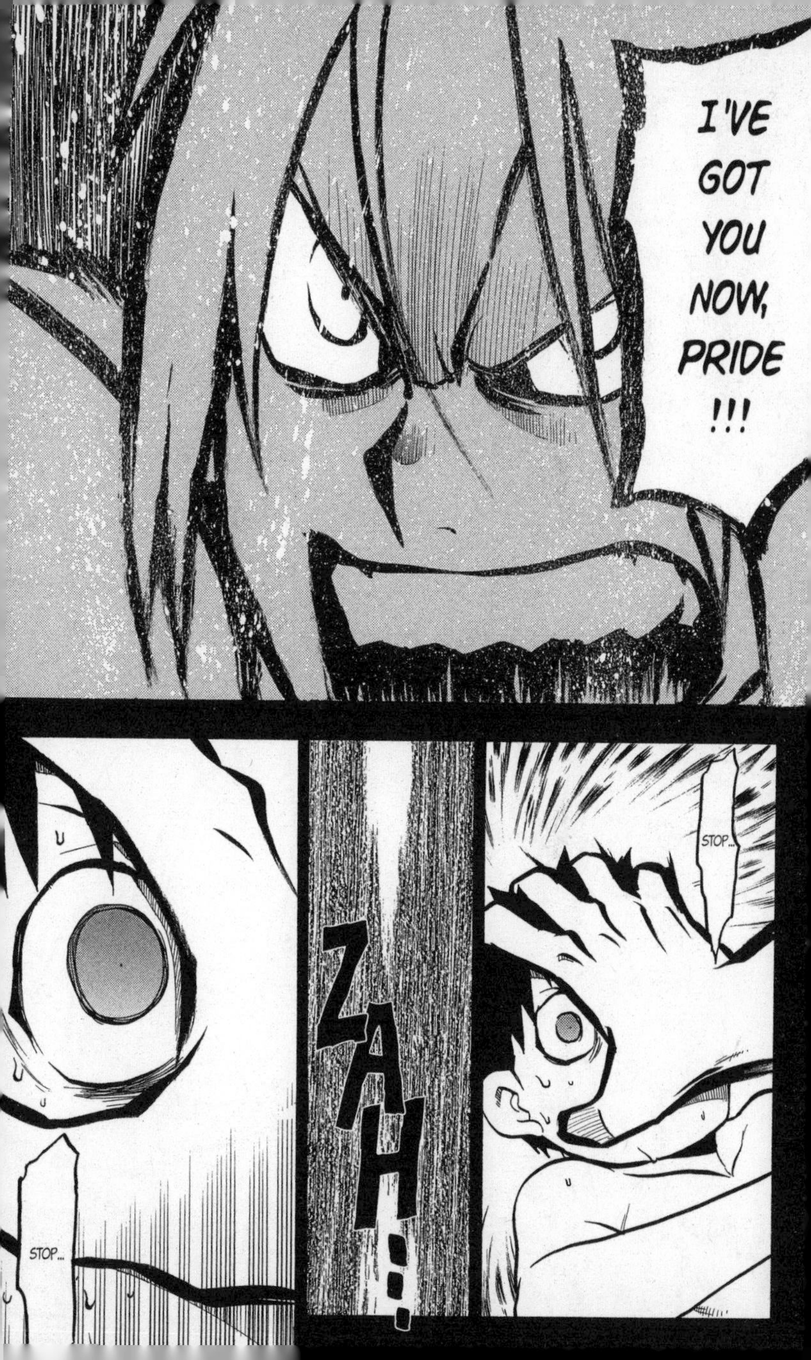
I'VE GOT YOU NOW, PRIDE!!!
STOP...
ZAH...
STOP...

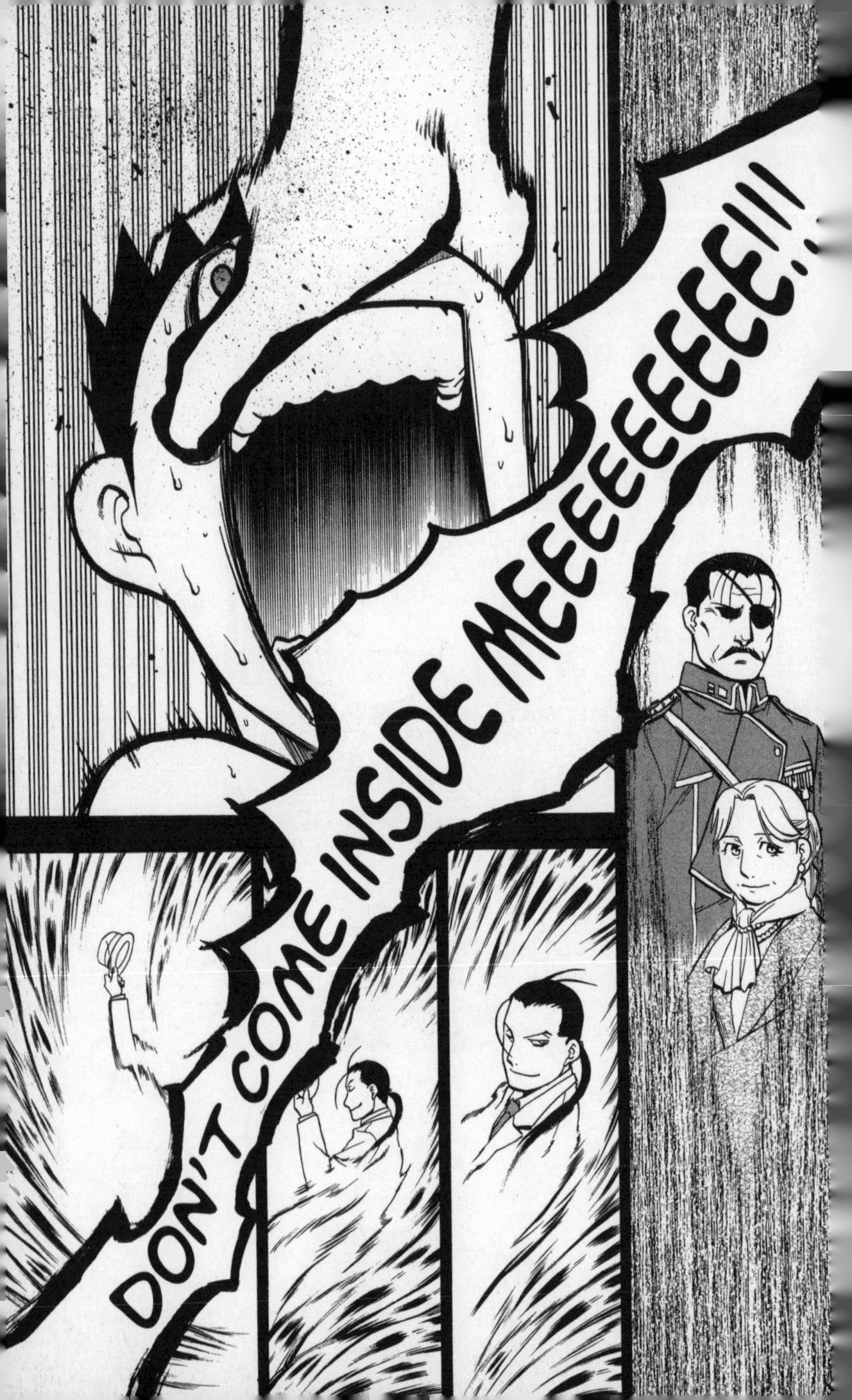
DON'T COME INSIDE MEEEEEEEEE!!!

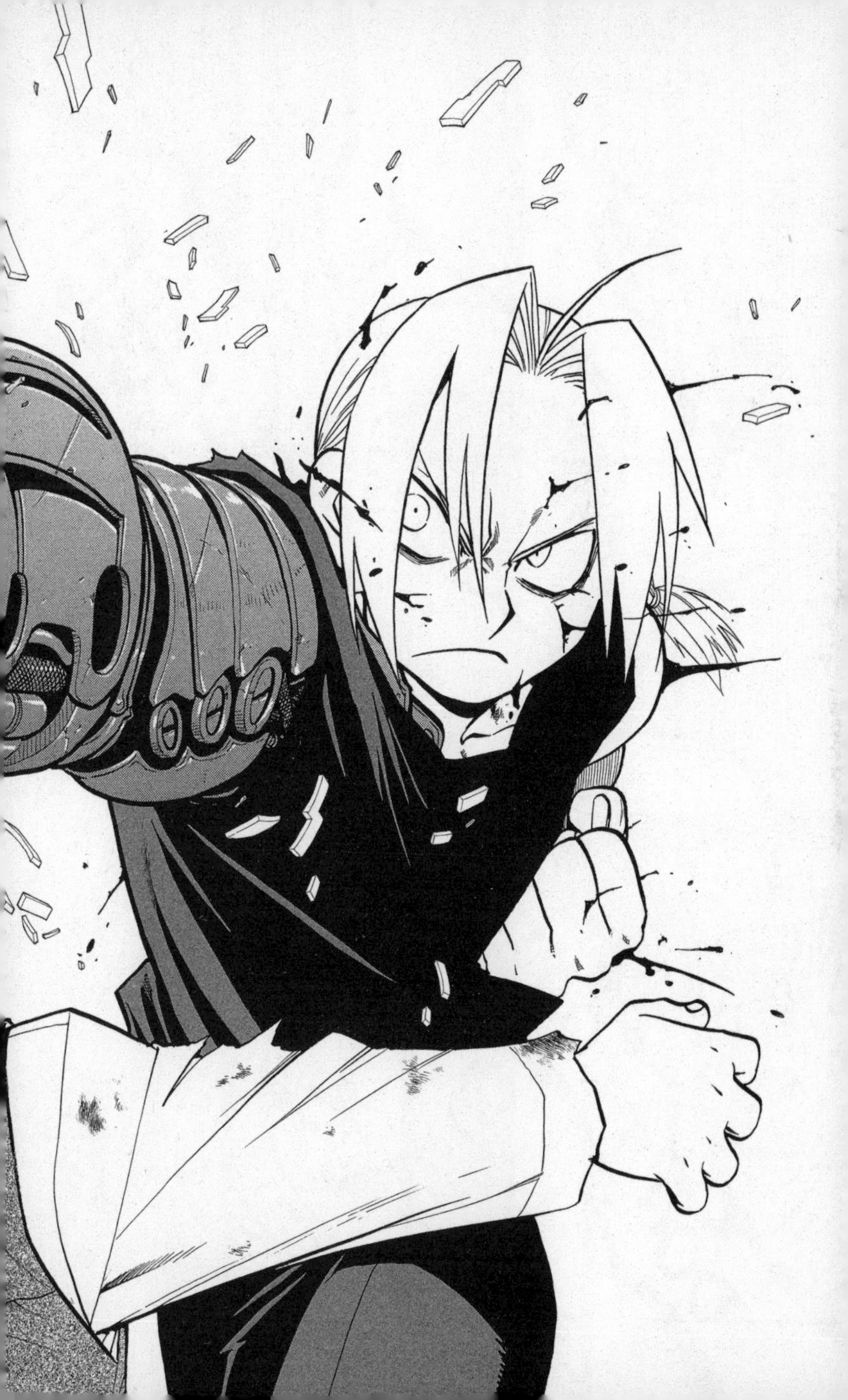

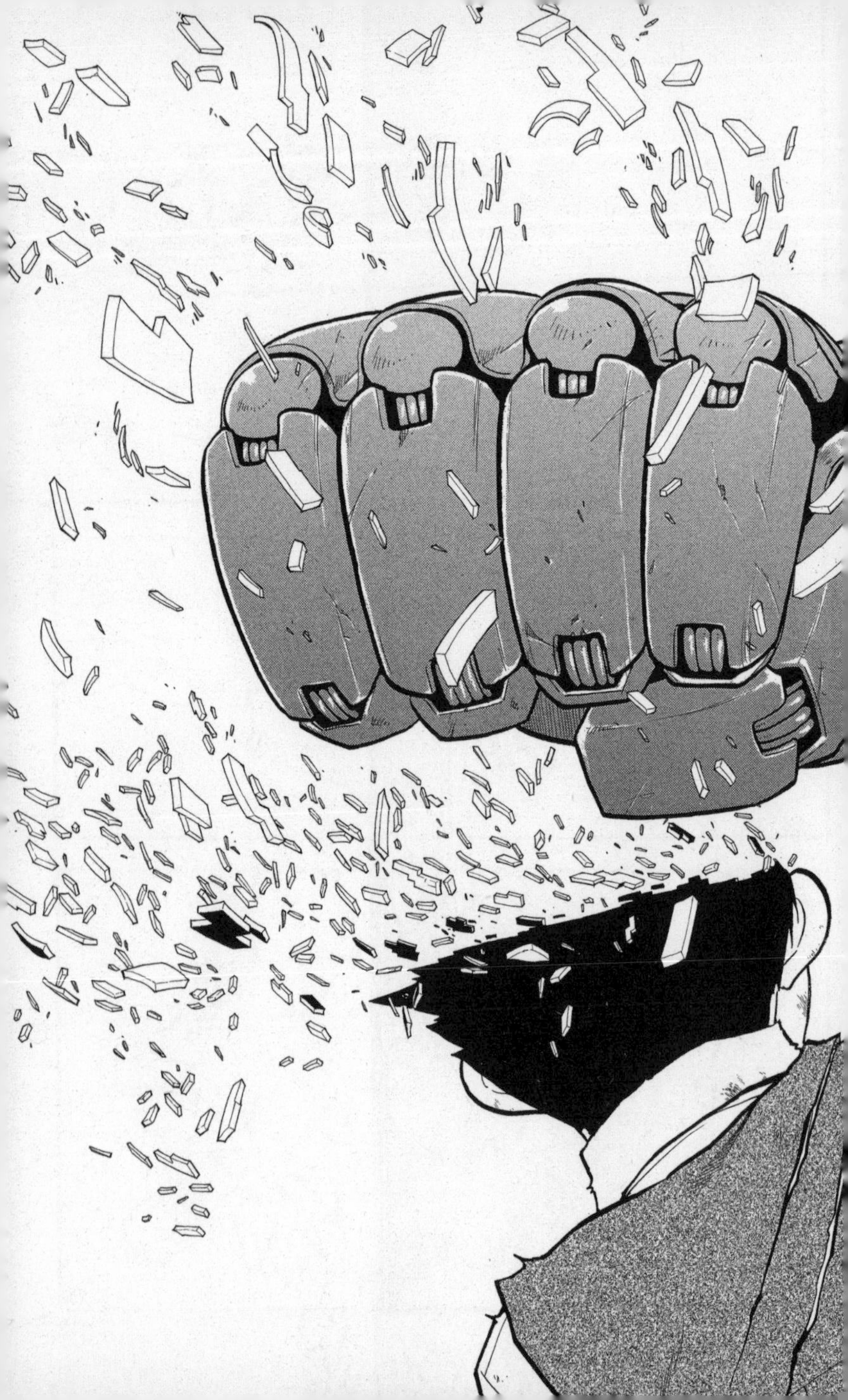

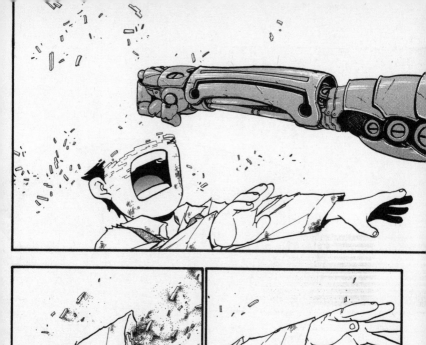

ZAH...

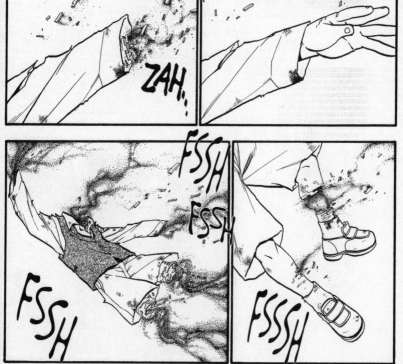

FSSH

FSSH

FSSH

FSSSH

178

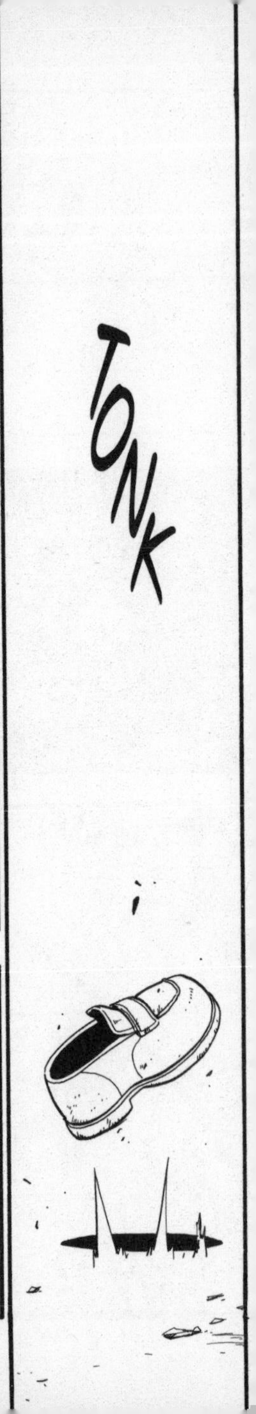
TONK

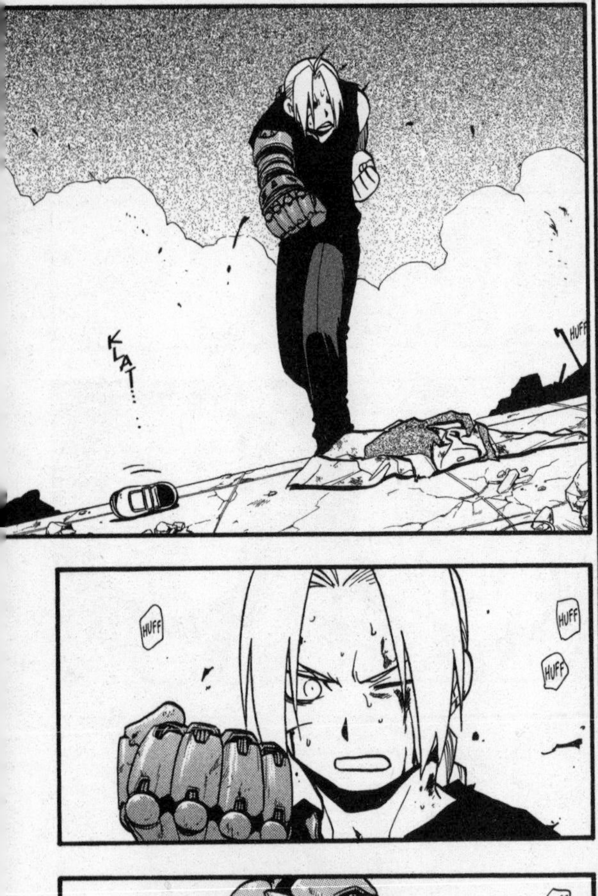
HUFF
KLAT!...
HUFF
HUFF
HUFF
HUFF
HUFF

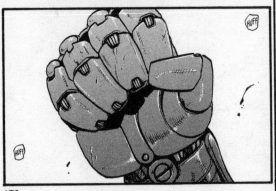

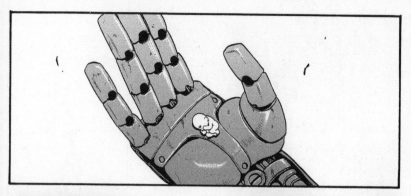

SO THIS IS YOUR TRUE FORM.

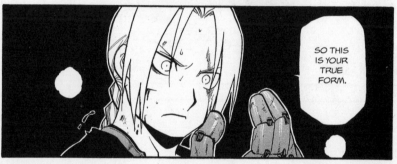

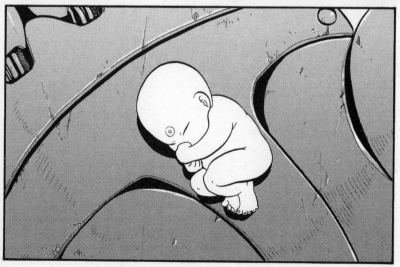

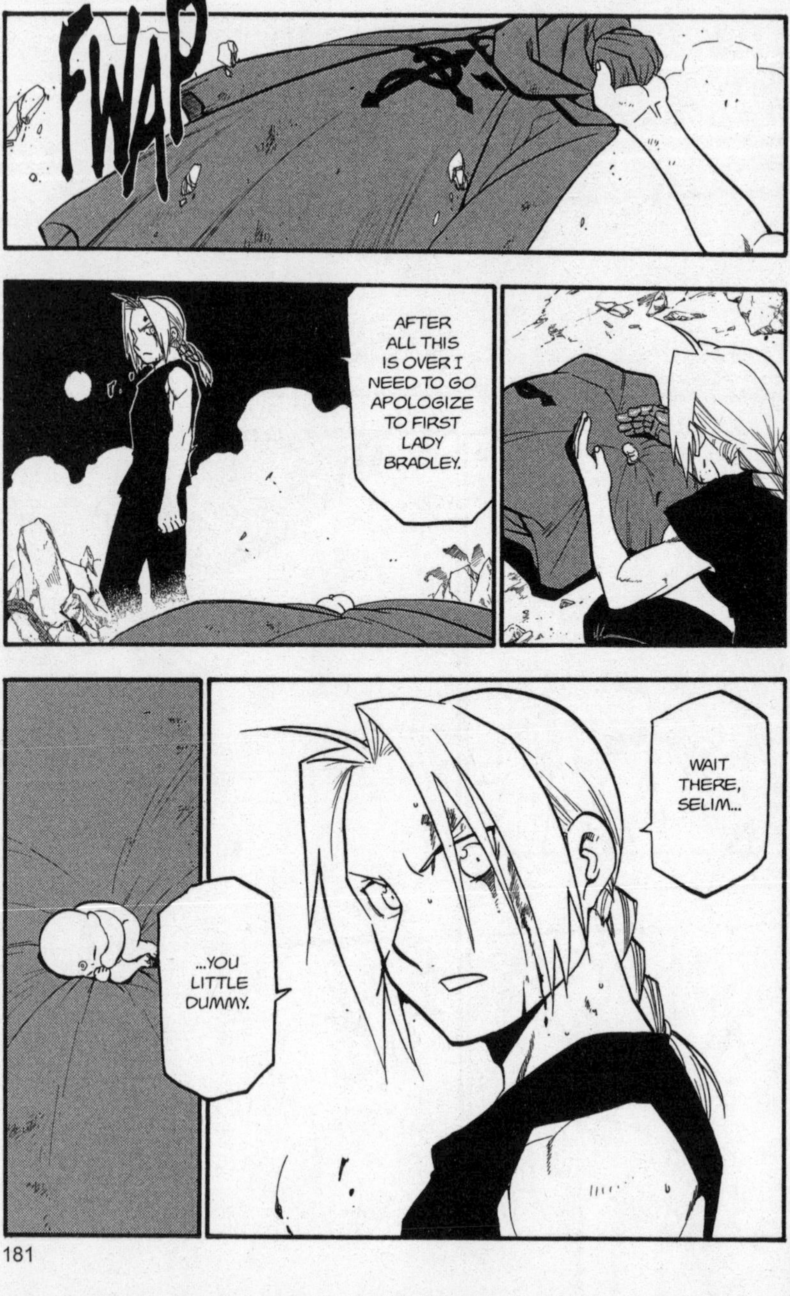
FWAP
AFTER ALL THIS IS OVER I NEED TO GO APOLOGIZE TO FIRST LADY BRADLEY.
WAIT THERE, SELIM...
...YOU LITTLE DUMMY.

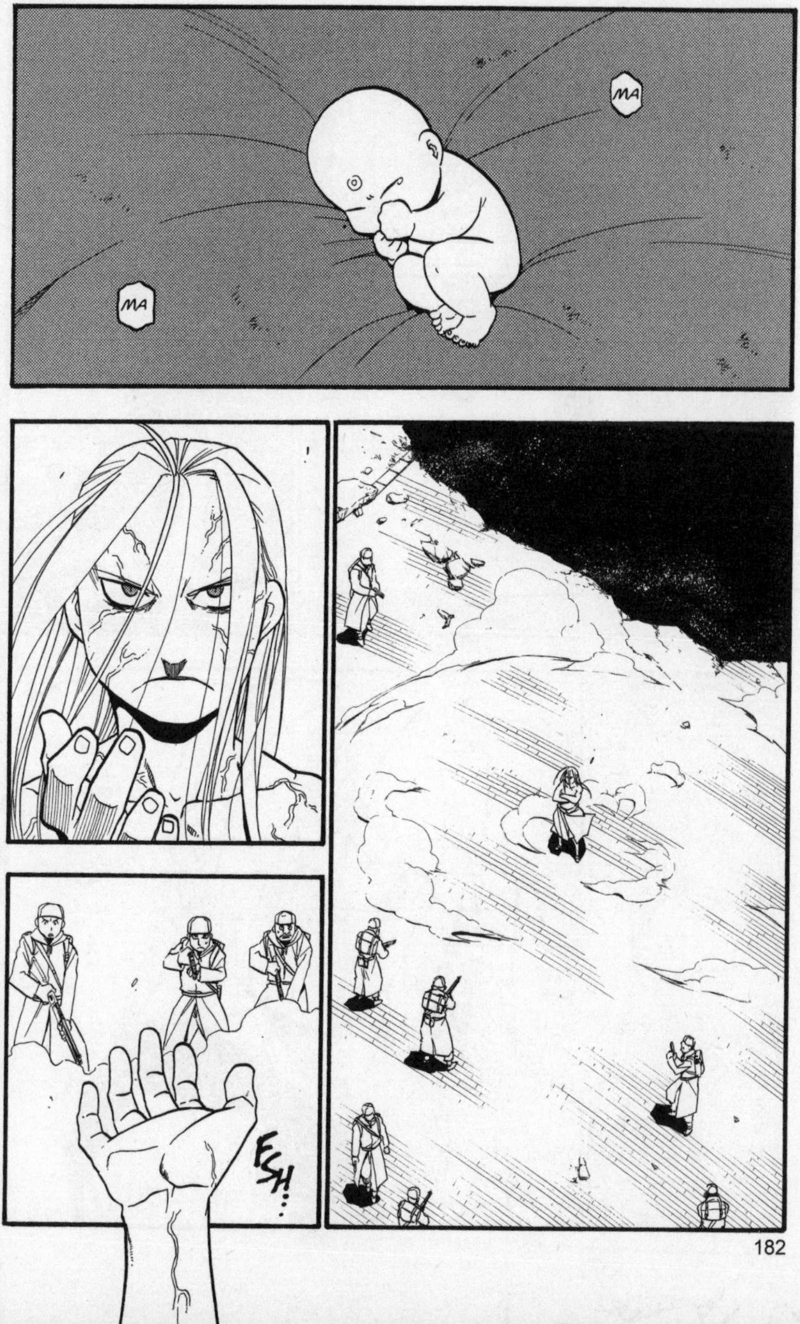
MA
MA
FSH!...

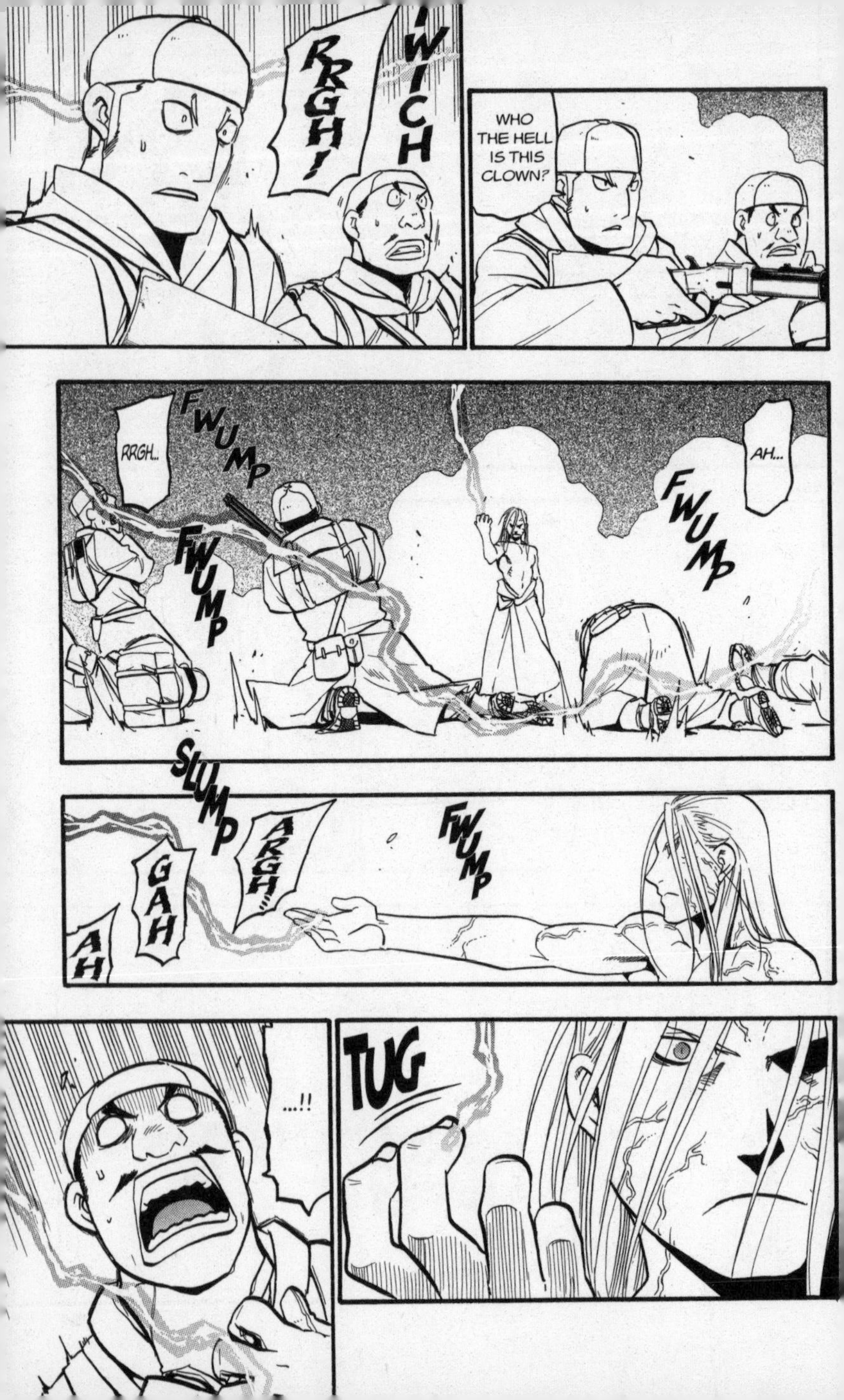
WHO THE HELL IS THIS CLOWN?
WICH
RRGH!!
AH...
FWUMP
FWUMP
FWUMP
RRGH...
FWUMP
ARGH!!
SLUMP
GAH
AH
TUG
...!!

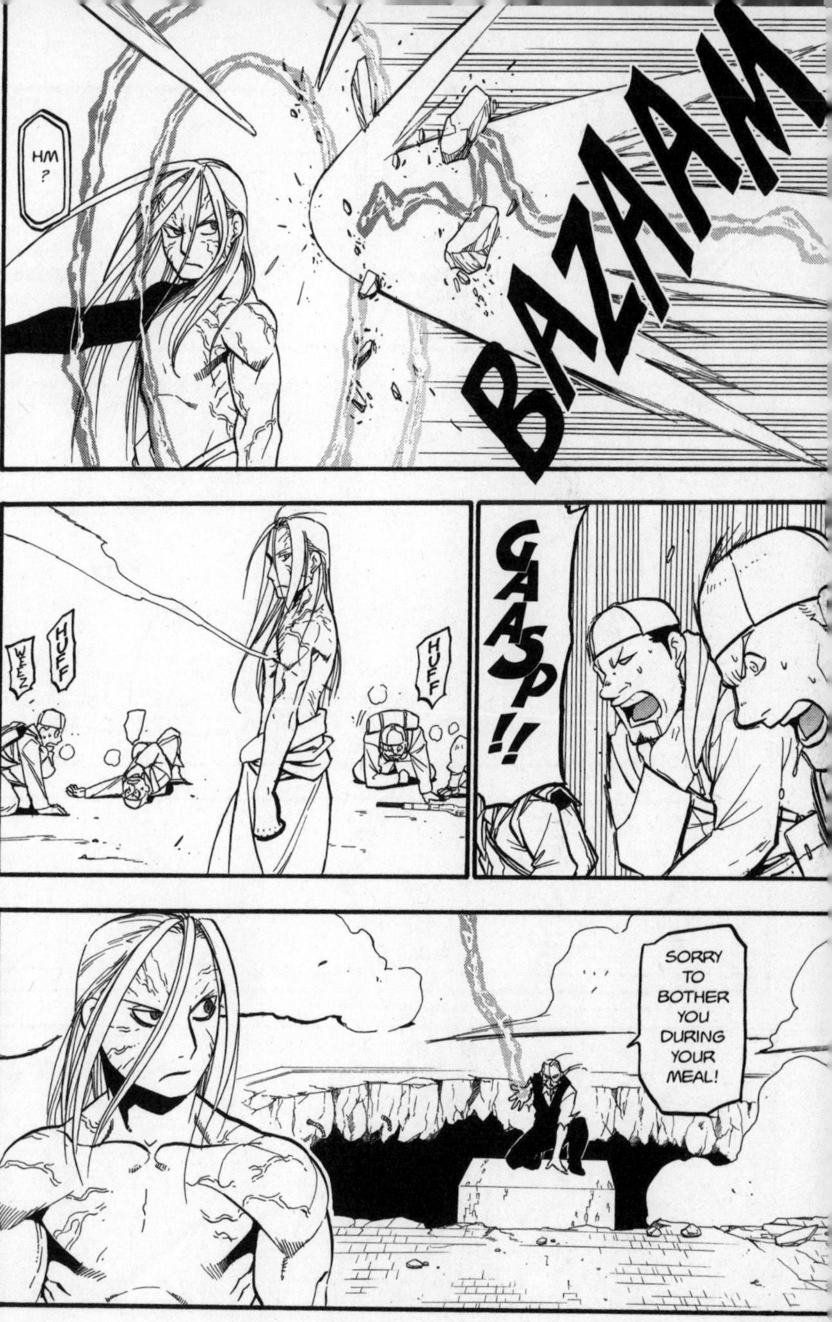
BAZAAM
HM?
GAASP!!
HUFF
HUFF
WEEZ
SORRY TO BOTHER YOU DURING YOUR MEAL!

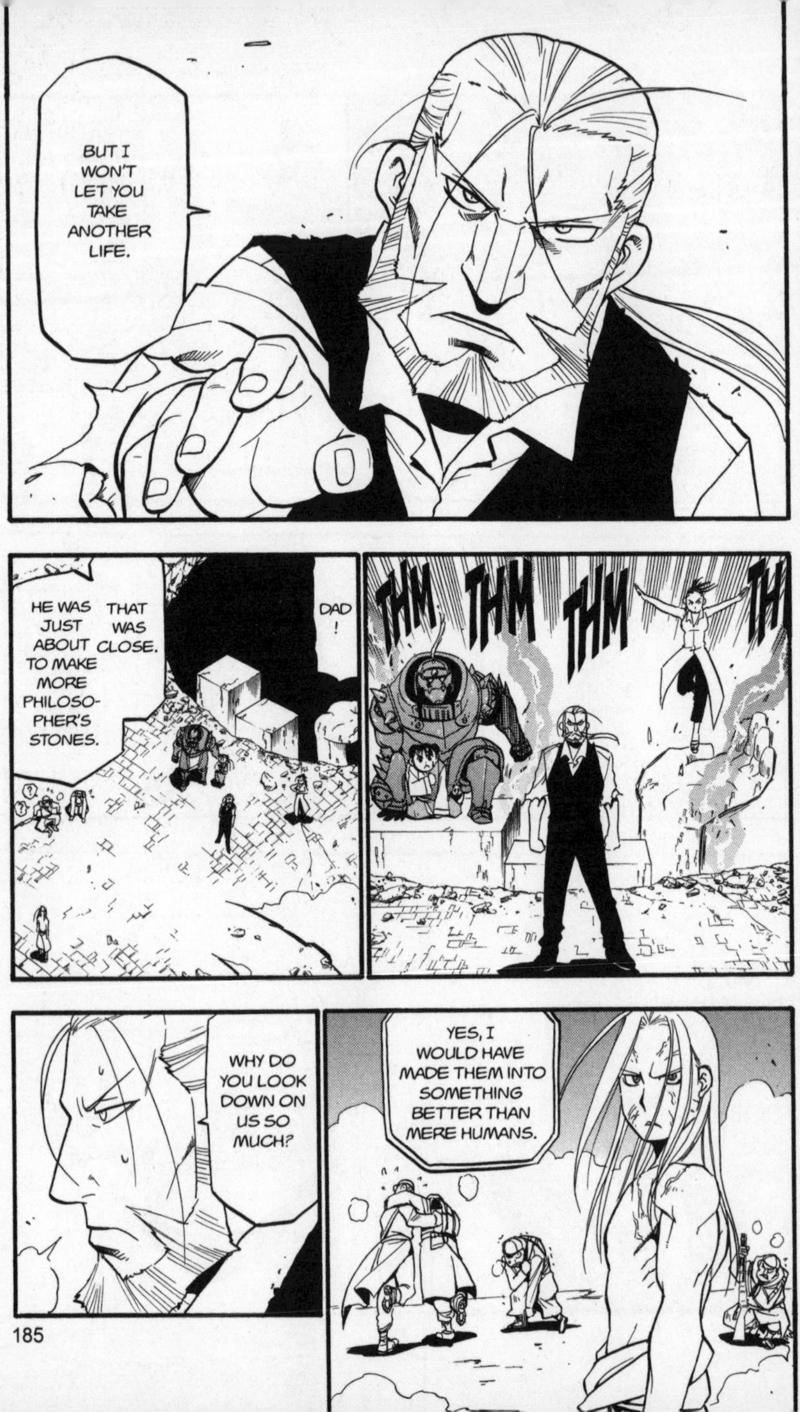
BUT I WON'T LET YOU TAKE ANOTHER LIFE.
THM THM THM TH
DAD!
THAT WAS CLOSE.
HE WAS JUST ABOUT TO MAKE MORE PHILOSOPHER'S STONES.
YES, I WOULD HAVE MADE THEM INTO SOMETHING BETTER THAN MERE HUMANS.
WHY DO YOU LOOK DOWN ON US SO MUCH?

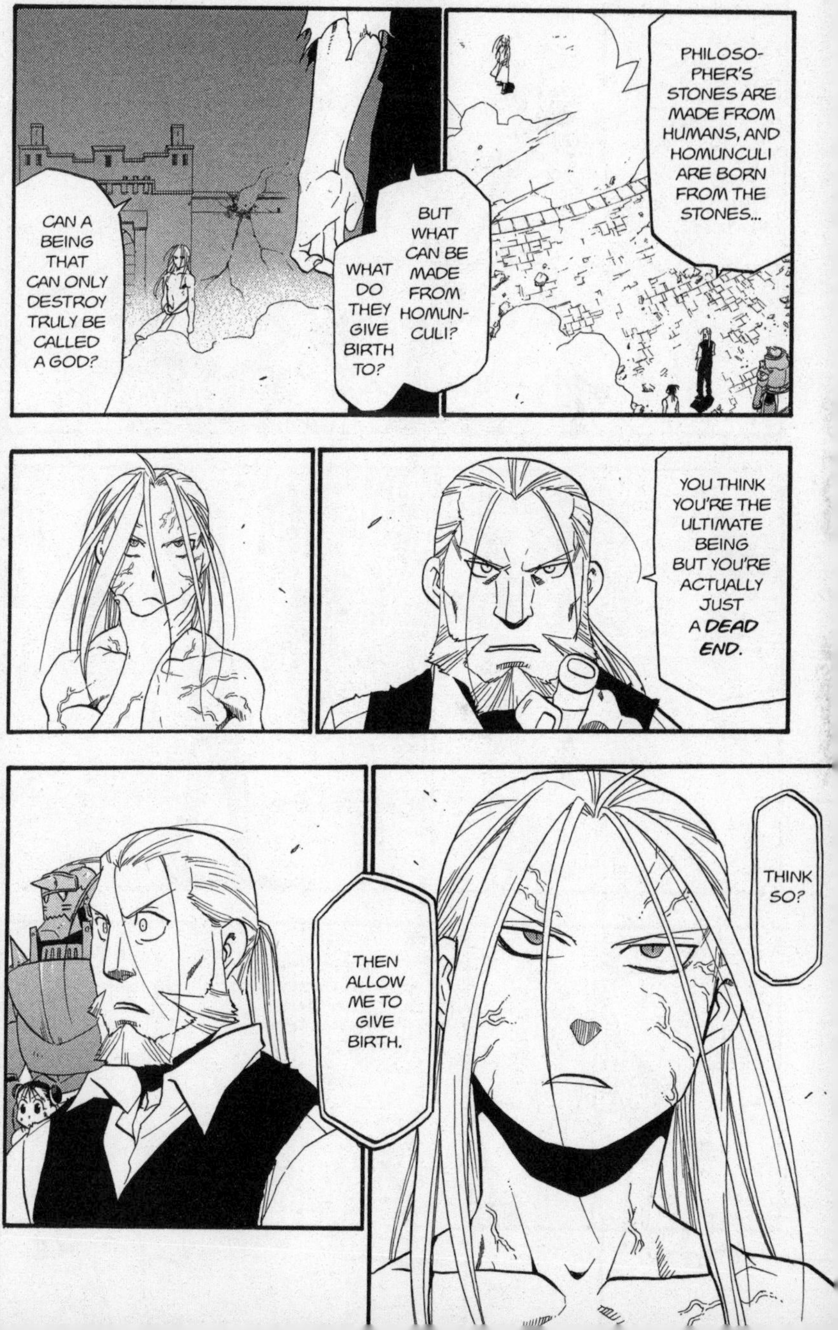
PHILOSO-PHER'S STONES ARE MADE FROM HUMANS, AND HOMUNCULI ARE BORN FROM THE STONES...
BUT WHAT CAN BE MADE FROM HOMUN-CULI?
WHAT DO THEY GIVE BIRTH TO?
CAN A BEING THAT CAN ONLY DESTROY TRULY BE CALLED A GOD?
YOU THINK YOU'RE THE ULTIMATE BEING BUT YOU'RE ACTUALLY JUST A **DEAD END.**
THINK SO?
THEN ALLOW ME TO GIVE BIRTH.

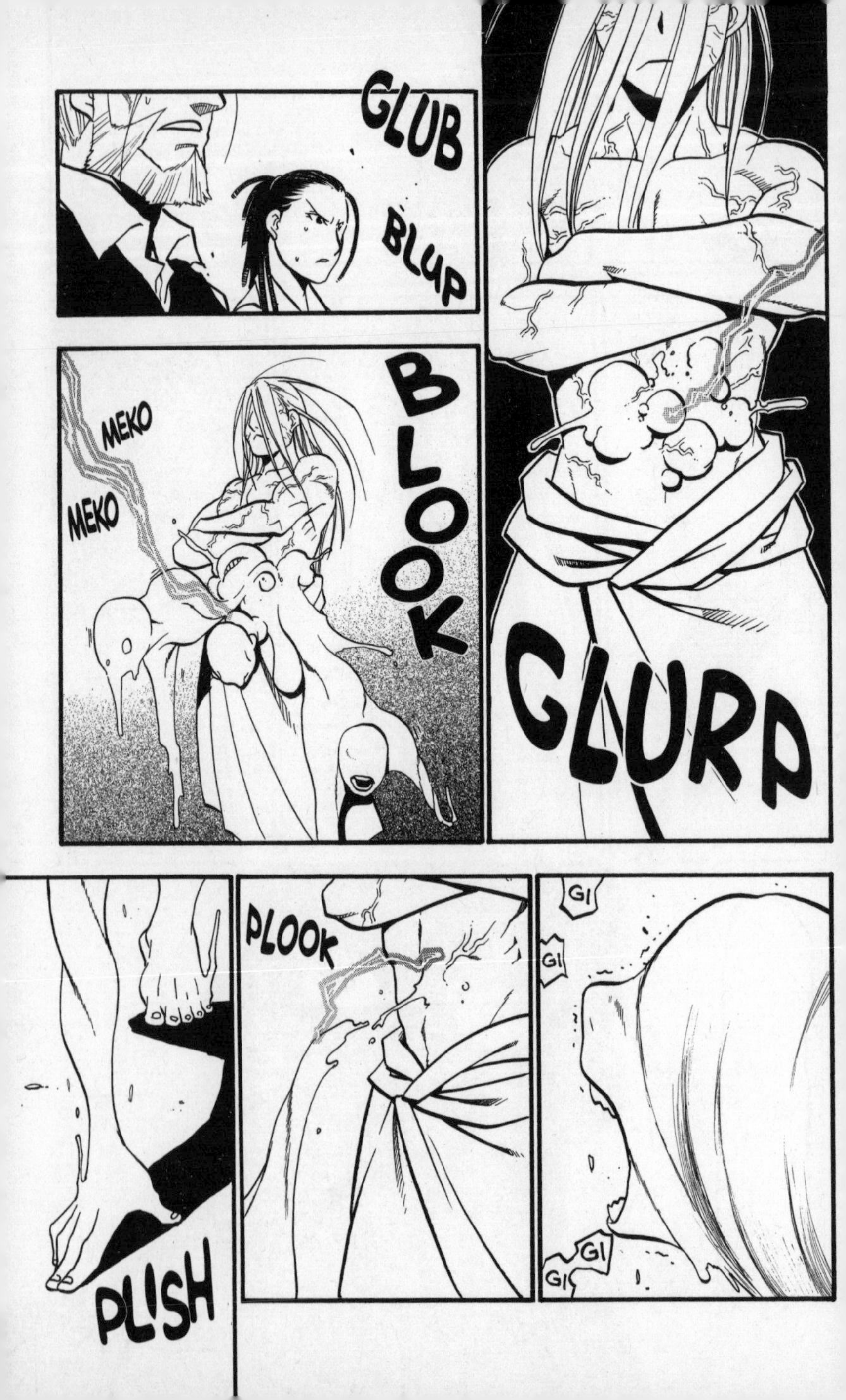
GLURP
GLUB
BLUP
BLOOK
MEKO
MEKO
GI
GI
GI
GI
PLOOK
PLISH

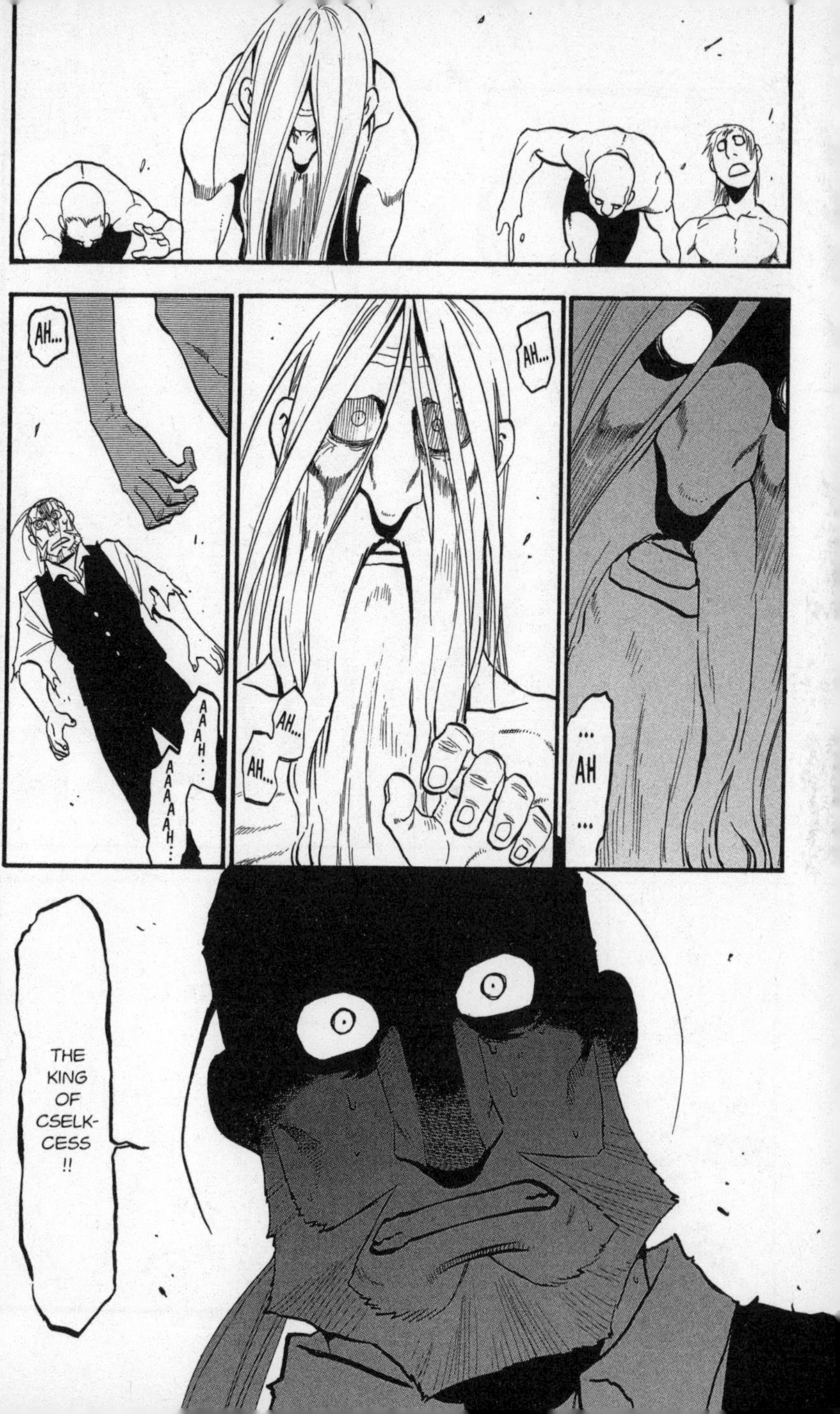

...AH...
AH...
AH...
AH...
AH...
AAAH...
AAAAAH...
THE KING OF CSELK-CESS!!

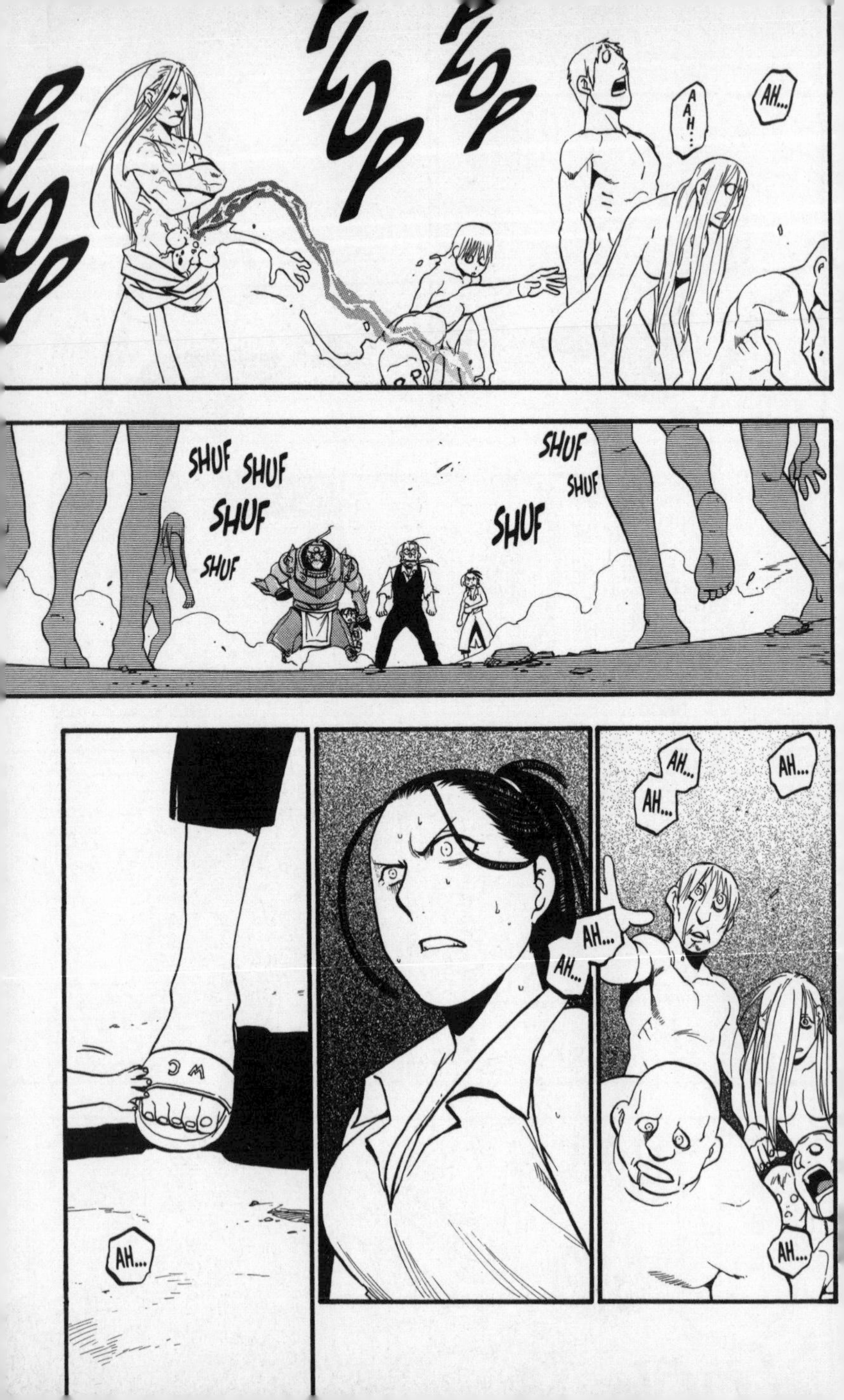
AH...
AAH...
PLOP
PLOP
PLOP
SHUF
SHUF
SHUF
SHUF
SHUF
SHUF
AH...
AH...
AH...
AH...
AH...
AH...
AH...

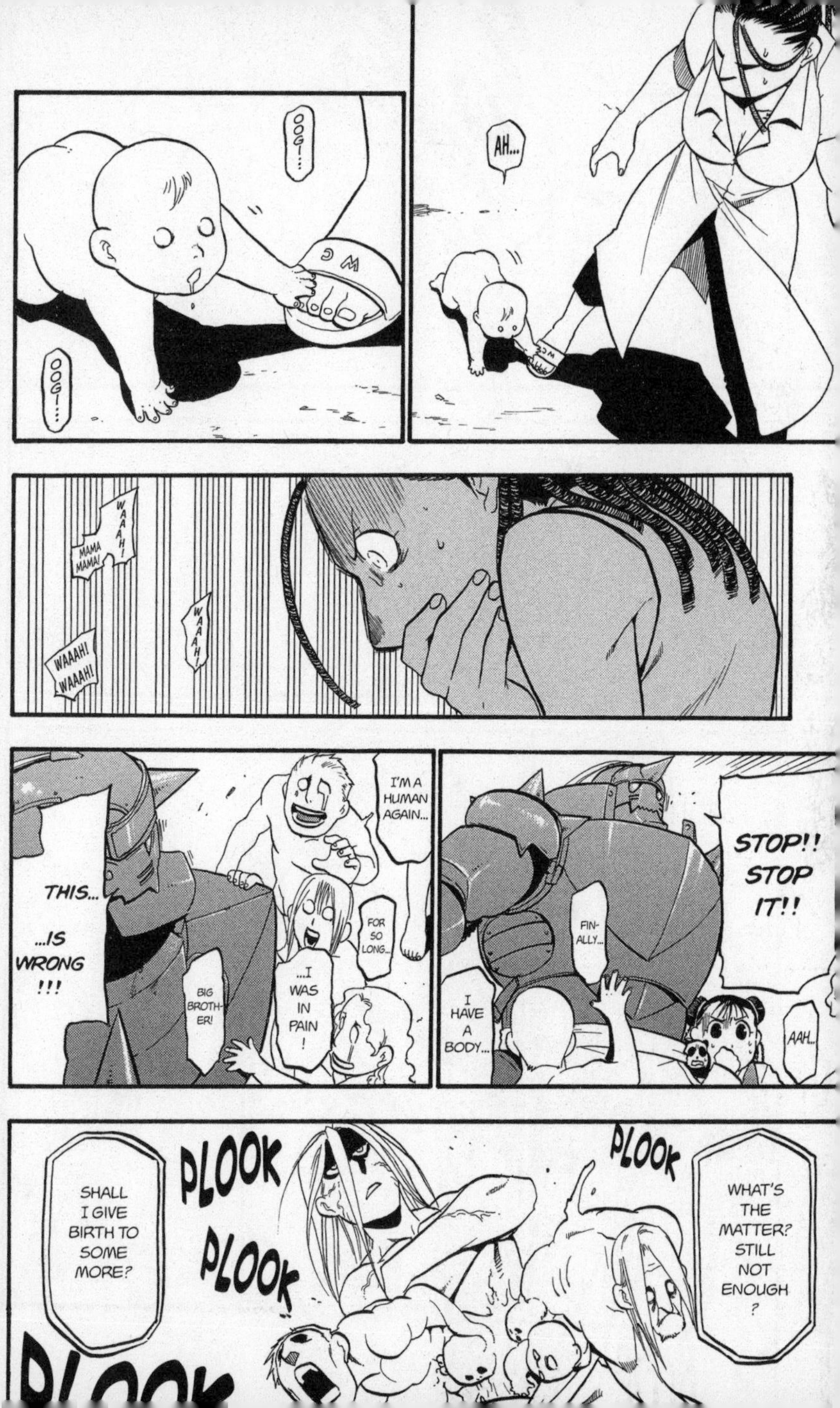
AH...
OOG!...
OOG!...
WAAAH!
MAMA MAMA!
WAAAH!
WAAAH! WAAAH!
STOP!! STOP IT!!
FIN-ALLY...
I HAVE A BODY...
AAH...
I'M A HUMAN AGAIN...
FOR SO LONG...
...I WAS IN PAIN!
BIG BROTH-ER!
THIS...
...IS WRONG!!!
WHAT'S THE MATTER? STILL NOT ENOUGH?
PLOOK
PLOOK
PLOOK
SHALL I GIVE BIRTH TO SOME MORE?

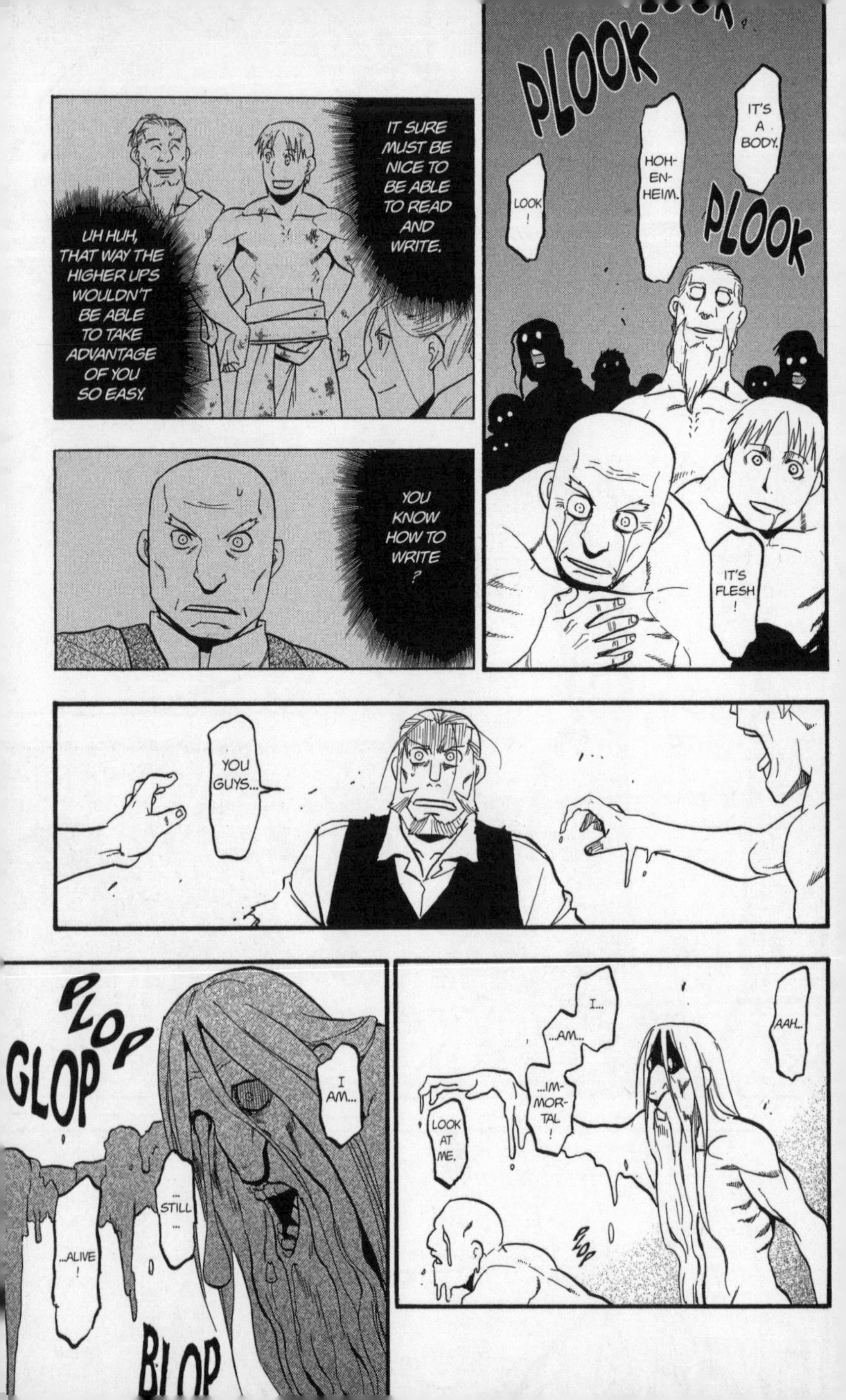
PLOOK
IT'S A BODY.
HOH-EN-HEIM.
LOOK!
PLOOK
IT'S FLESH!
IT SURE MUST BE NICE TO BE ABLE TO READ AND WRITE.
UH HUH, THAT WAY THE HIGHER UPS WOULDN'T BE ABLE TO TAKE ADVANTAGE OF YOU SO EASY.
YOU KNOW HOW TO WRITE?
YOU GUYS...
AAH...
I...
...AM...
...IM-MOR-TAL!
LOOK AT ME.
PLOP
PLOP
GLOP
I AM...
...STILL...
...ALIVE!
BLOP

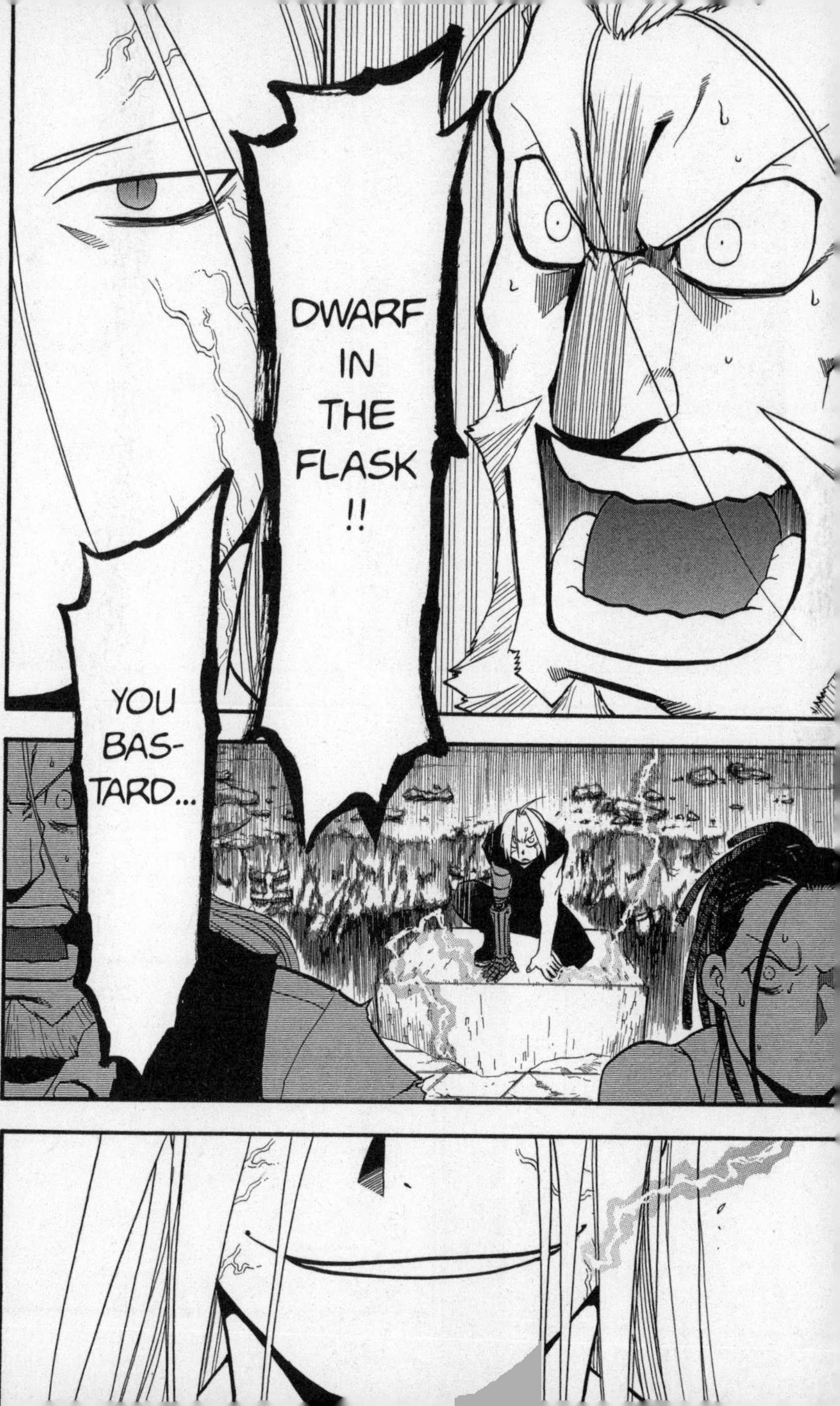
DWARF IN THE FLASK !!
YOU BAS-TARD...

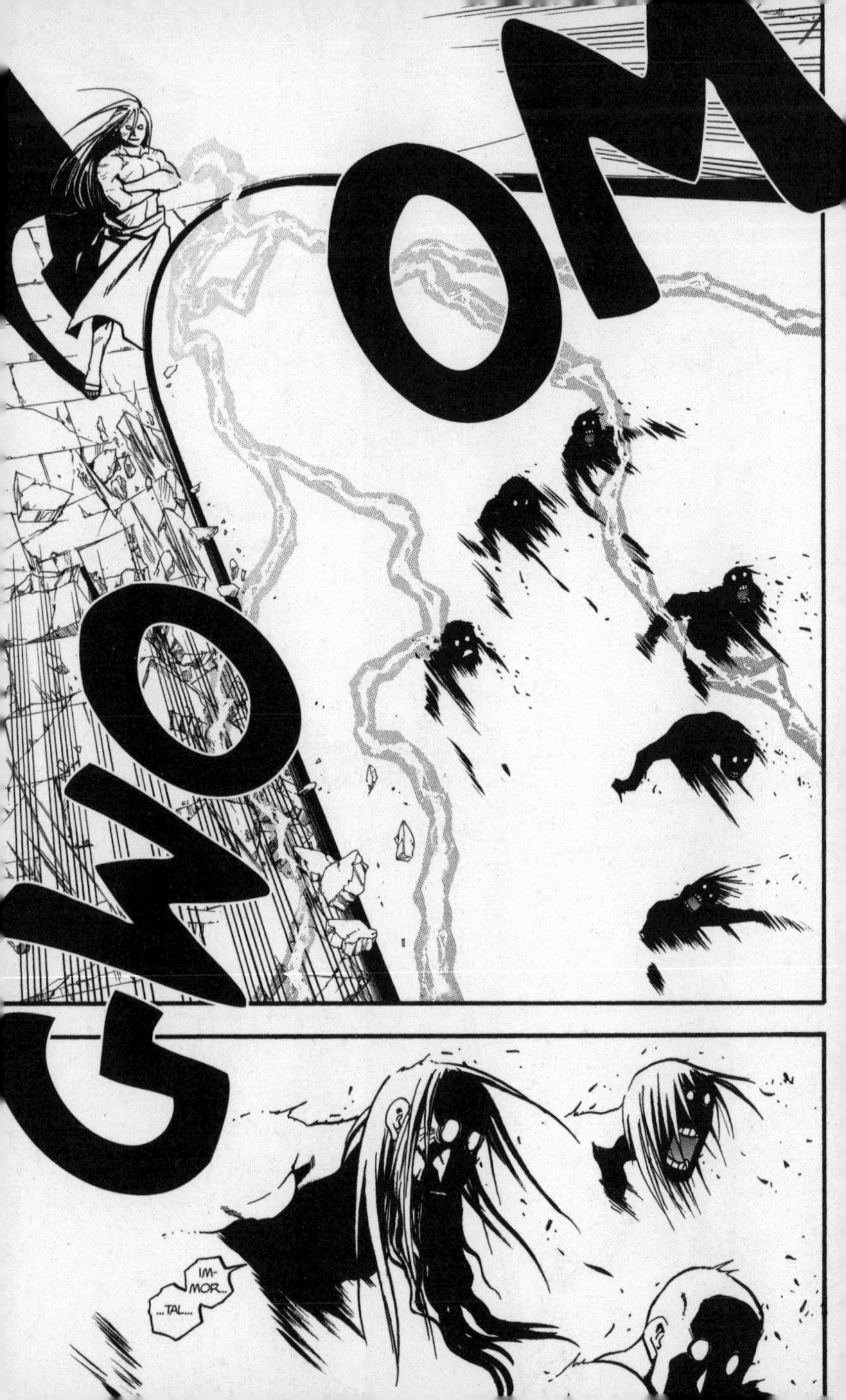
GWOOM
IM-MOR...
...TAL...

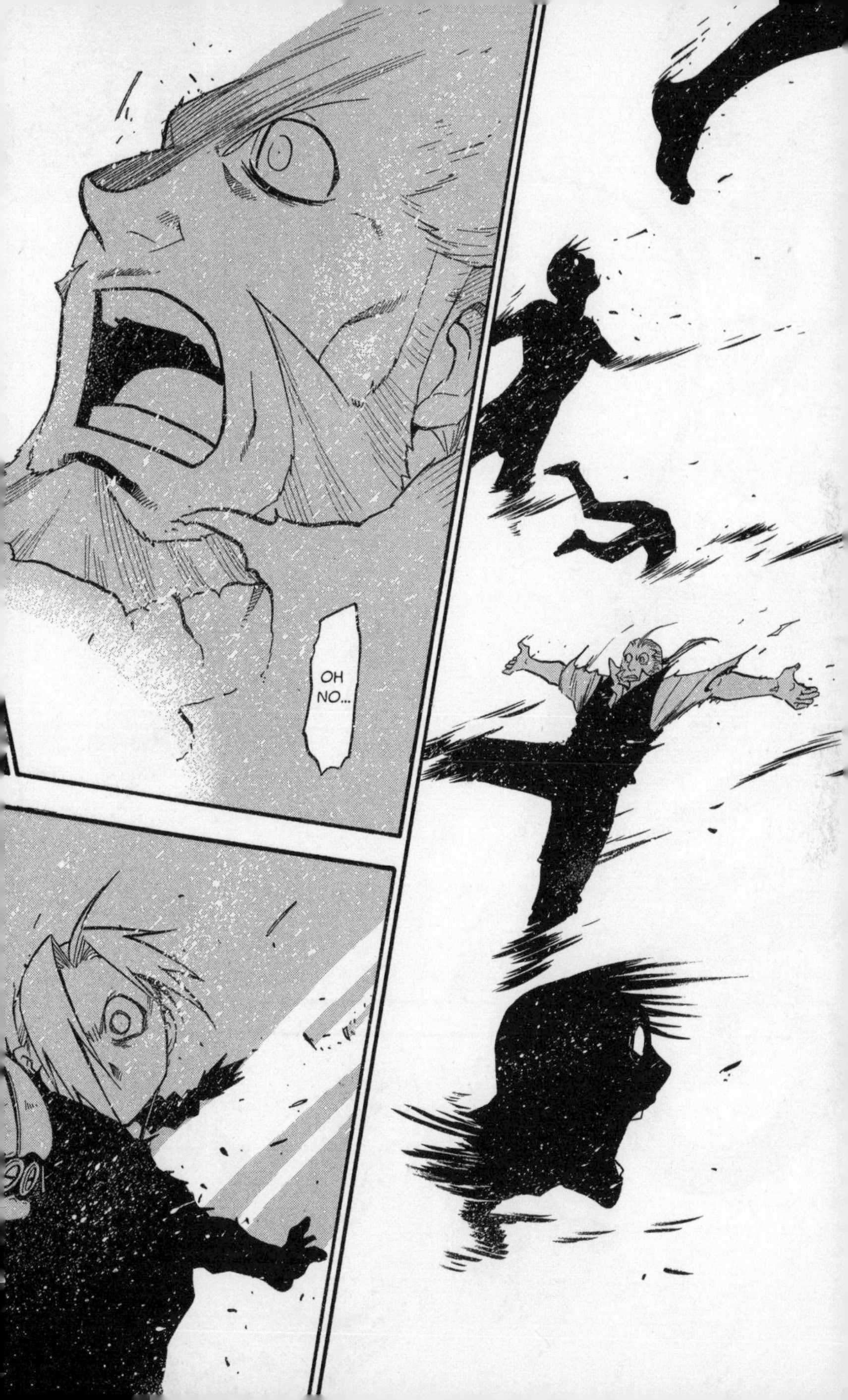
OH NO...

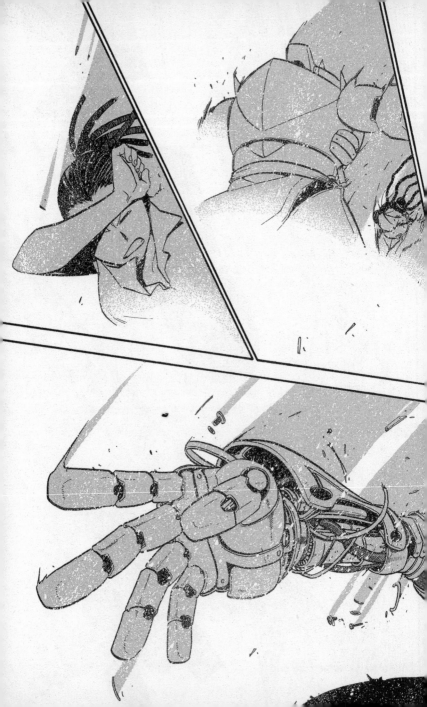

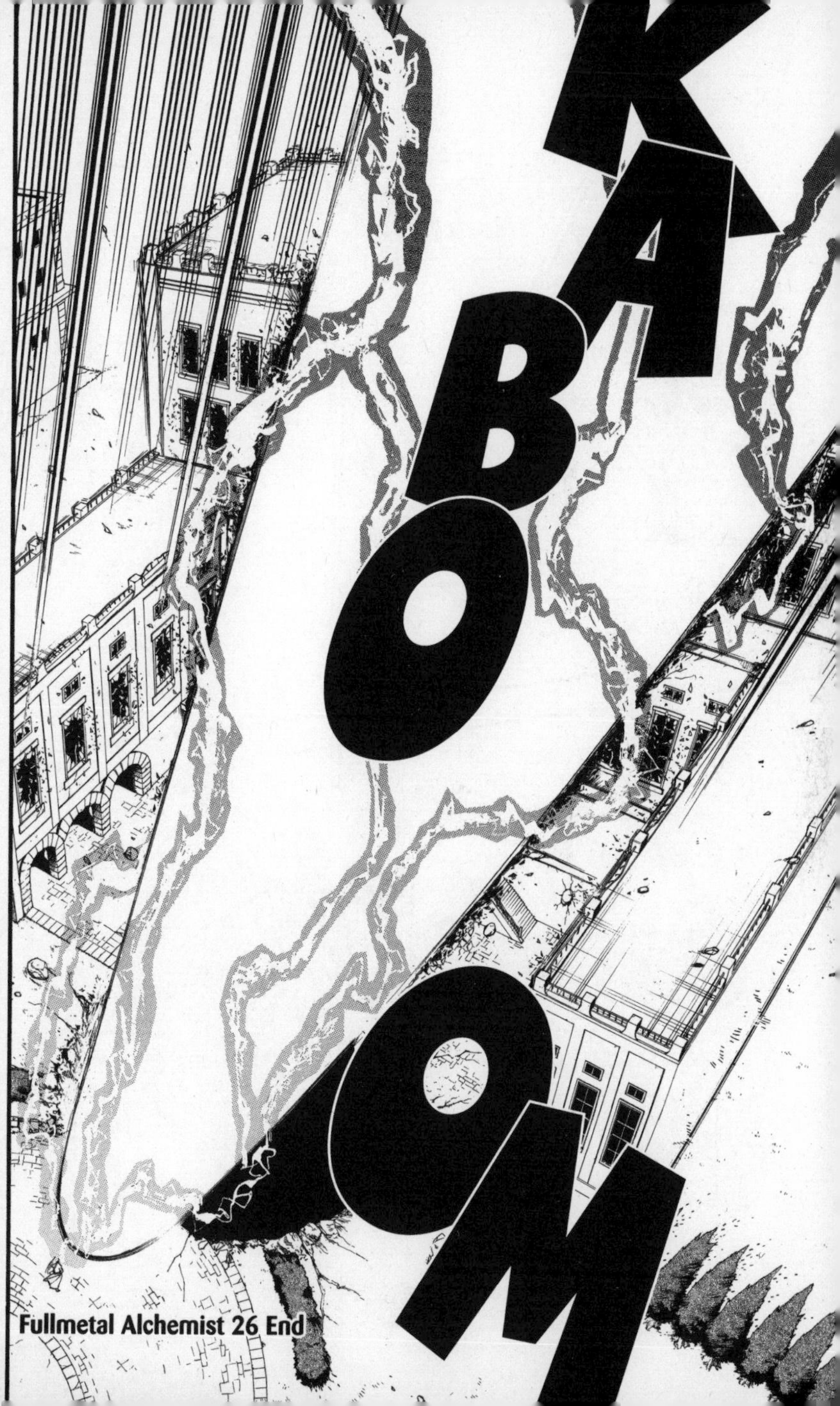
KABOOM
Fullmetal Alchemist 26 End

EXTRAS

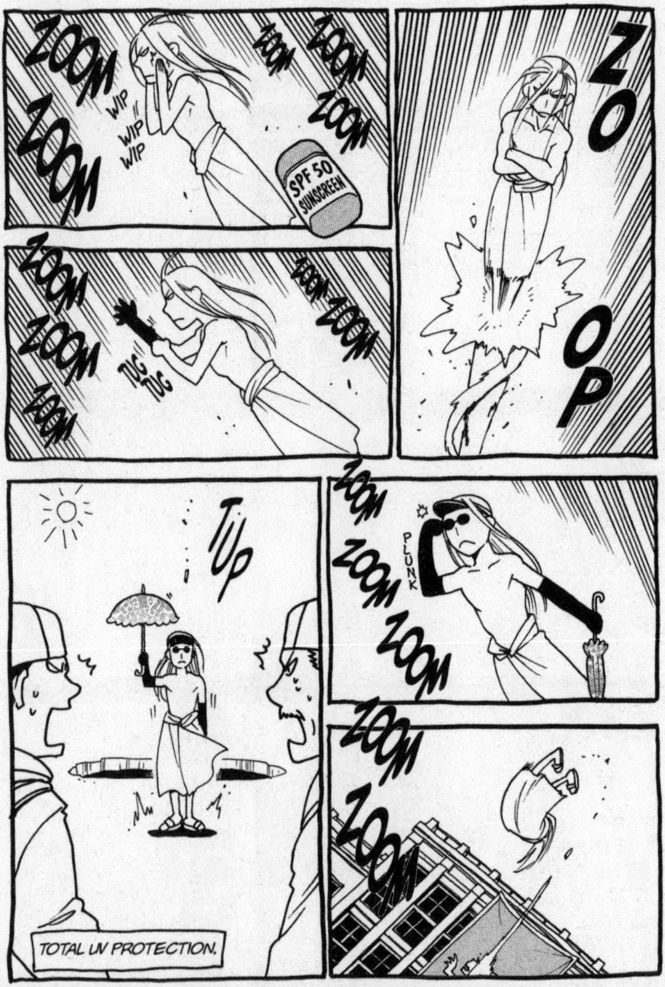
ZOOP
ZOOM ZOOM ZOOM ZOOM ZOOM
WIP WIP WIP
SPF 50 SUNSCREEN
ZOOM ZOOM ZOOM ZOOM ZOOM
TUG TUG
ZOOM ZOOM ZOOM
PLUNK
ZOOM ZOOM
TIUP
TOTAL UV PROTECTION.

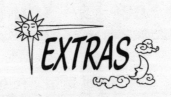

You Brute!!

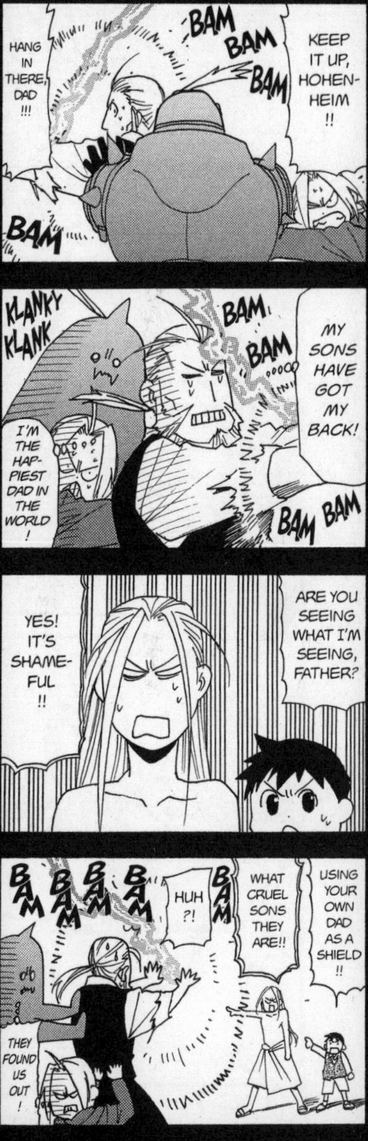
KEEP IT UP, HOHENHEIM!!
BAM BAM BAM
HANG IN THERE, DAD!!!
BAM
MY SONS HAVE GOT MY BACK!
BAM BAM
KLANKY KLANK
I'M THE HAPPIEST DAD IN THE WORLD!
BAM BAM
ARE YOU SEEING WHAT I'M SEEING, FATHER?
YES! IT'S SHAMEFUL!!
USING YOUR OWN DAD AS A SHIELD!!
WHAT CRUEL SONS THEY ARE!!
BAM
HUH?!
BAM BAM BAM BAM
THEY FOUND US OUT!

I Want To See

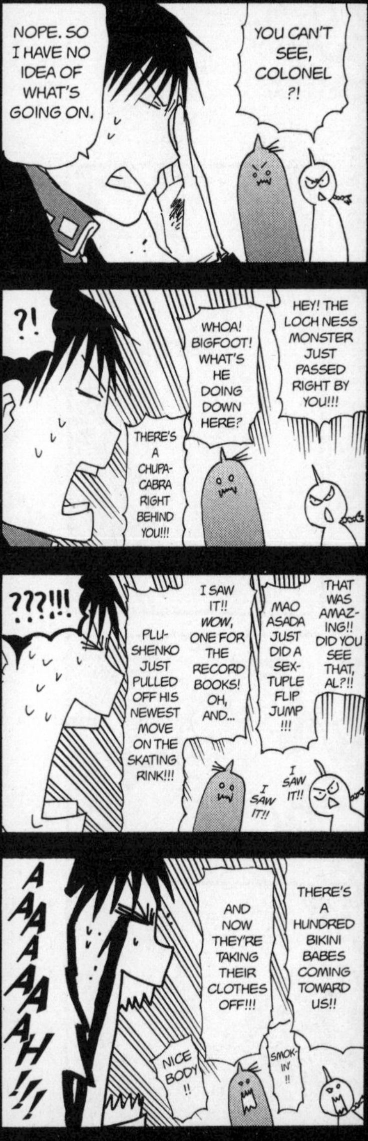
YOU CAN'T SEE, COLONEL?!
NOPE. SO I HAVE NO IDEA OF WHAT'S GOING ON.
HEY! THE LOCH NESS MONSTER JUST PASSED RIGHT BY YOU!!!
WHOA! BIGFOOT! WHAT'S HE DOING DOWN HERE?
?!
THERE'S A CHUPACABRA RIGHT BEHIND YOU!!!
THAT WAS AMAZING!! DID YOU SEE THAT, AL?!!
MAO ASADA JUST DID A SEXTUPLE FLIP JUMP!!!
I SAW IT!! WOW, ONE FOR THE RECORD BOOKS! OH, AND...
???!!!
PLUSHENKO JUST PULLED OFF HIS NEWEST MOVE ON THE SKATING RINK!!!
I SAW IT!!
I SAW IT!!
THERE'S A HUNDRED BIKINI BABES COMING TOWARD US!!
AND NOW THEY'RE TAKING THEIR CLOTHES OFF!!!
SMOKIN'!!
NICE BODY!!
AAAAAAAAH!!!!

The Promised Day

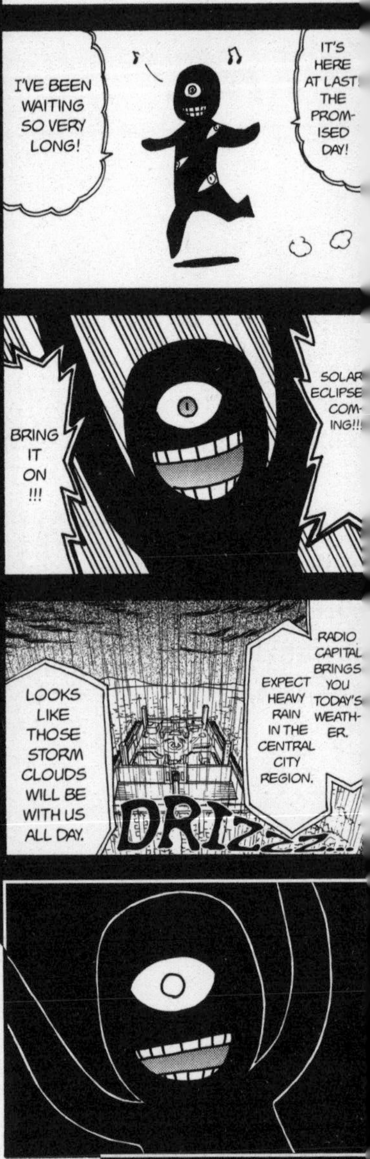

IT'S HERE AT LAST! THE PROMISED DAY!
I'VE BEEN WAITING SO VERY LONG!
SOLAR ECLIPSE COMING!!!
BRING IT ON!!!
RADIO CAPITAL BRINGS YOU TODAY'S WEATHER.
EXPECT HEAVY RAIN IN THE CENTRAL CITY REGION.
LOOKS LIKE THOSE STORM CLOUDS WILL BE WITH US ALL DAY.
DRIzzz...

FULLMETAL ALCHEMIST 26

SPECIAL THANKS to:

Jun Tohko
Masashi Mizutani
Mr. Coupon
Noriko Tsubota
Kazufumi Kaneko
Kori Sakano
Manatsu Sakura
Keisui Takaeda
Yota Arao
Haruhi Nakamura
Soichi Kurose

In cooperation with the National Astronomical Observatory

My Editor, Yuichi Shimomura

AND YOU!!

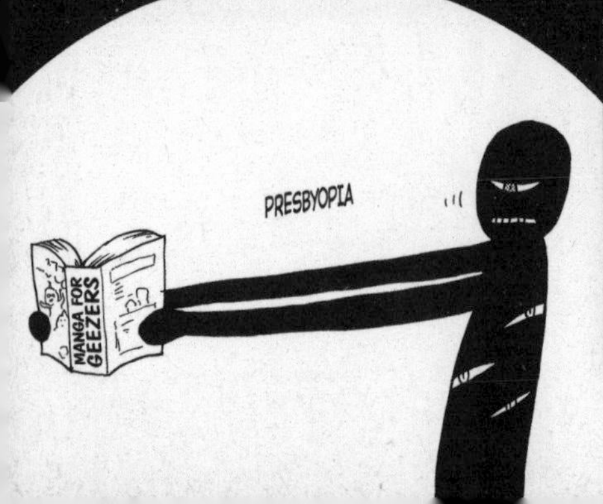

PRESBYOPIA
MANGA FOR GEEZERS

FULLMETAL ALCHEMIST

**THE FINAL VOLUME,
ON SALE NOW!**

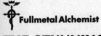 Fullmetal Alchemist

THE STUNNING CONCLUSION

FAREWELL...

AN UNFORGETTABLE END AWAITS...

Parable of the Woodcutter

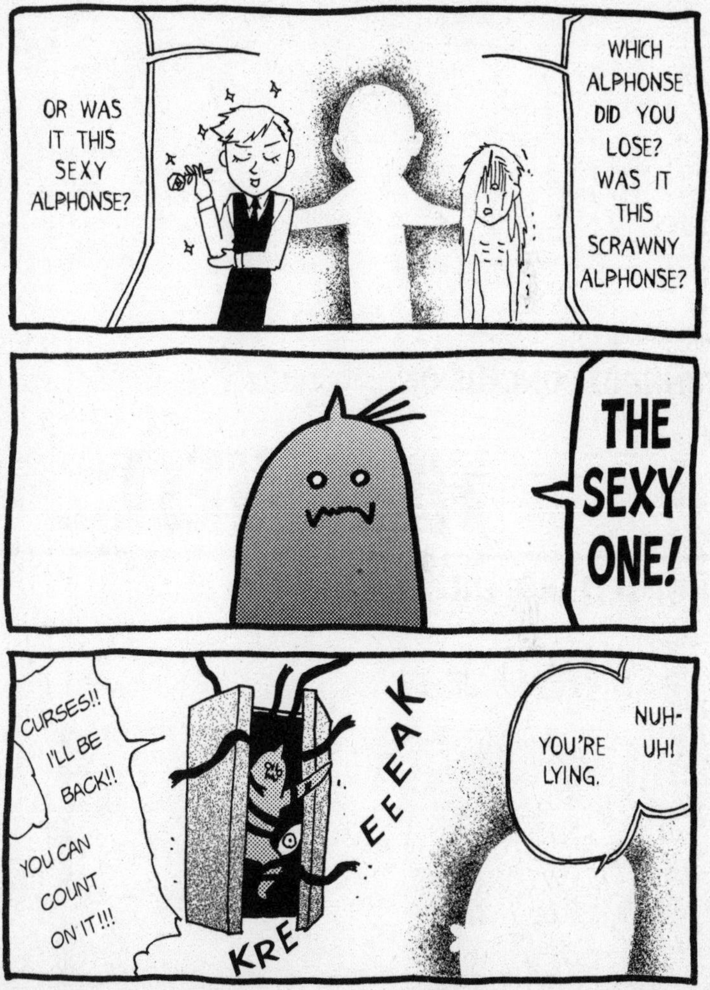
WHICH ALPHONSE DID YOU LOSE? WAS IT THIS SCRAWNY ALPHONSE?
OR WAS IT THIS SEXY ALPHONSE?
THE SEXY ONE!
NUH-UH!
YOU'RE LYING.
KREEEEAK
CURSES!! I'LL BE BACK!!
YOU CAN COUNT ON IT!!!

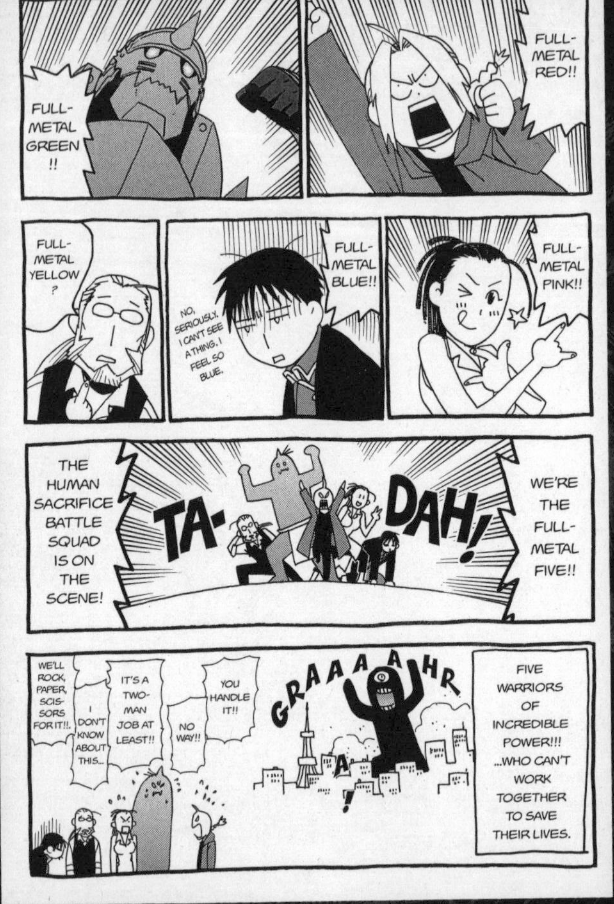
FULL-METAL RED!!
FULL-METAL GREEN!!
FULL-METAL PINK!!
FULL-METAL BLUE!!
NO, SERIOUSLY, I CAN'T SEE A THING. I FEEL SO BLUE.
FULL-METAL YELLOW?
WE'RE THE FULL-METAL FIVE!!
TA-DAH!
THE HUMAN SACRIFICE BATTLE SQUAD IS ON THE SCENE!
FIVE WARRIORS OF INCREDIBLE POWER!!! ...WHO CAN'T WORK TOGETHER TO SAVE THEIR LIVES.
GRAAAAAHR
YOU HANDLE IT!!
NO WAY!!
IT'S A TWO-MAN JOB AT LEAST!!
I DON'T KNOW ABOUT THIS...
WE'LL ROCK, PAPER, SCISSORS FOR IT!!

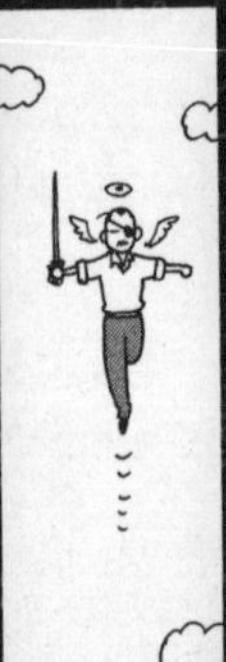

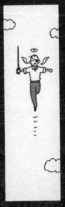

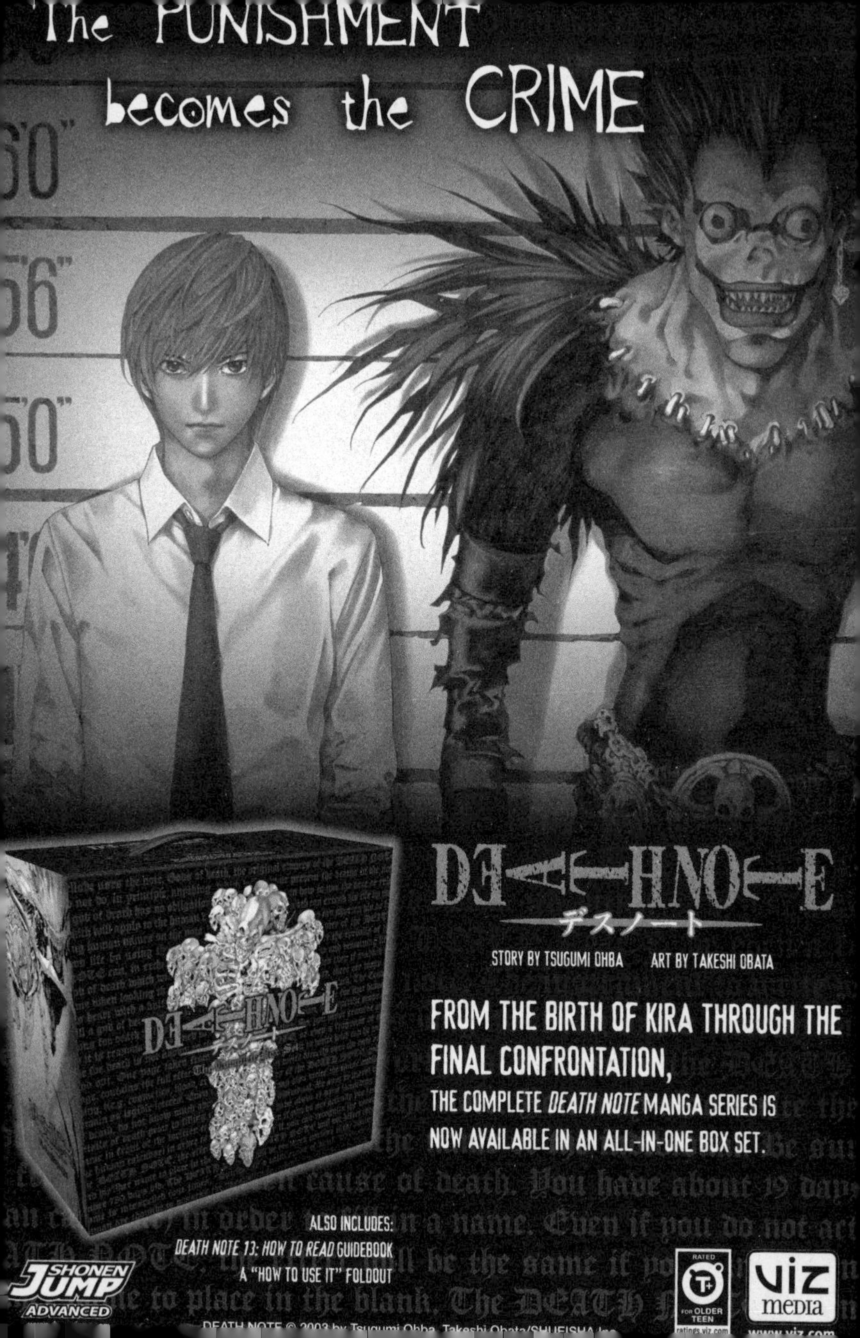
The PUNISHMENT becomes the CRIME
DEATH NOTE
デスノート
STORY BY TSUGUMI OHBA
ART BY TAKESHI OBATA
FROM THE BIRTH OF KIRA THROUGH THE FINAL CONFRONTATION,
THE COMPLETE *DEATH NOTE* MANGA SERIES IS NOW AVAILABLE IN AN ALL-IN-ONE BOX SET.
ALSO INCLUDES:
DEATH NOTE 13: HOW TO READ GUIDEBOOK
A "HOW TO USE IT" FOLDOUT
SHONEN JUMP ADVANCED
RATED T+ FOR OLDER TEEN
ratings.viz.com
viz media
www.viz.com
DEATH NOTE © 2003 by Tsugumi Ohba, Takeshi Obata/SHUEISHA Inc.

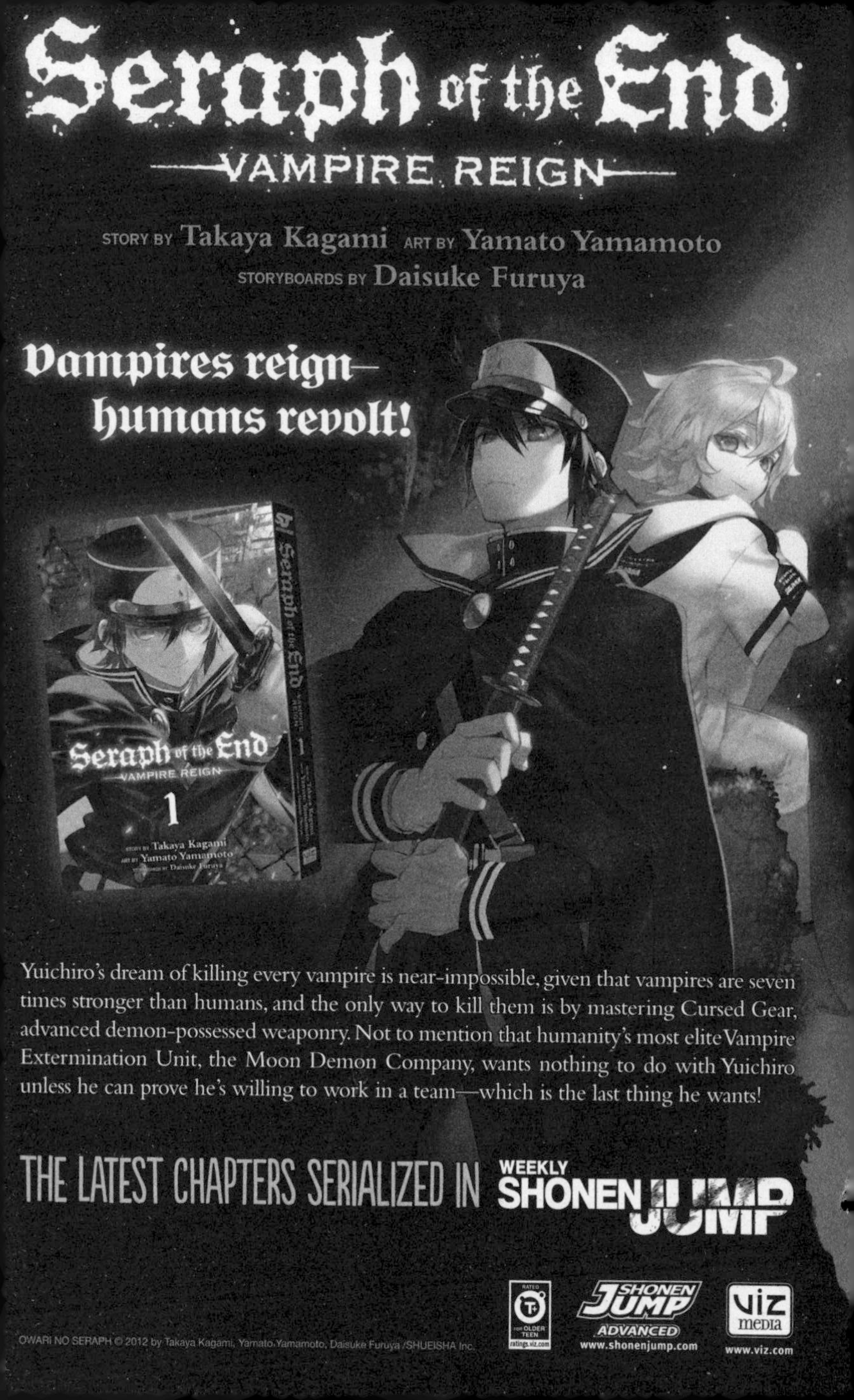
Seraph of the End
VAMPIRE REIGN
STORY BY Takaya Kagami ART BY Yamato Yamamoto
STORYBOARDS BY Daisuke Furuya
Vampires reign—humans revolt!
Seraph of the End
VAMPIRE REIGN
1
STORY BY Takaya Kagami
ART BY Yamato Yamamoto
Yuichiro's dream of killing every vampire is near-impossible, given that vampires are seven times stronger than humans, and the only way to kill them is by mastering Cursed Gear, advanced demon-possessed weaponry. Not to mention that humanity's most elite Vampire Extermination Unit, the Moon Demon Company, wants nothing to do with Yuichiro unless he can prove he's willing to work in a team—which is the last thing he wants!
THE LATEST CHAPTERS SERIALIZED IN WEEKLY SHONEN JUMP
RATED T+ FOR OLDER TEEN ratings.viz.com
SHONEN JUMP ADVANCED
www.shonenjump.com
VIZ media
www.viz.com
OWARI NO SERAPH © 2012 by Takaya Kagami, Yamato Yamamoto, Daisuke Furuya /SHUEISHA Inc.

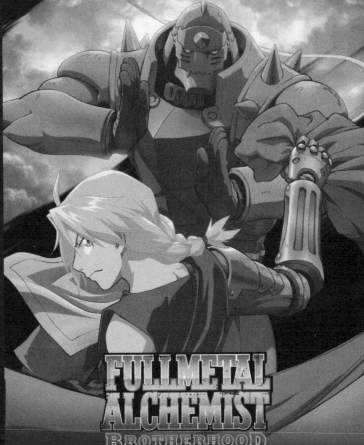

Hey! You're Reading in the Wrong Direction!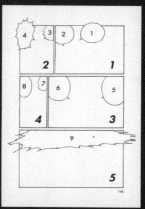

This is the **end** of this graphic novel!

To properly enjoy this VIZ graphic novel, please turn it around and begin reading from **right to left.** Unlike English, Japanese is read right to left, so Japanese comics are read in reverse order from the way English comics are typically read.

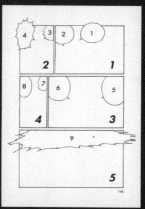

Follow the action this way

This book has been printed in the original Japanese format in order to preserve the orientation of the original artwork. Have fun with it!